A POET'S WAY WITH MUSIC:

Humanism in Jorge de Sena's Poetry

Francisco Cota Fagundes

Gávea-Brown
Providence, Rhode Island

Cover and Design
   Teófilo Ramos

Published and Distributed by
   Gávea-Brown Publications
   Center for Portuguese and Brazilian Studies
   Box O, Brown University
   Providence, R. I. 02912

Library of Congress Catalogue Number: 88-72191

ISBN: 0-943722-15-2

For my wife, Maria Deolinda,
and our son, Evan Anthony

ACKNOWLEDGMENTS

I owe the existence of this book to three people: to Mrs. Mécia de Sena, to my colleague Professor George Monteiro, and to my wife, Maria Deolinda.

Mrs. Mécia de Sena deserves a very special thanks. The first person who read the original draft of my manuscript, Mrs. de Sena not only went through the entire work in the amazingly short period of three weeks—no small feat, considering that the manuscript contained over 500 pages—but she read it as thoroughly as anyone could hope for. I have twelve typed letters from Mrs. de Sena, filled with practical comments pertaining to almost every page of the manuscript, as well as numerous suggestions for its improvement. Her substantial editorial advice was incorporated in the revision and is acknowledged in the text. Mrs. Mécia de Sena's contribution to this book—not only in the form of comments and suggestions, but also by her making available to me her husband's as yet unpublished works—clearly bespeaks her totally unselfish commitment and her unconditional availability to students of all aspects of Luso-Brazilian studies.

George Monteiro's contribution to my book was unique and extends far beyond what is reasonable to expect from a colleague. George read my manuscript in a little over two weeks. And he not only read—but practically copy-edited it. His constructive comments and suggestions contribute greatly to the content of the book. George's input in matters pertaining to English and style accounts, to a large degree, for the readability of the text, and his patient and thorough scrutiny of my translations of Sena's prose and poetry was such that I can say, without exaggeration, that in many cases those translations are as much his as mine.

I also wish to express my appreciation for Onésimo T. Almeida's generosity in offering to publish my book while leaving open for me the option of publishing it in a Portuguese translation.

Finally, I wish to thank my wife, Maria Deolinda. She never faltered in her encouragement and moral support—seeming intangibles without which small projects usually do not get done on time and long ones remain, very often, only prospects.

To all these very special people I convey my deepest gratitude. Needless to say, any mistakes or less felicitous translations of mine are solely my responsibility.

A note on the translations: Except where indicated all translations contained herein are my own; those of *Art of Music* belong to me and James Houlihan. Other translations of Sena's poetry are taken from either of the following volumes: *The Poetry of Jorge de Sena,* ed. by Frederick G. Williams (Santa Barbara: Mudborn Press, 1980) and *In Crete, with the Minotaur and Other Poems,* by George Monteiro (Providence: Gávea-Brown, 1980). All translations acknowledged by name in the text, except for George Monteiro's, are contained in *The Poetry of Jorge de Sena.*

I opted for a translation of all titles—whether books of poetry, poems, or critical works—to facilitate reading of the text. The titles of poems are as literal as possible for quick identification with the originals. All poems quoted in this book, whether by Sena or not, are given in the original language, followed by the English translation. All quotations of prose works, on the other hand, are cited only in English translation.

The punctuation in the titles of Sena's poems, particularly those of *Art of Music,* is often inconsistent; for example *"Water Music,* by Handel"* (title of the musical work *underlined*), "'Requiem' by Mozart" (title of musical work in quotation marks, no comma), but "'Má Vlast,' by Smetana" (comma after the title of the musical work). For the most part I have followed Sena's own practice. In other cases the practice established by other translators is used.

F.C.F.

CONTENTS

INTRODUCTION

This study of Jorge de Sena's *Art of Music* follows two widely held assumptions in which I firmly believe: 1) To be acquainted with a poet's philosophy of life is to be in possession of one of the major keys to the understanding of his poetry. This is particularly true in the case of a poet who, like Jorge de Sena, believes humankind to be the noblest model for art, and human experience, in most of its ramifications, to be the highest subject for poetic treatment. 2) In order to undertake a study of an author's work one must place it within the context, as widely as possible, of his other productions, creative as well as extracreative. That is why, although this book deals specifically with *Art of Music,* I do not even begin to discuss the latter until Chapter IV.

Chapter I outlines Sena's philosophy of life from the viewpoint of its underlying principles and also as that philosophy is revealed in the poet's very choice of, and relative importance given to, different orders of subject matter. Attention is also called to the close interrelation of Sena's humanism as revealed in his poetry and other creative works, as well as extracreative writings. This chapter is not meant as an exhaustive study of Sena's humanism. Indeed, the latter is best understood and appreciated when it is seen mirrored in concrete works like *Art of Music.*

Chapter II provides a schematic survey of Sena's poetic corpus both from the perspective of general themes, as well as from a diaristic viewpoint. The latter category, which comprises the majority of Sena's poems, is based on identified (in the poems themselves, or in

13

notes to the poems) or extrapoetically identifiable lived and/or witnessed experiences, ranging from an incident observed by the poet on a street of Oporto to the complex reaction to a work of visual or musical art. Again no attempt is made to provide an exhaustive survey of all the themes to be found in Jorge de Sena's over one dozen books of poetry. My purpose is to show the thematic evolution, as well as continuity, in Sena's experiential poems. In Sena's early books these experiential poems draw largely upon lived and/or witnessed experiences. The poems of *Metamorphoses* and *Art of Music* are based, for the most part, on experiences derived from works of visual art and music, respectively. *Art of Music* represents a high point in these series inspired by *Bildungserlebnis,* as far as the poet's optimistic view of life is concerned. Following *Art of Music,* Sena continues his poetic diary based mostly on lived and witnessed experiences: *Peregrinatio ad Loca Infecta, Exorcism, I Know the Salt... And Other Poems,* and *Over This Shore.* These books, however, as well as *40 Years of Servitude, Sequences,* and *Perpetual Vision,* do contain numerous examples of poems inspired by art and also many poems that can be considered non-experiential in the sense defined and explained in Chapter II.

Chapter III deals with some of the major processes involved in the transmutation of lived/witnessed and art-derived experiences into poetic substance. Once again this chapter can, at best, schematize these metamorphic processes. The discussion of the latter will prepare the ground for a much more thorough elaboration of the metamorphic processes operative in the conversion of a musical experience into poetry.

Chapters IV and V dwell on Sena's own ideas, as he put forth in the postface to the book, regarding the philosophical and aesthetic foundation of *Art of Music.* In Chapter IV, I will also place my critical approach to *Art of Music* within the perspective of current musico-literary studies. In his *Tones into Words,* Calvin S. Brown, the foremost musico-literary authority writing in the English language, measures the success of the poems he analyzes, not by their intrinsic literary merits—which he finds relatively lacking—but solely by how well the poems reproduce musical effects. My analyses of Sena's poems will aim—but only in part—at determining how he adapts musical forms and structural techniques. However, in the overall study of the poems this will be one of the least important considerations. More important to this study is to determine Sena's success on the basis of how he combines various approaches to the experience of music and produces poems capable of standing on their own as poetry. Most important, the poems of *Art of Music* will be analyzed with the purpose of determining how coherently Sena brings poetized musical experience into harmony with his humanistic outlook. Accordingly, Chapter V will discuss well-known theories of musical origin and meaning and relate those theories to Sena's own views of music, as the latter are stated and elaborated in the postface and as they are mirrored in the poems themselves.

In Chapters VI, VII, and VIII, a widely representative selection of the three groups of poems of *Art of Music*—and this division is based on the kinds of music that inspired the poems, e.g., program music, absolute music—will be discussed primarily for their humanistic content. And this brings us to the legitimacy of the title of this study, *A Poet's Way with Music: Humanism in Jorge de Sena's Poetry.* As I hope to show, humanism is an important and justifiable perspective from which to view *Art of Music.* My critical approach to these poems is also consistent with one of the most frequently employed musico-literary approaches, as we shall see. But the present angle of study is not the only one possible, nor is it necessarily the most fruitful. I am perfectly aware—and make no apologies in this regard—that this study, although it places much emphasis on the *aesthetic* and *formal* dimensions of *Art of Music,* nevertheless is heavily oriented toward *content*: a study of humanism as it is mirrored in these poems inspired by music.

In the postface to *Art of Music*, Jorge de Sena writes: "I wish to focus briefly on two points. To what extent are poems such as these outside the reach of the common reader of poetry? To what degree are they unimportant to the conscientious and educated music lover or, still less important, to the professional of music?" Sena adds that the answers to these questions are not up to him. They are, however, questions that every serious reader of *Art of Music* must ask (and answer) himself or herself. Jorge de Sena was an extremely well-informed "sort of professional music lover" (his words). As the poems of *Art of Music,* as well as the notes that accompany them and the postface, reveal, Sena's knowledge of music extended well beyond mere acquaintance with music as an aesthetic and cultural phenomenon to the point of enabling him to penetrate, to a considerable degree, the area of technical knowledge. Earlier in the postface, Sena had stated that the reason he includes in the notes to the poems the information pertaining to the specific interpretation of a given composition is that "Perhaps . . . there are specialists interested in discovering to what extent a particular concert performer or a certain conductor, at that moment, influenced my view of the work by his interpretation of it."

Art of Music is a book which lends itself—and Sena's postface as well as the poems themselves reveal this very well—to a variety of readers and critical approaches. The professional musician probably would find in it much to delight him: from poetic descriptions of the music, to ingenious techniques of poetic transposition of musical phenomena, to provocative interpretations of universally known works. To what extent does the information contained in these poems represent a valid contribution to musical knowledge? What is the worth of Sena's musical interpretations—for many of these poems do strike critical poses—independently of their viability as poetic statements? Do Sena's descriptions of the musical models respond accurately to the tonal and rhythmic configurations, i.e., to what the music is doing? These questions can be answered only by a professional musician or musical critic. But were the question regarding Sena's contribution to musical knowledge answerable in the affirmative, would the poems of *Art of Music,* as poems, gain anything beyond what they are worth as poetry in their own right, i.e., as artistic crystallizations of the complex experiencing of music, as distinct from being verbal re-presentations of the model compositions or musical criticism in stylized form? To me the answer is "No"—even though much would be gained for an overall understanding of *Art of Music* and for our knowledge of Sena's musical expertise if that and similar questions were competently answered.

The musically limited reader, however, need not despair. And the reader of Sena's poetry need not bypass *Art of Music*—as has been the case thus far, with precious few exceptions. For the poems of *Art of Music*—like the poems of *Metamorphoses,* which are largely based on works of visual art—are, first and foremost, poems. Their primary affinity is with literature, not music. In other words, in order to penetrate some of their secrets and beauty, they require on the reader's part more sensitivity to, and familiarity with, literary culture than they do a technical knowledge of music. Nevertheless, the safest way to read *Art of Music* is, I believe, to strike a medium between the two extremes: between the technical musical approach (and the professional of music is not likely to become the most common reader of *Art of Music,* anyway) and the musically incognizant approach. That is to say, the reader of poetry who is also a lover of music and who has a fair knowledge of music as an aesthetic and cultural phenomenon, even though he or she may not possess a technical knowledge of the most technical of all the arts, is in a position to derive a great deal of information and pleasure from critically reading *Art of Music.* To be sure, there are many subtleties which this reader will miss that would probably be readily apparent to the musically better informed; but there remains much left upon which he can feast the intellect, emotions, and aesthetic sensibility. My reading of *Art of Music* seeks, first of all, to provide an account of Sena's work as poetry. However, it does not, nor should it, forget that the poems are based on works of art whose "content" and formal make-up enter very often into the very substance of the poems. As the last chapter will attempt to demonstrate, the present approach to a study of *Art of Music*—the pursuit of Sena's humanism as it informs his poetic crystallizations of his *experience* of music—is thoroughly defensible. For, despite the fact that Sena's book is inspired and to a large degree conditioned by the content (understood in musical and extramusical terms, as we shall see) of the inspiring works, nevertheless the overall thematic profile of *Art of Music* does not differ significantly from that of Sena's entire poetic corpus, which, except for a few poems on music and *Art of Music* itself, has ostensibly nothing to do with music as such. We shall also see in this chapter that the humanistic outlook that feeds Sena's entire poetic corpus bears its ripest fruits in this work inspired by music.

One of the challenges to Humanist writers and artists will be to embody in artistic and literary work the general point of view for which Humanism stands; to express that sense of the beauty and glory of life . . .

(Corliss Lamont, *The Philosophy of Humanism*)

I

Jorge de Sena: A Philosophical Profile

Jorge de Sena (1919-1978) was a humanist. His philosophy of life informs his immense and varied extrapoetic corpus (fiction, theater, essay, cultural history, literary criticism) and is stamped upon the overwhelming majority of his poems from those based on the most concrete lived or witnessed experience, to those, such as the poems of *Art of Music,* which are inspired by the most impalpable of the arts: music. Sena's humanism is even reflected in the choice of works of poetry and fiction he translated. These extremely numerous translations often reflect world views and thematic concerns akin to Sena's own. They range in chronological scope from the writings of ancient Greek and Roman humanists (Sappho, Euripides, Catullus, etc.) to works of modern fiction, such as Hemingway's *The Old Man and the Sea.* Sena's humanism, although it grew in depth and expanded in scope along the years, was already quite evident in the two short stories, "Paradise Lost" and "Cain," written when he was less than twenty, and published under the collective title *Genesis* (Lisbon: Edições 70, 1982).

Humanism, however, can be a very vague and even misleading term. It has been used to refer not only to love of letters in general, but to the professional activities of those who teach letters without necessarily loving them. The term has been used most frequently to designate the different historical humanisms: the humanism of ancient

Indian philosophers; that of Chinese Taoists and Confucianists; the philosophy of the Sophists in the Athens of the fifth century B.C.; the humanisms of the Renaissance and Enlightenment; those of the democratic revolutions of the eighteenth and nineteenth centuries; and the New Humanism of Irving Babbitt and Paul Elmer More. And the list could be greatly increased without being exhaustive. The label "humanism" has been pinned to or assumed by philosophical stances as radically different as those of Aquinas and Erasmus; as irreconcilable as those of the materialist Karl Marx and the naturalist Corliss Lamont and the Christian Jacques Maritain. So varied and often contradictory can "humanism" be that Jean-Paul Sartre has written a book to demonstrate in part that, contrary to the opinion of some, *Existentialism is a Humanism.*

For the infinitely rich but highly ambiguous term "humanism" to begin to have any validity, it must be clearly and carefully modified by adequate delimiting adjectives. For the wide and dynamic concepts that humanism can and does embody to possess controllable applicability to a study of Jorge de Sena's poetry, the term has to be carefully defined and explained—as it applies specifically to Sena. The adjectives that most aptly qualify Sena's brand of humanism are *secular, naturalistic,* i.e., in accordance with the laws of nature, *materialistic, scientific, democratic,* and *socialist.* Not all of these adjectives serve equally well when applied to designate the world view reflected in a body of poems or in a single poetic text. Taken together, however, these are the most appropriate adjectives to guide a discussion of Sena's humanism. Sena, who called himself "philosophically a Marxist," would probably prefer the adjectives *democratic* and *socialist. Democratic* and *socialist,* besides encompassing, in my view, all the other adjectives mentioned, are also used by Sena (as nouns) in the most complete autobiographical statement he left us (to be quoted and discussed below). But these two adjectives possess connotations that are much too political to accommodate the present discussion of Sena's overall commitment to life as revealed in his poetic corpus in general, and in *Art of Music* in particular. Due to their overly materialistic (in the non-philosophical sense) and quantitative implications, the adjectives *materialistic* and *scientific* will likewise be avoided, despite their appropriateness in connection with many of the ideas that inform Sena's poetry. *Secular* is a most justified modifier for the philosophical stance of a poet who, in numerous poetic and extrapoetic instances, emphatically and even combatively affirms this-earthly realism in opposition to supernaturalism. Even so, this adjective connotes polemically too narrow an attitude vis-à-vis theology, a posture which Sena's poetry, for the most part, clearly transcends.

Naturalistic, the term favored by Corliss Lamont in his *The Philosophy of Humanism,* is the adjective I shall use to refer to Sena's humanistic view of and attitude toward life. Lamont's definition of naturalistic humanism necessarily encompasses all the adjectives mentioned above and has the added virtue of avoiding entangling connotative webs, as well as restricting labels. "To define twentieth-century humanism briefly," Lamont writes, "I would say that it is a philosophy of joyous service for the greater good of all humanity in this natural world and advocating the methods of reason, science, and democracy."[1]

A concise definition of Sena's humanism—and one which, like most definitions of such loaded terms, is necessarily susceptible of improvement—could be formulated thus: Sena espouses an essentially man-centered philosophy of life—with its cosmological, ethical, and aesthetic implications—which is for all practical purposes opposed to supernaturalism and philosophical idealism. Like any responsible humanism, Sena's does not exclude ideality, i.e., the ability to conceive of and strive for ideals for mankind in this-earthly reality; nor does his fundamentally naturalistic view of life preclude an interest in spiritual values. But it does mean that Sena conceives of the latter as being attainable in our spatial and temporal world. Susan Stebbing dispells the erroneous notion that spiritual excellences are assignable only to another world. She writes:

> These spiritual excellences are intellectual and moral capacities, lacking which the life of human beings would be nasty and brutish . . . They include love for human beings, delight in creative activities of all kinds, respect for truth, satisfaction in learning to know what is true about this world (which includes ourselves), loyalty to other human beings, generosity of thought and sympathy with those who suffer, hatred of cruelty and other evils, devotion to duty and steadfastness in seeking one's ideals, delight in the beauty of nature and in art—in short, the love and pursuit of what is worthwhile for its own sake . . . These excellences are to be found in *this* world; no heaven is needed to experience them.[2]

Fernando Pessoa's (1888-1935) famous statement, "I was a poet animated by philosophy, not a philosopher,"[3] could have been made by Jorge de Sena. Like Pessoa, Sena left us no philosophical system, no self-contained structured world view or *Weltanschauung.* It is possible, however, as is also the case with Pessoa, to outline Sena's view of life by bringing together his most pertinent philosophical statements which are profusely scattered throughout his essays, such as *Machiavelli and Other Studies,* those collected in *The Kingdom of Stupidity* (2 vols.), and his critical and theoretico-critical works, for example *"The Poet is a Feigner,"* *Theoretical Dialectics of Literature* and *Applied Dialectics of Literature.* More important, expressions of his philosophical beliefs are to be found in autobiographical statements contained in interviews, such as the one published by *O Tempo e o Modo,* in a special number dedicated to Sena,[4] and "Jorge de Sena Reads His Own Poetry," a videotape interview by Frederick Williams (conducted 4 May 1978). More important still, Sena's view of life and of his art's place in it is abundantly contained in all the prefaces and postfaces to his creative works. Finally, and most important of all, Sena's philosophy of life is to be abstracted or inferred from his creative works, where his humanism is not only *explained,* for example in statement poems like "Letter to My Children on the Shootings of Goya" *(Metamorphoses),* but is actually most emphatically *applied,* as it were, as in *Art of Music.*

A study of those extracreative and creative sources, but particularly the latter, reveals that Jorge de Sena, with minor deviations or momentary exceptions, subscribes to the ten major tenets of naturalistic humanism as identified, outlined and discussed by Corliss Lamont in *The Philosophy of Humanism.* I did say *with minor deviations or momentary exceptions,* and this point needs to be emphasized right from the outset. This profile of Sena's humanism is meant to provide an ideological perspective—an angle among several that could have been chosen—to glimpse Sena's poetry in general and to view *Art of Music* in more detail. It is not meant as an exhaustive exposition and critique of Sena's philosophy of life in all of its creative and extracreative ramifications. It only aims to identify and discuss briefly the concepts, attitudes and ideals mirrored or embodied in his poetry to which the designation humanistic can and does legitimately apply. A given poem, to the extent that it is affected, and to some degree effected, by particular circumstances, may depart from and even contradict—as Sena's poems often do—the principles or propositions that the poetic corpus, seen in its totality, embodies. It is a truism to say that all poetry worthy of the name is necessarily ambiguous. Sena, in both thought and style, can be a very ambiguous poet indeed. What I seek to establish, therefore, is not a reduced number of philosophical propositions from which Sena *never* departs, but the seminal philosophical ideas and ideals that inform the overwhelming majority of his poems, or those principles to which the poet inevitably returns after brief excursions into other realms.

Sena's poetry reflects a truly remarkable philosophical consistency. *Fidelity* (the title of one of his poetical works) meant to Jorge de Sena both loyalty to his poetic calling and faithfulness to his humanistic principles. We must remember, however, that the earliest poem of *Persecution* (1942), "Stains," is dated 7 December 1938; and that the last poem Sena set down, "Warning to Cardiacs and Others Afflicted with Like Diseases" *(40 Years of Servitude,* 1979), bears the composition date 19 March 1978. However remarkably consistent a poet may be, as he converts forty years' worth of human experiences (for Sena's is essentially an experiential poetry) into poetic substance, he is bound to momentarily detour without ever abandoning the direction in which he is moving. I do contend, however, that, notwithstanding some hesitancies, primarily in his early books of poetry, in regard to these humanistic tenets, *Art of Music* is absolutely unshakeable in its philosophical consistency.

According to Corliss Lamont (op. cit., pp. 12-14), the central propositions of naturalistic humanism are: 1) acceptance of a naturalistic cosmology or metaphysics of the universe and opposition to all supernatural explanations or views; 2) the belief, in accordance with the discoveries of science, in the evolutionary theory of human life and a concomitant acceptance of a monistic or unitarian relationship between body and mind (or what is supernaturalistically called soul); 3) reliance upon reason and the scientific method as the most useful and adequate tools for solving problems and achieving reliable truth; 4) the belief that man is the master of his destiny, in opposition to views that uphold universal predestination, determinism and fatalism; 5) belief in and practice of an ethics of morality that is exclusively man-based, i.e., one "that grounds all human values in this-earthly experiences and relationships; and that holds as its highest loyalty the this-worldly happiness, freedom and progress—economic, cultural and ethical—of all mankind, irrespective of nation, race or religion"; 6) belief that the good life is attainable via self-development as well as commitment to one's community and to humankind as a whole; 7) belief in the development of art and awareness of beauty both man-made and natural so that an aesthetic component be made an integral and enriching part of human experience as a whole; 8) belief in democracy and peace for all mankind; 9) "humanism believes in the complete social implementation of reason and scientific method; and thereby in the use of democratic procedures, including full freedom of expression and civil liberties, throughout all areas of economic, political, and cultural life"; 10) humanism rejects all types of dogmatism. "Humanism, in accordance with scientific method, believes in the unending questioning of basic assumptions and convictions, including its own. Humanism is not a new dogma, but it is a developing philosophy ever opened to experimental testing, newly discovered facts, and more rigorous reasoning."

The differences between Marxist humanism and the milder

Lamontian humanism are significant. An exhaustive study of Sena's Hegelian and Marxian philosophical background would have to take these differences into consideration. For purposes of the present study of *Art of Music,* however, I do not believe them to be crucial. Howard L. Parsons, in his *Humanism and Marx's Thought,*[5] outlines Marxist humanism thus: 1) Marxist humanism is concerned with *all of man,* i.e., it is a total commitment "with the *total* man and his *total* fulfillment"; 2) it is a universal concern, i.e., one which encompasses all of mankind; 3) it is scientific; "truth is the grounding totality of men's responses to the world, rendered consistent and mutually reinforcing, and progressively brought into kindred relations to the world"; 4) "Marxist humanism discriminates *means* from *ends* and strives to relate them so that each signifies and requires the other. It is intensely focused on *all* of man and *all* men, is committed to man's fulfillment, and in using a dialectical, scientific method in understanding man is able to grasp the conditions and relations that define man"; 5) "Marxist humanism is *revolutionary.* It should be contrasted with *contemplative* humanism, or *conservative* humanism, which knows nothing of the principle of *practice,* of changing present circumstances in the direction of man's progressive improvement." Parsons is careful to point out, however, that "Marx's *revolutionieren* carries the Hegelian notion of annulment, absorption, and supersession, i.e., creative, transformation." For Marx, *revolution* does not necessarily imply bloodshed. Parsons quotes the *Standard Dictionary of the English Language* definition of "revolution," which reads in part, "while such change is apt to involve armed hostilities, these make no necessary part of a *revolution,* which may be accomplished without a battle"; 6)"Marxist humanism is *progressive, i.e.,* must be opposed to all fixities in thought and practice" (Parsons, pp. 178-89).

As we can see and deduce, two of the major differences between the two humanisms are Lamont's implicit versus the Marxists' explicit idea of revolution, and Lamont's stress on the biological explanation of human evolution versus the Marxian emphasis on material production as the main basis for the understanding of human evolution and history. Lamont himself points out what he perceives to be the major differences between his and Marxist humanism:

> On economic, political and social issues the Marxist Humanists are of course much to the left of the other types of Humanists I have described. Ordinarily they use the formidable phrase *Dialectical Materialism* to designate their philosophy, though they often talk in a general way about the *Humanist* civilization of Soviet Russia and of the socialist world. The Marxist materialists disagree sharply on certain philosophic issues with me and with other Humanists, particular-

ly in their ambiguous attitude toward democracy and their acceptance of determinism. They are, however, unquestionably humanistic in their major tenets of rejecting the supernatural and all religious authority, of setting up the welfare of mankind in this life as the supreme goal, and of relying on science and its techniques. (Lamont, pp. 26-27)

As noted earlier, for purposes of this study of humanism in *Art of Music,* these differences are not of great importance. Indeed, the only reason why I dwell on them is that Sena calls himself a Marxist. The essential point is that whether we choose to label Sena's humanism Marxist, or whether we prefer, as I do, the more neutral but nevertheless all-encompassing term *naturalistic* (bearing in mind the applicability of all the other adjectives mentioned to portions of Sena's corpus), Sena's humanism, as it is specifically revealed in his poetry, is a view of life that has extremely deep roots in the distant and recent past, as well as in the present. It is a view that, save the extremely important characteristics peculiar to Sena's poetic personality, has been defended by philosophers, statesmen, men of letters, scientists, as well as by countless common people who, without even being aware of it, have practiced many of the principles of naturalistic humanism in their daily lives. Naturalistic humanism is a view of life that has characterized, albeit to varying degrees, with more or less emphasis on a given tenet, e.g., modern scientific method or socialism, every man-centered and humankind-oriented philosophy of all times and places: from Protagoras who formulated the famous dictum "Man is the measure of all things"; to Terence who, although no naturalistic humanist himself, nevertheless contributed the immortal sentence, "I am a man, and nothing that concerns a man do I deem a matter of indifference to me"; to Lucretius whose *De Rerum Natura* is not only a song of Nature but constitutes an attempt to free man from the shackles of supernaturalistic views; to Giordano Bruno who died to safeguard the "heresies" of naturalistic humanism; to Spinoza who wrote his *Ethics* steeped in the humanistic spirit; to Darwin who gave humanism a monumental impetus with his *Origin of Species;* to Ludwig Feuerbach whose *The Essence of Christianity* laid the cornerstone of Marx's socialist humanism. Sena, as a thinker, is a brother to all these men and countless other kindred spirits throughout the ages. Sena rejects, as he so often states or implies, all views, institutionalized and otherwise, which displace man from his rightful and ennobling place in the universe and persuade or force him to look away from this his earthly home—the only one he knows and perhaps will ever know; the only place where he can not only aspire to but actually achieve a measure of self-fulfillment and happiness.

As far as his humanistic stance is concerned, the most complete of Sena's extrapoetic autobiographical statements is included in the preface to the second edition of *Poetry-I*.[6] Because it contains or implies most of the humanistic propositions outlined by Corliss Lamont (and some of those discussed by Howard L. Parsons), this statement deserves to be quoted in full. Sena prepares this brief philosophical autobiography by saying that his poetry, for better or for worse, reflects these convictions. He writes:

> I am personally against any organized church or organized party, but I recognize the right of any person to be a member of anything whatever, provided that my personal liberty is not thereby affected. Religiously speaking, I can say that I am a Catholic but not a Christian—which means that I respect in the Catholic Church all the old paganism that the Church preserved in its rituals, dogmas, etc., under several disguises, which the protestant Reformation did not know how to preserve. I believe that the gods exist under the One, but in this One I do not believe because I am an atheist. However, an atheist who, in a manner somewhat Hegelian, placed his life and destiny in the hands of this God whose existence and non-existence are the same meaningless thing. Philosophically, I am a Marxist for whom modern science erased any antinomy between the antiquated concepts of matter and spirit. But, politically, I am against any type of dictatorship (whether it be of majorities or minorities), and in favor of representative democracy. I have no illusions whatsoever regarding the latter—it can be a mask for the most unmerciful of imperialisms. But other systems can be that also. I am in favor of peace and understanding among nations, and I hope that socialism will prevail everywhere, maintaining liberty and representative democracy. I do not subscribe to the view which divides the world between Good and Evil, between God and the Devil (no matter what the philosophy involved may be). Despite my Hegelian and Marxist education, or even because of it, to me contraries are more complex than an opportunistic acceptance of simplistic Manicheisms. Morally speaking, I am a married man and the father of nine children, someone who has always lacked the patriarch's vocation, and who has always been in favor of the most complete freedom in all forms of love and sexual contact. No freedom shall ever be secure, anywhere, so long as a church, a party, or a group of hypersensitive citizens is allowed the right to govern someone else's life. Likewise, we must never consent to the idea that there is any reform whatever worth the price of a human life. Now more than ever, in a world in which human lives have become so cheap that they can be wasted by the millions, it is the writer's duty to resist. We may have revolutions: but let us hope that in them people may die accidentally, never by assassination.

As stated above, Sena's humanism presupposes the belief in the scientific explanation of the origin and nature of the universe. Although this view can be inferred from extrapoetic statements such as the one just quoted, Sena was interested in establishing this naturalistic principle from the outset in poetic terms. According to Alexandre Pinheiro Torres, in *Persecution,* the first of Sena's poetical works, the poet is "particularly sensitive to a cosmogonic-metaphysical speculating that is marked by implications derived from the most recent /knowledge/ of Celestial Mechanics."[7] Pinheiro Torres reminds us of Sena's study of physics in Liceu de Camões in Lisbon, where he had, as teacher of science, Rômulo de Carvalho, better known today by the literary pseudonym António Gedeão. "An examination of Sena's academic records," Pinheiro Torres goes on to say, "reveals that he had already completed the courses in General Physics and Thermodynamics preparatory to the Course of Study in Engineering at the Department of Sciences /at the University/ of Lisbon, before the publication of his first book /of poetry/. And this educational background on Sena's part would decisively influence his later studies. Hence the need for a scientific decoding of *Persecution*—which will permit access to the foundation of his poetic edifice" (p. 24).

Whether Sena's cosmogonic and cosmological views derive from Newton and Kant, or whether they follow more closely Einstein's theory of a curved universe, as Pinheiro Torres attempts to demonstrate through a detailed analysis of the poem "Collecting" ("Arrecadação"), is really not of great importance for us here. Suffice it to reiterate that Sena's humanism rests in part on the solid foundation of the modern scientific explanation of the origin and functioning of the universe, the true and only home of man. I shall return to Sena's poetic encounter with science later.

A rejection of the existence of God, i.e., of a supreme being who created all things and of supernaturalism in general would seem to be the logical concomittant of this cosmogonic and cosmological position. However, despite extrapoetic statements such as the one quoted above ("I am an atheist"), the general problem of religion in Sena's poetry—and within the general problem of religion that of the existence versus non-existence of a supreme deity—remains a very thorny one indeed. For the most part Sena believes, with all naturalistic and socialist humanists, that the physical universe is all there is, and that "The supreme being for humanity is humanity itself—not as it is at any given stage, but humanity in the making, humankind as it can and will be."[8] This is the belief that triumphs in Sena's poetry, one which finds its most unequivocal expression in *Art of Music.* But there are two other attitudes regarding the existence of God and a hereafter which compete with this one in Sena's poetry, particularly although not exclusively in his first books. In a few poems, notably the series of six sonnets entitled "Genesis" *(Crown of the Earth)* and the beautiful sonnet "Dawn" *(I Know the Salt...)* Sena comes very close to expressing orthodox theistic views even though it would be difficult and risky to justify in their regard a label such as Christian. Let us read "Dawn," where the belief or hope in a hereafter would not be unsustainable:

> *Há que deixar no mundo as ervas e a tristeza,*
> *e ao lume de águas o rancor da vida.*
> *Levar connosco mortos o desejo*
> *e o senso de existir que penetrando*
> *além dos lodos sob as águas fundas*
> *hão-de ser verdes como a velha esperança*
> *nos prados de amargura já floridos.*
>
> *Deixar no mundo as árvores erguidas,*
> *e da tremente carne as vãs cavernas*
> *aos outros destinadas e às montanhas*
> *que a neve cobrirá de álgida ausência.*
> *Levar connosco em ossos que resistam*
> *não sabemos o quê de paz tranquila.*
>
> *E ao lume de águas o rancor da vida.*
>
> (*III*, p. 212)

> (One must leave on earth the weeds and sorrow,
> and on the water's surface leave the gall of life.
> We should, when dead, take with us the desire
> and sense of our existence which, while reaching
> out beyond the mire below the deepest waters,
> shall be as green as age-old hope eternal
> upon the bitter meadows now in bloom.
>
> One must leave the trees on earth erect,
> and, of trembling flesh, the foolish caverns,
> destined now for others and for mountains
> which snows will cover with their chilly absence.
> To carry in our high resistant bones
> an unknown quantity of tranquil peace.
>
> And on the water's surface leave the gall of life.)
>
> (trans. Frederick G. Williams)

The other attitude—this one much more prevalent throughout Sena's poetic corpus—is the opposition between the tradition-bound emotional self who desires and seemingly needs to believe in the supernatural, and the man- and earth-oriented rational self who cannot or will not believe. Many of Sena's poems, once again particularly in early works, are dedicated to this personal drama. In other words, the religious doubts, hopes and quests that Sena, like most human beings, harbored, were not put aside for the sake of expressing a thoroughly secular humanism: they were made an integral part of his poetico-metaphysical drama. Naturalistic humanism triumphs in the end not because the poet determined aprioristically that it should; it does because the poet's search for the truth, meaning and joy of living inevitably lead him to the humanistic path—as it might have led him elsewhere.

No poetical work of Sena's deals more intensely with the question or problem of God than does *Persecution,* followed closely by *Crown of the Earth* and *The Evidences,* although the poet returns to this topic again and again in the course of his forty-year "poetical servitude." In the sonnet "Transept" *(Persecution),* Sena's denial of the existence of God, particularly the God associated with the Christian religion, is unequivocally expressed. Although it is true that the door remains open for a search for, and possible discovery of, a personal God, it is also apparent that the poem rings with the definitive echo of Nietzsche's "God is dead":

> *Volteei lugubremente pela nave.*
> *Deus estava aceso a cada canto.*
> *Havia cheiro a túmulo e, enquanto*
> *a ele se ia somando um fresco suave...:*
>
> *as pedras roxas... e, ao meio, a trave*
> *onde balouça levemente um santo*
> *sem feições e sem braços—só um manto*
> *esculpido no olhar que se lhe crave.*
>
> *Depois um silvo... e cada vez mais forte*
> *o cheiro antigo e tenro a tanta morte!*
> *(O santo alastra dúvida esgotada!)*
>
> *E o fio do juízo amortecendo, tenso...*
> *O céu de pedra anoiteceu imenso.*
> *Então?... Deus apagou-se... Não é nada.*

(*I,* pp. 77-78)

(I circled lugubriously about the nave.
God was lit at every corner.
There was a smell of tombs and, while
a fresh breeze slowly mixed with it...:

the purple stones... and, in the middle, the beam
where a saint lightly swings
featureless and without arms—only a cloak
sculpted in the eyes of the onlooker.

A whistle is heard... and growing stronger
a smell ancient and recent of so much death!
(The saint spreads exhausted doubt!)

And the thread of understanding grows dim, strained...
Night fell on the heaven of stone—immense.
And now?... God is extinguished... It is nothing.)

From the ashes of so much death; from the prison of this "heaven of stone," the poet will emerge to the fresh air of humanism, to the latter's affirmation of things living. Still, the very fact that Sena needs to ask himself the question "And now?" and proclaim his "discovery" that "God is dead"; and, more important still, the fact that he returns again and again to the question and quest of God, suggests that in his mind the problem is far from settled. In the long poem "Declaration" *(Persecution)* the conflict between the God- and religion-seeking emotional self and God-weary and God-denying rational self achieves a truly dramatic expression. The poem gives us the feeling that Sena's naturalistic humanism struggles, as it were, to emerge free from what may be termed an atavistic residue of the idea and need of God, especially God conceived in orthodox Catholic terms. Reading the beginning of the poem, one almost senses the reconversion of a man who, having wandered away from organized religion, is returning, prodigal son-like, to its bosom. Once again, perhaps even more so than in "Transept," we see Sena poetizing his problem of religion and God not with the detachment befitting a philosophical problem, but with the human emotion appertaining to a truly existential drama. By the middle of the poem those residual feelings of and for religion and God clash with the rational humanistic *need* not to give in to supernaturalism. The power of this need is expressed with one of the greatest forces the poet can graphically command: with the shout of capital letters. After having maintained for fifty-three lines that he was going to (re)turn to God as conceived by Catholicism, the poet, i.e., his rational, humanistic self, rebels in this fashion (English version quoted is by F. G. Williams):

E SEI QUE ENTÃO ME HEI-DE RENEGAR E ESTE POEMA À FRENTE.

(AND I KNOW THAT THEN I WILL DISOWN MYSELF AND THIS POEM
FIRST.)

"Declaration" points to the strictly humanistic path the poet wishes to follow. The poem also suggests that this path can be costly. How much easier it is to give oneself to comfortable beliefs: "e nessa crença ⌐em Deus⌐ encontrarei a alegria / de quem encontra paredes verdadeiras / só do seu lado, / encontrarei uma alegria de sedução poética..." ("and in that belief ⌐in God⌐ I will find the joy / of one who contemplates real walls / only on his side, / I will find a poetically seductive joy...") But the poet prefers the more arduous human way, the path of human freedom, the one that brings pain but also joy. This poem represents the triumph of reason over emotionality; of ennobling self-reliance over comfortable servility; of the open-ended search for truths over the codified and stultified ready-made Truth.

It is very befitting that the last three poems of *Persecution* should contribute to clarifying the poet's "new" freedom from supernaturalism. In the antepenult poem, "Pentecost," the poet neutralizes the idea of the supernatural by thoroughly humanizing God (in a manner reminiscent of Alberto Caeiro's poem VIII of "The Shepherd") and celebrating the life and freedom lacking in the stifling atmosphere evoked in "Transept." However, there is one major difference between Caeiro's and Sena's poems that is worth noting. Pessoa humanizes the Child Jesus, who in the Catholic tradition is already conceived of in very human terms. At the end of the poem, Caeiro writes:

> *Quando eu morrer, filhinho,*
> *Seja eu a criança, o mais pequeno.*
> *Pega-me tu ao colo*
> *E leva-me para dentro da tua casa.*
> *Despe o meu ser cansado e humano*
> *E deita-me na tua cama.*
> *E conta-me histórias, caso eu acorde,*
> *Para eu tornar a adormecer.*
> *E dá-me sonhos teus para eu brincar*
> *Até que nasça qualquer dia*
> *Que tu sabes qual é.*[9]

> (When I die, my child,
> May I be the child, the smaller one.
> Take me in your arms
> And carry me into your house.
> Undress my tired and human self
> And lay me down in your bed.
> And tell me stories, should I awake,
> That I may again fall asleep.
> And give me your dreams to play with
> Until I am born on some day
> Known to you.)

That is to say, despite the irreverent humanization of an already humanized Jesus turned child again, Caeiro still deals most reverently and deferentially with Him. It is he, the poet, who shall rest in His arms, "Until I am born some day / Known to you ⌐implication: and not to me7." Sena's poem is much more iconoclastic: it addresses the First Person of the Holy Trinity. It is He, God, who will be aided by the poet—the poet who knows that neither he nor God "shall cry about anything in any verse" written by the poet! Furthermore, Caeiro's encounter with the Child Jesus is conceived as taking place within a dream:

> Num meio-dia de fim de Primavera
> Tive um sonho como uma fotografia.
> Vi Jesus Cristo descer à terra.

> (At noon of an end-of-Spring day
> I had a photograph-like dream.
> I saw Jesus Christ come to earth.)

By conceiving the poem as a dream vision, the poet further implies that his irreverent poem is an experience that happened to him, as distinct from one that he consciously thought of. The encounter envisioned by Sena, on the other hand, is conceived within waking reality. The poet assumes full responsibility for it.

> Estranha fidelidade!
>
> Apreensivamente, um dia,
> ultrapassarás Tu, meu Deus, a primeira vidraça
> e dar-Te-ei a minha mão para desceres do espaço.
>
> Estaremos logo os dois num poema sem lágrimas,
> nenhum de nós chorará de nada em nenhum verso.
>
> Quem sabe?—por memória do tempo anterior—
> guardarei fechada a mão que Te ajudar.
> Mas estaremos os dois nesse poema,
> os dois num poema sem lágrimas.
>
> (I, p. 78)

> (Strange fidelity!
>
> Apprehensively, one day,
> You, my God, shall pass through the first window-pane
> and I shall give You my hand so that You may step down from space.
>
> We shall at once be in a poem without tears,
> neither of us shall cry about anything in any verse.
>
> Who knows?—for old time's sake—
> I shall keep closed the hand that helped You.
> But the two of us shall be in that poem,
> the two of us in a poem without tears.)

The penult poem of *Persecution,* "Ascension," is the joyous pro-
clamation of naturalistic truth, the truth of the earth and of
humankind rising to fill the heavens. This poem must be read, I
believe, as the logical conclusion to all the poems of *Persecution* (and
not only *Persecution)* that deal with the problem of supernaturalism.
It, too, deserves to be quoted in full. What is naturalistic truth? Does
the poet define it? No. Any definition would be too confining.
Humanistic truths are never ready made: they are constantly in the
process of being made. That is why the images of the poem are
dynamic, not static. Naturalistic truth is open-ended, ever in need of
being re-defined, perfected. But it exists; one can feel it; one has *faith*
in it. But it is a faith based on something tangible that touches our
bodies, that rises with us toward the sky:

> *Nunca estive tão perto da verdade.*
> *Sinto-a contra mim,*
> *Sei que vou com ela.*
>
> *Tantas vezes falei negando sempre,*
> *esgotando todas as negações possíveis,*
> *conduzindo-as ao cerco da verdade,*
> *que hoje, côncavo tão côncavo,*
> *sou inteiramente liso interiormente,*
> *sou um aquário dos mares,*
> *sou apenas um balão cheio dessa verdade do mundo.*
>
> *Sei que vou com ela,*
> *sinto-a contra mim,—*
> *nunca estive tão perto da verdade.*

(I, pp. 78-79)

(I've never been so close to truth before.
I feel it pressed against me,
I know I'm walking with it.

So many times I spoke always denying,
exhausting all the possible negations,
directing them at truth's encirclement,
and which today, concave so concave,
I'm entirely smooth within myself,
I'm an aquarium of the seas,
I'm only a balloon filled with those worldly truths.

I know I'm walking with it,
I feel it pressed against me,—
I've never been so close to truth before.)

(trans. F.G.Williams)

The feeling of concavity (regarding Absolute Truth? regarding interior truth, i.e., a purely rationalistic knowledge of truth?) is reminiscent of Alberto Caeiro's "Ser real quer dizer não estar dentro de mim. / Da minha pessoa de dentro não tenho noção de realidade" ("Being real means not being inside of myself. / Regarding my inner person I have no notion of reality") *(Poemas de Alberto Caeiro,* p. 91). Although in many respects no two poets could harbor more diametrically opposed world views than Jorge de Sena and Pessoa's heteronym Alberto Caeiro—Caeiro is a "poet of Nature without people"; Sena a poet who says "nature interests me if human beings or human marks are upon nature; otherwise, I'm not interested in nature at all"—nevertheless they touch common ground in looking outward in search of truths; in denying that truth can be attained by solely abstract reasoning; in denying that Absolute Truth is possible. Sena, however, goes much farther than Caeiro. For the latter, truth is, in principle, what one perceives with the bodily senses. Sena, while pointing to exterior reality in this poem, refrains from any hasty conclusions or definitions. Indeed, he refrains from telling us what truth is: he tells us only that he materially feels it pressing against him. For him truth, although connected with the *res extensa* in this case, remains an open-ended reality. The fact that truth is associated with the dynamic nature of water ("I'm an aquarium of the seas") and the fragility of a balloon bespeaks the ever-changing nature of naturalistic truth and the lack of absolute fixities in the humanistic path. But the overall optimistic tone underscored by the living waters and the rising balloon also belong to the humanist's way.

The last poem of *Persecution,* "Eternity," also bears an eschatological title—against which Sena asserts another important humanistic truth: the truth of human creation. In "Pentecost," the poet foresees the day when he and God will be together in a poem without tears, when he will maintain shut—"for old time's sake" (i.e., the time when he was a believer?)—the hand with which he helped God. In "Eternity," God *is* with the poet in a poem, in a manner of speaking:

> Vens a mim
> pequeno como um Deus,
> frágil como a terra,
> morto como o amor,
> falso como a luz,
> e eu recebo-te
> para invenção da minha grandeza,
> para rodeio da minha esperança
> e pálpebras de astros nus.
>
> Nasceste agora mesmo. Vem comigo.
>
> (I, p. 79)

36

(You come to me
small like a God,
frail like the earth,
dead like love,
false like the light,
and I receive you
for the creation of my greatness,
for the making of my hope
and the eyelids of naked stars.

You were born just now. Come with me.)
(trans. Helen Barreto)

Here God appears to be reduced to a simile for a poem; the earth is fragile; love can be dead; light can be false, i.e., all these symbols traditionally associated with God as his creation or attributes are robbed of their importance, of their aura of sanctity. Why? Possibly to make room for what, to the demiurgic poet, has come, momentarily, to stand for them: human creation itself. The latter, too, is an act of love, of giving birth; it is greatness; it is hope; it points to the heavens and humanizes them, i.e., gives them *eyelids*—light, life. In contradistinction to the "lack of correspondence" between heaven and earth, i.e., between the deity and man, dramatized in the poem "Stains" *(Persecution),* the ending of "Eternity" bespeaks companionship, friendship, sharing between the poet and his own creation. It bespeaks a true eternity: "You were born just now. Come with me."

Although *Persecution* suggests a kind of resolution of the religious problem in favor of secularism, still it would not be impossible to find in Sena's later poetical works ideas construable as beliefs in some sort of personal God, religious feelings, the notion that death is somehow not the end as far as human beings are concerned. What should be stressed is that the poems in which such ideas and feelings are detectable are relatively few in number and, more important, they are necessarily ambiguous poems. They are also far outweighed by poems where in Sena's unequivocal preoccupation is with this-earthly reality and the very denial of supernaturalism. One difficulty in determining Sena's stance vis-à-vis the supernatural is the fact that he often utilizes religious imagery and symbols to express naturalistic truths and beliefs. In the poems discussed above, for example, the eschatological titles ("Declaration," "Transept," "Pentecost," "Ascension," "Eternity") are used for two reasons: for their emotional power, and to contrast with the naturalistic truths and beliefs the poet wishes to communicate and celebrate. In other cases, however, the truth expressed can be so ambiguous that neither naturalism nor supernaturalism can be totally ruled out.

A case in point is "Glory" *(Crown of the Earth)*. "Um dia se verá que o mundo não viveu um drama" ("One day we shall see the world has lived no drama"), the first line reads (the translation is by James Houlihan). Following this the poet shows us what the world has indeed lived. The ten-line enumeration of dystopic images includes battles, crimes, "todas estas crianças que não chegaram a desdobrar-se em carne viva" ("all these children who could not unfold themselves in living flesh"), poets drilled by bullets, and culminates with "todo este sangue expressamente coalhado / à face íntegra da terra, / tudo isto é o reverso glorioso do findar dos erros" ("all this blood purposely clotted / on the whole face of the earth / all this is the glorious inverse of ending our errors"). And then comes the somewhat problematic utopic last line: "Um dia nos libertaremos da morte sem deixar de morrer" ("One day we shall free ourselves from death and not cease dying"). Possible reading: One day we shall free ourselves from death, or this type of so-called life, without ceasing to die a natural biological death. In other words, the world did not live a drama; it lived a "death," from which mankind will one day "resuscitate" (in accordance with Sena's Marxist hope of humankind's improvement, a hope based on the Marxian belief in the perfectibility of man) without ceasing to experience the inevitable death which "belongs to all and will come" ("Letter to my Children on the Shootings of Goya"). Supporting this naturalistic reading of the poem is the ironic phrase "the glorious inverse of ending our errors," which in turn renders secular the eschatological title "Glory" (i.e., heaven or its bliss). However, this interpretation does not fully preempt a supernaturalistic reading (which, in my view, is much less tenable): One day we shall rise from this cruel life into eternal life, without ceasing to die a biological death.

Still related to Sena's naturalistic conception of life are his poems on death. One of them, "Mortal Remains" *(Exorcism)* constitutes not only a celebration of the laws of nature but a denial of transcendence, i.e., an exorcism of supernatural hopes—hopes based in part on what Sena termed in the autobiographical statement quoted earlier "the antiquated concept" of dualism or the separability of body and spirit. With a good sense of humor, some metaphysical anguish, no supernaturalistic illusions, in a sense affirming life in the face of death, Sena writes:

O que de nós mais dura: só esqueleto
que nos fez ósseos mais do que moluscos.
O resto acaba tudo; quanto foi sentidos,
vontade, amor, inteligência, carne,
e sobretudo sexo, o sexo acaba
e se desfaz na mesma pasta informe
e fim de tudo que não é só ossos,
apenas os detritos da armação mecânica
de que se pendurou por algum tempo,
em sangue e carne, o porque somos vida.
E aquilo com que a vida se gozou
ou por acaso vidas foram feitas,
acaba como o mais—e os ossos ficam,
dos deuses esburgados. Porque os deuses temem
que sobreviva o sexo em de que morrem
na liberdade de existir-se nele.

(III, pp. 143-44)

(The lasting part of us: skeleton only
which makes us bonier than molluscs are.
The rest all goes: whatever has been senses,
will-power, loving, intelligence, flesh,
and, above all, sex, yes the sex goes,
unmakes itself to the same paste, shapeless
and end of all that is not only bones,
mere scrap of the mechanical armature
from which there dangled for a certain time,
by blood and flesh, the reason we are life.
And that with which life has enjoyed itself
or, fortuitously, lives have been made,
goes like the most part—and the bones remain,
peeled by the gods. Because gods are afraid
sex may survive in what they die of in
the liberty of being there in it.)

(trans. Jonathan Griffin)

As noted earlier, one of the major tenets of Sena's humanism—and, for that matter, of any responsible naturalistic commitment to life—is the reliance on reason and science. As George Novack says (op. cit., p. 133), "Socialist humanism believes firmly in the power of intelligence and reason and the cultivation of consciousness. But it does not err in making an ideal of reason detached from the social context, as do the idealistic humanists who believe in the omnipresence of intelligence regardless of time and place, and controlling circumstances." Jorge de Sena also believes that reason—applied to the limits of legitimacy, i.e., in association with concrete experience—is the natural weapon that has the potential of liberating man from the yoke of superstition. It is reason and freedom from any and all types of easy dogmas that the poet advocates and opposes to religious superstition ("alienation" in Marxian terms) in the poem "Pamphlet" *(Crown of the Earth),* a poem inspired by a procession in Oporto where people sang the "Ave."

Science, a product of applied reason, is the key with which humankind can open the doors to ever widening frontiers of knowledge; a tool with which man can increasingly gain control of his this-worldly destiny. One need but refer to a single poem of Sena's, "Death, Space, and Eternity" *(Metamorphoses),* to realize the promise that science holds for humankind in the opinion of Jorge de Sena. "Death, Space, and Eternity" can best be understood within the entire thematic framework of *Metamorphoses.* Because the book deals to a very large degree with the topic of death—for example "Pietà of Avignon," "Cephalus and Procris," *"The Dead Woman,* by Rembrandt," etc.—the poem, inspired in part by Sputnik I and dedicated to José Blanc de Portugal in memory of his mother, becomes a powerful statement against human death in general. More important still, it is an expression of the poet's hope, momentarily converted into poetic certainty or belief, that science will one day liberate men from death—if not individually, at least as a species—and impel them to the stars. Symbolically and most appropriately, this poem was written, as Sena is careful to point out, on *Sábado de Aleluia,* the day Christ is said to have risen from the dead. But in Sena's poem he who rises to Space and Eternity is man. Although an eschatological implication is probably unavoidable in this poem, nevertheless Sena makes it quite clear what kind of human life he foresees occupying Space and Eternity:

> A Vida Humana, sim, a respirada,
> suada, segregada, circulada,
> a que é excremento e sangue, a que é semente
> e é gozo e é dor e pele que palpita
> ligeiramente fria sob ardentes dedos.
>
> (*II*, p. 142)

> (Human Life, yes, the one that is breathed,
> Sweated, secreted, circulated,
> the one that is excrement and blood, the one that is seed
> and is pleasure and is pain and skin that throbs
> slightly cold when eager fingers touch it.)

Sputnik I, a fruit of modern science, becomes a symbol of the possiblities inherent in man's pursuit of knowledge through the scientific method.

It would be ludicrous, of course, to assume that Jorge de Sena was so naive as to believe that science is the panacea for all the problems facing humanity, the most important of which, nuclear destruction, hinges upon the potential misuse of science. Far from it, as Sena's often unflattering poetical portrayal of almost half a century of human experience amply demonstrates. But he was rational enough to recognize that the blame is not to be placed at the doorstep of science itself. He was honest enough to give science its due. It is science that has, to a large extent, lighted our way; it is science which in part substantiates the poet's belief, expressed in this poem, that death may be natural in nature but not natural for us humans. It is to science that we owe the supreme human triumph of being able to truthfully say, as Sena does in this poem, "de tanto que matava se não morre" ("of so much that used to kill we no longer die"). The end of this poem, I dare say, constitutes one of the most moving passages in all of Portuguese poetry, one which, because of its extreme optimism and faith in humankind, cannot fail to move any sentient human being:

> Para emergir nascemos. O pavor nos traça,
> este destino claramente visto:
> podem os mundos acabar, que a Vida,
> voando nos espaços, outros mundos
> há-de encontrar em que se continue.
> E, quando o infinito não mais fosse,
> e o encontro houvesse de um limite dele.
> a Vida com seus punhos levá-lo-á na frente,
> para que em Espaço caiba a Eternidade.

(*II*, p. 142)

> (To emerge we were born. Dread lays out
> before us this clearly visible destiny:
> worlds may end, but Life,
> flying in space, other worlds
> shall find in which to continue.
> And, if infinity should be no more,
> and if we should happen upon its limits,
> Life with its fists shall tear it open
> so that in Space Eternity will fit.)

A rejection (for all practical purposes) of supernaturalism leaves the humanist without any lofty agency to act as control tower for man's behavior. "Humanistic ethics," says Corliss Lamont, "draws its guiding principles *from* human experience and tests them *in* human experience" (op. cit., p. 232). Man is thus the sole pilot of his moral conduct. This does not mean, however, as is often supposed, that man is doomed to fight a no-win battle in the jaws of evil and social chaos. "Socialist humanism," George Novack rightly explains, "believes no less strongly than any other creed in human decency, dignity, and fellowship. But just as it is rational without being rationalistic, so it is moral without falling into empty moralizing. A genuinely practical and progressive morality cannot be separated from actual conditions, contending forces, and basic issues of class society." Novack goes on to add—and here Sena would agree with him only in part—that "According to the moral code of socialist humanism, whatever aids the exploited against the exploiter and the oppressed against their oppressors, and whatever actions clear the way to a free and equal society—whether these are directed against capitalists, colonialists, or usurping bureaucracies—are justified and morally right" (Novack, pp. 133-34).

Sena would agree with all these propositions, except one: the dangerous implications contained in Novack's "whatever aids," "whatever actions." We saw, in the autobiographical passage quoted above, that Sena does not believe that any reform whatever justifies the taking of human lives. He will not accept that a single human life be lost in any revolutionary effort, except accidentally. The "stern measures" (which may include killing human beings) for which, according to Novack, Bertold Brecht is apologizing in his poem "To Posterity," would not be condoned by Sena. In this particular Jorge de Sena is closer to the Existentialist view that nothing whatsoever is as important as a human life and "the joy of having it" (as Sena puts it in "Letter to My Children on the Shootings of Goya") than he is to socialist humanists like Novack and Brecht (if the former is correct in his interpretation of "To Posterity").

Sena's moral stance overlaps with his conception of poetry itself, as expressed in the following verses from sonnet VIII of *The Evidences:*

> *a pura liberdade do meu canto,*
>
> *um cântico da terra e do seu povo,*
> *nesta invenção da humanidade inteira*
> *que a cada instante há que inventar de novo.*
>
> (*I*, p. 182)

> (the genuine freedom of my song,
>
> a canticle of the earth and its people,
> in this invention of the whole of humanity
> which at every instant must be invented anew.)

Humanity, this excerpt indicates, is never static: it is a dynamic collective entity, one to which the humanist poet must forever be attuned.

Therefore, morality, the principles that act as beacon for man's behavior, must also be dynamic, not entombed in some frozen code. Because it serves the cause of humankind, and not any mythical higher principles, man's behavior must be guided, first and foremost, by respect for humanity and not by fear of retribution; the Golden Rule and not narcissistic self-interest (in this case naturalistic humanism gladly joins hands with Christianity and other religions in the *what* if not in the *why*). With the humanist John Dewey, humanists believe that the ethical truths of yesterday are not necessarily the truths of today; those of today may not, and most likely will not, hold sway in the different tomorrow of a different humanity.

The poem most likely to be considered the maximum, most unequivocal and deeply felt expression of Sena's humanistic ethical standing is "Letter to My Children on the Shootings of Goya." Again we must remember that the two thematic poles of *Metamorphoses* are the joyous experience and celebration of life, as represented for instance in *"The Swing, by Fragonard,"* and the theme of death. The poem inspired by Goya's *Third of May,* which is conceived by Sena as a letter to his children but is indeed addressed to all of humanity, brings these two extremely important Senian themes together and, I might add, most of the major tenets of Sena's humanism: love and celebration of life and hatred of life-denying cruelty; belief in an open society and defense of all kinds of legitimate freedoms, including religious, and condemnation of intolerance, dogmatism, and oppression, particularly oppression in the name of God; affirmation of earthly reality and personal denial or repudiation of the supernatural; a humanistic view of art and an implicit repudiation of the mere aesthetic or detached contemplation of same; commitment to human history—past, present, and future. In fact, in answer to a question posed to him by a group of students in one of the last classes he taught at the University of California, Los Angeles, Jorge de Sena singled out "Letter to My Children on the Shootings of Goya" as particularly illustrative and all-inclusive of his humanistic position.

Sena stated that he was an atheist who, "in a manner somewhat Hegelian, placed his life and destiny in the hands of this God whose existence and non-existence are the same meaningless thing." This does not mean, of course, that Sena literally believed that all human events are determined by fate or somehow preordained by destiny, however one conceives of the latter. It is undeniable, though, that Sena was something of a fatalist and that he believed in some sort of *destino.* He repeatedly acknowledged that the latter played a major role, not always positive, not always painless, in his life as a man and as an artist. "'La Cathédrale engloutie,' by Debussy" attests to this fact, as we shall see in a later chapter. "Soube-me sempre a destino a minha vida" ("My life always smacked to me of destiny"), Sena tells us in "Andante" *(Persecution)*. Both of these titles, the title of the poem ("Wanderer") and that of the book *(Persecution)*, as well as dozens of other similar titles easily collectable in Sena's corpus, underscore the life of the wanderer and emigrant—in every possible sense of these terms—that he lived. In "Ode to Destiny" *(Philosopher's Stone),* he writes resignedly:

> *Destino: desisti, regresso, aqui me tens.*
>
> *Em vão tentei quebrar o círculo mágico*
> *das tuas coincidências, dos teus sinais, das ameaças,*
> *do recolher felino das tuas unhas retrácteis*
> *—ah então no silêncio tranquilo, eu me encolhia ansioso*
> *esperando já sentir o próximo golpe inesperado.*
>
> (*I,* p. 174)
>
> (Destiny: I gave up, I return, here I am.
>
> I tried in vain to break the magical circle
> of your coincidences, of your signs, your threats,
> of the feline retracting of your retractile claws
> —alas! in tranquil silence, I would shrink uneasy
> already expecting the next unexpected blow.)

"Destiny" seems to have meant for Sena the collective name for the chances of life, for contingency, the "monster" who, in the course of our existence, often betrays our hopes and disheartens our spirit. "Humanism takes the position," writes Corliss Lamont, "that human life, like Nature as a whole, is shot through with contingency. When chance manifests itself in human affairs, we frequently describe it as accident or coincidence or luck—good luck or bad luck" (Lamont, p. 156). "Destiny" for Sena is not always negative, although it is nearly always painful. As the profusion of antithetic images at the end of "'La Cathédrale engloutie'" suggests (they will be discussed later), it was destiny that thwarted Sena's dream of a Navy career—but it was the same destiny that led him to the at once painful and joyous path of Art. Seen as a whole, though, Sena's gigantic production as a writer—in its quantity, quality, and content—is a monument to the humanistic proposition that man is the sole capable master of his ship even though many of the perils in the sea of life are beyond his control. But these unavoidable perils do not lead to defeatism, nihilism or solipsism: they lead to reaction and provoke rebellion, which is another name for commitment to, and affirmation of, life.

Sena's naturalistic philosophy of life results in an attitude of joyous affirmation and in a celebration of all of life's gifts: from wholesome sexual love, to holistic love, to love for humankind as a whole; from the enjoyment of Nature to the supreme rejoicing in the experience of art: from movies to a Beethoven quartet. Understandably, Sena condemns and does fierce battle with all forces that interfere with the sanctity of life and the freedom to enjoy and relish it. Sena celebrates life without the abashed subterfuges of moralists and pseudo-moralists, but also without the rosy-eyed awe of many romantics. He neither camouflages nor hyperbolizes the wonderful bounty and beauty of life. He is also not the kind of poet much given to metaphorizing the essential pleasures of living. More often than not they flow from his conscience and his pen with the unencumbered fluidity with which they overcome us, if we allow them. Sena experiences, he reasons. He respects because he loves the natural world with his senses, his emotions, his intellect. He delights in unusual beauty, in usual or trivial epiphanic moments, e.g., watching his baby daughter prattle at his feet; he is capable of relishing to the fullest the simple but grand pleasure of just being alive. Those who are afraid of life, and who may even deep down despise it, will probably be shocked at some of Sena's poems based on a "libertine conception of love" (the words are applied by him to his own poetry[10]). Those who love and respect life as he did will partake of the exultation in naturalness that the poet felt when he wrote *"The Swing, by Fragonard"* (*II,* p. 111), "Four Sonnets to Aphrodite Anadyomene" (*II,* pp. 151-53), "Love" (*III,* p. 75), "Art of Love" (*III,* p. 125), "Double Puzzle" (*III,* pp. 126-27), "Undress Someone" (*III,* p. 220), and "Those Legs that March" (*III,* p. 199). Sena's poems on sexual love can be as graphic as pictures, as shockingly honest as the feelings that inspired them. What greater honesty could we demand of a poet than that conveyed by the scene and accompanying meditation that comprise "In the Train from Edinburgh to London" (*III,* p. 234)? But Sena's poems on love do not dwell exclusively on "libertine" love: they cover the whole range of human love. What could be more tender than the exquisitely tender if totally unabashed "I know the Salt" (*III,* p. 236)? What could be a more forceful expression of love in a holistic frame than "The Death of Isolde," one of the greatest love poems of *Art of Music?*

One's spirit rises with Sena's songs of hope as he meditates, for example, on the future of Portugal, which the poet, like few others in Portuguese literature, repeatedly chastises and verbally batters to death, but which he, despite himself, deeply loves. Who has poetically photographed Portugal in darker colors than Jorge de Sena—in poems such as "The Artificial Paradises," "The Five Senses" (*I*, pp. 131; 208), "Refuse from an Empire," "Lisbon, 1971," "The Ballad of Gnawing Bones," "L'été au Portugal" (*III*, pp. 174; 175; 178; 179), "To Portugal," "Stop Pretending," and the utterly brutal "In the Land of Pricks" *(40 Years,* pp. 89; 130; 155)? Yet, in the midst of the seemingly unending fascist nightmare that had already lasted for over a quarter of a century when the next poem was written in 1956, Sena could muster enough hope, optimism and prophetic vision to write "Those Who Have It" (*II*, p. 44):

Não hei-de morrer sem saber
qual a cor da liberdade.

Eu não posso senão ser
desta terra em que nasci.
Embora ao mundo pertença
e sempre a verdade vença,
qual será ser livre aqui,
não hei-de morrer sem saber.

Trocaram tudo em maldade,
é quase um crime viver.
Mas, embora escondam tudo
e me queiram cego e mudo,
não hei-de morrer sem saber
qual a cor da liberdade.

(I will not die without knowing
The color of freedom.

I cannot be other than
Of this land of my birth.
While belonging to the world,
And since truth will always out,
What it will be like to be free here
I will not die without knowing.

So evilly has everything been changed.
It is almost a crime to live.
But even though they hide everything
And would have me blind and dumb,
I shall not die without knowing
The color of freedom.)

(trans. George Monteiro)

Fortunately, Sena lived to see the color of freedom in his country. He celebrates this event in the poem "April Song" *(40 Years,* p. 184), which is dedicated to the Portuguese Armed Forces and to the Portuguese people. The poem contains as epigraph the first two lines of the above quoted "Those Who Have It." "What is the color of freedom?"—Sena asks in "April Song." It is the color of the Portuguese flag; it is the color of hope (and hope is what the poet stresses) and that of struggle: "It is green, green and red." Sena goes on celebrating the freedom of the Portuguese nation in several other poems that comprise the series "'Political and Other Related' Poems" *(40 Years)*. He composed the poem "So, We Are Finally Free" on 2 May 1974, a week after the April 25 Revolution, still thinking of the poem "Those Who Have It," written eighteen years earlier. But Sena is cautious. His is not a blind trust in the freedom already won. It is also a warning to his countrymen to keep up the struggle to preserve what had already been gained and to gain what still remained to be won. He ends "So, We Are Finally Free" thus:

> *De todo o coração, gritemos o nosso júbilo, aclamemos gratos*
> *os que o fizeram possível. Mas, com toda a inteligência*
> *que se deve exigir do amadurecimento doloroso desta liberdade*
> *tão longamente esperada e desejada, trabalhemos cautelosamente,*
> *politicamente, para conduzir a porto de salvamento esta pátria*
> *por entre a floresta de armas e de interesses medonhos*
> *que, de todos os cantos do mundo, nos espreitam e a ela.*
>
> *(40 Years*, p. 188)

> (With all our hearts, let us raise our voices and rejoice, thankfully
>   praising
> those who made it all possible. But, with all the good judgement
> that must be exacted from the painful ripening of this freedom
> so long awaited and desired, let us work cautiously,
> politically, to bring this country safely to port
> through the forest of arms and frightul self-interests
> which, from all corners of the world, have their eyes on us and on
>   her.)

Being a socially oriented poet, Sena could not help but experience deep frustration, feel anger and even reach extremes of hopelessness in face of the calamities that befell humankind in this century and to many of which his poetry bears faithful witness. Before the poet departed for Brazil in 1959, for what he was to term a "self-imposed exile," he had experienced some of the worst years of fascism in Portugal, and had witnessed and to a large degree experienced himself the effects of the Spanish Civil War and World War II. The social, economic, political, and moral repercussions of fascism, the Spanish Civil War and World War II, as these affected Portugal and as they impinged upon the fate of humanity in general, constitute both the ostensible and underlying thematic thrust of Sena's first five books of poetry. The subject of fascism itself recurs throughout most of Sena's

47

poetry—even penetrating one of the poems of *Art of Music,* as we shall see. The Spanish Civil War and fascism are also at the core of such fictional, albeit autobiographically inspired, works as *The Grand-Captains* (1976), the novel *Signs of Fire* (1978), and other works of fiction. In Brazil, Sena did enjoy, as he himself said, "the experience of living in the full democracy that was, with all its defects and limitations, the government of President Kubitschek, and in the magnificence of the government of João Goulart." However, this was only until, as Sena puts it, "it was evident what was going to happen /with the Revolution of 1964."[11] Sena's experiences in Brazil are partially documented in the series "Brazil (1959-65)" of *Peregrinatio ad Loca Infecta,* as well as other poems scattered throughout the Senian corpus.

Ever in pursuit of a route to freedom, Sena emigrated to the United States and lived here for the rest of his life. In the United States, Jorge de Sena shared in the atmosphere brought about by the War in Vietnam, which was not destined to play a major role in his poetry,[12] but to which he alludes in the same interview published in *O Tempo e o Modo* in 1968: "Likewise, I find it invaluable to live in the United States, in the crucial moment the country finds itself in, *even though my liver suffers humanly all the time"* (my italics).

It is quite justifiable, then, that in light of all these events a committed humanist poet should experience the disillusionment and bitterness that characterize, among others, the series of poems on Christmas scattered throughout his poetical works, as well as poems such as "Ode to Destiny" (*I,* p. 174), "Requiem For the World" *(40 Years,* p. 94), "So Complicated" *(40 Years,* pp. 120-21), the already mentioned and appropriately entitled "Dead End, or in Sum" contained in a book also significantly entitled *Exorcism,* and the poem "Distich" *(40 Years,* p. 122). This two-line poem epitomizes epigrammatically a prevalent attitude running the entire course of Sena's poetry. It reads:

> De uma palavra sei que tem sentido:
> é desespero: não importa a causa.
>
> (Of one word I've known the full meaning:
> it is despair: no matter the cause.)

However, Sena always bounces back to a posture of guarded but confident optimism in the future of mankind—a guarded optimism which at times, as noted earlier, breaks down any reservation barriers. Illustrative of this optimistic hope is, for example, "A Very Little Light" (*II,* p. 52), which is perhaps Sena's best-known expression of hope for freedom, converted into poetic certainty, for all mankind. To this poem we may add several others whose very titles bespeak Sena's optimistic outlook: "Eternal Hope" (*I*, p. 149), "Peace" (*II*, p. 40), and "I Cannot Lose Hope in Humanity" *(40 Years,* p. 103). "Message For the Dead" (*II*, pp. 49-51), besides containing magnificent lines such as the opening ones—

> *Não desesperarei da Humanidade.*
> *Por mais que o mundo, o acaso, a Providência, tudo,*
> *à minha volta afogue em lágrimas e bombas*
> *os sonhos de liberdade e de justiça*

> (I shall not lose hope in Humanity.
> No matter if the world, chance, Providence, everything,
> around me should drown, in tears and bombs,
> the dreams of freedom and of justice)

—also contains extremely important statements regarding the poet's cosmological and ethical views.

Sena left us enough statements scattered in essays, prefaces, postfaces, notes to poems, and of course poems whose subject matter is poetry itself to allow us to assemble a complete and coherent poetics. It is not my intention to discuss exhaustively Sena's poetics (although I shall return to this topic in the next two chapters), but many of its concepts have a direct bearing on the discussion of his humanism. Sena's poetry from *Persecution* to *Perpetual Vision* constitutes a systematic application of his ideas on literature in general and poetry in particular. All of Sena's works, creative and otherwise, reveal a truly remarkable philosophical consistency, as stated earlier. Not only does his poetry exemplify aesthetic ideas extrapoetically elaborated—sometimes in connection with studies on the poetry of other poets—but these aesthetic ideas bear an organic relationship to his humanistic philosophy as a whole. Sena once wrote: "As a critic, I have never demanded of anyone more than I demand of myself: fidelity to a world view, a view as lucid as a fidelity to it must be complete; and I believe that the lucidity of one is the condition for the completeness of the other."[13]

Sena's ideas on poetry are intended by him as philosophico-aesthetic guidelines or theoretical explanations of the kind of poetry he writes or criticizes. They are not meant as universal dogma. The author of *Metamorphoses* believed, as he stated in the essay "Love of Literature,"[14] that everything we say about literature must be referred to the person we are and to our philosophy of life. That is why he left us a clear explanation of what constitutes the philosophical and aesthetic (and very often historical and autobiographical) groundwork of his poetry. Indeed, his essayistic and pre- and postfactory explanations provide indispensable keys to the reading of his poetical works. The more chronologically advanced Sena was in his poetical career, the longer and more elaborate his prefaces and postfaces grew; the more copious his notes to poems became, often incorporating explanations as to the sources of poems originally published without notes. Perhaps consciously, perhaps unconsciously, Sena felt the need to leave ajar the door to the understanding of his poetry. He probably did this for three reasons: he believed in openness and artistic honesty; he wanted to provide an aid to critics (often indispensable, considering the cultural wealth which informs his poetry); and as a safeguard against misinterpretation of his works. Sena was painfully aware of—indeed a bit paranoid about—the possibilities for misunderstanding and critical bad faith. And he considered himself, very often with reason, a victim of both. Sena warns in the postface to *Metamorphoses* that these poems are not "literary essays, moralistic meditations, impressionistic art criticism, all this dressed up in metrics and some emotion" (*II,* p. 162). He calls the poems of *Metamorphoses* "applied meditations" (p. 163). He also cautions against the interpretation of his place and travel poems as "touristic" ("Note" to *Exorcism, III,* p. 115). There are, in his prefaces, postfaces and notes to poems, several other such admonitions and interpretive hints.

Perhaps the most succinct and yet far-reaching definition of literature in general that Sena left us is contained in the above-mentioned essay, significantly entitled "Love of Literature." In this essay, Sena outlines what he considers to be the four basic attitudes assumable toward literature: to know it, to study it, to teach it, and to live it. Then, he defines literature thus: "the products of writing which, consciously or occasionally, go beyond the threshold of aesthetics to delight (sometimes how painfully!) in the act of creating, and not to delight in anything other than ⌊the fact⌋ that written language is but a means and a tool" (p. 116). This definition contains one two-pronged idea which Sena so often reiterates and which his own creations exemplify: literature is not, as some would have it, primarily a self-contained and self-sufficient aesthetic entity somehow divorced from or alienated from life; literature is, without ever surrendering its aesthetic integrity, a means to an end. Perfectly conscious of the heretical if not original character of this statement—proferred *after* and *amidst* so many consummate aestheticisms, both foreign and domestic—Sena insists in the same essay: "literature is not self-sufficient, and it only is *literature,* true and authentic literature, that is, when, by its very essence, it goes beyond the perimeters within which it is defined as autonomous and independent" (p.124).

What, then, is this higher cause to which literature renders service and from which it draws sustenance and meaning? Sena's entire literary corpus provides the answer: the cause of human life, the pursuit of human freedom, dignity, earthly happiness, and the creation of life-enhancing beauty. Literature is a "form of living," a way of being in life that, without ever forsaking or betraying the framework of Art, exposes and denies everything that may impede the fulfillment of these humanistic goals.

In this same essay Sena goes on to warn that the didactic function of literature or what he terms, less dogmatically, its "intentionality," is not tantamount to placing literature at the service of any specific ideology, or any restricted or self-serving morality. T.S. Eliot, in his essay "The Social Function of Poetry,"[15] states that "The meaning of the term *didactic* poetry has undergone some change. Didactic may mean 'conveying information', or it may mean 'giving moral instruction', or it may mean something which comprehends both" (p. 4). Sena understood the "intentionality" of literature as encompassing both of these functions (in accordance, of course, with what he terms "a sociologically enlightened morality"[16]), but also as going beyond them. To Sena literature is not the safeguard of values of any *status quo:* it is, much to the contrary, a revolutionary activity in the broadest sense of the term. Literature, he says, aims to "betray any and all securities, in the name of a broader security which it is our human mission to constantly reestablish" ("Love of Literature," p. 118). A page earlier Sena had written:

> Literature is, as it must be, a poison wisely administered; a juggler's art, capable of elegantly or violently raising an individual above the ground or of pulling the ground, as one pulls a rug, from under his feet; and literature is not at all obliged to maintain the individual suspended in midair, in any case. The intentionality of literature consists, in fact, in suspending the magical action and in letting him fall, bewildered and lost, from as high up as possible.

Sena's "intentionality" is thus more and less than a restrictive and restricting ideological didacticism—a role too often assumed by art, which he deeply despised. Less because it remains on this side of propounding static social, political and moral views to which one could readily pin a label—other than the all-encompassing and all-saying term "humanism." More because it is precisely on guard against such confining labels—be they philosophical or aesthetic. What underlies and in part explains Sena's forty years of poetic servitude is this humanist's deep conviction—a conviction which he defended against all modish currents—that Art, if it immerses itself in life, reflects it, and is not afraid to expose and accuse, but also praise and rejoice when it finds something praiseworthy and a true reason for rejoicing; if, in short, it is not afraid to proclaim the desire to see man totally and truly free; most of all, if it sets itself up as an unwavering example of that freedom, Art can be a guiding force in humankind's destiny without ceasing to be Art. Art can make a contribution, and perhaps not a small one, to help prepare the way toward a future full of promise and further hope. It will not make, perhaps, the impact often claimed for the books that changed the world. Very few, if any, literary works have done that. But as it works on the individuals who come in contact with it, they become—as they must if that contact is guided by openmindedness—changed, a bit lost perhaps, but also a bit more cleansed and hopeful and determined than before. Art, in short, is commitment for Jorge de Sena. It is not commitment to narrowly defined ideologies, religious or secular, of the right or of the left. Art must be committed to the ultimate and the ultimate, as Sena saw it, is life: the life that has been (his poetry is forever mindful of the past), the life that is (his poetry is forever attentive to the present), to the life that could be—for the sake of all those who call themselves human.

From the viewpoint of subject matter, Sena's poetry is fundamentally a transmutation of lived and/or witnessed experiences, not imagined experiences tailored to illustrate aprioristically conceived ideas or ideals. Therefore, his poetry draws thematic sustenance and points its guiding beacon at ever-changing life. That is why Sena defines poetry—his own poetry included—as "the recording, for a few centuries, or for a brief span of time of much or of little that happened to us."[17] Of course, Sena does not mean that the poet is a mere recorder of events, a disinterested seismograph that preserves the imprint of historical happenings. Sena's conception of the poet, as we shall have plenty of occasions to see, is that of recorder plus interpreter of what life presents him with. Sena grounds his poetry in reality, which is not to say that he buries it there. He is a creator, but his creation is always rooted in life; he upholds the aesthetic integrity of art, yet he conceives of the latter as inseparable from life. In his essay "The Humanist Frame," Sir Julian Huxley describes the role of the humanist artist in a way that is entirely applicable to Jorge de Sena:

> The individual artist has two main functions—that of creator and that of interpreter. As interpreter, he translates complex and emotion-tinged experience into directly communicable forms and so is able to express what otherwise would remain unexpressible. He bears witness to the variety of the world and its significance, to its wonder and beauty, but also to its horror and nastiness. His witness may be by way of affirmation or by way of protest. But his function, even when he is not conscious of it, is to interpret the world to man, and man to himself. As creator, on the other hand, he provides experiences of stimulus and enjoyment, sometimes enlargements of experience itself . . .[18]

Of course, Sena's humanistic ideas and ideals influence to some degree *which* experiences he poetizes and to a large degree *how* he poetically transforms the interior experiences, the incidents, the social and political events, the travels, and the works of art that his muse converts into poems. Although in the next two chapters I will deal in greater detail with Sena's poetics, let me hasten to add that the nature of Sena's poetical inspiration is neither entirely volitional nor mysterious. He always claimed that poems "happened" or "occurred" to him, and that he always remained much influenced by surrealism, without having ever officially belonged to this or any other -ism. Surrealism contributed to his freedom of poetical thought and is also revealed in his poetic imagery. On the subject of poetical inspiration, a comparison between Jorge de Sena and Fernando Pessoa is useful. Fernando Pessoa used the verb "to happen" in connection with poetical inspiration. There is, however, a great difference between Sena's type of inspiration and the kind that Pessoa claims in the famous ortonymic poems "Passos da Cruz" ("Stations of the Cross") that begin "Aconteceu-me do alto do infinito / Esta vida ⌐de poeta?⌐" ("This ⌐poet's?⌐ life / Happened to me from the heights of infinity") and, more unequivocally, "Não sou eu quem descrevo. Eu sou a tela / E oculta mão colora em mim" ("I do not describe. I am the canvas / And an occult hand paints on me").[19] Poetical inspiration is, by definition, always somewhat mysterious in its psychological implications, yet Sena's poetry reveals that, despite the fact that poems do "happen" or "occur" to him, the nature of this happening is, by his own admission, more akin to Goethe's and Rilke's type of inspiration than it is to Pessoa's occultist type, i.e., the one type that Pessoa mentions in these poems. (As we know, there are many other types of inspiration as far as Pessoa's other poets are concerned.) In other words, if not the full thematic implications or the form, at least the seed of what happens to Sena as poem has, for the most part, already happened or is happening as vital lived experience. (We shall see later that Sena quotes both Goethe and Rilke to this effect.) Therefore, inspiration for Sena is not a volitional act, but neither is it a calling of unfathomable mysterious origin, or the weaving of experiences out of a void.

A general principle always presides at the choice or "happening" and handling of poetical subject matter: an unwavering commitment to life. Sena generally shunned topics where human presence was lacking. In the videotape interview with Frederick G. Williams, previously alluded to, Jorge de Sena states, for example, that "Nature interests me, but nature interests me if human beings or human marks are upon nature; otherwise, I'm not interested in nature at all."[20] Some of his poems belie this statement, if what he meant to say was that Nature *only* interested him if human presence were evident or strongly implied. There is, first of all, undoubtedly a little of *boutade* in that statement, as Mrs. Mécia de Sena herself admitted to me in private conversation. And Professor George Monteiro also has shared with me his opinion that "this over-statement was meant probably as a corrective to those who glorify Nature at the expense of the human, those to whom a tree is more to be valued than a human life." About a dozen poems can be found in Sena's corpus that could be properly classified as Nature poems, for example "Two California Seascapes," one of which, "Big Sur" (*III,* p. 155), reads like a verbal photograph, where the only human presence is implied in the poetic use of language itself:

> Do alto da escarpa escarpas se prolongam
> em que de praias se entrelaça o mar
> sobrevoado de aves. Os rochedos
> somem-se e brotam de sem espuma em volta
> que só ressaca é depois deles areia.
>
> (From high atop the escarpment escarpments extend
> in which the shore has interlaced the sea
> overflown by birds. The rocks
> disappear and gush forth without foam around them
> since after them the receding tide leaves only sand.)
>
> (trans. F.G. Williams)

It is true, however, that in most of his Nature poems human life is read into the landscape, as in "Spring in Wisconsin" (*III,* p. 89), where "naked and motionless trees" "are like nerves or expectant veins":

> Na limpidez tranquila da manhã diáfana
> em que as despidas árvores imóveis
> são como nervos ou expectantes veias
> no corpo transparente do azulado ar,
> as águas quietas, mas não tanto que
> pareçam gelo perto as águas mais distantes,

pousam na margem delicadamente
como na mesma terra infusas se dispersam
dos ramos e dos troncos sombras confundidas.
A terra se amarela de ante-verde
e, sêca, espera, entre a neve que foi
e o ténue estremecer da seiva que desperta.

(In the peaceful clear of the shimmering morn
where naked and motionless trees
are like nerves or expectant veins
in the translucent body of the bluish air,
the still waters (not so still
as to mirror more than the concentrated hue
of the tranquil air nor yet less so that
the most distant waters should seem ice nearby)
pause daintily on the bank
as sunken in the very earth are spread
the wavy shadows of branch and trunk.
The earth yellows to its pre-green
and, dry, it waits somewhere between the snow that was
and the subtle tremor of awakening sap.)

(trans. Jack E. Tomlins)

There is, of course, nothing incompatible between humanism and a love of Nature. Quite the contrary, as Corliss Lamont points out and as Lucretius, long ago, demonstrated in his *De Rerum Natura*. And there is in Sena's poetry and in numerous passages of his fiction plenty of proof that Jorge de Sena enjoyed the spectacle of Nature and reacted to its beauty with the sensitivity of the true poet he was. It is also undeniable, however, that when he drew inspiration from beautiful objects, he preferred to concentrate on man-made ones, such as works of art. He looked for man in a landscape, as we saw; in the statue of a gazelle, as we shall see; and in a work of absolute music from which, as some have claimed, nearly all vestiges of human life have been removed. For when he poetically approached a work of art, it was not solely or even primarily for its beauty, although he was most capable and intellectually equipped to appreciate beauty. It was for art's human charge, the fact that art objects are repositories of human experience. He poetically approached art objects not for purposes of passive contemplation, but in order to bring to life, through the revivifying power of poetry, the life force that he knew the artists had invested in their works, as well as the life force that he, as experiencer of art,[1] was most willing to invest in it. In whatever Sena makes into poetry, if he does not find man—man will be there when he is done with the poem.

There is very little that is earthshakingly original in humanism, a philosophy of life whose roots are ancient and everywhere—except that it is constantly incorporating what is new and in harmony with its eternal principles and constantly on guard against what may be new but noxious to those principles. Yet, there is something most original and refreshing in Sena's humanism as mirrored in his poetry: it is this search, this quest for humankind, this breathing of life into everything that his muse comes in contact with.

II

The Poet as Diarist

Although some of Sena's philosophico-aesthetic ideas recur from preface to preface and from essay to essay, none does so with greater frequency than the idea which states that his poetical works constitute a "diary turned poetry" and that he, the poet, is both an actor in the experiences he poetizes and a witness to what happens around him. In the preface to *Poetry-I*, Sena refers to the poetry he wrote between 1936 and the eve of the 1974 Portuguese Revolution as

> the "poetical diary" of a *witness,* as I always wanted to be, of 38 years of Portuguese life, from the time fascism installed itself with the outbreak of the Spanish Civil War until it fragilely collapsed, blown by the contradictory and complex breezes of the April 1974 Revolution, which I felt would never come to pass. What I wrote or will write after that span of time already belongs to a distinct world and a different experience—but what I lived within myself, as a poet, as a human being, as a citizen, as a politically involved albeit always independent person . . ., is what's represented and distilled in these books, which I published from 1942 to 1974, containing poems written from 1938 to 1974. (*I*, p. 11)

In the preface to *Poetry-III,* Sena again alludes to his book *I Know the Salt... and Other Poems* as the "continuation of my diary turned poetry that the writing of poems has always been for me, even when the poems deal with what happened long ago" (*III*, p. 15). And several other statements could be quoted to show that Sena always conceived of his poetry as a diary.

Viewed generally, the differences between the diary and lyric poetry are so great and the similarities apparently so few that, barring Sena's statements, any approximation of the two genres might seem inappropriate. To compare painting, music, or any of the "higher" literary genres with lyric poetry is to compare art forms that occupy more or less equal planes of aesthetic excellence. But to compare the relatively minor art of the diary with lyric poetry—the ultimate in verbal expression—does indeed seem farfetched. "A good diary is not necessarily literature," says Kate O'Brien. She explains why: "Vision, imagination, passion, fancy, invention, scholarship, detachment, and the steely restraints and consciously selected embellishments of form and of design—none of these has a vital place in diary-writing."[1] In fact, Alain Girard goes so far as to say that "To speak of art with respect to the intimate diary would constitute a kind of nonsense, except if one wishes to deny its specificity and that which lends it a unique value."[2] Given Sena's statements, however, a comparison between his poetry and the diary, for purposes of an inventory of his poetical subject matter, is not only in order but actually necessary.

The diary may be defined as a day-to-day record of experiences both public and private, reflecting the point of view of the journal keeper. (In this study the terms diary and journal will be used interchangeably.) Entries are usually in prose, although some diaries—Miguel Torga's and Vergilio Ferreira's, for example—alternate prose entries with poems. The latter are sometimes independent of the subject matter of the prose entries. At other times the poems constitute meditations on themes derived from the experiences recorded in prose. Most diaries have not been avowedly intended for publication. Many have indeed appeared posthumously. But many diarists also have written their journals with publication in mind. Amiel himself, whose *Journal intime* is of the most intimate kind, seems to have contemplated publication of at least some portions of the work. Anaïs Nin, although she thought about burning her diary at some point, actually ended up investing much time and energy readying it for publication. And Miguel Torga thinks of his *Diary* as a book both for the public and for the self: "Being a work for the public—unfortunately, all I write is for the public—it is also meant as a book for me, something which rarely happens to an author."[3]

The idea expressed by Kate O'Brien and Alain Girard, as well as other critics, that the diary is a para-literary art form or no art form at all, must also be revised in light of many works. Amiel's *Journal intime* has always been read as much for its literary style as for its content. Torga's *Diary,* in its combination of poetry and poetic prose entries, is as much a work of art (I dare say, one of his best!) as it is a huge anthology of experiences, a partial repository of a human life, a literary portrait of an era. And referring to Anaïs Nin, Robert A. Fothergill writes: "Existing in an intermediate zone between living experience and the formal work of art, the diary threatens to encroach upon both, becoming a substitute for life and a deflection from art; the resolution of this problem is one of her central themes."[4]

When speaking of the diary it is important to distinguish among the several principal types or forms that this most versatile and Protean of genres can and does assume. There are at least five major types of journals, keeping in mind that none is absolutely pure or totally excludes elements more typical of the others. They are: the public diary, the intimate, the religious, the travel, and the heterogeneous diary. The last named generally includes, in greater or lesser proportions, elements typical of the others. It is important to elaborate on these differences for a comparison (and later for a contrast) between the diary and the poetry of Jorge de Sena with its various types of subject matter. *Metamorphoses,* the book of poems inspired by works of visual art, and *Art of Music* constitute special sequences of Sena's poetic diary.

The fundamental characteristic of the public diary is its emphasis on outward rather than inward experience. This does not mean, however, that the diarist dwells exclusively on major public occurrences, such as political changes, wars, and natural disasters. It also does not imply that the writer is a mere recorder, a self-styled newsman, of what is happening around him. The public diarist is all this, to be sure. But the bulk of his journal may still be, and more often than not is, a repository of the keeper's day-to-day personal experiences, which generally encompass the *minutiae* of everyday living. The time element is very important to the diarist (as we shall see, it is also of extreme importance to Sena). Events are recorded usually as they are happening, as they have recently happened or, if they occurred long ago, they are often communicated with a present-like vividness. What is perhaps most important to stress is the fact that the self-image projected by the diarist is that of the social being in interaction with his fellow man rather than that of the introvert. The public diarist is a person committed, in the broadest sense of the term, to his spatio-temporal reality. He is a witness of his times, a recorder but often a re-creator of events. But he is simultaneously the major character in the life drama(s) that he so assiduously commits to paper. For what happens, happens to and through him.

Perhaps no writer in any literature is more prototypical of this type of diarist than the Englishman Samuel Pepys. His *Diary,* first published in part in 1825 but written in 1660-69, gives a vivid picture of those years at the same time that it reveals numerous aspects of the author's personality. "To read Pepys is to be transported immediately into his own world," writes Robert Latham. And he adds: "His diary is not so much a record of events as a re-creation of them. Not all the passages are as picturesque as the famous set-pieces in which he describes Charles II's coronation or the Great Fire of London, but there is no entry which does not in some degree display the same power of summoning back to life the events it relates."[5]

Unlike the public diary, the intimate journal is a record of mental history. It is the book of the introvert who generally shuns collective experience and social analysis in order to concentrate on personal experience and self-analysis. The intimate diary is not a record of the times, but a mirror of the soul. In this type of diary, says Alain Girard (op. cit., p. 16), "The circumstances, the events, if they are recorded in an intimate diary, it's never for their own sake. They are only a reason for the author to reflect on himself, to take to his conscience the reflection of the exterior world, to provoke a feeling or a thought, to clarify an aspect of his being, considered for purposes of analysis as the only reality." To say, therefore, that the intimate diary is a record of personal memoranda may not be enough. The public diary is that, too. The journal intime is, above all, the chronicle of day-to-day experiences and thoughts so private that one would hesitate to share them with others. If there is a bedroom book, the intimate journal is it. It is usually the type that its authors are, understandably, most reluctant to publish. "This literary form, . . . is characterized first of all by its specific 'intimacy,' by the fact that the text is not written to be read by anyone except the writer."[6]

In Portuguese literature, the intimate diary is well represented by the fragments of self-analysis left by Fernando Pessoa and published in the volume *Páginas íntimas e de auto-interpretação (Intimate Journal and Pages of Self-Analysis),* posthumously published in 1966. Famous intimate journals have been left by, among other well-known writers, George Sand, André Gide, and Cesare Pavese. The prototype of the intimate diary, however, is Henri Frédéric Amiel's *Journal intime,* the first part of which was published in 1822, about a year after the author's death. The bulk of this work consists of philosophical reflections, meditations, inward soliloquies, numerous notes on readings (which are also typical of all the other types of diaries), self-reproaches, reflections on the meanings of holidays, and the like. True that Amiel's diary contains brief entries on travels and sporadic references and commentaries on public events. But entries of these types are relatively rare. "I have just heard of fresh cases of insubordination among students,"[7] he writes in an entry dated 20 March 1865. Elsewhere he notes: "I have just read the *procès-verbal* of the Conference of Pastors held on the 15th and 16th of April at Paris" (op. cit., p. 160). He comments briefly on some religious controversy of his day; he mentions, without further comment, the death of an important public figure such as Sainte-Beuve. But then he quickly retreats into his inner world. "Instead of only seeing the world," he says, "I analyze myself" (op. cit., p. 246). Amiel defines himself and the intimate diarist when he writes: "I am a spectator, so to speak, of the molecular whirlwind which men call individual Life; I am conscious of an incessant metamorphosis, an irresistible movement of existence, which is going on within me. I am sensible of the flight, the revival, the modification, of all the items of my being, all the particles of my river, all the radiations of my special force" (op. cit., p. 167).

The religious diary is a variant of the intimate diary. The major difference between the two is that the "reader" of the religious diary is not the self, but God. As the name implies, it is a type of journal characterized by adherence to activities, thoughts, reflections and feelings related to devout life. It can be a well-structured spiritual autobiography, as Saint Augustine's *Confessions*; it can be a more conventional diaristic work, such as *The Diary of Richard Kay* (1737-50). Robert A. Fothergill (op. cit., 103) characterizes Kay's journal thus: "That Kay's 'reader', the object of his address, is a personal paternal God cannot be doubted. The general tone displays to a marked degree the presentation of the self in a humbly filial role, and every entry concludes in a prayer. Each day he furnishes a polite account of his expenditure of time and expresses a renewal of his religious commitment."

In the travel diary we return to outward experience once again. It constitutes a subcategory of the public diary just as the religious may be construed as a particular mode of the intimate diary. The travel diary is also related to the travelogue or memoir, that type of literature inspired by and dealing with experiences related to travel. In order to characterize the travel diary, one has to distinguish among at least three related types of travel works. I shall call them the subjective travel narrative, the objective memoir, and the travel diary itself. The differences among the three reside, on the one hand, in the literary manipulation of events experienced and, on the other, in the kind of didactic purpose to which those experiences and the reactions they provoke are put. One aspect that all travel works have in common (perhaps to a greater degree than any other type of diary) is didacticism: from imparting of information about places to ostensible moralizing. Being faced with new places, different peoples, new and varied customs—which one instinctively compares and contrasts with those of one's own country—perhaps accounts in part for this moralizing. The natural human tendency to show "I was there," perhaps contributes a great deal.

In the subjective travel narrative the events connected with a voyage or trip are little more than a pretext for meditations, reflections, satire, moralizing, etc. In some extreme examples of the subjective travel narrative, the trip itself may be partially or wholly imaginary, as is the case, respectively, with Sterne's *A Sentimental Journey* (1768) and De Maistre's *Voyage au tour de ma chambre* (1794). Examples of subjective travel narratives based on real travels are Fernão Mendes Pinto's *Peregrinação (Peregrination),* published in 1614, and Almeida Garrett's *Viagens na minha terra (Travels in My Country),* which appeared in 1843-45. Rebecca Catz has persuasively argued that *Peregrinação,* while adopting the framework of Pinto's 21-year peregrination throughout the Orient, is a work of satire in the vein of Jonathan Swift's *Gulliver's Travels.*[8] In Garrett's *Viagens*, the events of the trip from Lisbon to Santarém function primarily as points of departure for commentaries on the most diverse aspects of human experience. Garrett, who was inspired by the works of Sterne and De Maistre, dabbles in an extremely wide variety of subjects ranging from socio-political impressions to impressionistic literary criticism. Today *Viagens na minha terra* is revered for its stylistic innovations (in this particular it is a masterpiece) and for the histórico-sentimental-autobiographical novelette included as part of the narrative.

The objective travel memoir is a lot closer in content and intent to the travel diary than is the subjective narrative. However, the objective memoir constitutes a much more carefully constructed work than the diary generally is. The depth of treatment of geographical, historical, and cultural information that goes into the objective travel memoir is also greater than it commonly is in the diary. The author of the memoir may depart from the experiences at hand in order to reflect on the nature and meaning of what is being seen and heard. But when he includes interpretations, comments, reflections and personal reactions they are presented as being based on the factual evidence at hand, on the information obtained, not on the author's fancy or imagination. His general comments, in other words, are meant to serve an objective rather than a subjective purpose, even when subjectivity enters into the narrative. Travel memoirs, unlike diaries for the most part, are usually written some time after the travels take place. The information contained in such works may derive as much from a library as it does from the actual lived or witnessed experiences. Examples of objective travel memoirs are Joaquim de Paço d'Arcos's *A floresta de cimento (The Cement Forest)* (1942), based on travels in the United States, and Ferreira de Castro's *A volta ao mundo (Voyage Around the World)* (1944).

The travel diary, as represented for instance by Montaigne's *Journal de voyage en Italie* (based on travels undertaken in 1580-81, but only published in 1774), is a chronicle of day-to-day activities and events experienced during a trip and written down as they are happening or soon thereafter. Because Montaigne's diary was not intended for publication and was composed *in locu,* it lacks any rigorous artistic organization. The primary concern of the author seems to be to record as much as possible of what he experiences during the trip. The entire journal constitutes a minute account of Montaigne's and his retinue's day-to-day passage and brief sojourn in parts of France, Switzerland, Germany, and Italy. The usual order of activities is for the group to arrive at a city or town and seek lodging. Following this, Montaigne almost invariably meets with the local seigneur—priest, dignitary, learned personage—with whom he engages in conversations. The latter may dwell on contemporary events of local interest, or may deal with history and art. The diary also records visits to monuments; includes comments on culinary arts; the beauty of women. Montaigne often compares what he sees and hears with their counterparts back home in France. Although the travel diarist like Montaigne often engages in meditations and reflections of all types, he differs from the subjective narrative writer in that the former's primary aim is to record experiences, not to use them as mere pretexts for philosophizing. The travel diarist also differs from the objective memoir writer in that the former person always occupies center stage. The objective memoir writer concentrates, at least in principle, on the world out there. He maintains a considerable distance between what he reports as facts and what he relates as subjective impression. He plays the historian, in other words. The travel diarist, on the other hand, is not only close to, but actually immersed in, the experiences he relates.

In this characterizaton of the different types of diaries we now come to the heterogeneous diary, which is the type probably most widely cultivated by twentieth-century writers. Miguel Torga's *Diary* (12 volumes, 1941-1977), and *The Diary of Anaïs Nin* (6 volumes, 1966-1977) are excellent examples. One way to define this kind of diary is to call it a repository of everything that happens around and within the writer which the latter deems worthy of being recorded and preserved. Heterogeneity, however, does not mean that equal importance is given to public, intimate, religious, and travel experiences.

Emphasis may lean more heavily on one or the other of those areas. Although Anaïs Nin's diary includes much information on public events and travels in the United States, Mexico, and Europe, we can nevertheless say that its primary orientation is psychological. Given Nin's deep interest in psychology and psychoanalysis, her diary is particularly rich in self-exploration and in psychological portraits of people she came in contact with. In this particular, no diarist (and perhaps not many writers of any kind) has surpassed her. A large portion of her diary is dedicated to accounts and analyses of her own dreams. Nin herself realizes the overwhelming preponderance of inward scrutiny in her journal over her interest in the outside world. She writes in the winter of 1955-56: "Now I do realize that my physical world is subjected to such an intense emotional lighting that it is for most people invisible or abstract. And it is in the realm of emphasis on the physical world that I want to round out my work. I worked too much like an X-ray, taking photographs of the psychic self."[9]

Miguel Torga, too, records in his diary much private memoranda, travel notes; there are plenty of insights into his and the national psyches. But what essentially characterizes his prose entries—and even his poems, as far as their subject matter is concerned—is a keen attention to what is happening around him in Portugal—from an incident or accident in the street, to a major socio-political event. Nin represents the psychologist and psychoanalyst; Torga assumes the role of the socio-political observer and commentator. (Let me mention in passing that, given their similar world views and the fact that they lived through some of the same public events in Portugal, a comparative study of some of Sena's Portugal-oriented poems and Torga's *Diary* might prove very fruitful and revealing indeed.) Torga describes best the thematic range of his diary when he writes:

> I have at least one consolation. There was no fact of my time, nor nook of this country that didn't engage my attention as if they were matters of life and death. I was no believer, but I believed in the concrete every-day reality as if it were a daily eternity. Therefore, I never let the great and small world happenings pass me by without meditating on them, nor did I fail to visit the plains and the little hillside fields of my country, following my stubborn and honest effort to be at once a man and Portuguese, while assuming the voluntary responsibility of being both.[10]

It is, therefore, evident that the most basic characteristic of all types of diaries is the utilization of actual experiences, both exterior and interior. The same is also true, to a very large extent, of Sena's poetry. "I have always understood poetry as a process of bearing witness," Jorge de Sena writes, "whose best art consists in giving expression to what the world (the inner and the outer) reveals to us." (Preface to 1st ed., *Poetry-I,* p. 26). The experiences Sena transforms into poems may be lived, and they may be witnessed. They may be experiences derived from his involvement in the common business of living; they may be experiences extracted from his encounter with works of art: literature, movies, painting, architecture, sculpture, music. The diarist may, and for the most part does, re-create or transform experiences; he may use them as points of departure for meditation or reflection. However, he usually does not invent or tailor them. Jorge de Sena *always* transmutes the inspiring experiences—because it is in the nature of poetry to do so, and because Sena conceives of poetry as a metamorphic art—but in the overwhelming majority of cases he does not snatch "experiences" out of a vacuum.

At least twice Sena quotes, with approval and admiration, major poets who, like himself, believed, at least at some point in their careers, that poetry ought to be rooted in real experience. These poets, as previously noted, are Goethe and Rilke. Sena quotes as epigraph to the section of *Philosopher's Stone* appropriately entitled "Circumstance," part of Goethe's famous statement to Eckermann: "The world is so big and so rich, and life is so full of variety, that motives for poems will never be lacking. But they must be always circumstantial poems, that is, reality must supply the motive as well as the subject matter" (*I,* p. 129). The reference to Rilke occurs in Sena's essay "Sobre a poesia, com variações sobre a sinceridade de um poema de Cavafy" ("On Poetry, with Variations on Sincerity in a Poem by Cavafy").[11] Rilke's comment, which is voiced by the protagonist of *The Notebook of Malte Laurids Brigge,* reads in part as follows: "For verses are not, as people imagine, simply feelings (we have these soon enough); they are experiences."[12]

I estimate that about half or slightly fewer of Sena's poems (published as of August 1983) cannot be said to be based incontrovertibly on lived and/or witnessed experiences or works of art that could be extrapoetically identified or pinpointed. In the case of these poems, the referents are thoughts, feelings, Sena's philosophical views, aspects of his personality, momentary emotional attitudes and moods whose causes or reasons are not made clear either in the poem or in notes. Most of Sena's statement poems in which he explains or otherwise projects his philosophical stance (including ethical and aesthetic views), and the majority of his love and other abstract poems are all cases in point. We could not claim, for example, that the poem "I Know the Salt" is based on any *lived* experiences, that the "you" of the poem is any real person—although chances are that it was, and that it is. The essential point here is that these are experiences so private, so intimate, so interior that the poet understandably left us in the dark as far as their extrapoetic identity and character are concerned. In the case of these poems, rather than talk about divisions of subject matter in terms of extrapoetically identifiable or identified experiences, we have to talk about general themes. I do maintain, however, that these general themes bear an intimate relation to the subject matter of the poems clearly identified by Sena as experiential, and that they are in perfect harmony with Sena's world view as a whole. More important still, they have about themselves an aura of *lived* experiences. They speak to us with the voice of things done, seen, felt, suffered or enjoyed. They lack, for the most part, that halo of universalistic nowhere which can be a mask for one's not having lived or experienced what one is talking about; or for one's fearing to face up to what one has undergone in thought or in deed. Some of the most common of these themes—all of which also recur in poems based on clearly lived experiences and experiences derived from works of art—are love (in most of its ramifications), death, the experience of time in many of its human implications, and religion. I shall return to the most common general themes of Sena's poetry and how they are also mirrored in *Art of Music* in the last chapter of this book.

The other half, or slightly more, of Sena's poetry, however, is based on real experiences in the sense that *Webster's Dictionary* defines "experience," i.e., "an actual living through an event or events; personally undergoing or observing something or things in general as they occur." One knows that these experiences are real, as opposed to invented or tailored, not only because of Sena's numerous pre- and postfactory statements to that effect, but because the poet identifies many of these experiences in numerous notes to poems. In addition, the poems often refer to public events or circumstances in Sena's life which are extrapoetically documented and therefore verifiable. Cases in point are the poems on the Portuguese Revolution and those based on travels undertaken by Sena throughout Europe. In other cases the poems' frame of reference is the well-known social, economic, and moral reality of a specific time and place. Sena's poems commenting on Portuguese life during the fascist regime, for example "The Artificial Paradises," fall under this category.

About 400 poems out of a total of 900 (the approximate number of Sena's poems as of August 1983) are identified by the poet (in prefaces, notes, etc.) as being based on real experiences—ranging from a visit to the grave of Karl Marx in England to listening to Schoenberg's *Concerto for Orchestra*. But it is fair to assume that at least another 150 poems are topical even though Sena chose to leave the incident or circumstance extrapoetically unidentified, either to evade possible censorship (this is the case, for example, with the poem on Karl Marx) or else because in the beginning of his poetical career Sena published all his poems without notes and a large number of them without dates (although he always followed the practice of dating them in the manuscripts).[13] The poems contained in *Poetry-I* were published twice without any notes. It was years later that Sena supplied an explanation and notes to a number of them in a note to his short story "A campanha da Rússia" ("The Russian Campaign"). Part of this note, although long, is worth quoting:

> Some passages of this short story (especially the evocative parentheses), in light of what they bring to mind of works of mine published earlier, or of other writings that came to light afterwards, perhaps deserve a brief commentary. Thus, for example, gardens and plane trees (cf. "Ode to the Plane Trees" in the section of poems *Philosopher's Stone,* 1950, and "The Plane Trees Revisited" in *Fidelity,* 1958), evoke above all the Garden of Cordoaria to whose plane trees the word expressly refers, even though that may not be "obvious." The horrible wound of the human creature who was a shadowy beggar had appeared like a flash, less graphically described, in the poem "Nuptials," of *Crown of the Earth* (1946). The tubercular dying on a chair that could be seen from the bridge had been described, of course, in the poem "Cubicle" in *Persecution* (1942). The square overflowing with people howling "Aves" is the so-called Square of Bacalhau, or Avenida dos Aliados—and the scene inspired the revolt of the poem "Pamphlet," also of *Persecution.* The gaping tunnel entrance and the circumstances surrounding it, in reverse, would form one of the most revolting scenes in my short story "Child's Cry," 1962, published in *The Grand-Captains* (1976). But the children, who carry another in a coffin along the promenade Fontainhas, and the scene itself had been the substance of the poem "Sunny Day," in *Crown of the Earth,* published many years earlier. Thus it can be seen that what the author lived, experienced and observed and what he created in poetry and prose are intimately connected. In *Monte Cativo (Captive Mountain),* if it is ever concluded or at least gets past the first stages, there will be much more material that was scattered (or condensed, if you will) throughout my poetry and short stories. Needless to say, in the case of the present notes, it would be necessary to mention things connected with Oporto, where "Russian Campaign" takes place, and where many of the author's poems, *which are sometimes more topical than may seem at first,* have been written. (my italics)[14]

Thus, we may think of the greatest majority of Sena's poems as constituting a huge anthology of transmuted vital experiences. The span of time covered in his poetic diary begins, as noted before, in 1938 (date of the oldest poem of *Persecution)* and ends with the poem "Warning to Cardiacs and Others . . ." *(40 Years).* According to Mrs. Mécia de Sena, "This was Jorge de Sena's last poem, written when he was still unaware, as he would discover two weeks later, that he had so little time to live."[15] If one knew nothing of Sena's life except for the autobiographical information crystallized in his poems, it would be possible to infer from the latter not only the poet's humanistic stance, as previously stated, and many aspects of his personality, but also his experiences and reactions to socio-political events in Portugal, the Spanish Civil War and World War II. One would be able to follow Sena's move in 1959 to Brazil and some of his experiences in that country; his subsequent emigration to the United States; Sena's travels throughout Europe with periodic trips to Portugal and then Portuguese Africa. It would be possible, furthermore, to accompany Sena's vicarious experience of, and concomitant reaction to, events in Portugal, such as those of the 1974 Revolution. Sena left numerous poems inspired by, and commenting on, books he read and movies he saw. Poems inspired by works of visual art and music are scattered throughout the corpus. Many of the poems inspired by the arts gravitated together to become *Metamorphoses* and *Art of Music*. Had Sena wanted to, he could have published a substantial volume of poems inspired by specific works of literature, for there are sufficient poems in the corpus to warrant it. He comments retrospectively on impressions, experiences and reactions poetized years before. "June Song" and "Christmas 77" *(40 Years)* are two examples among many of poems inspired in part, or referring to, other poems of Sena's. Sena talks poetically about his private life, seeing himself primarily as an exile from his country. In his last poems Sena anticipates his own death, a topic that had obsessed him intensely all through his poetical career.

Sena's corpus harbors a mass of experiences which, in their quantity and variety, would fill to the brim two or more lives. His books of poems, which draw on these experiences, very often as they are happening, must perforce lack the thematic unity typical of the carefully constructed work, whether the latter be wholly fictional or veridical. In fact, one of the major differences between the genre autobiography and the genre diary is that the latter does not possess the thematic and structural organization of the former. St. Augustine's *Confessions,* an outstanding example of autobiography, is a deliberately constructed narrative in which the author's life experiences are selected and shaped into a coherent introspective analysis of the soul's journey to the discovery of God. The diarist, on the other hand, while including in his or her diary innumerable fragments of experience present and past, does not attempt, at least ostensibly, to impose any artificial order upon them through selection. If and when a portrait of the writer or the times emerges from the thematic collage that is the diary, it is the reader, not the writer, who has assembled the pieces in his or her mind into coherent patterns.

In this particular, too, Sena's poetical corpus resembles the diary. His attention to dates—almost obsessive at times—is also akin to the diarist's. (Let it be said in passing that his autobiographical fiction, for example *The Grand-Captains,* is closer to autobiography than it is to the diary.) Sena himself stated that, with the exception of *The Evidences* (I would also include *Metamorphoses* and *Art of Music,* with some reservations), "only in a very special sense do I consider my books *books* of poems, with their own unity." He adds:

> The poems appear, are written, put in the drawer, and an opportunity for publishing them in book form presents itself. It is then that a selection and an arrangement of the poems selected are made. It is in this selection and arrangement, just as in the titles of the books, that a certain intentionality insinuates itself, which theretofore had not existed except as it pertains to the act of writing itself. This intentionality is one of clarifying some dominant aspects of the spiritual itinerary of the witness I have been of myself and of my world. (Preface to 1st ed., *Poetry-I,* p. 27)

Although Sena offers, in the continuation of this passage, a coherent allegorical interpretation of this "spiritual itinerary," based primarily on the titles of the books, a thematic analysis of his poetical works will reveal, I think, more the heterogeneity of life's varied experiences than the thematic cohesion of the deliberate artistic construct. In other words, if we exclude *Evidences,* which Sena called "a poem in 21 sonnets," *Metamorphoses,* and *Art of Music*—which, in the latter two cases, derive their thematic homogeneity respectively from works of visual art and music—Sena's books of poetry reveal the wide and random contours of the poet's own life experiences. In these books it is life itself that dictates poetical subject matter by forcing itself upon the poet.

There is an expansion or branching out of subject matter in Sena's poetry to accompany or parallel the poet's geographical and spiritual peregrinations and his ever increasing interest in poetizing experiences derived from his encounter with the arts. One can easily identify three major experiential thematic periods in Jorge de Sena's poetry. It is important to point out, however, that this division into thematic moments or periods takes into account only those poems based strictly on identifiable or identified experiences. Poems that deal with non-experiential sources (in the sense defined above), for example, poems that constitute statements of Sena's humanistic position, run the entire length of the poet's career. Philosophically speaking, there are no periods or phases in Sena's poetry, as I suggested in

Chapter I. He began his career with a basic philosophical outlook which never changed. Sena started out by revealing himself a humanist poet and remained one to the very end of his life. José-Augusto França, writing of Sena's early books, probably has this same idea in mind when he states that Sena's is "A corpus which shows no evolution because the author had no adolescence to outgrow, and therefore all that he experienced seems to have been, sadly, a state of adulthood. Like Pessoa, Sena could rightfully say, 'I do not evolve, I travel.' Only adults travel, adolescents flee from home."[16]

The first thematic period comprises the works written and published before the poet's departure for Brazil in 1959, i.e., the books up to and including *Fidelity* (1958). The primary geographical setting for the experiential poems contained in these works is Portugal, even though certain experiential thematic strands, such as the Spanish Civil War and World War II, encompass the entire European stage. Indeed, the geographical setting for the majority of the topical poems in *Persecution* and *Crown of the Earth* is not even Portugal in general, but the city of Oporto, where Sena resided for years. *Crown* is dedicated in part to Oporto where, as Sena says, "the majority of poems contained in this book were experienced and written" (*I,* p. 82). In the passage quoted earlier from the note to "The Russian Campaign," we were also told that many of the poems of *Persecution* are results of experiences in the Northern Capital.

From the viewpoint of experiential subject matter, the second period of Sena's poetry is represented by *Metamorphoses* (1963) and *Art of Music* (1968). This period covers the years from 1958, date of the oldest poem in *Metamorphoses,* to 1974, the most recent date borne by several poems of *Art of Music.* These two books, for the human content they embody, are perhaps the most universal of Sena's works. In the temporal sense, they encompass thousands of years of human experience. Geographically, they "cover" the entire Western World. As Sena states, had he not left Portugal many of these works of art could not have been seen by him except in prints (although Sena had seen many in his trips to England and Spain before departing for Brazil). Many of the works of music which are now included in his excellent library could not have been acquired, for simple financial reasons, had Sena remained in his country.

The third experiential thematic period of Sena's poetry includes the rest of his books, starting with *Peregrinatio ad Loca Infecta* and ending with *40 Years of Servitude. Sequences* (1980) and *Perpetual Vision* (1982) contain poems belonging to the first and second periods. There is, chronologically speaking, considerable overlapping among these three periods. What makes this third period, for example, differ substantially from the other two is the overwhelming preponderance, in the books starting with *Peregrinatio,* of poems derived from experiences Sena had outside Portugal. His experiences in Brazil, the United States, and many European countries during his tours supplied material for a vast number of poems. What is important to remember is that Portugal always looms as one of the omnipresent thematic constants. Sena repeatedly returned to Portugal, after the first ten years of absence, and wrote many poems *in locu.* But even when he was abroad, Portugal was forever on his mind. Sena left his country physically, but spiritually it never left him. Let us recall that, despite his humanism, despite his constant alertness to what was happening to human beings everywhere, the War in Vietnam left relatively few vestiges in his poetry, judging from what has been published thus far. (It seems that Sena always considered himself a guest in the United States. As such, he probably felt uneasy or that he did not have the right to poetically scrutinize America. Of course, he did leave some violent protest poems about the U.S. However, even though his sojourn in Brazil was a lot shorter, the poems inspired by the Brazilian socio-political reality appear to be greater in number than those derived from his observations of life in America.) On the contrary, Sena *lived through* the 1974 Portuguese Revolution, not in Portugal, but in Santa Barbara, California. Yet few persons who trod the streets of Lisbon during those memorable days felt that major event for Portugal more intensely and more personally than did Jorge de Sena. His poems inspired by the Revolution are ample proof. Sena used to say that he was a Brazilian citizen, an American professor, and a Portuguese writer. He also was fond, with reason, of comparing himself to Camoens in the sense that he, just as the epic poet, had left his "life parcelled out throughout the world in bits and pieces" ("In Crete, With the Minotaur"). However, in the deep sense of the terms, Sena always remained a citizen of Portugal and a teacher to the Portuguese who bothered to read him. Almost a third of his life was spent in Brazil and the United States. But a lot of his artistic and professional energy was channeled toward building a better Portugal insofar as creating and teaching literature and culture can do this. And teaching Portuguese culture and literature in the United States is no small undertaking—even if one's name is Jorge de Sena.

More useful than this division based on chronology, geography, and extremely broad areas of subject matter, however, is a classification of Sena's poetical subject matter according to its diaristic orientation, i.e., taking into account as a basis of comparison the different types of diaries discussed above. If we exclude momentarily *Metamor-*

phoses and *Art of Music* (which will be treated as special sequences of experiential poems in the next chapter), the entire remainder of Sena's experiential poetry may be grouped into wide but fairly well-defined thematic series that closely parallel the public, intimate, religious, and travel diaries. These diaristic series or sequences cut across all of Sena's books, i.e., they disregard chronology. Thus, public and intimate poems appear from *Persecution* to *Sequences,* and travel poems are scattered throughout all the books, starting with *Peregrinatio* (although some place poems do appear earlier). This division of Sena's experiential poems into public, intimate, religious, and travel sequences is established primarily for expository convenience. We must bear in mind that, as far as the scope and variety of subject matter are concerned, the only sort of diary that can begin to match Sena's corpus is the most heterogeneous of the heterogeneous diaries. Another point that must be emphasized is the fact that, as is the case with the diary, none of these sequences is thematically pure or independent of the others. Some of the public poems contain elements of a personal or intimate nature and vice-versa; and not a few poems associated with travels could be easily categorized as belonging to either the public or intimate sequences.

Of the four diaristic sequences, the public is the one comprising the greatest number of poems and the one that persists in almost all the books of poetry Sena published (I am, of course, excluding *Metamorphoses* and *Art of Music*). In these poems Sena is a witness to events, an observer of life around him, not an actor in the occurrences. That is to say, his own self does get involved—but only through his reactions, explicit and implicit, to the experiences poetized. A good example of a poem based on a factual occurrence observed by Sena and in which the poet also registers his reaction is "Cubicle" *(Persecution)*. This poem will be discussed in Chapter III. It is in this public sequence of poems that Jorge de Sena projects his clearest image as a social poet even though his poetry, to the extent that it is preoccupied with humankind in history and with earthly existence, may be said to be, all of it, social poetry. Sena's poetry, as revealed in the public sequence, is social poetry in the sense that Pedro Salinas defines the term in regard to some of the poetry of Rubén Darío: "Social poetry does not derive from an experience affecting that part of the poet's life that is personal, unique, inalienable and individual. Rather, it stems from an experience that affects the poet in that mode of his existence by which he feels he belongs to an organized community, a society, a realm where his acts are always related to someone else's."[17] Sena's community is never restricted to Portugal or any other of the two countries in which he lived for long periods of time, but all of the earth and all of humanity.

Within this broad sequence of public poems, at least four sub-categories can be identified. I shall call them the daily experience mode, the national experience mode, the political mode, and the universal mode. To be sure, they are all public and all interrelated. Yet, all reveal certain peculiarities which set them apart from the others and therefore justify the division. As the phrase suggests, the daily experience mode comprises those poems based on quotidian incidents or occurrences that the poet observes as he goes about the business of living. The following poems, which by no means exhaust the list, are good examples of this mode: "Well," "Cubicle," "The Last Day" *(Persecution)*; "Nuptials," "Sewer," "Sunny Day," "Pamphlet," "Lullaby" *(Crown of the Earth)*; "Rain, Twilight and Suburbs—Municipal Fancies," "I Who Went By," "Immense Fields of Wheat" *(Philosopher's Stone)*; "Income," "Alentejo, at a Glance" *(Post-Scriptum)*. Most of the poems in this mode deal with life in Portugal, although quite a few are inspired by incidents that Sena witnessed in other countries as well. When I discuss (Chapter III) the processes by which factual experiences are transmuted into poetic substance, we shall see that despite the fact that these poems are inspired by daily occurrences, they gain their true significance only when integrated in the wider context of national or even universal human experience.

What I have called the national experience mode is made up of poems not necessarily based on unique day-to-day experiences, but rather wider collective ones. These poems represent attempts on the part of Sena to paint general poetical portraits of life in Portugal, Brazil, or the United States on the basis of all-encompassing, but never vague, impressions. "The Artificial Paradises" *(Philosopher's Stone)* is a good example. The poem will be discussed in the next chapter. Other examples of poems based on broad collective impressions of life and which seek to give synthetic portraits of Portuguese national life are "Ode to the Future," "Ode to Lying" *(Philosopher's Stone)*; "The Five Senses" *(Post-Scriptum)*; "Vampire," "The Emperor's Bones and Other Bones," "L'été au Portugal" *(Exorcism)*; "In the Land of Pricks" *(40 Years)*. Some poems based on impressions of Brazilian and American life—for example "Civic Vigil" *(Peregrinatio)* and "The Waltz of Democracy" *(Sequences)*—also belong to this mode.

The political mode includes poems specifically inspired by political events, or else current events with wide political repercussions, such as the Brazilian coup of 1964 and the Portuguese coup of 1974. The latter inspired, as we know, the whole series of poems included in the section "'Political and Related' Poems" of *40 Years of*

Servitude. Other examples of political poems include some of the poems in the section "Brazil" of *Peregrinatio* and the poem "Hymn to the 1st of April" of *40 Years.* Once again it must be emphasized that this category of political poems can only be justified on the basis of expository convenience. Numerous other poems not necessarily inspired by specific or notable political events, and therefore excluded from this category, are, and were considered by Sena to be, socio-political in nature. The poet writes in the preface to the second edition of *Poetry-I* that the entire *Crown of the Earth,* "without abandoning—and even by refining—surrealistic techniques that I have not abandoned even today, reflected the anguish of the war years, to which it corresponded, and the socio-political preoccupations that, now as then, I have always felt" (*I,* p. 15).

What to a large degree characterizes the poems within the political mode is direct statement, i.e., discursive affirmations without the benefit of suggestive images or symbols. Apparently Sena felt, for example in the poem "No, No, I Don't Subscribe" *(40 Years),* that the human concerns involved were so important and pressing, and that what he, the poet, had to say must be said so unequivocally, that the end of this poem constitutes both a justification of the latter and a rebuttal to those who may accuse it of being unpoetic. Sena concludes the poem by addressing it, in the manner of the classical *canção:*

> *E tu, canção-mensagem, vai e diz*
> *o que disseste a quem quiser ouvir-te.*
> *E se os puristas da poesia te acusarem*
> *de seres discursiva e não galante*
> *em graças de invenção e de linguagem,*
> *manda-os àquela parte. Não é tempo*
> *para tratar de poéticas agora.*
>
> *(40 Years, p. 204)*

> (And you, message-song, go and tell
> what you've just said to whoever wants to listen.
> And if poetry's purists accuse you
> of being discursive and unrefined
> graceless in invention and style,
> tell them to go you know where. Now
> is not the time to attend to poetics.)

Without question a humanistic preoccupation with any segment of humanity is a preoccupation with all of humanity. But lest it be thought that, in the poems comprising the public sequence, Sena is primarily interested in what is happening immediately around him or to his country, I call attention to the vast number of poems belonging to what I termed the universal mode. In these poems the stage is the entire world and the poet's concerns encompass all of humanity—even

74

when the events that motivated the poem are of a local character. A case in point is the poem "Glory," discussed in the previous chapter. Among many others, the series of poems inspired by Christmas and scattered throughout Sena's corpus (these poems could, of course, be included under the heading "religious diary"), fall within this mode. Against the backdrop of the traditional association of Christmas with birth and renewal, peace and love, Sena's attention is drawn to what he sees happening to humankind, year after year: hatred, war, and death. As Frederick G. Williams points out, Sena "would often reflect on the human condition generally—but nowhere better than in the series of poignant and often mordant 'Natal' or Christmas poems, which for him constitute a kind of exorcism; an annual, year-end, state-of-the-world review."[18] Echoes of the Spanish Civil War and World War II ring in his first Christmas poems. Other wars and acts of violence throughout the world serve as impetus to later ones, such as "Christmas 1971" *(Exorcism)*.

The second diaristic sequence mentioned earlier in this chapter is the one termed intimate, although the adjective "personal" would probably be more accurate to describe Sena's more private poems. For, despite the autobiographical and often extremely personal nature of these poems, they never, or seldom, attain the degree of intimacy, i.e., the self-analysis and confessions, to be found, for example, in most of the pages of Amiel's journal. Sena himself, although he repeatedly points to the diaristic nature of his poetry, nevertheless denies that it is an "intimate diary, or the recording of the significant facts of a spiritual autobiography" (I, p. 27). But it is true that Sena quotes as epigraph to *Fidelity* a very illuminating passage from St. Augustine's *Confessions* (Bk. X, 6). A careful study of the epigraphs Sena uses (and he is so fond of them) sometimes shows that the themes and concepts embodied in the epigraphs are partially or wholly negated in Sena's texts. In this case, however, the quotation from St. Augustine is not only true to *Fidelity,* but to much of Sena's poetry. It reads: "Such is the benefit from my confessions, not of what I have been, but of what I am, that I may confess this not only before you in secret exultation with trembling and in secret sorrow with hope, but also in the ears of believing sons of men, partakers of my joy and sharers in my mortality, my fellow citizens and pilgrims with me, those who go before me and those who follow me, and those who are companions on my journey."[19]

To what extent, then, are these poems personal or auto-biographical? I would say that the spiritual and intellectual image of the self cast in these poems is roughly equivalent to the public self of the man Jorge de Sena—with a difference of degree, not kind. In other words, the "I" in the poems and the poet's social self are basically identical. There is nothing in these poems that Sena would not have sustained extrapoetically if the opportunity presented itself. And there is relatively little in these personal poems that could not be deduced from an acquaintance with the man Jorge de Sena. Therefore, the only parallel existing between this sequence of poems and the intimate diary is the fact that both take what is perceived as the true self as the focus of attention. But the degree of intimacy, the exploration and exploitation of the recondite corners of the self achieved by both—once again taking Amiel as prototypical of the intimate diarist—is considerably different. Let us briefly outline some of the autobiographical elements contained in this sequence of poems. Later I shall return to the relationship between the poetical "I" or persona and Sena's social self. This point is of central importance, I think, for a discussion of Sena's poetry in general and of *Art of Music* in particular.

At least three broad thematic categories (and many subdivisions) can be identified within the 100 or so poems comprising the personal sequence: 1) self-characterizations as man and artist; 2) the personal experience of time; 3) miscellaneous personal memoranda. A unique example of self-characterization is the sonnet "One Who has Seen Much" *(Peregrinatio)*. Few others of Sena's poems come as close as this one to being a spiritual and experiential mini-autobiography. The seminal themes and personal attitudes herein contained—exile, sacrifice, joy of creation, bitterness against perceived injustice, irony, candor, pride and humility, uncanny prophetic vision—are all developed and exemplified in other personal poems and other writings. They were also mirrored to a very large degree in the public life and in the personality of the man Jorge de Sena. The sonnet reads:

> Quem muito viu, sofreu, passou trabalhos,
> mágoas, humilhações, tristes surpresas;
> e foi traído, e foi roubado, e foi
> privado em extremo da justiça justa;
>
> e andou terras e gentes, conheceu
> os mundos e submundos; e viveu
> dentro de si o amor de ter criado;
> quem tudo leu e amou, quem tudo foi—
>
> não sabe nada, nem triunfar lhe cabe
> em sorte como a todos os que vivem.
> Apenas não viver lhe dava tudo.
>
> Inquieto e franco, altivo e carinhoso,
> será sempre sem pátria. E a própria morte,
> quando o buscar, há-de encontrá-lo morto.

(*III*, pp. 50-51)

76

(One who has seen much, suffered much, undergone hardships,
Bruises, humiliations, sorrowful surprises;
And who was betrayed, and was robbed, and was
Deprived in extremis of the justice due him;

And who has wandered in lands and among peoples, experienced
Worlds and underworlds; and has had living
Within him the love of having created;
One who has read and loved all, who has been everything—

Knows nothing, not even winning, by chance
Befalling him as it does to all who live.
Only not living would give him life.

Restless and outspoken, haughty and endearing,
He will be homeless forever. And death itself,
When it comes, will find him dead.)

(trans. George Monteiro)

Two of the personal themes that obsessed Jorge de Sena the most were exile and his love-hatred for Portugal. By turns Sena sees himself as an exile from fascism, an emigrant, a man without a country, as he puts it in the poem "In Crete, with the Minotaur" *(Peregrinatio),* one who collects nationalities "like shirts that are shed." Portugal was nearly always on the receiving end of his anger. Sena seems to have, at times explicitly, often implicitly and perhaps even subconsciously, distinguished between two Portugals. On the one hand, there is the Portugal he knew socially, politically, culturally, and professionally. This is the Portugal he despised so thoroughly, the mediocre Portugal he chastises not only in many poems, but in the essays appropriately entitled *The Kingdom of Stupidity.* He hated this Portugal not because it was Portugal, but because it was not the Portugal he dreamt it could be. But coexisting with this one there was another Portugal for Jorge de Sena: the Portugal that Camoens, Eça de Queiroz, and Fernando Pessoa, among others, helped to create and sustain. This Portugal is symbolized for Sena in the Portuguese language. That is why he joins with Eça and Pessoa in saying "Eu sou eu mesmo a minha pátria. A pátria / de que escrevo é a língua em que por acaso de gerações / nasci . . ." ("I am my own homeland. The homeland / I write about is the language into which by the chance of generations / I was born") ("In Crete, with the Minotaur"; trans. George Monteiro).

The second thematic group within the sequence of personal poems has to do with the theme of time, more specifically with the idea of aging and the confrontation with death. Time is an extremely important thematic constant in Jorge de Sena's poetry. No wonder that even in his prefaces and postfaces he pays such an inordinate amount of attention to the chronological aspects of his poetry; that he was so obsessed with dating the poems, an obsession which he acknowledged but for which he made no apology. Given the fact that his poetry remains forever within time, forever attentive to the historical moment and to the present—even when it mines the past—it is not surprising that time should have forced itself thematically upon Sena's poetical works (as it does upon all his creative and extracreative writings). In fact, José-Augusto França opines that time is the single most important theme in Sena's poetry. "The desperate attempt to minimize the painful consciousness of temporal flow and the concomitant striving for permanency make up a dangerous adventure which takes place within the realm of poetry, and only within poetry does it seek resolution. This is Sena's theme, as I see it. Time—its opposition of permanence and flow both within time and of time's essence—is always there. It can be found in almost every poem."[20] França is writing in 1955. His comments, however, are applicable to much of Sena's poetry.

Concern with time in the poetry of Jorge de Sena does not take the form of a search for the paradisiacal suspension of temporal flow, as in Pessoa-Caeiro; not a recasting of the classical themes of transitoriness and *carpe diem,* as in Pessoa-Reis; it is not even a Proustian search for personal lost time associated with happy moments of childhood elevated to symbolic paradise, as in Fernando Pessoa and Pessoa-Campos. Time in Sena has to do with the present and the future. It is not an escape to a mythologized past, an impossible unidimensional moment, or a re-enactment of conventional classical attitudes. It is psychological time, *le temps humain.* Therefore, the theme of time, or better, the experience of time in Sena's poetry is related, understandably enough, to others of his humanistic themes: the love of life, the desire to go on living, the respect for his and other lives, the love of creation, the appreciation of beauty. The consciousness and explicit fear of aging and love of life are brought together in a poem inspired by an actual incident: the previously referred to incident of seeing and desiring a young and beautiful girl "In the Train from Edinburgh to London":

> Que coisas se fariam—tão de seios
> redonda e esbelta aqui sentada e loira
> e lendo um livro idiota à minha frente!
> As pernas que se juntam quando abri-las
> a duras mãos com dedos titilantes
> para depois se unirem apertando
> em húmidas paredes o que se entesa vendo-a...
> E ah como a boca se arredonda rósea!
> E os dedos que são esguios, serão sábios?
> Tão sábios como os meus e minha boca?

Que loura juventude nem me vê—quem pode
envelhecer sem raiva aos olhos dela,
se de alma e de entre pernas se é tão jovem sempre?

(III, p. 234)

(The things that might happen—so much breasts
girl rounded *and* svelte sitting here and blond
and reading an idiot book in front of me!
The legs held shut—to so far open them
with firm hands that have titillating fingers
for them then to unite grasping tight
within moist walls what stiffens seeing her.
And ah the way her mouth rounds rosily!
And will her fingers, so slender, be expert?
As expert as my own and as my mouth?
That golden youthfulness not even sees me—who
can grow old and not crazy at her eyes
if in soul and between legs one's this young still?)

(trans. Jonathan Griffin)

In the thematic group I called miscellaneous personal memoranda we have a series of poems covering a wide range of autobiographical information of the type which one would expect to find, and does find, in the average diary. "Complaints of the Head of a Family" *(40 Years)* is yet another poetic reflection derived from quotidian preoccupations. "It Happened One Hundred Years Ago in Luanda" and "In Memory of Adolfo Casais Monteiro" *(I Know the Salt...)* convey information regarding Sena's family history. In "Probably" *(Perpetual Vision)* one hears the same Senian voice of the prefaces and postfaces; that voice that, affectionate and sonorous, could become metallic and weapon-like and say things like

. . . Nunca leram nada.
E agora—ó esperteza de saloios—
até me atacam de tanto admirar-me
naquel' respeito silencioso e pio
em que jamais me defenderam. Doi-lhes
o pontapé no rabo? Hão-de apanhar
ainda muito mais—no grande estilo
com que em milénios a poesia deu
os pontapés devidos a uma tal cambada.

(Perpetual Vision, p. 149)

(. . . They never read anything.
And now—oh wisdom of hicks—
they even accuse me of self-admiration
with the quiet and pious respectfulness
they never used to defend me. Are they smarting
from the kick in the pants? They'll get
many more yet—in the grand style
with which for millenia poetry has dispensed
the kicks coming to such rabble.)

79

Of course, these poems very often transcend the mere anecdotal or personal level. Their aim, as we shall see, is not solely to impart or record autobiographical information. But the latter is an intrinsic and undisguised part of the poems and one can be absolutely sure that the voice in them is the voice of the man Jorge de Sena, not just that of a poetic persona.

This brings us to a discussion of the interrelationship between the "I" in Sena's poetry—not only in his more personal poems, but in *all* of his poetry—and the social self of the man. Lyric poetry and the diary have this very important aspect in common: both rely on the first person singular. In the case of the diary, it is safe to assume that the "I" and the social or historical one are identical or very close. But to what extent is it (still) legitimate to equate the poetic "I" with the poet's historical self? This question, which had been asked many times but which the New Critics asked and answered anew in favor of the "autonomous, fictional I," must be reformulated in the case of a poet like Jorge de Sena.

The history of poetry and literary criticism do show that, relative to the historical person, the "I" in a lyric poem oscillates or swings between a centrifugal and a centripetal tendency or degrees thereof. On the one extreme we have aesthetic distance, negative capability (Keats), poetic personae (Browning), poetic masks (Yeats), or, as Fernando Pessoa, the Zeus of the poetic "I's," preferred to say, "heteronyms." This is the type of poetic "I" that supposedly bears little or no relation to the poet's real self or only a distorted relation; this is the "I" that the reader of poetry is supposed to concentrate on and not equate with the historical person. It is true that bits and pieces of the true historical self may be present in the poetic persona—even the staunchest defenders of the separation of the "I's" admit this—but they fragment, scatter and sometimes reassemble at random. Thus we may have some particles from the authentic historical self but mixed with invented portions—rendering the sum total irreconcilable with the poet as man. This is what happens, we might say, in Álvaro de Campos's "Ode Marítima" ("Maritime Ode"), where Pessoa interweaves bits and pieces of autobiographical information with others that are totally invented—and then attributes everything to a fictional personality, Álvaro de Campos,[21] who in turn is not wholly fictional, but that part of Pessoa's personality which he prefers not to exhibit under his own name.

Unlike the centrifugal, the centripetal poetic self tends toward the center of the historical or social personality. It is the self traditionally associated with the Romantics, although it is the self of any poet of any epoch who rejects, in practice, the dissociation between a social and artistic personality—except perhaps in degree. In this case, art is an expression of the man, whether it be of his emotions or his philosophy of life. The question of sincerity, which has plagued Pessoan studies *ad nauseam,* becomes irrelevant. It does not mean that the centripetal poet is monochordic as far as his human personality is concerned. He may have, and all true writers do have, multiple personalities, but he integrates them. More important still: he accepts and respects them. And is not afraid to call them his. He treasures all his personalities too much to allow any one of them to stray or camouflage itself. When and if one strays, it inevitably comes back to join hands with the others, its sisters. Sena is an outstanding example of a centripetal poet. In this particular, Fernando Pessoa (who has often been compared to Sena) and the author of *Art of Music* are as unlike as any two poets could possibly be. Of course, this observation does not in any way imply any value judgment as to their respective greatness as poets. Each in his own way was sincere. But both conceived of and practiced sincerity in totally different ways. Sena equates his poetic self with his social self so much that he actually quotes passages from his poems in support of autobiographical facts; and not a few statements made in interviews bear a remarkable resemblance to poetic ones.

In the preface to the first edition of *Poetry-I,* Jorge de Sena explains that poetry is not direct confession. When it is confession, it is tranformed or metamorphosed confession. But he adds in the same breath, "But to me poetry is not *feigning (fingimento)* either." Following this he refers to Pessoa's heteronymic practice in these terms:

> If sometimes I tried to explain and defend the poetics that constitute the basis of Pessoa's artistic being, even when they were contrary to my own views, I always did it moved by the feeling that it is imperative to understand and accept each person as he presents himself, before moving on to express ideas more in accordance with one's personal views. It is true that his "feigning" is not strictly an art of deception, but rather the just affirmation, set forth by an eminently analytical individuality, that all the potential personalities that dwell in us are more than the being that contains them, and that poetic activity surpasses what we precariously determine to be at any given moment. His "feigning" served as a lesson and as an example, both of which are far from being understood in a country where to be a poet is to be a professional of the expedient emotion. But the element of artifice was always repugnant to me, in the highest sense of the technique of grasping those potential personalities, which such "feigning" implies. Because only artificially, even though on the plane of poetry and not on that of the entertainment arts, is it possible for us to assume extrinsically, exteriorly, the multiplicity of personalities which, within us, is

a bothersome family, a restless company, an anguished world. There is a lot of boundless arrogance in that "feigning" which contrasts, as far as I am concerned, with the expectant humility, the judicious attention, the watchful availability with which, giving of ourselves more than we are capable, we bear witness to the world that surrounds us, a world that, because we live in it, we surround with maternal care.

(Poetry-I, pp. 25-26)

As Fernando Guimarães states, "Jorge de Sena's poetry constitutes an attentive, lucid and permanent dialogue established between the objective and subjective worlds. 'Um só poema basta para atingir a terra' ('A single poem suffices to accomplish the world'); and, in this line, the poet points to a verticality, a descending road that will open up contact with that reality of circumstances, which, following the advice he learned from Goethe, 'supplies the motive' for the poems."[22]

In this book I will always assume, at whatever risk, that Sena's poems project the voice of the man Jorge de Sena. At the same time it will never be forgotten that a poem crystallizes a highly privileged moment in a man's life. A poem is a type of utterance that concentrates or synthesizes diverse emotions and may reach heights of intensity and passion that can significantly alter, if not destroy, one's "true," i.e., extrapoetical, feelings and beliefs.

A close interrelationship between the poetic "I" and the historical self also exists in the diaristic sequence I termed religious and which may be considered a subdivision of Sena's poetical *journal intime.* As noted in Chapter I, where the topic has been sufficiently discussed, Sena's corpus contains dozens of poems that can be construed as his "religious" diary. However, what the poet records, in contradistinction to what is recorded by diarists like Richard Kay, is his voyage away from God and into the arms of humanity. Some of these poems, too, are addressed to God which, as noted before, is one of the outstanding characteristics of the religious diary: "Sinto que vou voltar-me para Ti" ("I feel that I am going to turn to You") ("Declaration," *I,* p. 71), "Meu Deus... como posso eu falar-Te" ("My God... How Can I Speak to You") ("Unity," *I,* p. 73), "Oh Deus! que um dia adormeceste nos meus braços" ("Oh God! You Who one day fell asleep in my arms") (*I,* p. 107).

The last diaristic sequence to be discussed is comprised of those poems inspired by travels. Quantitatively they represent a series of about sixty poems primarily, although not exclusively, contained in *Peregrinatio, Exorcism, I Know the Salt..., 40 Years of Servitude,* and a few in *Sequences* and *Perpetual Vision.* This sequence, except for a few poems pertaining to travels within the United States or Portugal itself (and I did include those for Portugal in the category of public diary), was inspired by Sena's two grand tours of Europe. The first took place between September 1968 and February 1969, after Sena's nearly ten years of residency in Brazil and the United States. During this first trip Sena revisited England and traveled in France, Germany, Austria, Holland, Belgium, Italy, etc. His second tour occurred between January 1972 and March 1973. He visited England again, and toured Italy and Greece. He also traveled to Africa, where he spent time in Angola, Mozambique, the Island of Mozambique, and South Africa. During these two trips several months were spent in Portugal.

Sena's travel poems are among the most topical he ever wrote. The titles of the poems usually suffice to point out to the reader the referents under poetic focus. In most cases one need not even refer to the notes that the great majority of them carry, except for clarification of particularly difficult allusions. In a prefactory note to *Exorcism* (*III*, pp. 115-116), Sena defends the referentiality of these travel poems, warns against their being taken as "touristic," and ends by saying that to write referentially or topically does not preempt flights of imagination or linguistic experimentation. Sena is absolutely right. We shall see in the next chapter that some of these poems have much to do with things other than those seen and heard during the trip. One poem, which ostensibly purports to be the minute enumeration of places and objects seen, turns out to possess a level of meaning that has absolutely nothing to do with life in "Antwerp."

The similarities between these poems and the travel diary are indeed striking, both from the viewpoint of chronology and subject matter. Most of the poems not only accompany the chronological order of the travels, but convey the notion of having been written *in locu* (when we know that many, perhaps most, were not). This happens even with a poem like "Athens" *(I Know the Salt...),* which Sena says is a poetization of earlier experiences. Nevertheless, the poem contains passages that denote contemporaneity, a feeling of being there right now, which is one of the fundamental characteristics of the travel diary:

> Desçamos tristemente a escadaria
> do Propileu que se abre para baixo,
> para as cidades rentes à traição divina.
>
> (*III*, p. 218)

> (Sadly let's descend the stairway
> of the Propylaeum that leads downward,
> towards the cities close to divine treason.)

But it is the subject matter of the poems that truly recall to the reader's mind the travel diary. In Sena's poems this subject matter may be grouped into four major areas, which often coexist in the same poem: 1) descriptions of places or monuments; 2) association of places with great men who lived there; 3) meditations, reflections or flights of imagination occasioned by places visited; and 4) searching for Portugal in foreign lands.

Although some of these poems—for example "Islands of Santa Barbara" (*III,* p. 155), "Gregynog Hall" (*III,* p. 234), "Spring in Wisconsin" (*III,* p. 89), "Calvaries" *(40 Years,* p. 59)—are ostensibly descriptive, they are seldom exclusively so. It is more than obvious also that these descriptive travel poems, whether they be of landscapes or monuments, never fail to strongly imply human presence. This point was discussed in Chapter I and I shall return to it in Chapter IX. The aesthetic nature of description in one of these poems will be dealt with in the next chapter.

Another aspect that Sena's travel poems have in common with the travel diary, for example Montaigne's, is the fact that the portions of the trip that end up being recorded are seldom totally restricted to the geographical and temporal planes occupied by the traveler. It is also a journey into past history, a search for great men associated with a given place. "Encounter with Vermeer in Delft" *(Peregrinatio)* and "Rotterdam" *(Exorcism)* are good examples of Sena's "encounter with" or "search for" historical figures (Vermeer and Erasmus) associated with those places. At times the physical place itself seems to vanish and only the historical figure draws the poet's attention—another example of Sena's greater interest in people than in places. "Homage to Spinoza" *(Exorcism),* inspired by Sena's visit to Amsterdam, is indeed not a travel poem, but a salute from one humanist to another.

Traveling is as much geographical as it is temporal; as much a touristic as an intellectual adventure. Many of these poems even belie the notion of spatial topicality. They constitute miniature syntheses of historical and cultural interest far beyond the circumstantiality of the inspiring site; they are poems of vision rather than poems of sight. In poems such as "Köln" and "Bruges" *(Exorcism),* Sena is indeed far from taking the poetic equivalent of pictures. In these poems his are not the eyes of the tourist, however well informed, however adept with the camera; they are those of the historian and poet. This enlightened and heightened vision brings into focus the most diverse associations and shapes them into authentic poetic jewels. One such jewel is "Scotland" *(I Know the Salt...).* Another jewel, with irony and humor added, is the already mentioned "Antwerp." For all this, although the designation of poetic travel diary remains the most appropriate, Sena's travel poems often seem to encroach on the territory of the subjective travel narrative (in their temporal flights, in their didactic nature in the broad sense of the term) and the objective travel memoir (they are always learned poems, always well informed about history, art, life). Sena reads things out of but also into what he observes—as he does with works of art, or any type of experience he poetizes. He does not record reality; he reads and interprets it.

In several travel poems the search for the historical past is limited, or almost, to a search for Portugal away from home, i.e., for historical figures and moments associated with Portugal or Portuguese history. These poems once again indicate that wherever Sena went Portugal went with him. "Florence Seen from San Miniato al Monte" and "The Angel-Musician of Vienna" *(Exorcism)* are examples of this search for vestiges of Portugal's historical past. In "Ravenna" *(Exorcism),* the Portuguese province of Alentejo acts as a point of comparison for what is being looked at, in a way reminiscent of Montaigne's comparisons and contrasts between the lands he visited and France.

Sena's travels also constitute a search for himself. He ends the poem "Crossing," which opens the section "Notes of a Return to Europe" *(Peregrinatio),* this way:

> Desci porém a terra, tonto como uma criança,
> pousando com cautela os pés no cais.
> Não por ser a França o que pisava na calçada suja:
> Europa
> *(mais velha, como eu, quase dez anos).*
>
> *(III,* p. 103)

> (I got off on land, though, giddy as a child,
> cautiously stepping on the pier.
> Not because the dirty cobblestones were France.
> Europe, it was—
> (older, like me, by almost ten years).

In "Lusitanian Oecumenicalism or Double Nationality" Sena synthesizes two personal vignettes: one is an encounter with a Brazilian nun who, upon discovering his status as a naturalized Brazilian citizen, denies him that nationality; the other is a similar encounter in Hamburg with a Portuguese emigrant who, discovering he was a naturalized Brazilian, denies him any nationalistic ties with Portugal. Both of these people echo, although not for the same reasons, Sena's own feelings about his own citizenship as expressed in "In Crete, with the Minotaur." "It Happened One Hundred Years Ago in Luanda" *(I Know the Salt...)* recounts part of his own family roots in Angola.

Some of the poems inspired by travels in Spain constitute vicarious encounters with beloved fellow poets: "San Juan de la Cruz in Segovia," "Antonio Machado and San Juan de la Cruz" *(40 Years)*. In "Roaming Around Europe, Nothing Sentimental" *(Exorcism),* where he enumerates, diarist-like, some of the places he visited, Sena is glad to return home, where family love permits him not to find himself so old after all:

> *O amor me espera em casa.*
> *Ardente antigo e ansioso.*
> *Não envelheço nunca*
> *sobre este seio tépido.*
>
> (*III*, p. 170)

> (Love awaits me at home.
> Ardent long-lived and anxious.
> I don't ever grow old
> resting on this warm breast.)
>
> (trans. F.G. Williams)

In conclusion: Sena's poems, individually and collectively considered, exhibit many similarities with the different types of diary discussed in this chapter. These similarities have to do primarily with subject matter in its raw state, i.e., before it undergoes poetic metamorphosis. The differences between the different types of diary and Sena's poems—which are even more important than the similarities—will be considered next. In the next chapter I will also dwell on the place that Sena's poems based on art—literature, the visual arts, and music—occupy within his overall poetic diary.

III

Poetry as Metamorphosis

The cornerstone of Sena's poetics is, as has been shown, the idea that poetry must be rooted in real experience in the broadest sense of the term. He also believes, however, that the poet is not a mere recorder of experiences. As the poet bears witness to life in himself and around himself he is, first and foremost, a transformer of experience, nay, of the world. Sena writes in the preface to the first edition of *Poetry-I:*

> More so than any other form of communication, poetry has the capability, beyond understanding the world, of transforming it. If poetry, in the relations of the poet with himself and with his readers, is above all an *education,* it is also in the relationship of the poet not only to that which he transforms into poetry, but the act of transformation and the very product of that transformation—the poem—a revolutionary activity. If "feigning" is, without a doubt, the highest form of education, liberation and enlightenment of the spirit as an educator of itself and of others, "bearing witness"—expectant, discrete, watchful—is the highest form of transformation there is. In, with and through "bearing witness," which is above all *language (linguagem),* one effects the modification of ready-made schemes, accepted ideas, unanalyzed social habits, and conventionally standardized feelings. *(Poetry-I,* p. 26)

Sena's poetry serves both, and equally well, the cause of Life and the cause of Art. Unlike the extremist adherents of art for art's sake and pure poetry, for example, Sena does not see any incompatibility between a poetry committed to life and at the same time to an idea of poetic purity; a poetry that, root-like, grips reality while retaining artistic substance. When asked what he thought his own poetry represented, Jorge de Sena replied in part:

> I believe that my poetry has been an attempt to overcome contradictions in the current consciousness, contradictions which are precisely reflected in the diverse "paths" of modern Portuguese poetry. If my poetry represents anything, representing me, it represents a desire for an independence allied to social poetry, a desire for human commitment to pure poetry, a desire for perfect, classical expression, for surrealistic liberation, a desire to destroy by means of an uncommon tumult of imagery any outdated discipline (e.g.: Aristotelian logic must give rise to Hegelian logic; a sociologically enlightened morality must replace the morality of legalistic prohibition), and, above all, a desire to express what I believe to be human dignity. In short, a total fidelity to the responsibility of our being alive in the world, even when everything tries to convince us that we are one too many... or too few.
> *(Kingdom of Stupidity, I,* pp. 212-213)

This statement summarizes much of what has been discussed thus far regarding Sena's philosophy of life and the nature of his poetry. As for his concept of "pure poetry" vis-à-vis the traditional concept of same, the key phrase in the above quotation is: *human commitment to pure poetry,* i.e., the significant pairing of *human* and *pure.* From Gautier's theory of art for art's sake, to the Abbé Batteux's theory of pure poetry, to Mallarmé's theorizing and practice, to the disciples or adherents of those aesthetic views, the underlying idea is the cutting off of poetry from its roots in life. Technical perfection and self-containedness as far as content, i.e., the absence of referentiality, constitute the supreme objectives of purist poetics. Poetry for these purists is poetry aiming to become as abstract and "pure" as pure music. In the preface to *Mademoiselle de Maupin* (1835), Gautier insists on the closed poem, on its detachment from life experiences, human emotions and psychology. In his book *Pure Poetry,* D.J. Mossop writes that "The Abbé Batteux evidently measured the purity of poetry by the extent to which the content was removed from the reality of life."[1] Referring to Mallarmé, Mossop says that by the year 1866, or the end of Mallarmé's first stage of poetic development, one finds the author of *L'Aprés-midi d'un faune* "withdrawing ever further from life in pursuit of an ever more 'unearthly' and therefore purer content for a poetry which was already as technically pure as he could make it in light of the theory to which he then subscribed" (op. cit., p. 128).

In contradistinction to adherents of art for art's sake and pure poetry, when Sena claims a human commitment to purity he is implying that the latter does not mean a rejection of life experiences or any kind of referent as subject matter for poetry. What he means by purity, his entire corpus demonstrates, is the degree to which poetic expression transmutes experience until the latter becomes allegorical, symbolic, etc., and aesthetically satisfying, i.e., viable poetic substance. The adjective *human,* in the phrase *human commitment,* however, suggests that the poem must remain somehow connected or attached to the original experience, the same way that a flower remains part of the plant and root to which it is attached without being less of a flower for that. Sena's experiential poetry is, thus, experience stylized, purified, transformed—not experience denied. The processes of purification have to do with the transformation or metamorphosis of referents, not with their elimination.

A parenthetic historical note is necessary here. Although Sena's committed poetry is explainable solely on the basis of his humanism, there are historical reasons, to which Sena alludes in the passage quoted above, that account for his often polemical insistence on that commitment vis-à-vis aestheticist trends within Portuguese literature in the '30s and '40s. Jorge de Sena, although his poetry reveals deep affinities with contemporary -isms—Surrealism, even before it officially began in Portugal (1947), and Neo-Realism—never belonged to any literary movement or school. His affiliation to *Cadernos de Poesia* (the second series, 1951-53, was co-organized by him), is the closest he ever came to belonging to a literary group. However, as Sena is careful to point out in the opening statement to the second series, *"Cadernos* never constituted a literary group, not even an association of poets. *[Cadernos]* represent, that they did and still do, an attitude of lucidity, understanding and independence."[2] Almost from the outset the motto of this review, and one to which Sena subscribed, was "A poesia é só uma" ("There is only one poetry"). The polemic nature of this motto represented in part a reaction against the group of *Presença* (last number, 1940), which defended the idea of art for art's sake and whose mentor, José Régio, had proclaimed that "The ideal of the Artist has nothing to do with that of the moralist, the patriot, the believer or the citizen." But the *Cadernos* group also rejected the often simplistic manicheisms of Neo-Realism, although it did not oppose the motto that guided *Sol Nascente* (1937), which read "The end of all human culture consists in understanding Humanity." Fernando J.B. Martinho, in his "Breve enquadramento da poesia de Jorge de Sena" ("A Brief Framing of Jorge de Sena's Poetry"), synthesizes the role and contribution of the *Cadernos* to the resolution of the debate between the adherents of art for art's sake and the exacerbated social humanitarianism of the Neo-Realist movement. What Martinho writes regarding *Cadernos* in general, also applies to Jorge de Sena:

> *Cadernos* steered attention away from the ping-pong table that Portuguese poetry was fast becoming. They rendered a service to the idea of modernity which, to the most clear-headed of those who engaged in the dispute of pure art versus committed art, was an idea that had not been betrayed. More than explicitly, that is to say, more than on the level of proclamations and manifestos, the writers of *Cadernos* accomplished their intentions by bringing about a dialogue among the living voices of their time and in a judicious selection based soundly on a criterion of quality.[3]

The kind and degree of metamorphosis operated by Sena's poems over raw experiences depends, ultimately, on the nature of the inspiring model. Sena's entire corpus, as I suggested earlier, may be divided into two broad categories of experiential poems, only the first of which has so far been dealt with at length: poems derived from life experiences, and poems inspired by the experience of works of art. The latter include a few dozen poems (scattered throughout Sena's corpus) inspired by literature and movies, visual arts, and music. Drawing on life's experiences is quite different from drawing on works of art. The latter are in themselves distillations of life experiences (in Sena's poetical view, at any rate). To transmute an incident witnessed on a street of Oporto into a poem requires in most cases a different type of poetic technique from that employed in extracting a poem from the experience of seeing and meditating on Van Gogh's *The Yellow Chair* or listening to and living through a performance of Handel's *Water Music*. I will deal first with some of the major metamorphic processes employed in the poems based on life experiences. Afterwards, I shall discuss the transformational techniques that Sena utilizes as a poet of art. The latter discussion will lead directly to the study of *Art of Music*.

Before discussing any of these metamorphic processes, however, something must be said regarding the nature of poetry as a medium supremely endowed with the capability to transform the experiences it absorbs. One way to define poetry is to adapt Ezra Pound's definition of great literature. The author of the *Cantos* stated that "Great literature is simply language charged with meaning to the utmost possible degree."[4] Much of the kind and degree of transformation in Sena's poetry—as of any poetry whatsoever—is attributable to this expressive charge of poetic language. Most of this power is under the control of the poet. That is to say, it is the poet who chooses the words for the poem and who, depending on how he manipulates words, instills greater or lesser charge in them. However, a great deal of the power of language in poetic discourse stems not from the poet but, through him, from the expectations that the reader places upon the institution of poetry. For example, the same incident recorded by a diarist and a poet within their respective genres is read differently in part because of the conventions surrounding the two genres. This truth is easily verifiable if one compares the poems of Wordsworth and Coleridge based on entries recorded in Dorothy Wordsworth's journal. Most, if not all, readers will be satisfied if the diarist records or verbally re-creates the experiences in question. The reader can, of course, read "higher" meanings into what is presented, but it is fair to assume that in most cases he or she is not predisposed to doing so. In the case of poetry, on the other hand, the reader is usually not content with mere discursive statement or mere denotation. He expects the language of the poem to be malleable to suggestion, connotation, symbolization, allegorization; he is accustomed to imagery, rhythmical patterns, as well as many devices of sound manipulation. Thousands of years of poetical tradition have conditioned the reader not to confine himself to literal meaning. Barring the inevitable exceptions—there are, for instance, most viable statement poems—traditional genre expectations clip the reader's wings or give them the capacity to soar high, as far as reading meaning(s) into or out of a text is concerned.

While discussing the poetics of the lyric, Jonathan Culler refers to this well-known expectation on the part of the reader of poetry. He writes that "If one takes a piece of banal journalistic prose and sets it down on a page as lyric poem, surrounded by intimidating margins of silence, the words remain the same but their effects for the readers are substantially altered."[5] Culler illustrates his assertion by graphically writing and then reading as poem this 23-word journalistic report of an automobile accident:

> *Hier sur la Nationale sept*
> *Une automobile*
> *Roulant a cent a l'heure s'est jetée*
> *Sur une platane*
> *Ses quatre occupants ont été*
> *Tués.*

Culler's comment on the "poem," although long, is worth quoting in full:

To write this as a poem brings into play a new set of expectations, a set of conventions determining how the sequence is to be read and what kind of interpretations may be derived from it. The *fait divers* becomes a minor but exemplary tragedy. "Hier," for exámple, takes on a completely different force: referring now to the set of possible yesterdays, it suggests a common, almost random event. One is likely to give new weight to the willfulness of 's'est jetée' (literally 'threw itself') and to the passivity of 'its occupants', defined in relation to their automobile. The lack of detail or explanation connotes a certain absurdity, and the neutral repertorial style will no doubt be read as restraint and resignation. We might even note an element of suspense after 's'est jetée' and discover bathos in the possible pun on 'platane' ('plat' = flat) and in the finality of the isolated 'tués'. (pp. 161-62)

Later in this same chapter ("Poetics of the Lyric"), Culler is careful to point out that this way of reading poetry is not peculiar to any critical approach, but universal. "The lyric has always been based on the implicit assumption that what was sung as particular experience would be granted greater importance" (p. 176). Goethe also stressed this heightening power of poetry to which Ezra Pound's definition of great literature refers and which Culler's poetic reading of a news report corroborates. In his statement to Eckermann, quoted in part by Sena as epigraph to the section "Circumstance" of *Philosopher's Stone,* Goethe did say that reality must provide both impulse and material for the production of poems. But he adds in the same breath that "A particular case becomes universal and poetic by the very fact that it is treated by a poet."[6]

Even though the conventional expectations on the part of the readers may and do work in favor of the poet who draws inspiration from experience, the selection process, i.e., the choice of elements from reality that enter into the body of the poem, is still entirely up to him. If his choice of experiences is not 'right' and his handling of it is inadequate, no amount of *reading into* what is presented can save the poem. For example, what makes Jonathan Culler's news piece an acceptable poem is not only the organization or distribution of the words on the page or in time, but also the very incidents or reality that those words denote and connote. In other words, the *how* and the *what* are inextricably interconnected. Let us set aside for the time being any considerations of strictly formalistic exigencies—strophic, metrical and stylistic—and focus only on the selection of experiences to be poetized. In order for the experiences to be poetically significant, they must possess in and of themselves a certain resonance susceptible of conversion into poetic meaning. They may be trivial, but they must not lack a considerable deal of human interest. That is why, although he repeatedly refers to his poetry as a "poetic diary," much of the passing trivia abundantly found in diaries is conspicuously absent from Sena's poetry. The selection of source experiences by the poet is, in a very meaningful way, already part of the meaning(s) of the poem even before the poet decides how the former is going to be written. Here we have a fundamental difference between the diarist and the poet, despite the fact that both may draw from the same or similar pools of experience. The diarist may decide to be selective regarding what he or she includes in the work and, of course, all diarists are selective to a greater or lesser extent. But in theory the diarist need not be so, since his genre does not necessarily depend on the connotative or symbolic implications, i.e., the representative or universal character, of the experiences recorded. The same cannot be said regarding the poet. Theoretically, everything can be poetized, as Jorge de Sena maintains. But the very fact that only a portion—a relatively small portion at that—of Sena's life experiences became poems suggests that, in practice, only those experiences bearing latent poetic possibilities—or, as Sena might say, those that "happen" or "occur" to him as truly significant—can eventually blossom into poems. Of course, what is considered "significant" will vary widely from poet to poet, from reader to reader, and from epoch to epoch.

Although it is not my intention here to analyze exhaustively all the processes and effects involved in the leap from raw experience to poetic substance, the following devices and corresponding effects are involved and can be detected easily in the poems to be discussed later. These processess can be divided into two broad categories. The first is selection. Whether the latter is a wholly conscious and volitional process, or whether it is attributable to what is traditionally called inspiration—however one chooses to conceive of the latter—is not of great importance here. The second process is, of course, stylization. Stylization is the poet's second contribution (the rest, as we saw, is reader response, which is based in part on conventional expectations); it is what produces heightening of the raw materials from mere facts into rich poetic meaning(s) and effects. Stylization involves, among others things, the following in varying degrees of combination: repetition (of sounds, words, phrases, images, patterns, etc.), compression (through deletion of syntactical nexuses, for example), and positioning (distribution of the linguistic elements so as to force them into often unexpected relations with other elements). The end result is that the original raw materials of experience are intensified, metaphorized, allegorized, personified, forced into analogies between the circumstantial and the representative, the particular and the universal, between what is fact and what is truth. Usually overriding these processes is conjoining, i.e., the bringing together into association of elements from different spheres of experience (vital, literary, artistic) which may produce, among others, the effect of ambiguity. The latter is the primary vehicle of polyvalence—without which poetry is greatly impoverished and experiential poetry often reduced to little more than the embellished record of facts. The selection of raw materials and the degree of stylization to which those materials are submitted ultimately depend, of course, on the poet's point of view or his subjective response to experience. The poet can present the facts quite directly, objectively, discursively—allowing them to speak for themselves, as it were. On the other hand, he can shape and manipulate them in such a way that they end up approximating or matching his own "reading" of the raw experiences. In other words, through point of view, the poet can lean toward the side of the disinterested historian or recorder of experience, or the *engagé* observer and interpreter of experience. Needless to say, Jorge de Sena is generally on the side of the latter. His poems on experience are nearly always interpretations or "readings" of experience, not merely disinterested renditions of it. This reading of experience is completed by the reader's own reading.

Let us turn to the poems based on incidents of the type covered by the daily experience mode poems within the broader category of Sena's public diary. One of the processes most frequently employed in these topical poems is allegorization. In fact, there is a sense in which all of Sena's poems based on real episodes or vignettes are allegorical. Applied to Sena's public-diary poems based on everyday-type incidents, what I mean by allegorization is the process by which a particular occurrence or event witnessed by the poet is raised in the poem to the level of the representative. The source experiences, without losing their documental value necessarily, become root metaphors for wider meanings, microcosms begging to be read as macrocosms. The latter, in the case of most incidents dealing with Portugal, is the socio-economic-political-moral reality brought about by fascism. What lends to these poems a significance beyond the circumstantiality in which they are rooted, therefore, is the reader's knowledge of the Portuguese history of the time. To cut the poems off from this latter context would be to render them partially ineffectual. It would also mean a disavowal of the poet's acknowledged intention to bear witness to his times. And in the case of a poet like Jorge de Sena to commit intentional fallacy is to commit a far lesser sin that intentional neglect.

A typical example of allegorization of a witnessed incident (in the city of Oporto) is the poem "Cubicle" of *Persecution*. The occurrence—a tuberculose man dying in a chair on a sidewalk in the presence of bystanders—had it taken place anywhere else in the world or even in the post-Revolution Portugal, would without a doubt have a different meaning from that which it acquires when set, as it must be, against the backdrop of the Portuguese socio-political-moral history of the 1940s. I hope I am not belaboring the point by saying that recognition on the part of Sena of the relationship or parallelism between the factual experience and its potentially transcendent meaning must be considered an integral part of the total poetic act. As for the reader, if he must penetrate one of the primary levels of meaning of "Cubicle," he must allow that wider historical context to guide his reading.

> Gente pára curiosa
> ante uma cadeira onde agoniza alguém.
>
> (E, do mesmo modo que os papéis descem do ar,
> eu penso que circula, assim, um ódio feito por medida,
> um ódio que o tempo não transformará em réplica
> mas cansaço de ódio.)
>
> Lá, dentro de casa,
> não podia morrer.
> A luz entrava só pela porta
> como qualquer de nós.

(I, p. 44)

(People stop curious
before a chair where someone agonizes.

(And, in the same way that paper comes down from the air,
I imagine the circling, in like manner, of a hatred made to measure,
a hatred which time shall not transform into reply
but into a surfeit of hatred.)

There, inside the house,
he couldn't die.
Light came in only through the door
like any of us.)

For purposes of analysis we may divide the poem into three distinct but interrelated components: the action of the bystanders and the sick man; the nouns *chair, light,* and *house,* which in the whole context of the poem gain profound symbolic and allegorical meaning; and finally the response of the poet to the entire episode. This response acts as a catalyst for the conversion by the reader of the incident into allegory. The poem does not begin by focusing on the man, but instead on the people who are watching him. The reference to the man comes in second place. Even in this detail Sena is faithful to reality. We recall that in the note to "The Russian Campaign," quoted earlier, Sena states in regard to this poem that "The tubercular dying in a chair that could be seen from the bridge had been described, of course, in the poem 'Cubicle' in *Persecution.*" This strongly suggests that the poet witnessed the incident from the bridge. Therefore, it is quite logical that he should see the crowd first. This vantage point on the part of the poet is very important, as we shall see in due time.

It is only in the last four lines of this ten-line poem that the reader is told why the man was there:

> There, inside the house,
> he couldn't die.
> Light came in only through the door
> like any of us.

We thus have a dying man who is impelled from his house onto the street by his need for *light* (and breath, as the note to the poem further explains), a universal symbol of hope and freedom (cf. "A Very Little Light" of *Fidelity).* The light he could obtain at home was something physical: It "came in only through the door." The *light* he needs is out there in the street, among the people (again one is reminded of "A Very Little Light," whose intertextual relation to "Cubicle" is indeed striking). The man provokes in the passersby not compassion, not rebellion, but curiosity. His need for *light* at the hour of death (he "agonizes") is most telling. If it is essential now, how much more so it must have been as he carried on the business of living! The *house,* i.e., the nation, in which he lives has become a prison—a *cubicle*—into which only a ray of physical light can penetrate. The very *chair* in which he "agonizes" suggests an instrument of death, of execution. The bystanders are watching his execution; nay, their own execution, because the man is each and every one of them.

The third component of the poem—which is really the second section of the poem—constitutes the poet's reaction to the episode. It can also be construed as the poet's interpretation of the reaction of the bystanders. It is by reading these lines that the reader begins to suspect why the bystanders reacted with curiosity to the man's plight, an attitude which is understandable but hardly sufficient under the circumstances. The reason—the poet suspects—is fear on the part of the bystanders. The latter perhaps feel a sense of compassion for the man. But this feeling does not compel them to act on his behalf. Due to fear, this sense of compassion in the face of moral injustice—the moral injustice of a country reduced to a concentric layer of prisons—is converted into self-contained and emasculating hatred—"a hatred made to measure"—outwardly disguised as curiosity. This hatred is like a contagious disease—and it has become as epidemic as the fascist terror that bred it. For the *paper* which the poet, from the bridge, as he surveys his country, could see floating in the breeze, is strongly suggestive of fascist propaganda, blowing everywhere, falling from the air, i.e., the sky. The poet seems to partake of the spectators' fear, which he "feels" circulating like the paper blown by the wind. But he, unlike the bystanders, purgates himself by writing the poem.

Positioning is also an important component in the entire process of transformation of the vignette into far-reaching dramatic allegory. We note that the poem is conceived and develops as a mini-drama—where suspense plays an important role. Indeed, the poem may be construed as a series of concentric dramatic actions, where the roles played by the characters change as the poem develops. The suspense is in the delayed information, i.e., the subjective parenthetical intervention on the part of the poet before he give us the end of the story (last four lines). First, we are introduced to the audience watching the drama (first line). But soon these spectators, too, become actors—with the poet as audience. In the end, the very poet becomes an actor—"I imagine the circling"—with the reader as audience. But the reader, too, realizes that he has played an active role in the entire story, as he is led by the poet's hand into the story's true meaning.

Jorge de Sena has thus manipulated the reader, as it were, into converting a street incident into a powerful allegory: the story of a moribund nation desperately searching for the light of freedom and hope but rendered impotent and helpless by fear and misguided, even though justifiable, anger. Poetry has forced, through its heightening and metamorphic power, the circumstantial to soar onto the plane of the representative. We might, in fact, say that it has raised it to the level of the universally symbolic. For the reading just given is not the only one possible. One could, for example, interpret the man's action (without preempting the above interpretation) by saying that freedom and hope are so important to the human being that even in the hour of death he is compelled from within to seek them. But I believe the first reading to be more correct—because it can account for all the elements of the poem.

In "Cubicle," what started out as raw experience ends up being converted into true poetic substance. The poem's relation to reality is not mimetic, but transformational. The poet does not use experience as a model for imitation, but as a stimulus for creation. Reality has given way to another complementary and expanded reality, where neither historical nor aesthetic truth are betrayed. Sena has seized upon a deeply human situation and extracted from it its ultimate implications and significance—in both artistic and human terms. As Adolfo Sánchez Vázquez writes, in his *Las ideas estéticas de Marx (Marx's Aesthetic Ideas),*

When the artist comes face to face with reality, he does not do so in order to copy it, but to appropriate it, to convert it into the foundation of a human signification. To aesthetically appropriate reality is to integrate it into a human world; forcing it to lose its self-sufficing nature, transforming it into a humanized reality. That which, in the name of realism, limits itself to copying or imitating reality is neither realism nor art. True realism is always a transformation of reality and the creation of a new reality.[7]

A page later Sánchez Vázquez adds that

The principle of the creative essence of art doesn't operate in an absolute manner. It fuses . . . with the socio-historical conditioning of artistic creation to become a dialectical interplay whose just understanding will allow us to avoid two pernicious extremes: socialization, on the one hand, which ignores the specific and relatively autonomous character of art, and, on the other, aestheticism which turns art into an absolutely unconditioned and autonomous activity.

The conversion of circumstance into universal allegory is typical of other poems based on incidents witnessed by Sena. An example is "Sunny Day" *(Crown of the Earth)* which, as Sena indicates in the note to the short story "The Russian Campaign," is based on real events. The poem reads:

Sob a teia de sombra dos galhos outonais,
passaram crianças
guiando na aragem
a outra já morta.

Não era a mãe nenhuma das mulheres.
Falavam tranquilas;
quase não vivera,
tão pequeno ainda.

E, rio acima, iam subindo barcos,
hora a hora menores,
na distância tão grande,
que alisava as águas.

(*I,* p. 97)

(Under the web of the autumn branches,
children passed
guiding in the breeze
the other one already dead.

Of the women none was the mother.
They spoke calmly;
he had hardly lived,
still so small.

And up the river, boats were sailing,
getting smaller and smaller,
in the huge distance,
that smoothed the waters.)

(trans. Helen Barreto)

The death of the child and the theme of abandonment ("Of the women none was the mother") suggests yet another allegory for Portuguese national life. The fact that the women "spoke calmly" invites the reader to conclude that, in this society, infant mortality, the death of innocence and promise for the future, is already accepted matter-of-factly. However, the poet (without preempting this reading of the poem) also raises the incident to a much more universal allegory—one which transcends the socio-economic-moral reality of any time and place to become a statement about life and death in general, which accords with the faith and hope inherent to Sena's humanism.

In the first line the theme of transitoriness of all life is subtly introduced: "Under the web of the autumn branches." Autumn will lead to winter and the latter to spring again—a spring which will not be shared by the young child. But then Sena brings in another element: the boats in the river. This process of conjoining, whereby a second element alters the meaning of another, is typical of Sena, as noted above. Since the incident takes place in Oporto, the reference could be to boats plying the Douro. But this is of no consequence, because "river" is strictly used in this poem in its traditional symbolic sense. We note, however, that the boats do not glide downriver, but *upriver,* i.e., against flow, against time or transitoriness. Life goes on against all odds, the poet suggests. Despite setbacks such as the death of a child, humankind continues and, as the direction of the boats implies, with some success. A note of hope, so characteristic of Sena, thus pervades this scene of death in a stifling social environment—a death which was foreshadowed in the first line of the poem, brought before the reader's eyes with reportorial matter-of-factness. But the symbolic implications of the child's death are considerably attenuated at last as the poet sets his hopeful sight towards the future.

Numerous other poems inspired by factual incidents witnessed by Sena can be read as partial or full verbal snapshots of Portuguese national life, for example "Sewer" and "City" *(Crown of the Earth).* Very often the poet acts as a sensor, capturing visual, audial and olfactory images which his muse converts into far-reaching metaphors. Just as vignettes are allegorized, so scattered impressions are metaphorized in Sena's public-diary poems. *Crown of the Earth,* above all other books, abounds in imagery of darkness, filth, and children screaming in the dead of night. All these impressions are gathered and alchemized by the poet. The latter's role in many of these poems is that of wanderer, spy for human justice in a kind of decaying moral world; of surveyor and interpreter of lives, as a man determined to report the truth as the rest of the city, i.e., the country, slumbers.

In his first books of poetry—and also in short stories dealing with this same period of time (the 1940s) and locale (Oporto)—Sena is totally obsessed with the allegorical and symbolic implications of children's activities: children crying, children playing in the dark, filthy streets, children dying. All these poems suggest that Jorge de Sena probably had in mind the Declaration of Geneva on the Rights of Children (1923). All of its propositions are upheld by him. In certain poems, such as the one appropriately entitled "Pamphlet," Sena sets aside all poetic subterfuges (subterfuges that were most likely as much poetic as they were a means to evade censorship) and makes direct statements. "Pamphlet" is a direct attack on religious superstition; a condemnation of the waste of human energy that could be used to open the "way of life" (*I,* p. 112). In other poems Sena intersperses verses that can be construed as interpretations of the very imagery used in the poem. "Nuptials" and "Sewer" *(Crown of the Earth)* are cases in point. In the second strophe of the latter poem, one reads:

> *Alegremente o esterco toma formas náuticas;*
> *um murmúrio de água incita-o com ternura,*
> *um murmúrio no cano coberto de lajes gastas,*
> *um ciciar de restos não comidos, restos digeridos, vidas não geradas.*
>
> (*I,* p. 93)

> (Happily filth assumes nautical forms;
> a murmur of water impells it tenderly,
> a murmur in the pipe covered with worn-out flagstones,
> a whisper of uneaten scraps, digested scraps, lives never begotten.)

This image of "nautical forms" fulfills a double function: it is a reference to the children's play; but it may also be construed as a subtle and ironic allusion to the Portuguese maritime enterprises so often vaunted about by fascists. The nautical future of *these* children is the filth in which they are immersed. Unlike the yet unborn children of the fisherwomen in Cesário Verde's poem "O sentimento de um ocidental" ("The Feelings of a Western Person"), those who "will one day perish in the storms at sea," these will not even get that far. As Sena tells us in the poem "Glory," they are the children who "could not unfold themselves in living flesh."

A scene inspired by the drip-drip of the sewer pipe in Oporto mentioned in the quoted passage of "Sewer" appears in the short story "Child's Cry" of *The Grand-Captains.* In this story, too, the sight is converted into allegory and Sena intersperses asides similar in content and intention to the last line of the passage of "Sewer": "um cheiro de amarguras, um cheiro de vidas cortadas, um cheiro de esperanças traídas, um cheiro de promessas não cumpridas, um cheiro de carne saudosa, de posses que não houvera, adiadas, recusadas, ou não conseguidas" ("a smell of sorrow, a smell of lives cut short, a smell of betrayed hopes, a smell of unfulfilled promises, a smell of flesh yearning for the love that wasn't, the love postponed, refused, not consummated").[8]

The overall impression of Portugal left by these poems—when they are read allegorically and metaphorically, as most were meant to be—is that of a social and moral wasteland, a land of hopelessness or where hope survives precariously; a land where children age before growing up, where they die before they live; a land where adults wallow in superstition and where those who do not are rendered impotent by fear; a dark place where the sun of life seldom shines; a land, in short, before which—as Sena tells us in the allegorical poem "City" *(Crown of the Earth)*—the very sea, a symbol of life, retreats in discomfort:

> *Imersa, troglodita, ambiciosa,*
> *vai a cidade até à praia;*
> *perdeu no campo as rochas cor-de-rosa,*
> *e o mar, se a busca, evita-a, não desmaia,*
> *antes se ergue negro contra o desconforto.*
>
> (*I,* p. 93)

> (Immersed, troglodytic, ambitious,
> the city goes down to the beach;
> losing in the countryside the pink-colored rocks,
> and the sea, when seeking it, avoids it, doesn't swoon,
> but rears black in discomfort.)

Although Portugal at large is implicated in the poems comprising the daily mode of Sena's public diary, the poet left us a large body of poems where the experiential impetus comes not from particular incidents but from his overall impression of life in his country. However, even in these poems the referents are always veridical. "The Artificial Paradises," the opening poem of *Philosopher's Stone,* falls within the category of what I termed the national mode of Sena's public-diary poems. Although it is inspired by the socio-economic-political reality of the Portugal of the 1940s, the poem also engages intertextually two well-known literary works. One is Baudelaire's *Les paradis artificiels* (1860), a book in which the author of *Les fleurs du mal,* as he himself stated, retells in a shortened form De Quincey's

Confessions of an English Opium Eater (1822). The other work less directly present in Sena's text but still quite discernible is the famous poem "To Portugal" by the ultraromantic Portuguese writer Tomás Ribeiro (1831-1901). Although he is best known for his patriotic epic poems, Ribeiro also gained notoriety as a singer of the natural beauty of his country. A series of clichés from "To Portugal" became extremely famous during Ribeiro's lifetime and were, later, much quoted and paraphrased by Portuguese fascists, one of whose patriotic slogans was "A tua Pátria é a mais linda de todas as Pátrias: merece todos os teus sacrifícios" ("Your Homeland is the most beautiful of all Homelands: it deserves all your sacrifices"). The portion of "To Portugal" most directly implicated in Sena's poem is the third strophe:

> *Jardim da Europa à beira-mar plantado*
> *De loiros e de acácias olorosas;*
> *De fontes e de arroios serpeado,*
> *Rasgado por torrentes alterosas;*
> *Onde num cerro erguido e requeimado*
> *Se casam em festões jasmins e rosas;*
> *Balsa virente de eternal magia,*
> *Onde as aves gorgeiam noite e dia.*[9]

> (Europe's garden, planted by the sea,
> With laurel and sweet-smelling acacia-trees;
> Its fountains and meandering small streams,
> Ripped by lofty rushing torrents;
> Where on a high and sun-scorched hillock
> Are joined in wreaths jasmins and roses;
> Verdant cork-tree of eternal magic
> Where birds sing by night and by day.)

By entitling the poem "The Artificial Paradises" Sena engages the sarcastic tone implicit in the noun and also the theme of artificiality explicit in his and Baudelaire's title. Indeed, the major thematic thrust of Sena's poem concerns artificiality. As the poem develops, however, so do the semantic frontiers of "artificial," which progressively expand to encompass ever wider circles of meaning. The latter range from "made by humans as a substitution for the natural" to "deliberate deception." A veritable imagistic tour de force, the poem can be read at three different even though interrelated and complementary levels. On one level it is an ecologically minded protest against the violation of Nature. In this sense "The Artificial Paradises" reveals a marked resemblance to the poem "Born in the City" *(Perpetual Vision),* which begins with the lines

Nascido na cidade de árvores sem nome,
de flores no jardim municipal,
sem animais além de ratos e baratas,
e com um turvo céu quase sem estrelas,
à beira de um rio já estuário
salgado e baço como estanho sujo.

(Born in a city of nameless trees,
of flowers in the municipal garden,
without animals except for rats and cockroaches,
under a turbid and almost starless sky,
by the side of a river already estuary,
salty and muddy, like dirty tin.)

On the other level, "The Artificial Paradises" is a sarcastic refutation of the pristine paradises sung by Ribeiro. On a wider and more profound level still, the poem is a satire against official fascist propaganda in general.

I believe, though, that the poet's protest against the ecological consequences of modern progress functions more as a decoy for the more important (in the poem, at any rate) comment Sena makes on the national socio-economic-political-moral reality than it does as an end in itself. The first three lines of the poem support this assertion:

Na minha terra, não há terra, há ruas;
mesmo as colinas são de prédios altos
com renda muito mais alta.
(I, p. 131)

(In my country there is no country, there are streets;
even the hills are high buildings
with rent and rates much higher.)
(trans. Jonathan Griffin)

Although the poet calls attention to the macadamization of the land and the presence of tall buildings where hills used to be (cf. Ribeiro's "Where on a high and sun-scorched hillock / Are joined in wreaths jasmins and roses"), the point he is really keen on making only becomes clear by the third line: "with rent and rates much higher." Sena exploits the double meaning of *renda:* "rent" and "income." In other words, the "paradises" are "artificial" not only, or primarily, because "progress" has cast a cement and iron mask upon the face of pristine Nature: they are "artificial" because they constitute masks meant to disguise socio-economic inequality and inequity.

In the next six lines of the poem Tomás Ribeiro's clichés continue to be implicated even though the underlying intention of the imagery is less and less applicable to the destruction of Nature as such, and

103

more and more concerned with the violation and brutalization of basic human needs and rights. The theme of calculated deception, always complemented and reinforced by ecological nuances, is particularly stressed in the reference to the songs of the birds: "O cântico das aves—não há cânticos / mas só canários de 3°. andar e papagaios de 5°." ("The song of the birds—there are no songs, / only 3rd-floor canaries and 5th-floor parrots") (cf. Ribeiro's "Where birds sing by night and by day"). As the wild flowers became immured within precarious gardens and the trees succumbed to the brutal and extremely efficient—"especialíssimas" ("very special")—machines of the State, so the songs of the free birds were replaced by those of domesticated canaries. (In Portuguese, "to speak like a canary" means to make good speeches, to speak well; to be pompously rhetorical by implication.) And the canaries' sweet talk is further echoed and artificialized by echoing parrots. In this rigidly stratified, topsy-turvy order of artificial song—where one never knows whose is the true voice and whose is the mere echo—even the most glaring of realities is "sweet-sung" out of existence. As the poet sarcastically remarks, parodying the songs of the canaries and the grunts of the parrots,

> Na minha terra, porém, não há pardieiros,
> que são todos na Pérsia ou na China,
> ou em países inefáveis.

> (In my country, though, there are no slums,
> those are all in Persia or in China,
> or in ineffable countries.)

The title that Baudelaire chose for his book is most significant, writes Enid Starkie, "for it indicates that, in spite of its great joys, he wanted to condemn the machine-made heaven, the fool's paradise, which can be reached by means of drugs."[10] The artificial, machine-made paradises Jorge de Sena condemns are those of pseudo-progress and caged existence. Images of prison punctuated by violence run the entire length of the poem in an ever tightening circle: streets, gardens, cages, slums. So much so, to such an ironic degree in fact, that the very "canaries" and "parrots"—instruments of the machinery of incarceration—are themselves incarcerated. Most of all, the poet exposes the fool's paradise induced by the opium of propagandistic deception—a deception that pervades all of life and stifles genuine speech. So much so that the very poet—the supreme singer of humanity—is forced to combine more or less direct statement with imagistic subterfuge in order to lay bare the truth about the "ineffability" of life in his country.

Turning now to a discussion of the personal poems, we may begin by asking: Do Sena's personal experiences, i.e., those in which he was not primarily the spectator but actor, achieve a representative or allegorical dimension? Or do they remain personal materials mostly of interest to the biographer and the biographical critic narrowly defined? In answer to these questions we could say that there is a convergence or interpenetration of personal and public experiences in Jorge de Sena's poetry. There is a private or personal quality to all of his public poems to the extent that they bear the imprint of his personal response to experience, his philosophy of life, and his personality. By the same token, there is something public in his private or personal experiences in the kind of representativeness they attain in the poems. Perhaps it was in part this desire to lend the more personal poems this representativeness that made Jorge de Sena shun the intimate-type experiences and bedroom-type confessions that constitute the *sine qua non* of a journal such as Amiel's. At any rate, there is in Sena's experiential poetry a marked tendency to personalize the impersonal and impersonalize the personal experiences that constitute the raw material of the poems. Here again Sena is not deviating from a well-established poetical tradition. Jonathan Culler states that "even in poems which are ostensibly presented as personal statements made on particular occasions, the conventions of reading enable us to avoid considering the framework as a purely biographical matter and to construct a referential context that the rest of the poems make" (op. cit., p. 167). But I must stress that this impersonalization of the private experiences does not rob the latter of their autobiographical, human integrity. The range of meaning of the personal matter is poetically extended and metamorphosed, but never completely neutralized.

Sena's poems on aging, on being a poet, on being a wanderer *("andarilho")* or exile are all examples of poems based on concrete personal experiences—but reaching out to encompass wider meanings. His poems of exile, for example, are poetic statements regarding not only his own situation but that of other Portuguese (and not only Portuguese) intellectuals who, now as in the past, due to one kind of oppression or another, were compelled to leave their country, voluntarily or involuntarily. Explicitly or implicitly Sena strikes analogies between his own and the lives of these exiles and *estrangeirados,* thereby placing his experience within a nationally representative context. In the poem "In Crete, with the Minotaur," Sena evokes Eça de Queiroz, Fernando Pessoa, and Camoens, all of whom were exiles or *estrangeirados* in one way or another. Like Camoens, Sena considers having left his "life parcelled out throughout the world in bits and pieces" (a literal quotation from Camoens's *canção* "Junto de um seco, fero e estéril monte"—"As I Stand by this Dry, Wild and Sterile Mountain"). And "having collected several nationalities"—as did, in their own way, Eça de Queiroz and Fernando Pessoa—Jorge de Sena, too, is left, as they were, with the Portuguese language for a country.

Although Sena addresses the theme of exile in several poems, in none does the theme achieve such profound resonances as "In Crete, with the Minotaur." It is most significant that the poem should begin with concrete autobiographical information:

> Nascido em Portugal, de pais portugueses,
> e pai de brasileiros no Brasil
> serei talvez norte-americano quando lá estiver.
>> (The whole poem appears in *III*, p. 76-78)

> (Born in Portugal, of Portuguese parents,
> The father of Brazilians in Brazil,
> I shall become, perhaps, an American when I'm there.)
>> (trans. George Monteiro)

Starting from a well-defined nationality and a clear sense of identity, the poet soon begins to lose his roots. The "perhaps" of the third line of the poem already bespeaks a condition of uprootedness, of uncertainty as to where he belongs. In the very order of these elements—Portugal, Brazil, United States—we have an exact parallel to his real life. By the end of the poem, the poet finds himself

> Em Creta, com o Minotauro,
> sem versos e sem vida,
> sem pátrias e sem espírito,
> sem nada, nem ninguém,
> que não o dedo sujo,
> hei-de tomar em paz o meu café.

> (In Crete, with the Minotaur,
> Sans poems and sans life,
> Sans homelands and sans spirit,
> With nothing, nor anyone,
> Except for that dirty finger,
> I shall drink my coffee in peace.)

Unlike the geographical entities already mentioned, Crete must not, of course, be viewed in geographical but symbolic terms. It is the archetypal island of rest. It is the ultimate result of the progression announced in the first three lines of the poem: Portugal-Brazil-United States-island of rest, which is more wishful thinking than anything else, as Sena himself indicates in the poem "On a Strophe By Jorge de Sena" *(Sequences)*. The poet ends up drinking coffee with the

106

Minotaur, i.e., in the company of a mythological beast—part man, part bull, as Sena says earlier in the poem—the kind of "beast" he often encountered in his *peregrinatio ad loca infecta* of this world. In the poem, Crete also represents a refuge from the world of art, from all things cultural. As Sena says in the poem, "O Minotauro / não falava grego, não era grego, viveu antes da Grécia, / de toda esta merda douta que nos cobre há séculos" ("The Minotaur / Did not speak Greek; he was not Greek, having lived before the time of Greece, / Before all that learned shit that has covered us for centuries"). This feeling of cultural saturation, this attitude on the part of Sena to befoul that which he held as most sacred will be repeated in "Final 'Potpourri,'" the last poem of *Art of Music*. It presents Sena's desire to knock down all absolutes, all gods, even those he revered.

The poet's condition is not as negative as one might be led to conclude. True that he is in the company of a beast; he has, as he tells us, no poems and no life because he has "cast off" the former and feels he is nearing the end of the latter; he has no country and no spirit (desire to go on living?). But he does have two very important things: relative peace and quiet; and a "dirty finger" from, as he puts it, "probing for the origins of life." In other words, the poet has reached a stage of his life, a bitter-sweet stage, where he can, if nothing else, rest in the consolation of having borne witness to his times, to his own life, nay, of having delved as poet to the very origins of life—in all the acceptations of this, the most daring image in all of Sena's poetry. Although, humanly speaking, the loss of one's country may be tragic (and in the case of Jorge de Sena it seems to have been), poetically speaking it seems to be the fate of many men. And Jorge de Sena accepted this fact. His abode is with all of humanity—that humanity that is sometimes more human than bull, and all too often more bull than human. And to commune with all of humanity one has to move away from home. Once having left, there is no way back. The poet is left to his own resources: to dream an island of rest—not a paradisiacal island for that would never be Sena's way, but an island at once real and symbolic of our human, all too human condition.

In his travel-inspired poems Sena always avails himself of every opportunity to transform factuality into allegory, metaphor or symbol by utilizing the alchemic power of poetry. A case in point is the poem "Meditation at a Corner on King's Road" (*II*, p. 46), which, according to the note (*II*, p. 228), "was inspired by the author's observing King's Road, the central axis of Chelsea, London, in 1957—at the moment the traffic lights turned green." The indecision to cross or not cross the street at a traffic light is raised to the level of a meditation on human choice, on human destiny. The poem reads in part:

Solícitas de mim, como de mim ou fora,
oferecem-me os caminhos que desdobram
ante os meus gestos, a que me convidam.
Ou não convidam—antes eu à beira
da rua já não posso recuar,
acesas que já estão por só momentos
as luzes verdes. . . .

(Solicitous of me, as in me or out of me,
they offer me the ways that open out
before my gestures, to where they beckon me.
Or do not beckon—rather, I
at the edge of the street cannot recoil,
now when the green lights are lit . . . .)
(trans. Jean R. Longland)

The poem ends with the lines, "Acesos os sinais—mas por qual delas?— / não tenho tempo já senão de atravessar" ("The signals are lit—but toward which of them?— / now I have no time but to cross"). Given the poet's emphasis on the *green* lights, the poem is relatable to the theme of hope so often expressed in Sena's poetry. His indecision, his lack of volition and his unpreparedness to cross the street and, finally, his surrender to the hazards of the traffic—all suggest Sena's attitude toward destiny. The most arduous but also rewarding paths one takes at the crossroads of life are often unpremeditated. But neither are they left entirely to chance. After all, it was the poet who pressed the button for the lights to change.

In some of these travel poems allegorizing and analogizing attain remarkable, totally unexpected, and, in some cases, humorous results. "Antwerp" is an excellent example:

Na catedral o Cristo faleceu atlético
e tomba de ouro em Rubens por sempre.

Na casa dele patrício, Sir, Grande de Espanha,
a magna oficina tem balcão e tudo
para o grande espectáculo dos heróis e deuses
e as deusas adiposas rubicunda esposa.

Plantinos imprimiram e um soneto
diz aurea de Cristóvão mediocritas

le bonheur de ce monde: avoir une maison...
(*III*, p. 224)

(In the cathedral the Christ died athletic
and he tumbles in gold by Rubens forever.

In the house of nobleman, Sir, *Grande* of Spain,
the magnificent atelier has counter and all

108

for the great spectacle of heroes and gods
and adipose goddesses rubicund wife.

Plantins engraved and a sonnet
says aurea of Christopher mediocritas

le bonheur de ce monde: avoir une maison...)

As Sena indicates in the note to "Antwerp," "The poem starts with
an allusion to *The Descent from the Cross,* the magnificent painting
that is in the cathedral. Afterwards it refers to the manorial home, a
splendid mansion, and to the atelier of Rubens himself, both of which
survive. I then quote the famous sonnet by one of the Plantins" (*III,*
p. 268).

There are other identifiable allusions in the poem. All of
them—which superficially appear to constitute a haphazard collage—are logically and organically interconnected and motivated by
Sena's visit to the three great tourist attractions in Antwerp: the
cathedral, Rubens's house, and the Plantin-Moretus Museum. In addition to the allusions mentioned by Sena in the note, there is a
reference in the poem to Rubens's title ("Sir"), an evocation of the
Duke of Lerma, the Great Man of Spain, minister of Philip III. As is
well known, Rubens worked temporarily for Lerma and left us a
magnificent equestrian portrait of the influential man. In the sixth and
seventh lines of the poem Sena recalls aspects of Rubens's subject
matter—"the great spectacle of heroes and gods / and adipose goddesses rubicund wife." According to tradition, Rubens's first wife was
the model for his Magdalens, including the one in *Descent from the
Cross.* The reference to the famous printer Christopher Plantin
(1520?-1589) and his equally famous sonnet, "Le bonheur de ce
monde," may seem quite arbitrary in a poem that apparently concerns
itself primarily with Rubens. But again, the enumeration is chaotic only apparently: it follows a perfectly logical line of associations. As
noted earlier, the reference to Plantin was probably motivated in part
by Sena's visit to the museum—where a copy of the sonnet hangs. We
might also add that even if that visit had not taken place, the association between Rubens and Plantin would have forced itself almost inevitably upon the poet. Moretus, Christopher Plantin's grandson, was
Rubens's schoolmate. It is also well known that the painter left several
portraits of members of the Plantin family.

A still more important connection between *The Descent from the
Cross* and Christopher Plantin, however, is the latter's given
name—Christopher. The painting, as we know, is the central piece of
a triptych. The two volets are *The Visitation* and *The Presentation in*

the Temple. The entire work had been commissioned by the Brotherhood of Arquebusiers for the altar of the cathedral and was meant to glorify St. Christopher. When the painting was finished and no St. Christopher was to be seen, the arquebusiers protested. Rubens explained that the characters shown in the triptych were all "carriers of Christ"—which is the meaning of *Christopher* in Greek. The mention of "Christopher" in Sena's poem can thus be construed as doubly referential: it is an allusion to the general theme of the painting as well as a reference to Plantin. Most logical also is the ending of Sena's poem with a quotation from Christopher Plantin's sonnet. The Portuguese poet quotes the title plus part of the first verse, which reads, in a continuation of the title phrase, "Avoir une maison commode, propre et belle."[11] The reason for associational logicity in this case is that the *aurea mediocritas* expressed in Plantin's sonnet is precisely that of Rubens's philosophy of life, as two plaques attached to his princely house with a couple of quotations from Juvenal clearly show. One of these quotations reads: "We should pray for a healthy body. Ask for a brave spirit, with no fear of death... let it know no anger and covet nothing." These and other ideals are expressed in Plantin's sonnet, whose last line is "C'est attendre chez soi bien doucement la mort."

Although these are the empirical elements and logical associations in Sena's poem, they are far from being presented in logical and syntactical sequence. The experiential raw materials of the poem are all dismembered, fragmented, and then reassembled following a process akin to that of free association and chaotic enumeration. Inspiring reality is submitted to a kind of surrealistic automatism as far as its verbal expression is concerned. The empirical referents are not negated, but they are forced into totally unexpected interrelationships. And here we have a major difference between Sena's travel poems, as far as content, and the travel genres, particularly the diary, which they superficially resemble. The travel diarist observes the present, often recalls the past, and may even utilize momentary impressions gathered from visits to historical or artistic sites. He may use these as the basis for meditations or reflections. But he usually keeps observation, temporal digressions and reflections logically separated, compartmentalized. In "Antwerp," however, Sena's approach to reality does not follow this conventional compartmentalization of experience. It is not a verbal duplication of empirical reality, but a total re-creation of it. The poem does not bear a direct relation to the vital experiences on which it is based, except at one level of meaning. At another level, this relation to concrete reality is a very oblique one indeed. Although the poem is ostensibly a recording of impressions plus historical associations gathered during a visit to Antwerp, it also becomes a testing ground for syntactical experimentation and, more important still, an outlet for flights of further daring associations for which the original experiences in the Belgian city only provide a frame of thematic reference.

For, as farfetched as it may seem, the choice and disposition of empirico-thematic elements assembled allow the poem to be read as a sarcastic and highly humorous depiction of some of the major philosophical tenets of Salazar's Estado Novo. In other words, "Antwerp" is both a portrait of Sena's Antwerp and a caricature of Salazar's Portugal. This interpretation presupposes that the reader is aware, as most literate Portuguese were, of the well-publicized fact that, as Maria Filomena Mónica indicates, quoting António Ferro's *Portugal and Her Leader,* "A painting of the Sacred Heart of Jesus and a sonnet by Plantin ('Le bonheur de ce monde'), celebrating the 'aurea mediocritas,' decorated the austere office where Salazar daily diagnosed the Ills ⎾of the Country⏌."[12] Given this fact, which was unquestionably known by Jorge de Sena, it is easy to see how the poet most cleverly—and following the suggestion of Rubens's equally clever indirect depiction of St. Christopher in the triptych?—seizes upon the thematic material gathered during his visit to Antwerp to subtly reconstruct an aspect of reality back home (the poem was written in 1972; at a time, therefore, when Salazar's memory and legacy were still very much alive), thus exercising his common practice, as noted earlier, of always searching for Portugal in the most distant lands and under the most unusual of circumstances. The correspondence between Sena's carefully selected and carefully assembled experiences in Antwerp and their analogical counterparts back home is indeed uncanny: the picture of the Christ in the first two lines of the poem and the picture of the Sacred Heart in Salazar's office; the reference, which we now know to be sarcastic, to the Great Man of Spain (Hispania); to the "magna oficina" ("magnificent atelier") where Rubens practiced the artistic cult devoted to his heroes and gods and Salazar's "magna oficina" wherein he practiced the cult of devotion to the national heroes and gods of the past; the reference to the "rubicund wife" which refers to Rubens's wife but can also be construed as a supremely sarcastic allusion to Salazar's female companion; and, finally, the reference to Plantin's sonnet—a copy of which hangs in the Plantin-Moretus Museum and is implicitly present in Rubens's house—but also adorned the office of the Portuguese dictator, underlining and summarizing his paternalistic and outmoded view of life.

From poems dealing with vital experiences we now come to poems derived from *Bildungserlebnis,* i.e., to Sena as poet of works of art. The latter poems may be divided into three groups; poems inspired by literature, poems on works of visual art, and poems on musical compositions. In the group of poems inspired by literary works—which comprise a few dozen poems scattered throughout Sena's corpus—I also include the poems based on movies, such as "Battleship Potemkin" (*III,* p. 55), "Pornographic Movies" (*III,* p. 215), and "I Begin to Understand" *(40 Years,* p. 140).

A point that must be emphasized from the outset—and which is of key importance to our later study of *Art of Music*—is that Sena himself never entirely separated these two sources of inspiration, the vital from the artistic. To Jorge de Sena as poet, experiencing a work of literature, seeing and living a Fragonard and immersing himself in a work of music were experiences almost as vital as witnessing a child's funeral or watching a man dying of tuberculosis on the sidewalk. True that each of these experiences—and Sena's poetry shows that he knows this very well—is loaded with different kinds of meanings and the human dramas embedded in them can be very different indeed and touch the poet in radically different ways. Nevertheless, because the overwhelming number of Sena's art-inspired poems communicate precisely the human dimension embodied in the work of art, the differences between vital and artistic experiences are not as great as they may seem to be. For Jorge de Sena, poetizing art is very much being in close contact with life.

In the preface to the second edition of *Poetry-I,* Sena says of *Metamorphoses* and *Art of Music,* "the poems on aesthetic objects or considered as such, just as the poems on music, constitute autonomous sequences, while *Peregrinatio* was the continuation of the 'diary' whose publication had been initiated in 1942 with *Persecution,* a diary relative to which the meditating on those objects or those musical pieces was no more than the sequences of particular moments" (*I,* p. 12). That is to say, *Metamorphoses* and *Art of Music* are not entirely separate from Sena's diary: they constitute special sequences of it, sequences which the poet chose to isolate, as he could have isolated the poems inspired by specific works of literature and formed a book with them. All of the diarists discussed in Chapter II—Pepys, Amiel, Montaigne, etc.—also have entries in their diaries dedicated to works of art, ranging from attendance at a play to seeing an architectural monument. Sena's corpus, excluding *Metamorphoses* and *Art of Music,* also contains several poems that announce or foretell those two sequences: and, in the case of music, there are at least three poems that were to have been published in *Art of Music,* but which Sena finally decided to leave out. Anticipating *Metamorphoses,* we have, for example, the poem "Primitivos" ("Primitives") *(Philosopher's Stone);* two poems which anticipate *Art of Music* are "Fragment in Praise of J.S. Bach" *(Philosopher's Stone)* and "As of You..." *(Fidelity).* The latter is a poem which Sena dedicates "To the memory of Pope Pius XII who, when he was already on his deathbed, asked to listen to the 'Allegretto' of Beethoven's Seventh Symphony" *(II,* p. 53). The three poems that, according to Mrs. Mécia de Sena, were supposed to have been published in *Art of Music* are "Ray Charles" *(Sequences),* "Extemporaneous Indignation..." and "In the Corridor of the 'Metro'" *(Perpetual Vision).* At least three other poems of *Perpetual Vision* deal with music: "Music," "It's Late, Very Late at Night...," and the "Prince of Venosa . . ." And the poem "To Me, in My Hand,..." *(Perpetual Vision)* is clearly inspired, as Mrs. Mécia de Sena points out in a note *(Perpetual Vision,* p. 235), by António Pedro's painting *Noiva (Bride)* which hung by Jorge de Sena's work desk. The poem, dated 28 February 1974, could have entered into the republication of *Metamorphoses* (1978). As far as subject matter and treatment go, the poem belongs to that collection even though there is no indication that Sena ever contemplated including it.

When I discuss *Metamorphoses* and *Art of Music* we shall see that what Sena poetizes for the most part is his *experience* of the works of art. These books can, therefore, be considered special isolated sequences in Jorge de Sena's overall poetic diary. They too constitute examples of the poet's total commitment to poetizing human experience—whether the latter be derived from actual happenings or from the poet's contact with human creations.

Sena's poems on literature, the visual arts, and music, no matter what the specific transformational technique involved might be, constitute a metamorphosis of these three components in varying proportions: 1) the work of art as aesthetic entity, 2) the work of art as an object reflective of its creator's life and/or times, and 3) the work of art as producer and catalyst of a vital experience for the poet. (For this vital experience is always conditioned by the work of art, but may also awaken within the poet experiences extraneous to it.) The first of these components, i.e., the work of art as detached aesthetic object, is the least important as far as the poems are concerned. Indeed, most of Sena's poems on all of the arts may be construed as deliberate attempts on his part to bring works of art down from the autonomous pedestal on which many have been enthroned—and reinstate them in the vital stage of human experience from which they sprang and to which they remit. Thus, all of Sena's experiential poems undergo two apparently divergent metamorphic processes that eventually meet: the vital experience poems draw art, i.e., poetry, from life; and the poems based on works of art reinstill life into art. What Sena aims to do is reconcile life with art—cf. "human commitment to pure poetry"—by raising one to the bright universal light of the artistic plane, and respectfully lowering the other to the level of human experience. This image is of course figurative. What Sena does is actually *raise* art to the level of life, because, to him, life is always on a higher plane than anything else. I did use the adverb *respectfully* quite intentionally, though. For it is never Sena's intention, despite his interest in the human content of art, to betray art's basic aesthetic integrity.

As for any attempt to categorize them, the poems on literature pose a greater problem than those derived from the visual or musical arts. To begin with, there is a sense in which all poems can be said to derive from literature. By the very fact that Sena's poetic creations are part of literary tradition in general and that of poetry in particular, every one of his poems is to that extent based on literature. We must add to this the fact that all of Sena's creative works are informed by an extremely rich literary background, which manifests itself in a dense texture of allusions, dialogues with other texts, and use of epigraphs. Some examples among the dozens that could be cited are "The Artificial Paradises," already discussed; "For Whom the Bell Tolls, With Incidences of the Cartesian *Cogito,*" "Double Gloss," "Gloss of Menandro" *(Peregrinatio);* "Of Passing Birds" *(Philosopher's Stone);* "Of Docta Ignorantia" *(Fidelity).*[13] Therefore, by poems on literature I mean only those which draw their overall subject matter, not from literature in general, but from identified/identifiable literary works; not those merely containing allusions to a text, but those whose primary impetus stems from a literary work. In fact, at times Sena will base a poem, not on any specific work, but on the entire production and/or life of a given author. Cases in point are "To Dionisio Ridruejo" *(III,* p. 229), and "Pablo Neruda Died of Cancer" *(40 Years).* As we shall see, *Art of Music* also contains poems based on the entire production and life of composers.

Sena's poems on an author and his works include a wide range of names and titles. Some of these names are: Petronius, Sá de Miranda, Camoens, San Juan de la Cruz, Antonio Machado, Rilke, Kafka, Fernando Pessoa, Ridruejo, García Lorca, Manuel Bandeira, Carlos Drummond de Andrade, and Samuel Beckett. Included among the compositions are: *The Epic of Gilgamesh,* the *Satyricon, cantigas de amigo,* traditional ballads, Sá de Miranda's sonnet "O sol é grande, caem co'a calma as aves" ("The sun is big and the birds fall down due to the heat"), *The Lusiads,* several lyric works of Camoens and

Pessoa, Kafka's *The Trial,* and Beckett's *Waiting for Godot.* Poems on specific works of literature constitute meditations often based on a single episode, passage or verse, and less frequently on an entire composition. Inspiration derived from a single section of a large work also characterizes many poems of *Art of Music.* Examples of poems based on entire literary compositions are "As Silvana Stood" and "Two Songs of Camoens Sitting at a Table d'Hôte" *(40 Years),* which is inspired in part by a specific stanza of *The Lusiads.*

Thematically, Sena's poems on literature range from meditations on themes that, despite concerning humanity as a whole, were of especial interest to Sena himself (such as the theme of mortality), to reflections on life in Portugal. Therefore, in many cases these poems are not very different thematically from many of Sena's personal and public poems. This suggests once again that Sena's main preoccupation was always life—as it is being lived and as it is embodied in works of art. I will discuss briefly two poems derived from literature: "As To Gilgamesh" *(40 Years,* p. 146), as an example of a meditation on the problem of death; and "To Portugal" *(40 Years,* p. 89), as a reflection on Portugal, with autobiographical overtones.

"As To Gilgamesh" draws inspiration from two specific episodes of the ancient epic that implicate its entire thematic thrust: the human fear of death, a thematic constant in Sena's personal poems. These two episodes are the hero's crossing of the river or sea in hope of learning from Utnapishtin—the sage who had won immortality from the gods—the secret of eternal earthly life; and Gilgamesh's resolve to go home, i.e., to go on making the best of life after discovering that no man can escape old age and death. Sena's poem makes three essential points: 1) there are no entirely satisfactory metaphysical answers regarding the origins and ultimate purpose of life; 2) man must reconcile himself to the inevitable: death; and 3) despite this, man must never cease his search for the impossible or, as Sena puts it, "só um pecado existe e é não viver-se / em desafio sempre. A Gilgamesh foi quanto disseram" ("Only one sin exists—to fail to live life / as though it were a challenge. To Gilgamesh that's all they said"). This poem is thus an application of the thematic content of the *Epic* to a universal human concern, one which is addressed in personal terms by numerous other poems of Jorge de Sena. The overall positive view of life which Sena imparts to "As To Gilgamesh" is indeed reminiscent of "Death, Space, and Eternity."

"To Portugal" is simultaneously a very personal poem and a kind of state-of-Portugal address. Sena draws inspiration from a passage of *The Lusiads* where Vasco da Gama, after having described Europe to the king of Melinde, turns to a description of Portugal itself. In stanza 20, Canto III, Camoens had referred to the geographical location of Portugal as "cume da cabeça / De Europa toda" ("crown of Europe / it might be"). In stanza 21—which is the point of departure for Sena's poem—Camoens states' "Esta é a ditosa pátria minha amada" ("This is my well-loved country of content") and proceeds with the history of Portugal beginning with the historico-mythical "Esta foi Lusitânia, derivada / De Luso ou Lisa, que de Baco antigo / Filhos foram" ("And Lusitania traces her descent / From Lusus or from Lysa, who, we learn, / Were ancient Bacchus' sons") (*The Lusiads,* trans. with an intro. by Leonard Bacon. New York: Hispanic Society of America, 1950). Nevertheless, the title "To Portugal" also engages Tomás Ribeiro's poem of the same name, the poem in praise of Portugal already discussed in connection with "The Artificial Paradises." First, this reply to Camoens is put in personal terms. Sena writes:

> *Esta é a ditosa pátria minha amada. Não.*
> *Nem é ditosa, porque o não merece.*
> *Nem minha amada, porque é só madrasta.*
> *Nem pátria minha, porque eu não mereço*
> *a pouca sorte de nascido nela.*

> (This is my well-loved country of content. No.
> It is not of content, because it doesn't deserve to be.
> Neither is it well-loved, because it's only a step-mother.
> Nor is it my native land, for I do not deserve
> the misfortune of having been born in it.)

The "dialogue" with Camoens proceeds. In contradistinction to Camoens's historico-mythical origins for Portugal, Sena demythifies his country by calling it "Torpe dejecto de romano império" ("Ignoble excretion of Roman empire"); and to Camoens's "crown of Europe," Sena opposes "salsugem porca / de esgoto atlântico" ("saline filth / of Atlantic sewer").

Is Sena's poem, then, an attempt on his part to undercut Camoens's epic views of Portugal by inverting them? I believe it is, but only to a minor degree. More important than as a reply to Camoens, the poem is a refutation of the fascist epic glorification which often used and abused Camoens's statements by applying them out of their literary context. Thus, Sena's poem, more than a demythification of Camoens's epic views, is a denunciation of the fascist use to which that poet's ideas were put. The implication of Tomás Ribeiro's "To Portugal" corroborates this interpretation. Ribeiro's sentimental views of his country, too, were glossed *ad infinitum* for similar reasons. However, Sena's poem's essential thematic import is contained in its statements covering the overall state of Portuguese contemporary life—social, moral, religious, and cultural—in contradistinction to the epic portrait that, in Camoens's time, could still be justified in part. What started as a reply to Camoens, grows into an all-inclusive portrait of a decadent nation—one which attains all the more power for being contrasted with Camoens's epic statements. Sena, despite himself, belongs to this country—but he refuses to call it his own.

The rest of this chapter will deal with some of the transformational techniques employed in *Metamorphoses,* specifically in those poems which are based on identified works of visual art. My remarks on *Metamorphoses* constitute a synthesis of a recent study of mine, "History and Poetry as *Metamorfoses.*"[14] Therefore, the comments on this book will be kept to the bare minimum necessary for the later discussion of *Art of Music.* Although the poems of *Metamorphoses* constitute crystallizations of the poet's *experience* of works of visual art, Sena contrasts, at least implicitly, the attributes of his art, poetry, with those of the inspiring arts. (This same *silent dialogue* of attributes informs *Art of Music,* as we shall see in due time.) For Sena's poetry shows that he is always perfectly conscious of the fact that each art has attributes or strengths that the others lack or do not possess to the same degree; each art has weaknesses that constitute the appanage of the others.

Lessing has conclusively demonstrated in his *Laocoön* (1766)—despite numerous attempts to refute some of his arguments—that the primary strengths of painting and sculpture reside in their ability to depict *visibilia* or the visual dimension of reality. However, this strength is also, paradoxically, their main weakness; for, as Lessing says, painting and sculpture can only focus on the "single moment," not "progressive action."[15] The latter, as Lessing also shows, is one of the major attributes of poetry (and, of course, of any other literary art). Another principal distinction between poetry and the visual arts is that, as Matthew Arnold points out, "poetry thinks and arts do not."[16] The plastic arts show us pictures that may, and in the overwhelming majority of cases do, embody thought. Nevertheless, the latter can only be inferred from what is depicted on the canvas or sculpted in stone: thought is seldom, if ever, explicitly stated. Painting and sculpture can, for example, suggest the emotion of love; but they can hardly elucidate what specific kind of love, what its attendant circumstances are, what brought these about, and whether love is colored by other emotions. However debatable the point may be regarding the extent to which plastic arts can and cannot think, no one would deny that the medium of poetry by far surpasses painting and sculpture in its ability to communicate the products of the human mind and heart, just as the plastic arts surpass poetry in presenting the products of visual reality.

In addition to its greater ability in depicting successive action and thought, one may also add that poetry has a *voice* and the plastic arts do not. This truth is synthesized in the famous and influential dictum attributed by Plutarch to Simonides of Ceos that "painting is silent poetry, and poetry a speaking picture." In the famous statue, Laocoön—for the statement applies both to painting as well as sculpture, and Lessing, as we know, bases his arguments on the Laocoön group—opens his mouth to scream but no sound is forthcoming. Only in the medium of poetry could one hear his scream. True that Virgil cannot visibly present us the image that the *Laocoön* master depicts in stone. But, Lessing says, "Enough that *clamores horrendus ad sidera tollit* has a powerful appeal to the ear" *(Laocoön,* p. 23). In the sculpture, Laocoön opens his mouth but no sound is heard. It is Virgil, i.e., poetry, which allows him to scream. It may be possible to "hear" the sculpted Laocoön with one's "inner" ear. But poetry, because it has a voice and can think, is capable of communicating simultaneously the inner reverberations as well as the sound itself.

In the majority of cases, what Sena does in the poems of *Metamorphoses* inspired by plastic arts (for the book contains poems not inspired by identifiable/identified works, and one poem based on a picture of a male dancer published in a issue of the *National Geographic*), is to avail himself of these attributes of poetry to instill or breathe life into art. The attributes that the plastic art objects *gain*—as they are to some degree *filtered* through the medium of poetry—are some of the attributes of qualities of life itself: stasis gives way to movement; suggestive or implicit thought or emotions become unravelled and particularized; silence gains a voice. We could summarize these metamorphic processes by saying that their underlying thrust is revitalization or humanization of art. By this I mean one of two things (and in some poems both are used, one in conjunction with the other): either the poet, through his humanistic apprehension of the work of art, instills or infuses life where little or none might have existed before; or else he reawakens or vivifies the original vision, i.e., the historical and human antecedents, that inspired the work of art and continue to be embodied in it.

I will limit myself here to a brief discussion of four poems of *Metamorphoses:* "Gazelle of Iberia," *"The Swing,* by Fragonard," "Van Gogh's *The Yellow Chair,"* and "Camoens Addresses His Contemporaries." These four poems illustrate the attributes of poetry mentioned vis-à-vis the visual arts, as well as the processes of humanization of art just described. These brief analyses are not meant to be exhaustive; nor are they, together with these remarks on some of the principal metamorphic techniques of *Metamorphoses,* meant to suggest anything approximating an interpretation of a work which, in many respects, is probably the densest and most complex of all of Sena's works of poetry.

"Gazelle of Iberia" is a good example of the three components mentioned earlier: the work of art as autonomous aesthetic entity, as product of its time, i.e., as a human document, and as producer of an experience for the poet (and, of course, for the reader of the poem). Sculpture presents an image that one can both see and touch. Language can, within its limited capabilities for rendering the visual, either show or describe. Language's showing power, as far as *visibilia* is concerned, is by far weaker than sculpture's. Language's ability to describe is a kind of compensation for that other deficiency. Sena begins "Gazelle of Iberia" (*II,* p. 63) by doing what language does best as far as the presentation of the visual is concerned—describing:

> *Suspensa nas três patas, porque se perdeu*
> *uma das quatro, eis que repousa brônzea*
> *no pedestral discreto do museu.*
> *Ergue as orelhas, como à escuta, e os pés*
> *são movimento que ainda hesita. . . .*

> (Suspended on three legs, for the fourth
> was lost, behold it resting in bronze
> on the discreet pedestral in the museum.
> It raises its ears, as if to listen, and its feet
> Are movement still hesitant. . . .)

These and a few other descriptive lines throughout the poem constitute, we might say, the concessions that the poet makes to the work of art *qua* object. The phrases "focinho fino" ("thin snout") and "liso torso" ("smooth torso") are, we might add, some of the few concessions that Sena makes to the *Gazelle* as aesthetic object.

But more important to Sena than the art work as autonomous object of disinterested aesthetic contemplation is the work's contextual dimensions, i.e., its human antecedents. What are these? The antecedents of the bronze gazelle are unknown. The poet can only surmise as to what they might have been. This he does, not arbitrarily or impressionistically, but with a good deal of historical plausibility. Sena's poems on the plastic arts (and music, as we shall see) always reveal his profound knowledge and understanding of the history and criticism of art. The works of art are *never* mere pretexts for the exercise of poetic fancy. The poet proceeds to reconstruct in the poem the probable history of the people who hunted and sculpted the gazelle and some aspects of their culture—of which the work of art is an emblem. The attempt to humanistically, as opposed to strictly aesthetically, experience the work of art induces the poet to undertake a temporal voyage—for which the time-machine power of poetry is most suited—in an effort to discern what is hidden behind the sculpted object. "Acaso foi / a qualquer deus oferta?" ("Perchance was it / to some god an offering?")—the poet wonders.

The poem is not only a partial verbal translation (in the etymological sense of changing from one condition to another), as the descriptive lines might suggest; nor is it primarily an attempt to peer into its historical origins and human antecedents. It is both of these things. But it is also, and in part because it *is* those two things, an *experience* for both the poet and the reader. Description allows one to commune with the thing described; but it may also, paradoxically, set the describer apart from what he describes. It creates a kind of fence or barrier between the two. For to describe is to impart knowledge of or about; but it does not necessarily mean to enter into. Sena begins by describing but then goes on to break the fence created by the you-there-I-here dynamics of description. He enters, as it were, the world where the gazelle was sculpted; he gives us the gazelle in its living vitality; in short, he performs the miracle of resuscitation by employing the life-giving force of poetry. The gazelle *lives* once again:

> *Ergue as orelhas, como à escuta, e os pés*
> *são movimento que ainda hesita, enquanto*
> *o vago olhar vazio se distrai*
> *entre os ruídos soltos da floresta.*

> (It raises its ears, as if to listen, and its feet
> Are movement still hesitant, while
> its vague empty look is distracted
> among the loose noises of the forest.)

To see the gazelle in this fashion is not to have the common experience of visiting a museum in search of vestiges of the past; to read in the art objects the life that was. Nor is it to contemplate beautiful objects dissociated from their roots in life. It is, rather, an attempt (a most successful one) to recapture the life that was and transmute it into a life that still *is*. It amounts to having an art experience that is simultaneously, and primarily, a vital one. The poet's experience is also, needless to say, the reader's. The latter (at least this reader) has the feeling that he is not merely reading the results of the poet's perception—but actually following or participating in the processes or steps involved in that experience. The abrupt switches between the past and present tenses in the poem contribute to this feeling. It must be pointed out, however, that this poem is also a paean to the ultimate power of art, any great art—its ability to survive the ravages of time. It is important that Sena should stress the survivability of art *after* he experiences it as an emblem of the human beings who created it. Art does not survive because it springs from life and then somehow rises above it; it survives precisely because of the life it continues to embody and is capable of awakening in us:

> *Há muito tempo que esse povo—qual?—*
> *violado foi por invasões, e em sangue,*
> *em fogo e em escravidão, ou só no amor*
> *dos homens que chegavam em navios*
> *de longos remos e altas velas pandas*
> *se dissolveu tranquilo, abandonando*
> *os montes pelos vales, a floresta*
> *pelas escarpas onde o mar arfava*
> *nas enseadas mansas e nas praias,*
> *e as fontes límpidas por rios que,*
> *entre a verdura, sinuosos iam.*
> *Há muito, mas esta gazela resta*
> . . .

> (It's been long since that people—who?—
> were ravished by invasions, and in blood,
> in fire and in slavery, or only in the love
> of men who arrived in ships
> with long oars and tall swollen sails
> dissolved tranquilly, abandoning
> the mountains for the valleys, the forest
> for the escarpments where the sea heaved
> in the calm inlets and on the beaches,
> and the sparkling fountains by rivers that,
> amidst the greenery, meandering flowed.
> It's been long, but this gazelle remains
> . . .)

Two aspects of *"The Swing,* by Fragonard" are especially deserving of critical mention in the context of this discussion of metamorphic processes in *Metamorphoses:* the paraphraseable content of the poem, particularly when viewed in the entire thematic context of the book; and the metamorphic processes utilized by Sena to translate the painting's suggested motion to the verbal medium. As previously noted, and as Sena himself admits in the postface to the book, *Metamorphoses* is a work largely about death. Yet, it is far from being a morbid work. Counterbalancing the presence of death are the zest for living, the affirmation and celebration of life. In Chapter I, I discussed "Death, Space, and Eternity" in this connection. It is very significant that in the book *"The Swing,* by Fragonard" is made to immediately follow the poem *"The Dead Woman,* by Rembrandt." It is, so this order suggests, the erotic urge, the will to live, procreate, or merely enjoy the blessings of sex, contradicting or negating the presence of death.

The erotic element in this poem is, in part, a verbal transposition of the thematic content of the painting: the woman in the swing, her dress blown by the wind; the ogler stretching out his arm as if to touch her or arrest forever the marvelous vision; the very vegetation (Sena's interpretation) in a state of seeming sexual arousal, as if Nature, as if light itself, participated in the erotic glow that bathes the entire composition. Given painting's inability to depict movement (it can, at best, suggest it), however, the vision is a still picture of life, a frozen vision, except for the imagination of the viewer. Employing the kinetic power of his art, the poet sets the vision in motion. Description in successive stages, besides being the best substitute for painting's presentation of *visibilia* (Lessing), is also the best verbal conveyor of movement:

> *Como balouça pelos ares no espaço*
> *entre arvoredo que tremula e saias*
> *que lânguidas esvoaçam indiscretas!*
>
> (II, p. 111)

> (How she swings through the air in the space
> between groves of quivering trees and skirts
> that languidly flit indiscreet!)

Numerous other verbs of motion throughout the poem—together with strategically enjambed lines—extend this process of vivification and movement. We might say that the poet resets in motion the stream of time arrested in the canvas. A painting shows the frozen *present* but not the future. The poet, through the forward-looking power of his medium, not only sees the present but has the key to open the doors of the future:

> *Como balouça, como adeja, como*
> *é galanteio o gesto com que, obsceno,*
> *o amante se deleita olhando apenas!*
> *Como ele a despe e como ela resiste*
> *no olhar que pousa enviezado e arguto*
> *sabendo quantas rendas a rasgar!*
> *Como do mundo nada importa mais!*

(How she swings, how she flutters, how
gallant is the gesture with which, obscenely,
the lover delights by only looking!
How he undresses her and how she resists
with her looking slanted and argute
knowing how much lace to tear!
How nothing else matters in the world!)

(The reverse technique, i.e., the almost total absence of verbs and the preponderance of nouns and adjectives to communicate stasis, one of the principal attributes of architecture, is employed in the poem "The Nave of Alcobaça.")

In "Van Gogh's *The Yellow Chair*" we have one of the best examples in *Metamorphoses* of Sena's attempt to poetically read human presence where it is only vaguely suggested. In this poem Sena employs a technique of transposition which he also uses frequently in *Art of Music*. I call this the interpretive mode of poetically experiencing works of art. Although Sena explains in the postface to *Metamorphoses* that these poems are not art criticism in verse form (and he is absolutely right), nevertheless in this poem his experience of the work includes a coherent and very plausible interpretation of the painting. "Van Gogh's *The Yellow Chair*" begins, as do so many of these poems on the visual arts, with a detailed description of the object of art. As this description proceeds, the poet begins to associate the elements depicted in the painting—what seems to be tobacco, a pipe, etc.—with the man Vincent, whose signature appears on a box in a corner of the room. By about the second third of the poem, scenes from other Van Gogh paintings begin to merge with elements from *The Yellow Chair;* biographical elements become intermingled with both. History—past, present, and future—biography, and this specific work of art all come together as the poet uses the thinking attribute of poetry to break down the temporal and spatial confines of the canvas. *The Yellow Chair* undergoes a metamorphic process in the poet's mind. It is no longer a chair:

Não é, não foi, nem mais será cadeira:
Apenas o retrato concentrado e claro
de ter lá estado e ter lá sido quem
a conheceu de olhá-la como de assentar-se
no quarto exíguo que é só cor sem luz
e um caixote ao canto, onde assinou Vincent.

(*II*, pp. 119-20)

(It isn't, it wasn't, nor will it ever be a chair:
Only the concentrated and clear portrait of
there having lived and there having been one who
knew it from looking at it as from sitting on it
in the exiguous room that is only lightless color
and a box in the corner, where he signed Vincent.)

123

Sena's interpretation of *The Yellow Chair* parallels that of the art critic and aesthetician Theodor Meyer Greene: "Van Gogh's *Yellow Chair* . . . must be described *not* as a still life but as a portrait study . . . What makes it interesting as a portrait is the intimate individuality which the chair has acquired."[17] This poem is yet another perfect example of the three components which characterize the poet's humanistic approach to art: art as aesthetic object capable of attracting our attention; art as reflection of human experience; and art as vital experience. In this, as well as in the other poems of *Metamorphoses,* the reader experiences both the original work of art through the eyes and sensibility of the poet, and experiences the second work of art, the poem, springing to life from another, like Venus from the shell.

I shall return to "Camoens Addresses His Contemporaries" in later chapters. Suffice it to say here that this poem can be construed as the maximum exemplification in *Metamorphoses* of the audible voice power of poetry vis-à-vis the silent voice to which the visual arts are condemned. The poem is inspired in part by the bust of Camoens by the Brazilian sculptor Bruno Giorgi. The greatest source of its inspiration, however, is the very life of Camoens as Sena saw it. In the note to the poem Sena writes: "From the reading of this poem, one must not conclude that the author espouses the current disregard for the contemporaries of Camoens, whether it be for those who were themselves illustrious and knew it, or for those who, lost, forgotten, or unpublished, have been disqualified by Camonian idolatry. It is especially against this idolatry that, when it comes right down to it, corresponds to the indifference with which the poet was treated upon his return to Portugal—if that was the case, and we still have to discover to what extent—that in the poem the words are placed in Camoens's mouth" (*II,* pp. 230-31).

The poem can be read at two levels: On the one hand, it is the voice of Camoens as conceived by Jorge de Sena directed against his (Camoens's) contemporaries and later generations. At this level of meaning the poem might be thought of as the words that the bust of Camoens—whose reproduction in black and white appears on the preceding page to the poem—cannot speak. Even without the title, but with the picture of the sculpture, the poem would achieve its great communicative power. Without the picture, the reader would have to rely on the title to know that it is Camoens talking. This point is rather significant. Sena claims in the postface that the reproduction of the works of art do not contribute to the understanding of the poems. I disagree and so does Wilson Martins.[18] It is true that the poems are capable of standing by themselves as poems. It is also true, however, that the dialectical interchange, as it were, between source and derived poem is greatly enhanced by the presence of the reproduction—to say nothing of the overall aesthetic appearance of *Metamorphoses,* particularly if the reproductions were in color (as Sena so much wished).

But there is another possible reading for "Camoens Addresses His Contemporaries," a type of reading that Sena is also going to suggest for poems of *Art of Music* that purportedly and ostensibly represent artists' comments to their contemporaries and future generations. And this is an autobiographical reading. In other words, the hurtful, sarcastic, and prophetic words of Camoens are also to be construed as the hurtful, sarcastic, and intentionally prophetic words of Jorge de Sena directed at his (Sena's) contemporaries and future generations. The poem thus achieves a double meaning if read against the dual background of Camoens's life and Sena's own biography and personality. In the latter case it is particularly so when the poem is viewed in intertextual relation to other poems (for example "In Crete, with the Minotaur," "Camoens in the Island of Mozambique," and "To Portugal"), where Sena also relishes bringing forth similarities between his own and Camoens's life.

As we have seen, Sena's experiential poems—whether they be based on lived/witnessed experiences or *Bildungserlebnis*—are never attempts to merely record, communicate or verbally re-create events or happenings as a true diarist might do. Indeed, "poetic diary" should say it all as far as Sena's "entries" are concerned. In his experiential poems the experiences are building materials which the poet shapes into art, as a sculptor shapes marble into a statue. This analogy between poet and sculptor is actually suggested in the poem "Demeter" of *Metamorphoses.* But, outside the context of that poem, it must not be taken too far. Although no one would deny that a choice of material is essential to the sculptor, marble or bronze are dead matter until the sculptor endows them with form and breathes a species of life into them. The same is not true with regard to Sena's experiential poems. In this case, raw material—lived experiences or those derived from art—are already meaningful in their own right. What the poet does is release potential far-reaching meanings that were not present before he breathed his own poetic life into them; or else were present but in a different form or to a different degree. When the sculptor endows a piece of marble with form he denies or obliterates its pre-artistic formless state. On the contrary, when Sena expands on reality and transforms it he is not denying the model experience: he is metamorphosing it into new heights which remit back to the original inspiration. When he transposes from a work of art, he does not forsake or betray the latter's identity: he distills life from it or breathes life into it. How Sena uses poetry to breathe life and new experiences into the experience of the most impalpable of the arts, music, is what shall concern us for the remainder of this study.

IV

Sena as Poet of Music

It has been said that the "thought-essence of music contains within itself the promise of pictures and the potency of poems."[1] Jorge de Sena believed as much, for none of the sister arts inspired him to write as many poems as did music. Indeed, Sena's career as a poet is inextricably related to music. He tells us in the first poem of *Art of Music,* "'La Cathédrale engloutie,' by Debussy," that this work of music was responsible for his decision to become a poet. Although Sena had written poems before, it was on that day in 1936, as he tells us elsewere, that Sena "seriously" decided to commit himself to a poetical career that was to last more than forty years.

Art of Music, the eighth of Sena's books of poetry, was originally published in 1968. Then it contained 34 poems written between January of 1960 and June of 1967. The second edition, included in *Poetry-II* (1978), contains ten new ones written between November of 1971 and April of 1974. The majority of the poems are based on single or multiple compositions of art music, ranging from works of absolute or pure music, to lieder, an oratorio, masses, program music, and opera. A few poems draw inspiration from the entire production of given composers and aspects of their biographies and times. One poem deals primarily with the biography and impressions derived from the entire works of a personality associated with popular music, Edith Piaf. The three poems, mentioned earlier, which Sena thought at some point of including in *Art of Music*—"Ray Charles," "Extemporaneous Indignation," and "In the Corridor of the 'Metro' in Paris"—bear close thematic and other affinities with the poem on Piaf. I shall return to these poems in Chapter IX, but they will not be considered integral parts of *Art of Music*. The first and last poems of the book—"'La Cathédrale engloutie'" and "Final 'Potpourri'"—were considered by Sena to be "non-metamorphic," while the term "metamorphoses" was applied by him to all the other poems. Indeed, "'La Cathédrale engloutie'" is largely an autobiographical poem even though it draws inspiration to a very great extent from Debussy's Prelude. The poem is also a kind of introduction to *Art of Music,* as we shall see. "Final 'Potpourri'" is a kind of thematic summary of the book plus general commentary on it. Within the framework of the technique announced in the title, it includes a wide variety of thematic motives developed throughout the book, including the autobiographical element.

The titles of most of these poems are those of the pieces of music. At times the titles of the model compositions are slightly altered, as in the following examples containing the gerund *ouvindo* ("listening"): "Listening to Quartet Op. 131, by Beethoven," "Listening to Poems by Heine as 'Lieder' by Schumann," "Octaves: Listening to Brahms's First Symphony." The overwhelming majority of the poems, however, have titles like "Creation, by Haydn," "Mahler: Resurrection Symphony," "Concerto for Piano, Op. 42, by Schoenberg," etc. These two basic types of titles suggest two things: first, the temporal relation that exists between the writing of the poem and the hearing of the model composition; second, the nature of Sena's poetic relationship to the music. We are told in the postface to the book that the poems of *Art of Music* are based on repeated hearings of the inspiring works. Furthermore, given the amount of information about the music that the majority of the poems contain, it is fair to assume that they are the product of lengthy meditations. Indeed, the range and depth of the critical comments, as well as the historical and biographical information contained in the poems, could not, in the majority of cases, be the result of more or less extemporaneous writing or be the product of a first impression of a work heard for the first time. Nevertheless, many of these poems—including some based on acknowledged repeated hearings—were conceived and executed to convey the impression that they were written as the music sounded. In addition to the titles containing the gerund *ouvindo,* several verses indicate this simultaneity of hearing and writing: "Nesta fluidez continua de um tecido vivo" ("In this continuous flow as of a living weave") ("The Death of Isolde"); "Esta frase emerge subita no trio saltitado" ("This phrase emerges *subito* in the leaping trio" ("Mozart: Andante of the Trio K. 496"). This writing of the poem as the music sounds, communicates a feeling of immediacy to the poem; a feeling that the poet is translating a musical experience he is having right now, as opposed to recalling a prior experience. Because the temporal progression of the music is the map that points and delimits the poet's path, the reader, by referring to the music (or playing it as he (re)reads the poem), can follow the meanderings of the poet's mind. In other words, the reader bears witness to the poet's *modus operandi:* he realizes which tonal patterns the poet is or may be translating into verbal language; which dramatic episodes he is evoking; what in the music or drama motivates a given response. This poetic technique of following closely the temporal development of the model work is particularly suited for short compositions, such as the episodes of Wagner's operas. When poetizing an entire opera or a lengthy instrumental work, the poet has necessarily to condense his impressions and it is no longer easy or even possible for the reader to establish a one-to-one relationship between what music and poet are doing at a given moment.

As for the poems that bear simply the title of the inspiring composition, they strongly suggest that Sena's intention was to emphasize that the poems are totally conditioned by the work of art at hand. In fact, we shall see that Sena often departs from the musical into an extramusical realm as far as the content of the poem is concerned. However, whatever he says in the poem is always relatable in some way, usually in a very direct way, to the thoughts and feelings associated with the music or its textual content (in the case of music allied to texts). Music has meant many things to many people; it has awakened in listeners the most varied of responses. "Music does various things to me," writes Bernard Berenson. And he adds: "First and foremost, it liberates trains of thought. Then it encourages musing and daydreaming. Best of all, it conjures up worlds of marvelous possibility, conditions of ecstasy, visions of magical radiance of a universe permeated by divinely intelligent goodness, and of a Beyond surpassing all present powers of imagination."[2] Sena's poems illustrate that music does indeed 'liberate trains of thought,' and is an agent capable of setting the poetic imagination on fire. However—and this is a point I shall often emphasize—all these poems are, first and foremost, intelligential verbalizations—not attempts to communicate, through daring and synesthetic imagery or interjectional outbursts, the "ineffability" of music, which is common practice among many poets who have derived inspiration from music. Neither is music for Sena a vehicle that he rides into a world beyond. On the contrary, it is—without ceasing to raise the poet's spirit to great heights indeed—a vehicle that always conveys him into the midst of humanity; a catalyst that tightens his bonds with concrete human reality.

The 44 poems of *Art of Music*—which, except for the first and last, follow a chronological order based on the life of the composers—will be divided into three groups in this study. This division takes into account the kinds of music that the poet is dealing with. Since the nature of the inspiring work—absolute, program music, opera—determines to a large degree the content of the poem and often the very type of formal techniques Sena employs, this grouping is preferable, for expository and analytical purposes, to a study of the poems following the order in which they appear in the book. A thematic survey of all the poems of *Art of Music,* in accordance with Sena's chronological order, will be carried out in the concluding chapter of this book. What Sena said regarding most of his books—that they do not constitute *"books* of poems, with their own unity"* or, for I believe this is what he meant, that they do not contain a well-defined storyline to be abstracted from a global perspective—is also applicable to *Art of Music,* with minor reservations. The only storyline that these poems, seen as a whole, convey, rests upon the fact that the first and last poems are to a large degree autobiographical; and that this element also influences or is revealed in the "metamorphic" poems as such; and, finally, that *Art of Music,* seen in its chronological sweep of centuries, constitutes a sort of poetic musical survey of Western music, starting with the Renaissance and ending with our own century. This aspect of *Art of Music* will be dealt with in due time.

The following are the three groups of poems as they will be discussed in Chapters VI, VII, and VIII, respectively. First, we have the group of poems which, for lack of a better term, I shall call Miscellaneous. In this group are included, in addition to the first and last poem in the book, those based on art songs, the entire production of a composer, the poem on Piaf, and works of music inspired by a literary or liturgical text—but excluding program music and opera. This first group of poems includes the most heterogeneous variety of inspirational sources. The second group is much more homogeneous: it is based on programmatic compositions and opera. The third and largest group is comprised of poems on absolute music, ranging from works by Johann Sebastian Bach to a piano piece by Schoenberg. Thus, instead of a chronological order by composer or some thematic sectioning that could be used, I have opted to organize the poems on a scale going from the most general, to the more concrete insofar as the paraphraseable content of the model compositions (music allied to texts), to the wholly abstract (absolute music).

Any description of *Art of Music* would be incomplete if one did not mention the notes to the poems and did not comment at some length on the postface to the book. The notes range from brief statements identifying the live or recorded interpretation of the model composition, to Sena's opinions regarding a composer and his works, to critiques of a particular interpretation, to quite elaborate half-page statements situating a given composition or composer in the proper historical context. Sena writes in the postface, explaining the reason for the inclusion of these notes, that "because the premonitory state of spirit in relation to a work was sometimes brought about by an attentive listening to particular recordings of it, a list is provided, in the endnotes, of the musical interpretations to which the poems may especially refer." And the poet adds the words previously quoted: "Perhaps . . . there are specialists interested in discovering to what extent a particular concert performer or a certain conductor, at that moment, influenced my view of the work by his interpretation of it" (*II*, p. 218). In some cases, Sena identifies lines from other poets which he incorporates in his own poems, as well as less obvious literary and other allusions. The note to "Listening to 'Socrates' by Satie," for example, reads as follows:

> Inspired by the opera, particularly its text, which is based on Plato's "dialogues," the poem centers especially on Socrates (and on what Satie's music says about him, as synthesized in the last two lines). Let it be said in passing that the idea—in a manner more or less baroque—of having the famous characters represented by feminine voices (Alcibiades, Phaedrus, Phaedo, Socrates himself), as Satie has, seems to me incongruent, despite the beauty of the work and all the erudite (or less erudite) justifications he might have had for such an idea. (*II*, pp. 242-43)

In the 10-page postface, written in 1967, Sena delineates the historical, philosophical, and aesthetic background of the book. He tells us when and in what order the poems were written; he informs us regarding his background in music. He studied it as a child, owned a vast collection of records, and always listened to music, both for pleasure and poetic inspiration, whenever he could. In private conversation Mrs. Mécia de Sena has told me that he loved to sit at the piano and play his beloved *La Cathédrale engloutie*, which had so much influence on his life. It is also important to note, although this information is not contained in the postface, that Sena practiced musical criticism for a brief period of time. The *Gazeta Musical e de Todas as Artes* for May 1958 and February 1959 contains brief critiques by

Jorge de Sena of operas and other musical works performed in Lisbon theaters. Among the works critiqued are operas by Rossini, Verdi, and Puccini, although none of those that Sena would later poetize. It can be seen in the postface, and inferred from the poems and the notes that accompany them, that Jorge de Sena considered himself a non-professional but extremely well-informed music lover. Most important for the readers of *Art of Music,* however, is the fact that Jorge de Sena gives us some indications in this postface as to what the poems of *Art of Music* try to be and, equally important, what they are not.

To begin to find out what the poems of *Art of Music* are and are not we need to survey at some length the most prevalent current approaches to musico-literary criticism. Sena's poems respond well to all of these approaches, but especially well to one of them. First of all, it is important to differentiate two basic types of relationship between music and literature: 1) literature in music, and 2) music in literature. The former has to do with the alliance of music and literature (lied, oratorio, cantata) and the less obvious presence or influence of literature upon music (program music). This aspect shall concern us, but not for the moment. The second, music in literature, specifically in poetry, is the relationship we are after. It involves several types of imitation of music by the literary arts and the use of musical compositions (theoretically, real or imaginary) as subject matter for literature. Currently musico-literary critics distinguish among three quite distinct, although usually interrelated, ways in which literature can imitate or otherwise relate to music: word music; the literary use of large musical forms and structural techniques; and verbal music.

Word music: This can be defined as the imitation by the literary arts of the acoustic quality of music, as distinct from the adaptation of musical forms and structural techniques, and the use of musical experience as theme. Although I shall use the phrase "word music," the designation "phonetic music," applied to the same general concept, might be less confusing, given the similarity in name with "verbal music"—which is a totally different concept. As the prominent musico-literary critic Steven Paul Scher indicates regarding word music, "The most important constituents in both musical and literary treatment of sound are rhythm, stress, pitch, and timbre."[3] Musical rhythm—"the particular arrangement of note lengths in a piece of music,"[4] in the simplest of definitions—is infinitely more flexible and malleable than language rhythm. Yet, as Calvin S. Brown points out, it is easier for the literary arts to imitate musical rhythm than it is for them to approximate timbre or pitch.[5] The great variety of meters in *Art of Music* is an aspect of the book that deserves much more extended analysis than the orientation of this study allows for. For example, quite independently of any attempt to imitate the rhythms of the model compositions, poems such as "Brandenburg Concerto No. 1, by J.S. Bach" and *"Water Music, by Handel"* constitute extremely challenging opportunities for the student of poetic meter and rhythm.

Regarding stress, Steven Paul Scher states that the musical devices of *sforzato, subito piano,* or *subito forte* "can be approximated in literature to suggest comparable contextual emphasis or suddenness" *(Verbal Music,* p. 4). Stress is an element of some importance in *Art of Music.* It is suggested by proper manipulation of syntax, semantics, and meter. For example, "Wanda Landowska Playing Sonatas by Domenico Scarlatti" and "'Fêtes,' by Debussy" end in a series of progressively shorter enjambed verses which, coupled with adjectives, nouns and verbs denoting or connoting "end," convey the notion of *decrescendo* and the slow fading away of the music:

> *conclamar a que*
> *me submerja em vida*
> *percutindo*
> *a solidão*
> *triunfal.*
>
> ("Wanda Landowska")

> (shouting for it
> to submerge me in life
> striking
> the solitude
> of triumph.)

> *Mas o tempo falha*
> *para acabarem gestos,*
> *concluir a posse*
> *iniciada*
> *outrora.*
>
> ("'Fêtes'")

> (But there is no time
> to finish the gestures,
> or conclude the lovemaking
> initiated
> yesteryear.)

As for pitch, i.e., the high-low quality of sound, Scher considers it of minor importance in literature. He equates it with intonation in language and says that only when words are verbalized, for example in declamation, does language pitch play a role. However true this may be for the most part, the fact remains that most of us, even when doing silent reading, especially of poetry and dialogue, "sound" the words for ourselves mentally and can "hear" them in our inner ear. Bayard Quincy Morgan, in his "Musical Pitch in Goethe's Poetry," actually identifies three types of pitch-level in poetry: high, middle, and low pitch.[6] His ideas can be applied generally to a study of this much-ignored phenomenon of poetry. There is at least one instance, in "Bach: Golderg Variations," where Sena capitalizes a word, *COMO (HOW)*, for emphasis. This may be construed in part as an analogue of pitch, a high which even the silent reader can hear in his mind's ear. And even in silent reading one would probably not fail to mentally hear the various pitch-levels of the following verses (emphasis added for my own reading):

> *Neste silêncio, **que ficou, flutua?***
> **O quê?**
> **NÓS?**
> **Como tão pouco restaria?**

("Brandenburg Concerto")

> (In this silence, ***what remains floating?***
> **What?**
> **OURSELVES?**
> **How could so little remain?**)

Musico-literary critics differ widely regarding the element of timbre or tone color in literature. In *The Science of Verse,* Sidney Lanier writes: "It is thus that the voice produces those sounds of differing tone-color which we call vowels and consonants; for the voice is a reed-instrument which can alter the shape of its tube (the buccal cavity) at pleasure, and which in so doing alters its tone-color at pleasure."[7] One of the attractions that Góngora's *Polifemo* holds for C. C. Smith is precisely the immense variety of vowels and consonants, but particularly the former; or, as Smith puts it, "this phonetic music of echoes, of repetition, of similarities of rhythm and of extensions. . . . We shall be content to say that phonetic music satisfies us as such and that it contributes enormously to the artistic nature of the stanza and the poem."[8] Scher, however—obviously applying a more restricted definition of linguistic tone color than Lanier—opines that literary imitations of musical tone color "have met with limited success" *(Verbal Music,* p. 4). Scher excepts works like Verlaine's "Chanson d'automne" where, in the words of Alan G. Detweiler, "both sound and association of the words are welded into one musical effect."[9] Scher is careful to add that "the nominative use of timbre in the form of alliteration, assonance, and rhyme is purely literary" *(Verbal Music,* p. 5).

However, one of literary art's surest ways of approximating or imitating the acoustic quality of music resides precisely in the use of alliteration, assonance, rhyme, as well as other devices of sound repetition. Before turning to a brief analysis of word music in Sena's book, I should like to distinguish among three types of word music: independent, semi-dependent, and dependent. The first type is the liberal use and manipulation, conscious or unconscious, of linguistic sound patterns for general poetic effect, but without any avowed intent on the writer's part to imitate either a fictitious or real work of music. Most, if not all, poetry, as well as much literary prose, make use of this type of word music. Semi-dependent word music, on the other hand, might be said to represent a deliberate attempt on the writer's part to approximate pure music in general, but without any real piece of music as model, i.e., without involving a conscious effort to re-present a given musical model in the verbal medium. Much Symbolist and so-called pure poetry falls within this category. Semi-dependent word music is, therefore, an extreme example of independent word music, in which the writer may or may not have a specific composition in mind but is nonetheless intent on conveying the feeling of music. Verlaine's "Chanson d'automne" is a case in point. Few poets exemplify this extremely liberal repetition of sounds—in some cases one might even say for sound's sake—as does the "ortonymous" Fernando Pessoa. The titles of some poems of *Cancioneiro* indicate the poet's preoccupation with music: "Minuet invisível" ("Invisible Minuet"), "Trila na noite uma flauta" ("A flute trills in the night"), "Sorriso audível" ("Audible Smile"). A few almost random examples from *Cancioneiro* will suffice to illustrate several types of sound repetition:

> *E há nevoentos desencantos*
> *Dos encantos dos pensamentos*
> *Nos santos lentos dos recantos*
> *Dos bentos cantos dos conventos...*
> *Prantos de intentos, lentos, tantos*
> *Que encantam os atentos ventos.*

> ("Ficções do Interlúdio"—"Saudade dada"
> —"Interlude Fictions"—"Longing")

> (And there are misty disenchantments
> of the enchantment of the thoughts
> In the sluggish saints of the recesses
> of the saintly corners of the convents...
> Penitents in tears, lingering, legion
> Who enchant the attentive winds.)

Elas são vaporosas,
Pálidas sombras as·rosas
Nadas da hora lunar...

("Interlude Fictions"—"Invisible Minuet")[10]

(They are vaporous,
Sallow shadows the roses
Born of the lunar hour...)

Another Portuguese poet who readily comes to mind in connection with this type of word music is Camilo Pessanha. Particularly illustrative of consciously sought musical effects are his "Violoncelo" and "Ao longe os barcos de flores" ("Flower boats from afar").[11] And Jorge de Sena, who has so often been censured for his "unmusical" verses, writes poems like "Round Dance Song" *(Perpetual Vision),* from which I quote the first two strophes:

Minh'alma, não te conheço,
minh'alma, não sei de ti,
oh dança, minh'alma, dança,
por amor de quanto vi.

Não te conheço, minha'alma,
e nunca te conheci,
oh dança, minh'alma, dança,
dança por mim e por ti.

(*Perpetual Vision,* p. 202)

(My soul, I know thee not,
my soul, where couldst thou be,
oh dance, my soul, dance,
for the love of all I see.

I know thee not, my soul,
never have I known thee,
oh dance, my soul, dance,
dance for me and for thee.)

Finally, I would define dependent word music as the literary products resulting from the conscious effort to imitate, regardless of true success, the acoustic quality of a real work of music. Many of the poems analyzed by Calvin S. Brown in *Music and Literature*[12] and *Tones into Words* exemplify, among other elements of the interrelations of the two sister arts, this type of word music.

As far as word music is concerned, we can be absolutely sure only of the presence in Sena's *Art of Music* of independent word music. When it comes to the other two types we are on shaky ground indeed.

To begin with, Sena tells us in the postface that the poems of *Art of Music* are neither "music" nor "imitations of music." He adds: "Even when poetry only suggests or is but rhythm and sound, it still is not, nor can it be, music. The forms of expression may overlap and even fuse in some cases, but they cannot stand for one another" (*II,* p. 219). By "music" Sena means in this context something akin to semi-dependent word music. Let us dwell on this point a while. Music (and I am now referring primarily to pure instrumental music) is highly organized sound or, as Charles T. Smith defines it, "the art of reasoning with sounds."[13] Poetry (let us now exclude other literary arts) is highly organized language. Sound—pure unallied sound—is the most impalpable of all mediums. To be sure, music has meanings, but, as Leonard Bernstein points out, "music has intrinsic meanings of its own, which are not to be confused with specific feelings or moods, and certainly not with pictorial impressions or stories."[14] Language, on the other hand, has extrinsic meanings; it is the most precise system of communication known to man. It is true that the language of poetry and the language of music share some acoustic properties in common. To those mentioned earlier—rhythm, stress, pitch, tone color—we may add harmony and melody.[15] But when all the similarities and dissimilarities between what is meant by terms such as "harmony" and "melody" in the two arts are taken into account, and are specifically defined as to how they apply to music and to poetry, the net result is two entirely different systems of expression: on the one hand, the essentially self-referring audial substance of music; on the other, the referential concreteness of language. In his poetic handling of it the poet can, of course, make language more or less discursive or suggestive; he can treat it with an ear finely tuned to linguistic music, or not.

It is important to keep in mind Sena's words as to the impossibility of verbalizing music. Musico-literary critics are generally most emphatic on this point. Steven Paul Scher writes:

> No matter how similar to music purely verbal constructs may be, in the nature of their material they remain fundamentally different from works whose medium is primarily musical, such as absolute, vocal, or program music. Literary texts cannot transcend the confines of literary texture and become musical texture. Literature lacks the unique acoustic quality of music; only through ingenious linguistic means or special literary techniques can it imply, evoke, imitate, or otherwise indirectly approximate actual music and thus create what amounts at best to a verbal semblance of music.[16]

René Wellek's words are also most appropriate at this point:

> 'Musicality' in verse closely analysed, turns out to be something entirely different from 'melody' in music: it means an arrangement of phonetic patterns, an avoidance of accumulations of consonants, or simply the presence of certain rhythmical effects. With such romantic poets as Tieck and, later, Verlaine, the attempts to achieve musical effects are largely attempts to suppress the meaning structure of verse, to avoid logical constructions, to stress connotations rather than denotations. Yet blurred outlines, vagueness of meaning, and illogicality are not, in a literal sense, 'musical' at all.[17]

Calvin S. Brown notes the basic difference between the two sister arts: "Broadly speaking, music is an art of sound in and for itself, of sound *qua* sound. Its tones have intricate relationships among themselves, but no relationship to anything outside the musical composition. . . . Literature, on the other hand, is an art employing *sounds to which external significance has been arbitrarily attached" (Music and Literature,* p. 11). For poetry to approximate the non-referential, self-contained, self-sufficing nature of music, it would have to—in addition to utilizing its own repertoire of music-like properties such as alliteration, assonance, and rhyme—sacrifice or at least greatly compromise the one quality that defines it as language: extrinsic meaning, the kind associated with literature but not instrumental music, the absolute kind at any rate. But even if it were possible to make language entirely self-contained as far as semantic meanings are concerned—and Symbolist and pure poetry strongly suggest, to say the least, that the total nullification of referentiality is not entirely possible—we still would not end up with "music," as René Wellek points out. This non-referentiality, this creation of poetry for sound's sake, is also the primary reason why, even if it were possible for poetry to be entirely music-like, Jorge de Sena would most likely reject it, except in isolated cases, as experiments. Nothing could be further removed from Sena's philosophy of life and of poetry's place in it than a sound-serving, self-referring, self-sufficient kind of poetry. Examples of poems where Sena might be said to have created "music" with words are the "Four Sonnets to Aphrodite Anadyomene" *(Metamorphoses),* as well as other poems scattered throughout the corpus which use a similar "language." These sonnets are not written in Portuguese, but in a new "language" created by Jorge de Sena on the basis of Sanskrit, Greek, Latin, English and Portuguese words or word roots adapted to Portuguese phonology, morphology and syntax. But even in these extremely erotic four sonnets the referral power of words has by no means been severed or curtailed. We could only claim that meanings have been camouflaged and suggestiveness heightened in the process.

The idea of poetry as "imitation of music" is also disclaimed by Sena, as far as the poems of *Art of Music* are concerned. By "imitation" I take that he means duplication of the acoustic quality of the inspiring composition, i.e., something akin to what I termed dependent word music. This type of imitation, if totally successful, would consist in using poetry as a means of re-presenting the acoustic identity of the model work of music, in a way similar to that of a photograph reproducing or re-presenting an object or scene. The music piece, with its characteristic tone color, rhythms, melodies, would be readily recognizable in the poem. For the same reasons that poetry cannot be entirely music-like, so it cannot literally re-present music. We need not labor very hard at all to demonstrate that this is a clearly impossible feat to accomplish. Words are not substitutes for tones, the same way that tones cannot express concrete or particularized ideas and feelings—notwithstanding the temptation to establish one-to-one relationships between, say, musical notes and phonemes, motifs and morphemes, musical phrases and words, sections and clauses, etc. No poet could reproduce or re-present in the verbal medium the timbre or melody of the simplest of instrumental compositions, let alone the tone color of, say, Debussy's *Afternoon of a Faun* or a Wagnerian melody—to say nothing of all the components that comprise a musical composition. But even if poetry could do this, for a poet to limit himself to re-presenting another art's message would be both useless and servile. What one art is best at presenting, is best presented by that art, as Lessing taught us long ago. And sad would be the day for any art form when it bowed its head and placed itself at the slavish service of another. Jorge de Sena thinks too highly of poetry in general and of his own poetry in particular to make it serve any cause whatsoever—except the cause of life and the cause of poetry itself in the terms explained earlier. His sources are in reality—vital and artistic experiences—but the poems derived therefrom always re-create and transform; they do not serve any purpose best performed by the inspiring experiences; they always add to the original model: they are not mere recastings of it.

Returning to the sound-based word music that one *does find* in *Art of Music,* we encounter that the following claims can be made and substantiated: Sena's manipulation of linguistic sounds in *Art of Music* does not differ enough *in kind* from his use of identical and similar devices in other books of poetry, e.g., *Metamorphoses,* to warrant our considering them special techniques motivated by his conscious desire to imitate music in general and much less to duplicate or re-present the acoustic quality of the specific music models. However, the frequency with which these devices are used within a given poem and from poem to poem strongly suggests that the music might have acted as a powerful stimulus for the production of word music in the book. Sena's poetry has often been censured, as well as defended, for its prosaic nature. Gastão Cruz refers to "this kind of prosaism" in Sena's poetry (although he is careful to point out that this fact alone does not invalidate the poems), and singles out as particularly noteworthy examples the poems "In Crete, with the Minotaur," "To the Memory of Kazantzakis, and to All Those Who Made The Film *Zorba the Greek,* " and above all "Relatório" ("Report"). A poem of *Art of Music,* "Chopin: An Inventory," is pointed out as one of Sena's "greatest failures" as far as prosaism is concerned.[18] The critic João Camilo, on the other hand, while acknowledging Sena's prosaism, explains it as an essential feature of much modern poetry, and adds: "That prosaism, real or apparent, may well constitute a manifestation of a desire to create original, and freer, poetic forms, which become more difficult to understand because the regularity, the rhythm, and the very breathing appertaining to such poetry, are contrary to our reading habits and our conception of what poetry might be."[19] Another critic who mentions and understands the prosaism of many poems of *Art of Music* is Óscar Lopes. In the only noteworthy critical appraisal that *Art of Music* has evoked thus far (even though Lopes's study is but a review published in a newspaper of Oporto), he states that "certain poems may look like prose because of their discursive organization, their imagery . . . and their versification, but they have as a more obvious objective that of shaking, step by step, all complacent dormancy. There are rhythms that put you to sleep. This one wakes you up."[20] All these critics are correct in recognizing that, in many cases, the frontier in Sena's poetry between prose and poetry is not easy to find—which is of course not tantamount to saying that it does not exist. They are also correct who find that Sena's prosaism is intentional; that it is a feature of much contemporary poetry (and Sena's poetry is a poetry very much of its own time; he would have it be nothing less); and that it is functional, as João Camilo and Óscar Lopes rightly recognize. I would add, however, corroborating and extending Camilo's remark, that Sena's prosaism is sometimes more apparent than real, if by prosaism we understand the absence of the musicality traditionally associated with lyric poetry. For a musical quality is very often an important component of Sena's apparently more prosaic poems, including the very same "Chopin: An Inventory" censured by Gastão Cruz. I shall return to this poem a little later. However, in order for the musicality of Sena's poetry to be detected, for it is not always readily apparent, the poems must be read and savored aloud—as poems were ever meant to be. Sena himself was aware of the negative reaction to the "unmusicality" of his poetry when he wrote in the preface to the first edition of *Poetry-I:*

> As for the readers of poetry—among whom I don't include, of course, those fellow poets who think of me as their rival—the latter will read the poems, I am sure. And they shall read them as I always hoped they'd be read: not with their eyes, but with their ears, so that they be penetrated by the very music the existence of which they have denied; with their minds, so that the poems light up with the understanding they await; and with their hearts, so that these poems vibrate with the love and devotion to life which, imparted to them by me, shall vibrate free and living in the plenitude of their existence free from their creator. *(Poetry-I,* pp. 29-30)

Later on we shall see how word music functions, together with other components and techniques, some clearly imitative of specific aspects of the music, others not, to produce Sena's complex poetic expression of his equally complex experience of music. However, much of the beauty of *Art of Music* is derived from the manipulation of linguistic sound alone. For this brief analysis of word music in the book, I shall forego any comments on the conceptual content of the passages to be quoted and merely call attention to the poet's manipulation of sound patterns as such. Minoru Yoshida, in an article entitled "Word-Music in English Poetry,"[21] identifies and examines six types of "repetition of sound-tint" which characterize the writings of English and American poets. These six types of word music-producing linguistic sounds are all extremely frequent in *Art of Music.* Yoshida's terminology shall guide this survey as far as the six major categories are concerned. An exhaustive study of word music in *Art of Music* would reveal many others. Such a study, however, lies outside the scope of this book, for reasons that will become apparent.

Sound repetition: This category includes alliteration, i.e., the repetition of identical consonants in close proximity, and assonance or the repetition of identical or very similar vowels attached to different consonants. Although this type of sound repetition is common to all of Sena's poetry (indeed to all poetry), again I stress the fact that it is particularly frequent in *Art of Music.* A few random examples (which may include other types of sound repetition, as well) follow:

> *A brisa flui*
> *serena e fina.*
> > *("Water Music,* by Handel")

> (the breeze flows
> serene and fine.)
> > (trans. Jonathan Griffin)

Ouço-te, ó música, subir aguda
("'Requiem' by Mozart")

(I hear you, music, sharply rising)

Programas, poetas, sonhos de ópio,
pastores pipilando . . .
("Symphonie Fantastique, by Berlioz")

(Programs, poets, opium dreams,
shepherds piping . . .)

Even in the "prosaic" "Chopin: An Inventory" word music devices abound. Among these, we note a liberal use of alliteration and assonance:

> *. . . muitos sucessos mundanos; uma paixão infeliz;*
> *uma ligação célebre com mulher ilustre; outras ligações sortidas;*
> *uma pátria sem fronteiras seguras nem independência concreta.*

> (. . . many mundane successes; an unhappy passion;
> a celebrated liaison with a famous woman; other assorted liaisons;
> a country without sure borders or definite independence.)

Sound-group repetition: In this case, the repetition is not limited to single consonants or vowels but encompasses groups of consonants or vowels, for example /kr/, /ão/, /pa/, and /as/ in the following example also from *"Water Music,* by Handel":

> *Crepitam trompas e destilam flautas*
> *na crespa ondulação que as proas tangem*

> (Horns crackle and flutes distil
> on the crisp ripples the prows play)

Syllable repetition: There are two basic types: non-rhyming syllable repetition at the beginning or middle of a word; and syllable repetition at the end of a word, which can lead to beginning, internal, and end-line rhyme. An example of non-rhyming syllable repetition can be seen and heard in the following two lines from "Siegfried's Funeral March, of 'Twilight of the Gods'":

> *Na tarde que de névoas se escurece*
> *escuto a marcha que ao herói transporta;*
> *fúnebre e doce, tão violenta e fluida;*

> (In the afternoon darkening with mist
> I hear the march, funereal and sweet,
> fluid and violent, carrying the hero);

142

and these two from "'Fêtes,' by Debussy":

É como se as ruas de Florença se abrissem no espaço,
cheias de gente e colgaduras e festões de flores.

(It's as if Florentine streets opened out spatially,
full of people and tapestries and wreaths of flowers.)

Only three poems of *Art of Music* contain end-line consonant rhymes throughout: "D Minor Concerto, K. 466, by Mozart," "'Requiem' by Mozart," and "'Má Vlast,' by Smetana." The first of these three poems is one of only five sonnets in *Art of Music*. It contains the rhyme scheme *abba abba cdc ede*. The other four sonnets comprise the poem "'Requiem' by Mozart." These four sonnets all have different rhyme schemes; and the last sonnet contains fifteen as opposed to the traditional fourteen lines. The rhyme schemes of these sonnets—together with every other type of element of word music studied here—constitute a veritable tour de force of sound repetition and variation. The rhyme schemes are as follows: *abab abab cde cde; abcd abcd efg hfg; abba abba cde cde;* and *abba acca ded dede.* No scheme of an entire sonnet is ever repeated, and only the tercets scheme of two sonnets (1st and 3rd) are repeated, although the rhyming sounds are distinct. "'Má Vlast,' by Smetana" comprises sixteen metrically irregular lines with the following rhyme scheme, the conceptual function of which will be discussed at the appropriate time: *aabbccdaaeeggdff.* No other poem of *Art of Music* exemplifies end-line consonant rhyme throughout. However, some verses exhibiting end-line consonant rhyme can be found in "La Bohème,' by Puccini" and "'Listening to Quartet, Op. 131, by Beethoven." Examples of beginning and internal consonant rhyme can be seen in "Andante con Variazioni, in F Minor, by Haydn." As for assonant rhymes, they are numerous in *Art of Music*. This type of rhyme characterizes, among other poems or portions of poems, portions of "The Death of Isolde," "'Romeo and Juliet,' by Tchaikovsky," and "Erik Satie for Piano." A few examples of end-line assonant rhyme are also used in the four octaves that comprise "Octaves: Listening to Brahms's First Symphony." The overwhelming majority of poems (including poems containing portions with rhymes), however, is cast in ever-varying forms of free verse alternating, in some cases, with sections of regularized metrification. The repeated sounds these poems employ fall within types other than rhyme. However, all the poems employing non-standard meters exemplify several of the word-music devices outlined here. Also, every single poem that is cast in standard or regularized meters containing rhyme employs other devices of word music as well.

Word repetition: This is one of the most frequently used devices in *Art of Music*. Examples abound in nearly every poem:

vida minha, mas humana vida
    ("Again the Sonatas by Domenico Scarlatti")

(might be for me life, but human life)

Como se modulando neste espaço-tempo
que se desenha espaço em mero som contínuo
    ("Brandenburg Concerto")

(As if modulating in this space-time
that draws space in mere continuous sound)

Esta frase emerge súbita no trio saltitado
o violino pergunta de repente numa angústia
ansiosamente pergunta . . .
    ("Mozart: Andante of the Trio K. 496")

(This phrase emerges *subito* in the leaping trio
the violin asks suddenly in anguish
asks anxiously . . .)

Nem o Zaratustra de Zaratustra . . .
    ("'Thus Spake Zarathustra,' by Richard Strauss")

(Neither Zarathustra's Zarathustra . . .)

Word-group repetition: Although there are many types of word-group repetition, most involve some aspect of parallelism, anaphoric constructions and, in one case, the repetition of the same word but with a different meaning or gender *(diáfora)*. The following examples of word-group repetition could be greatly multiplied:

O velho honestamente escreve a História.
O jovem (falsamente) vai fazê-la.
Os boiardos (oligarcas) desfazê-la.
    ("Boris Godunov")

(The old man writes History honestly.
The young man (falsely) is going to make it,
The boyars (oligarchs) unmake it.)

Ouço-te, ó música, subir aguda
à convergente solidão gelada
Ouço-te, ó música, chegar desnuda
ao vácuo centro, . . .
    ("'Requiem' by Mozart")

(I hear you, music, sharply rising
to convergent solitude of ice.
I hear you, music, arriving naked
at the hollow center, . . .)

Tudo isso nada é perante
abstracção como esta
de morta música
num morto cravo
tocado pela morta

("Wanda Landowska")

(All this is nothing before
abstraction such as this
of dead music
in a dead clavier
played by a dead woman)

Mixed repetition: Several of the above types of sound repetition often occur in close proximity. The various combinations of different sounds—for example in *"Water Music,* by Handel" and "'Requiem' by Mozart" (in my view, the most "musical" of all the poems in the book)—produce the most effective and aesthetically pleasing type of word music. In the following two lines from *"Water Music,* by Handel" we note examples of alliteration, assonance, syllable repetition, and word repetition:

É como sol nas águas, no arvoredo verde
que as águas reverdece de verdura e sombra.

(It's like sun on the water, on the green grove
that greens again the waters with verdure and shadow.)
(trans. Jonathan Griffin)

In the following passage from "Andante con Variazioni, in F Minor, by Haydn" Sena blends alliteration, assonance, sound-group repetition, and beginning and internal consonant rhyme:

Firmemente suave e docemente atenta vai seguindo em variações
serenas
até que ao fim exclama resumidamente a mesma doçura
tenuemente harpejada que ao princípio dissera
como esta vida é uma simples coisa tão subtilmente amarga
que só variando em torno de perdê-la a toleramos toda.

(Firmly suave and sweetly attentive it flows on in serene variations
until at last exclaiming succinctly the same tenuously arpeggiated
sweetness

> that had at the beginning said
> how this life is a simple thing so subtly bitter
> that only by doing variations around its loss can we tolerate all of it.)

As a final example I quote five lines from "'La Bohème,' by Puccini," wherein are exemplified alliteration, assonance, sound-group repetition, syllable repetition in the form of end-line consonant rhyme, and word repetition, i.e., every one of the elements of word music just outlined:

> *jamais se foi tão fundo ao fundo da vulgaridade,*
> *jamais se fez tão terna e doce a irresponsabilidade,*
> *jamais se comoveu tanta gente dura com a realidade,*
> *transformando-as em convenções tão líricas.*
> *E jamais tão bem se anestesiaram as pretensões do gosto.*
>
> (never have we been so deep into the depths of vulgarity,
> never has irresponsibility been so tender and sweet,
> never have so many hardened people been moved by reality,
> transformed into lyric conventions.
> And never were pretensions of taste so well numbed.)

Literary use of large musical forms and structural techniques: While the verbalization of music and the re-presentation of the acoustic quality of a given composition prove illusory for the poet, the same is not true, at least not to the same extent, when it comes to the adaptation by poetry of the large musical forms. Consultation of the studies listed in the musico-literary bibliography will readily reveal that poets, as well as fiction writers, have an easier time finding close parallels to the musical forms of the rondo, fugue, and sonata or the structural device theme and variations than they do trying to establish convincing equivalents for tone color, melody, etc., i.e., dependent word music. The reason for this is obvious. Whereas the poet could not reproduce or re-present a single theme of a late Beethoven Quartet, say, it is relatively easy for him to suggest the latter's ABA or sonata form. Although one who does not know the music could never "hear" in Sena's poem the theme and variations which comprise Mozart's Piano Sonata in A (K. 331), yet it is easy to see that the structural device is at the root of Sena's poetic meditation on that composition. In "Sonata No. 11, for Piano, K. 331, by Mozart," Sena introduces a "theme" derived from his perception of the music—some of its identifying characteristics, e.g., the obvious *alla turca,* and its *Geistesgeschichte*—and then varies it in two other paragraphs. A series of appropriately recurring words and phrases are at the core of Sena's technique.

Poetry and music are both temporal arts. They present their

materials in temporal sequence. Both rely on the receiver's memory of what went on before, and, to some degree, on his anticipation of what will follow. The visual arts, on the other hand, present all their material at once. It is one thing, however, to organize a poem employing the ABA musical form—i.e., introduction of themes, development or churning up of those themes, and recapitulation—and quite another thing to translate or create a poetic analogue for a phenomenon like modulation, which the sonata form also presupposes. It may be possible to imitate the fugal devices of inversion and retrograde (Sena actually does, as we shall see momentarily). However, it is quite another thing to duplicate counterpoint or the simultaneous sounding of two, three or more melodic lines. And the fugue is, by definition, polyphonic. Commenting on the structural devices of tonality, tempo, balance and contrast, and repetition and variation, Calvin S. Brown states that "Tonality is essential for setting off contrasting sections and giving to each its individuality, but there is nothing quite analogous in poetry. Writers attempting sonata form may ignore key relationships entirely, or they may use shifts of meter, subject matter, or general mood, but none of these makeshifts is an unmistakable equivalent of tonality. Even the obvious difference between major and minor can be only hinted at by the poet."[22] At best, therefore, the poet can reproduce the architectural design or outline of sonata form, rondo, or theme and variations. As for the poetic imitation of strictly musical phenomena such as modulation and counterpoint, the poet can only provide approximate imitations or suggestions. As we shall see later, Sena, in two separate poems, succeeds in conveying a verbal notion or analogue of modulation and counterpoint. However, the very fact that other writers (including Sena himself in the case of counterpoint) have used entirely different devices to suggest the same phenomena, indicates that even these rough approximations are quite subjective and reveal a high degree of arbitrariness.

The adaptation of much-simplified musical forms is an element of some importance in *Art of Music*. It occurs, logically enough, in poems inspired by pure music. In the latter, content and form are one and the same thing to a much larger degree than in any other art medium. Poems based on musical works allied to texts—lieder, operas, and program music—do not reveal such preoccupation with musically inspired form even though they draw upon various other musical phenomena of the inspiring compositions. These poetic adaptations of musical forms will be studied in conjunction with the analyses of the poems in which they occur. For the time being, it is sufficient to point out the most common musical forms and structural devices adapted by Sena. In addition, we will look at some poems not from *Art of Music,* which employ musical forms or strongly suggest them. These poems supply a basis for possible explanation regarding why, in *Art of Music,* Sena chose to convey only *rough approximations* or *suggestions* of these forms and techniques rather than aim at nearly exact duplications of them.

Therefore, bearing in mind that the use of musical forms in *Art of Music* is only an approximation and not an attempt to literally translate the design of the musical model, we can easily detect in the book the forms and structural techniques of theme and variations, fugue, sonata, and suite. Logically, they occur in poems inspired by music employing the same forms or structures. Thus, an analogue of the technique of theme and variations informs "Bach: Goldberg Variations," "Andante con Variazioni, in F Minor, by Haydn," and the above mentioned "Sonata No. 11, for Piano, K. 331, by Mozart." A very simplified analogue of fugue is conveyed in, and will be discussed in conjunction with the analysis of, "Preludes and Fugues by J.S. Bach, for Organ." One of the most successful and poetically effective adaptations of musical form in *Art of Music* occurs in "Listening to Quartet, Op. 131, by Beethoven." As we shall see later, in this poem Sena not only creates a convincing and poetically functional analogue for the architecture of sonata form, but actually accomplishes an equally convincing and poetically viable suggestion of key change or modulation. *"Water Music,* by Handel" can be construed as a poetic suite. We shall see that in this poem Sena creates a closer equivalent of counterpoint than he had achieved in several apparent attempts at duplicating the same musical phenomenon in prose fiction.

"The usual method of the poetic theme and variations is identical with that of the musical form," writes Calvin S. Brown. And he adds: "a theme is given out simply and directly, and then followed by a series of reworkings in different moods, phrases and sometimes meters" ("Poetic Use of Musical Forms," pp. 93-94). Both composers and poets have used either their own themes or borrowed themes from other composers and poets. Sena's examples of the technique in works other than *Art of Music* can be found in *Sequences,* in a section of the book entitled "Inventions au goût du jour." All examples of "themes" are taken from literature. Sena entitles one of these poems "A Line by Bocage"—actually the last line of a famous sonnet in which the eighteenth-century poet compares himself to Camoens. Without adding any new words to Bocage's verse, but repeating or subtracting some and always changing their order and consequently their meaning and mood, Sena creates fifteen variations on the "theme" "Saiba morrer o que viver não soube" ("Let who knew not how to live know how to die"). The poem reveals an extremely interesting symmetry, strongly reminiscent of concrete poetry. All the lines end with the word "soube" ("knew"). Eight consecutive lines, including Bocage's "theme," begin with "saiba" ("know"); the other eight begin with "Não" ("Not"). The second word of the first four lines is always "o que" ("who"). In the next four lines "não morrer" ("not die") is always the second group and "o que" ("who") the third. "Saiba morrer" ("know how to die") is always the second group of words in lines 9-12 with "o que" ("who") always comprising the third group in the same lines. "Saiba não morrer" ("Know how not to die") is always the second group of words in the last four lines of the poem and "o que" ("who") always the segment that follows. Numerous other similar symmetrical patterns inform the entire poem, thus revealing Sena's extremely elaborate attention to technique. The important point, however, is that all the lines are replete with meaning. Logical meaning (at least in poetic terms) is never sacrificed for the sake of symmetrical effect. Following are the first four lines of the poem, including Bocage's:

> Saiba morrer o que viver não soube.
> Saiba morrer o que não viver soube.
> Saiba morrer o que não viver não soube.
> Saiba morrer o que viver soube.
>
> (Sequences, p. 16)

> (Let who knew not how to live know how to die.
> Let who knew how not to live know how to die.
> Let who not how to live knew not know how to die.
> Let who knew how to live know how to die.)

As the title of this section of *Sequences*—"Inventions au goût du jour"—suggests, these poems must not be taken for more than what they try to be. They certainly represent an extremely interesting and often humorous facet of this multifaceted poet who always availed himself of every opportunity for literary experimentation. True that experimentation for Sena was never an excuse for his disregarding the commitment he always lived. Some of Sena's most experimental works are also his best realizations at any level, as the novella *The Wondrous Physician* incontrovertibly demonstrates. Nevertheless, beyond their undeniable worth as experiments and as viable poems in their own right, Sena himself would not have dared equate them, qualitatively, with the noble poems of *Art of Music*. The adjective "noble" was used by Sena with respect to the poems of *Metamorphoses* and certainly does apply to the poems of *Art of Music* as well. In this poem, based on Bocage's verse, Sena achieves a closer rendition of the musical technique theme and variations than he does in the poems of *Art of Music* employing the same musical structural technique. This goes to show, I think, how careful the poet must be when imitating a musical phenomenon. If he is going to approximate any given musical constituent, he had better do so without allowing the seams of the device to show through in the end product and, more important still, without interfering with the poem's status as serious and viable art in and of itself. I believe that a general principle of the interrelations of the arts could be stated thus: If the literary artist must adapt techniques peculiar to other art forms, he must know how far he can go and when to stop. He does better by stopping short of what he could do than by going too far. He cannot give himself over to the luxury of literal translations as far as those techniques are concerned. He must content himself with free translation to allow his own art enough space for maneuvering. The integrity of his art demands no more and no less.

Regarding musical form in general and fugal form in particular, Jorge de Sena wrote in the postface to *Art of Music:* "Indeed, more than the other arts, music, being the most technical of all, contains neither limits nor exclusions for me—and my poems were perfectly aware both of this and that they could not be a catalog of something interminable." But Sena is careful to add: "There are things, however, which transcend, I suppose, any possibility of transposition: a case in point is the misnamed *The Art of Fugue,* which I am listening to now in Scherchen's orchestration" (*II,* p. 218). Perhaps this difficulty in transposing the fugue accounts for the fact that only one poem out of the 44 that comprise *Art of Music* is based on fugal works: "Preludes and Fugues by J.S. Bach, for Organ." Although the structure (and content) of this poem contains a suggestion of the form fugue (to be discussed in a later chapter), it is in the section "Inventions au goût du jour" of *Sequences* that we must look for a very close poetic rendition of the fugue. This poem is especially important for a discussion of poetic use of musical forms because it shows the limitations of poetry when it comes to the borrowing of musical phenomena. The poem is entitled "Fugue on a Strophe by Gastão Cruz" and reads:

> Que farei no outono quando ardem
> as aves e as folhas e se chove
> é sobre o corpo descoberto que arde
> a água do outono.

Ardem quando no outono que farei
se chove e as folhas e as aves
arde que descoberto o corpo é sobre
do outono a água.

A água do outono
é sobre o corpo descoberto que arde
as aves e as folhas e se chove
que farei no outono quando ardem.

Do outono a água
arde que descoberto o corpo é sobre
se chove e as folhas e as aves
ardem quando no outono que farei.

(Sequences, p. 26)

(What shall I do in autumn when the birds
burn and the leaves and if it rains
over the uncovered body that burns
the autumn water.

They burn when in autumn what shall I do
if it rains and the leaves and the birds
it burns that over the body uncovered
of autumn the water.

The autumn water
over the uncovered body that burns
burn and the leaves and if it rains
what shall I do in autumn when the birds.

In autumn the water
burns that the body uncovered is over
if it rains and the leaves and the birds
burn in autumn what shall I do.)

(The inversion of the words in Sena's "fugue" is impossible to translate, achieving the same exact effects that he attains in Portuguese. I give an approximate semantic rendition.)

In his *Music: An Appreciation,* Roger Kamien defines fugue in part as "a polyphonic composition based on one main theme, called a *subject*. Throughout a fugue, different melodic lines or 'voices', imitate the subject . . . A fugue's texture usually includes three, four or five voices. Though the fugue's subject remains fairly constant throughout, it takes on new meanings when shifted to different keys or combined with different melodic and rhythmic ideas" (pp. 131-32). Kamien goes on to mention the four ways in which a fugue's subject can be varied: inversion, retrograde, augmentation, and diminution. Only the first two types of variation need concern us. In Sena's poem,

Cruz's strophe is the main subject and each of Sena's three strophes constitute a different "voice," presenting three different variations of the main subject. The first two "voices" present two distinct types of inversion: the first inverts the order of the words of each line of the subject, but not the order of the lines themselves; in the second "voice," however, the inversion is no longer in the order of the words—but in the order of lines: the strophe begins with the last line of the "subject" and ends with the first. In the last strophe or third "voice" we have a perfect analogue of retrograde variation, which Kamien defines as "beginning with the last note of the subject and proceeding backward to the first" (op. cit., p. 133). Sena substitutes notes with linguistic segments—"do outono" ("of autumn"), "a água" ("the water")—and follows exactly the same retrograde motion.

Although we have to grant that Sena's poem is ingenious, we must conclude that his imitation of fugue is only partially successful. The most essential characteristic of the fugue—its polyphonic texture—is not, and could not be, duplicated in the poem—except if the latter were recited with four people reading each strophe in simultaneity. Whereas in the true musical fugue the four strands of melody would overlap as they sounded, in the poem we can only read the four stanzas sequentially, not simultaneously. It has been humorously stated that trying to pick out the subject in a fugue is like searching for a specific face in a highly agitated crowd of similar faces. In Sena's *fugue,* however, the "person" moves about a lot—forward, backward and sideways—but is always alone. It must be conceded, however, that despite the limitations of the poetic medium as a vehicle for re-presenting a technique that is music's alone, the poem still manages to convey a strong suggestion of the real thing. The crucial questions to be asked are: How successful, independently of its success as an experiment in translating techniques belonging to another art, is "Fugue on a Strophe by Gastão Cruz" as a poem? And, perhaps, more important still, Does the poem attract too much attention to its own experimental endeavors? The answer to the second question is, I believe, yes. The first question is probably unfair. The poem had modest ambitions and must not be judged for what it did not try to accomplish. Although Sena does achieve interesting poetic effects in the variation of the subject—again, the poem never entirely sacrifices intelligential meaning at the altar of technique—nevertheless, I do not believe it is as successful a poem as the overwhelming majority of the poems of *Art of Music* where musical techniques are used more subtly. To me, anyway, these two poems of "Inventions au goût du jour" contain an important lesson for *Art of Music.* They show that a slavish imitation of musical forms carries with it obvious dangers: it attracts too much attention to itself thus robbing the poem of its own identity and integrity as poetry in its own right. Sena was undoubtedly aware of this. That is probably why the adaptation of musical forms and structural techniques in *Art of Music,* when it occurs, is much more subtle than in these two poems. When it is present, it does not advertise itself as borrowed technique, but as an integral and inevitable component of the poem. It is almost inconspicuously blended with several other elements, structural and conceptual, which together comprise the poetic expression or translation, not of the music as it objectively exists independently of a subjective perception of it, but of Sena's rich and always complex experience of music.

Verbal music: For artistic repositories of Sena's intellectual and emotional, i.e., subjective, *experience of music* is what the poems of *Art of Music* fundamentally are. As the poet states in the postface, "These poems represent the *repeated experiencing* of a work or of a composer, which ended up by crystallizing verbally—and, while many times a first listening might inspire a few lines, it is no less true that in other cases crystallization reflects *impressions* of a musical piece heard repeatedly" (*II,* p. 217; my italics). A page later Sena refers to the poems as "objective correlatives of the emotions /that the musical compositions/ awakened within me." Sena used similar statements to explain the poems of *Metamorphoses.* Indeed, the similarity in technique of transposition (bearing in mind the different arts involved) between these two books is truly remarkable. It was the humanistic nature of this intellectual and emotional experience that I briefly touched upon when discussing poems of *Metamorphoses.* It is this same humanistic approach to musical experience that I seek to identify and analyze in relation to *Art of Music.*

Thus, although word music and the use of large musical forms and structural techniques constitute important components in Sena's overall poetic expression, the most important type of affinity between music and the poems of *Art of Music* falls within the category of what musico-literary critics have called verbal music. Steven Paul Scher defines verbal music as "any literary presentation (whether in poetry or prose) of existing or fictitious musical compositions: any poetic texture which has a piece of music as its 'theme.' In addition to approximating in words an actual or fictitious score, such poems or passages often suggest characterization of a musical performance or of subjective response to the music. Although verbal music may, on occasion, contain onomatopoeic effect, it distinctly differs from word music, which is exclusively an attempt at literary imitation of sound" *(Verbal Music,* p. 8). In a more recent study Scher adds the following comments to this definition: "The above definition indicates that verbal music is a *literary* phenomenon. Its texture consists of artistically organized words which relate to music only inasmuch as they strive to suggest the experience or effects of music, while necessarily remaining within the boundaries of the medium of literature. Realizing the ultimate impossibility of a transformation in basic artistic material, poets and writers who nevertheless attempt verbalizations of music must be content if they succeed in achieving a relatively true verbal semblance of the musical medium."[23] In the still more recent study, "Literature and Music" (p. 235), Scher offers these comments on the legitimacy, and especially on the viability, as far as the imitative approach to music on the part of literature, of word music, literary use of musical forms, and verbal music. "In many ways," he writes, "verbal music is the most genuinely literary among musico-literary phenomena, perhaps because successful attempts to render poetically the intellectual and emotional import and intimated symbolic content of music tend to be less specific and restricting in mimetic aim and thus less obtrusive than direct imitations of particular sound effects or elements of musical form." Although Scher's definition encompasses both poetry and prose fiction, it is applied by him to prose. Indeed, he states that "Verbal music in prose, however, possesses greater aesthetic potential" ("Literature and Music," p. 235). I maintain, though, that Scher's definition and explanation of verbal music does apply to *Art of Music* even though the particularities that verbal music assumes in Sena's book will have to be made clear in the rest of this chapter, in the next chapter, and in the discussions of the poems themselves.

The full title of Sena's book when it first appeared in 1968, as well as in the second edition of 1978, is *Art of Music: Thirty-Two Musical Metamorphoses and a Prelude, Followed by a "Potpourri," and with a Postface by the Author.* (Of course, when we include the 10 extra poems published in the second edition, there are 42 "metamorphoses.") As the subtitle indicates, Sena understood the poems of *Art of Music,* except for two, as involving some kind of transformation from music to poetry, the same way that *Metamorphoses* had dealt with the translation or transposition of certain aspects, formal and conceptual, of the visual arts into the poetic medium. It is important, however, to know specifically what is being transformed or metamorphosed and how.

Music, Sena notes in the postface (and in this case he is referring primarily to absolute music), "does not express anything except itself." He adds:

Music is, as no other art to such a high degree, its own technique. And this condition of being a refined technique, one that is useful for nothing except the creation of itself, raises music above everything and above us, despite the quantity of extremely circumstantial music that exists throughout its history. Meditating on this peculiar quality of music, which takes place on a superior and highly introspective level—and not on the level of note-taking, however learnedly—will tend necessarily toward poetic transmutation. (*II,* pp. 219-220)

This statement implies a distinction between two basic ways of experiencing music. One can experience music *qua* music, i.e., as a strictly musical phenomenon. And one can experience it poetically—which leads to some kind of transformation of the very phenomenon being experienced. Sena states in the same postface (p. 219) that there are two corresponding ways of communicating these two types of experience: technically (which is what music critics do) and poetically (which is, of course, what Sena does). Because the metamorphosis, i.e., the poem, is rooted (in the majority of the poems of *Art of Music*) in a specific composition or compositions, it possesses or reflects particularities (formal and conceptual) inherent to the model works. However, since it is a transposition and not a copy of the inspiring work, it is not the latter's verbal analogue. This is why Sena is careful to point out, as mentioned earlier, that the poems are neither "music" nor "imitations of (the) music." On this I insist, despite the fact that they possess some formal and conceptual residue of the model on which they are rooted—roughly to the same extent that the vital experience that inspired "Cubicle" is part of this poem even though it undergoes drastic poetic transformation. *Art of Music,* is, therefore, poetry communicating or synthesizing the poet's complex subjective perception or experience of the music. This experience incorporates meditations, reflections, opinions and, in some cases, approximate verbal renditions of elements derived from the direct or objective perception of the music as such. Sena also incorporates in the poems many other elements that, although related or relatable to the music in some way, are, properly speaking, extraneous to the musical compositions. Among these extra-musical elements are the poet's views regarding musical creation, the meaning of music in general and of this specific work in particular, the relationship between a given work of music and its composer and his times, the relationship between the concepts that this particular work of music embodies and Jorge de Sena himself and his times.

Thus, the poet communicates not only, and not primarily, the "objective" content of the musical composition as such, i.e., as it might be perceived and communicated by the professional critic (even though, as we shall see, Sena strikes very convincing and well-informed critical poses), but his poetic experience of the work. We must, therefore, dwell briefly on the different types of music listening in order to be able to determine 1) how much Sena's poems reflect or crystallize a common approach to music listening, and 2) what is it in what he experiences in music that makes his perception poetic and, more specifically for our purpose in this book, poetic and humanistic. In his *What to Listen For in Music,* Aaron Copland breaks up the listening process into three planes, which he calls the sensuous, the expressive, and the sheer musical.[24]

The sensuous plane is listening to music for the joy of immersing oneself in its unanalyzed, non-intellectualized sound. It means to forget or put aside, at least momentarily, the idea that music is "the art of reasoning with sounds" and to listen to it for sheer sensuous enjoyment, as one might derive intense pleasure from an aroma without scrutinizing the nature of the source of its provenance. This plane of listening characterizes, to a greater or lesser extent, all types of listening. In Sena's poems, however, it is more implicit than explicit. In other words, it is fair to assume that the poet is enjoying the music on this level, but relatively few indications to this effect are actually found in the poems. And even these few indications may be construed as indicative of the sensuous plane of listening only if isolated from the entire context of the poem. For example, when the poet writes, in "Preludes and Fugues by J.S. Bach, for Organ,"

> *Esta conversa harmónica que inventa*
> *as próprias frases com que Deus se cala,*
> *como me alegra! . . .,*

> (This harmonious conversation which invents
> the very phrases God did not speak,
> how it delights me! . . .),

the reader might be led to conclude that the exclamatory phrase "how it delights me!" is a reflection of the sensuous plane of listening. Upon closer inspection, however, the reader realizes that the poet's subjective reaction is not based on the music's sensuous but intellectual nature, i.e., "This harmonious conversation which invents / the very phrases God did not speak." The poet is thus enjoying not unanalyzed but highly intellectualized sound. His joy stems in part from the realization that the music is not a divine, but human creation; and that this creation constitutes a species of intelligential, not subliminal, discourse. Later on in the poem (which will be discussed later), Sena indeed states: "Alegra-me. Mas não para alegrar-me / foi concebida em racionais delírios / de pautas e compassos . . . ." ("It delights me! But it was not conceived / in rational ecstasies of staffs and lines / to delight me. . . .").

Thus, what superficially appears to be listening on a sensuous plane, is really listening on a level that partakes of Copland's expressive plane. The latter deals with the expressive or meaning side of music. What is the origin of music—divine or human? What does music communicate through its obviously purposive sound patterns? Can the listener's mind capture this meaning and can language express it? We shall see that Sena's poetic way of listening to music is very often interpretive, i.e., it consists in taking Copland's expressive plane of listening to its limits. We shall also see that when Sena's poems reflect this level of listening, they usually allude to well-known theories of musical origin and meaning.

Also important to consider in relation to *Art of Music* is the third or sheer musical plane. This one is limited to the province of music itself, without recourse to any extra-musical notions whatsoever. "Besides the pleasurable sound of music and the expressive feeling that it gives off, music does exist in terms of the notes themselves and of their manipulation. Most listeners are not sufficiently conscious of this third plane." Copland adds, however: "Professional musicians, on the other hand, are, if anything, too conscious of the mere notes themselves. They often fall into the error of becoming so engrossed with their arpeggios and staccatos that they forget the deeper aspects of the music they are performing" *(What to Listen For in Music,* p. 21). This plane of listening—unlike the first, and perhaps much more than the second—presupposes a great deal of knowledge about the art of music, from the nature and function of its elements (rhythm, melody, harmony, and tone color), to its creative process and historical development. Sena comes relatively close to exemplifying this plane of listening in passages of the poems that are essentially "objectively" descriptive of what the music is doing:

> *As notas vêm sós por harmonias*
> *como de escalas que se cruzam*
> *em sequências descontínuas de figuras*
> *singelamente acorde surpreendido*
> *de se encontrar num instante pensativo*
> . . .

("Erik Satie for Piano")

> (The notes go solitary through harmonies
> the way scales cross
> through discontinuous sequences of figures
> until a lonely chord is surprised
> finding itself in a pensive mood
> . . .)

However, the poet soon veers toward the expressive or meaning side of music, as the last two lines of this passage suggest. In quite a few passages of poems of *Art of Music,* particularly those inspired by instrumental music where there are no concrete textual or dramatic elements as in program music, Sena comes very close to dwelling solely on the acoustic substance of the inspiring work. But in no poem at all could he be said to limit himself exclusively to an account of what the music is doing while ignoring the composition's expressive dimension or extra-musical implications.

To be sure, Copland's planes of listening to music, particularly the second and to a lesser degree the third, are exemplified in *Art of Music.* Yet, in order to account for all the information and the kind of information that one finds in the poems, a fourth plane of experiencing works of music has to be postulated. I say *experiencing* instead of *listening* because this plane includes, but also goes beyond, listening as such. I call it the humanistic plane. This plane of experiencing and responding artistically to music, i.e., of deriving information contained or associated with the music and at the same time investing or projecting personal views onto it, incorporates many elements pertaining to Copland's planes. However, it also includes much material that is extraneous to the music as such. It is a mode of experiencing and responding to music that might not be expected, and perhaps should not be, of the average listener, no matter how well informed he or she may be. But it is a legitimate mode in Sena's case, considering that his intentions vis-à-vis music are not critical or historical, but essentially creative. All in all, his mode of experiencing and responding to music is one that might not be acceptable to purists, but probably entirely justifiable to critics and aestheticians who regard music from a humanistic standpoint—not as a self-contained entity but as a product of human experience as well as its repository.

V

Music on a Humanistic Note

It is fair to assume that no one approaches music with a blank mind, i.e., with one's faculties only attuned to the music and incognizant of everything else. Every person brings to the experience of music not only whatever understanding of the art he or she possesses, but also his or her views on life and of the place of music in it. What one experiences or perceives in music, regardless of one's philosophy of life, may of course be restricted to the music sphere, i.e., its more or less self-contained acoustic province. However, one may also experience the music—and express the products of that experience—as part of the wider circle of human experience as a whole. This way of experiencing music necessarily encompasses both audial and non-audial components. Among the latter may be one's views regarding the very origin of music, as well as its verbalizable meaning.

Although a thorough exposition of theories of musical creation is not possible or necessary here, an explanation of Sena's humanistic view of music requires a brief survey of some of these theories. As noted earlier, many poems of *Art of Music* contain important allusions to theories of the origin and meaning of the tonal art. The present discussion is limited to theories of musical creation. Theories of meaning (to the extent that the two types are separable) will be dealt with later in this chapter. This survey of theories of origin is, for the most part, a summary of the information contained in the excellent study by Julius Portnoy.[1]

From ancient to modern times, in the East and West, thinkers, ranging from theologians to philosophers, scientists and poets, have occupied themselves with the origin of music and have proposed diverse theories or explanations to account for it. These theories can be divided into two broad categories: divine-metaphysical and humanistico-empirical. In Western culture, the endowment of music with supernatural origin can be traced to the Greeks. Both Greeks and Romans associated the gift of music with Apollo and Hermes. Homer (*Odyssey,* Bk. VIII, 63), Plato *(Timaeus,* 47; *Laws.* Bk. III), and Plutarch *(Concerning Music,* 4)—all attributed the creation of music to the gods. In the Judeo-Christian tradition, divine attribution can be traced to the Bible (Chron., 2:7, for example), and is to be found quite frequently in the writings of Church Fathers and theologians from St. Chrysostom to St. Basil, and from Luther and Calvin to Charles Kingsley. The Rev. Kingsley, for example, writes that "Music has been called the speech of angels; I will go further, and call it the speech of God himself. . . . Therefore music is sacred, a Godlike thing: and was given to man by Christ /sic!/ to lift our hearts to God, and make us feel something of the beauty and glory of God, and of all which God has made."[2] Charles T. Smith quotes an even more recent theory of the divinity of musical creation—that of Cardinal Newman, who held that "musical notes, with all their power to fire the blood and melt the heart, cannot be empty sounds and nothing more; no, they have escaped from some higher sphere. They are outpourings of eternal harmony, the voice of angels, and the Magnificat of Saints" (apud Smith, p. 12). Poems *de laudabis musicae* are almost as old as poetry itself and almost as common as poems celebrating Nature. Among the poets who have sung the divine origin and essence of music is Robert Herrick (1591-1674):

> Musick, thou Queen of Heaven, Care-charming-spel,
>   That strik'st a stilnesse into hell:
> Thou that tam'st Tygers, and fierce storms (that rise)
>   With thy soule-melting Lullabies:
> Fall down, down, down, from those thy chiming
>   spheres,
> To charme our soules, as thou enchant'st our eares.[3]

And in his poem "Music," Shelley writes in part:

> I pant for the music which is divine.
>   My heart in its thirst is a dying flower;
> Pour forth the sound like enchanted wine,
>   Loosen the notes in a silver shower;
> Like a herbless plain, for the gentle rain,
> I gasp, I faint, till they wake again.
>
>   (Cited in *In Praise of Music,* p. 106)

More secular metaphysical explanations of musical origin are equally traceable to ancient Greece. However, as Julius Portnoy states, "We could no more separate the musical beliefs of the philosopher from those of the theologians in Greek antiquity than we can separate the musical beliefs of the philosophers, from those of the Christian theologians in the Middle Ages" *(Music in the Life of Man,* p. 6). One of the best-known theories of antiquity is that of Pythagoras and his followers who held that music reproduced the harmony of the spheres. Music, they thought, possessed ethical significance because it reflected universal order. Plato, as is well known, also followed the Pythagorean theory in believing that music possesses ethical implications. Echoes of these beliefs can be heard throughout the centuries.

The Pythagorean and Christian theories are found merged into one in Leibnitz (1646-1716), who claimed that music comes into being by imitating this-worldly order—an order that originates with God (Portnoy, p. 10). For Immanuel Kant, who concentrates on the genius of the composer, i.e., on a humanistic explanation, music is still endowed with a kind of metaphysical aura. Kant claims that the musician "does not himself know how he has come by his Ideas" (apud Portnoy, p. 11).

The humanistico-empirical theories of musical origin or creation have an equally long and distinguished career, ranging from ancient to modern philosophers, scientists, aestheticians and poets. In some cases, however, philosophical theories and poems in praise of music still hover on the borderline of natural, metaphysical, and, in some instances, partly religious explanations. According to Portnoy, "Philosophers, like Aristotle and Lucretius, held a theory that music grew out of man's desire to imitate sounds in nature, first with the voice itself and then with crudely-made instruments" (p. 5). With the coming of Renaissance humanism, says Portnoy, the idea of divine inspiration began to be employed, not in a literal but in a figurative sense. In "The Rise and Progress of the Arts" *(Essays),* David Hume denies outright that the composer's fire is kindled from heaven. "If anything, argued Hume, the *empirical* evidence is that 'it only runs along the earth'" (Portnoy, p. 11). Although Hegel still claims that the composer's art comes close to the "Ideal," he insists that music is an expression of the musician's reason and feelings. For Hegel, writes Julius Portnoy (p. 12), "The creation of music begins and ends with *dialectical* inevitability. The composer, in conflict with a world composed of contradictory forces, resolves opposing issues in imaginative musical forms to transform things as they are into something more ideal."

Unlike Hegel, both Schopenhauer and Nietzsche believed the creation of music appertains to the irrational in man. Like Kant, Schopenhauer concentrates on the musician himself who, according to the pessimistic philosopher, reveals "the inner nature of the world, and expresses the deepest wisdom in language which his reason does not understand; as a person under the influence of mesmerism telling things of which he has no conception when he awakes" *(The World as Will and Idea;* apud Portnoy, p. 12). In Nietzsche, says Julius Portnoy, "we have the most romantic version yet of artistic creation by the archenemy of romanticism himself" (p. 13). For the author of *Also sprach Zarathustra,* as for Schopenhauer, music transcends reason; it is an act of escape, an escape to a dream world in an attempt to reconcile the Apollonian and Dionysian—but an escape for which the composer would be totally unable to provide any rational explanation. Also, for both Bergson and Croce, music transcends reason to hover in the realm of mystery (Bergson) and intuition, which Croce equates with "expression" (Portnoy, p. 14).

It is with George Santayana and Jacques Maritain, among the theoreticians that Portnoy mentions in this book,[4] that the veil of mystery and irrationality is removed from explanations of musical creation. To Santayana, writes Portnoy (p. 14), "Music as a product of reason gives order and direction to our emotions and echoes our most primitive thoughts. 'Whatever writhes in matter, art strives to give form to.'" According to the Christian Jacques Maritain, music is also a rational phenomenon always rooted in an idea. As Portnoy points out (p. 14), for Maritain "The intellect acts as the moral sensor in guiding the musician's craft to beget the sort of music which will be pleasing to God."

Poets, too, have not remained silent when it comes to celebrating or dwelling on the strictly human origins and meaning of music. In Shakespeare, although he paid his poetic tribute to the music of the spheres by comments he placed in the mouths of his characters, *(Pericles,* V, 1), dramatic and lyric works abound in statements praising and exalting music, not as a divine but as human creation; not as a species of supersensuous ineffability, but as the expression of specific human feelings and passion. In *Twelfth Night* (I, 1), Orsino refers to music as "the food of love" and the "spirit of love," not as a product of divine love. One of the epigraphs to *Art of Music* is precisely the first line of Shakespeare's *Twelfth Night.* In sonnet VIII ("Music to hear, why hear'st thou music sadly"), Shakespeare uses similes of human love to describe the music:

Mark how one string, sweet husband to another,
Strikes each in each by mutual ordering;
Resembling sire and child and happy mother
Who, all in one, one pleasing note do sing.[5]

And Edna St. Vincent Millay (1892-1950), in her sonnet "On Hearing a Symphony of Beethoven," also concentrates on the human dimension of music, as the first quartet indicates:

Sweet sounds, oh, beautiful music, do not cease!
Reject me not into the world again.
With you alone is excellence and peace,
Mankind made plausible, his purpose plain.

(Cited in *In Praise of Music*, p. 119)

Among the explanations provided by modern scientists for the origin of music, Julius Portnoy mentions two main types of theories: psychological and sociological. The psychological theories are associated with Freud and Jung; the sociological receive impetus from Darwin, who himself proposed a (biological) theory of musical creation in his *The Descent of Man*. Although he did not originate the idea that musical creation is rooted in the unconscious life of the artist, Freud is the one who lent the theory scientific status by basing it on the practice of psychoanalysis. According to Portnoy (p. 20), Freud believed that the composer creates in response to one of the following: "a composer may create out of economic necessity, or he may attempt to call suggestive ideas from the unconscious, or a creative mood may come over him and force him to express himself." Though the music be based on a conscious idea or feeling, its true roots are deeply buried in the unconscious. When creating, the composer is in a mental state comparable to that of the psychic. However, whereas the latter produces fantasies or delusions, the musician's fantasies are converted into meaningful artistic forms.

Jung, like Freud, believed that music has its origin in man's unconscious. The two men part company on a very important point, however. Whereas Freud defends the individuality or uniqueness of each creator, Jung believes that each artist is, as far as the products of his unconscious are concerned, a repository of the collective psychic history of the race. In *Modern Man in Search of a Soul*, Jung explains his theory of artistic creation thus: "Art is a kind of innate drive that seizes a human being and makes him its instrument. The artist is not a person endowed with free will who seeks his own ends, but one who allows art to realize its purposes through him. As a human being he may have moods and a will and personal aims, but as an artist he is a 'man' in a higher sense—he is 'collective man'—one who carries and shapes the unconscious, psychic life of mankind'' (apud Portnoy, p. 24).

Sociological theories of musical creation ground the latter, not in the depths of the individual or collective psyche, but in social behavior. According to Portnoy, these sociological theories constitute applications of Darwin's theory of evolution. Thus, Spencer, echoing in part an idea already expressed by Theophrastus (see Portnoy, note 47, p. 53), ''believed that vocal music originated in impassioned speech, in the instinctive needs of man to express himself. The growth of music from a simple vocal utterance to a complex art paralleled the evolution of man and his institutions'' (Portnoy, p. 26). Schiller's art-as-play theory—which invokes Kant's remark ''Art compared to labor may be considered as a Play''—is applied to music by Konrad Lange. According to this theory, writes Portnoy (p. 26), ''The composer's creation and the child's fantasies are conscious forms of self-illusion, a necessary indulgence to grant them the means to equalize the balance between what society has deprived them of and what they required by nature.'' A third sociological theory is that of Carl Stumpf, who believed that music had its origin in early man's practice of sending signal calls from hilltop to hilltop. This feat, Julius Portnoy explains (p. 27), ''was accomplished by a man lingering on one tone so that his voice would be heard at a distance. This in turn produced a tightening of his vocal cords. The tautness of the cords produced a higher pitch. Sustaining the higher pitch developed a vibrato tone—the beginnings of music as compared to articulate language.'' Darwin's own theory, which, as Portnoy points out, is more properly speaking biological rather than sociological, also maintains that song preceded speech. I shall return to Darwin's theory in a later chapter when I discuss Sena's poem inspired by Beethoven's Quartet, Op. 131.

An important component of humanism in *Art of Music*—indeed one of the latter's philosophical and thematic pillars—is precisely the poet's stance vis-à-vis some of these theories of musical creation. In fact, ''Bach: Goldberg Variations'' and ''Listening to Quartet, Op. 131, by Beethoven'' constitute in part verbal crystallizations of the experience of music against the backdrop of theories of creation and meaning. In other poems—for example ''Preludes and Fugues by J.S. Bach,'' ''Octaves: Listening to Brahms's First Symphony,'' and ''Finale of Sibelius's Second Symphony''—Sena reacts against divine or metaphysical theories of music while upholding a humanistic explanation. Among the theoreticians discussed, Sena is on the side of those who, like Hume, Hegel, Santayana, Maritain, and modern scientists defend a man-centered explanation of musical origin. However, unlike some of them, Sena's views stop short of metaphysical and divine connections.

Although Sena's theoretical ideas do not amount to a structured and elaborate statement concerning the origin of music, the following ideas can easily be inferred from the poems of *Art of Music* in general, and, in particular, from those poems in which references to theories of musical origin are explicit or clearly implicit. Jorge de Sena is opposed to all divine-metaphysical theories of musical creation. He also does not subscribe to man-centered theories that hold for music a mysterious or irrational origin. For Sena music is neither a gift of God, the voice of God, or a path to God. It is neither a reproduction of the music of the spheres nor a species of supra- or infra-consciousness—although in one instance, "'Romeo and Juliet,' by Tchaikovsky," he does consider the composition an unconscious expression of its author's bisexuality. However, as we shall see when discussing the poem, Sena's interpretation is probably ironic and does not necessarily reflect an acceptance of the Freudian theory of musical creation. Freud's and Jung's theories can, I believe, be applied in part to poems such as "'Principessa di Morte'" and "The Death of Isolde," respectively. Music, Sena states or implies time and again, whatever the mechanics of its human origin—and it probably contains partly psychological and partly sociological roots, like any art—is, as we know it today, a form, a very special form, of human communication. It has its origin in human experience, in the broadest sense of this term, and is a receptacle containing vestiges, albeit altered or transformed, of that experience. There is no mystery in music as far as its origin is concerned, except the mystery that, through the musical medium, humankind sometimes surpasses, or seems to surpass, human limitations; or, as Sena puts it in "Bach: Golderg Variations," "o homem é, por vezes, / maior do que si mesmo" ("man is, sometimes, / greater than himself").

Although Sena's views regarding musical creation are extremely important, equally important, or perhaps more important still as far as humanism in *Art of Music* is concerned, is the poet's stance in regard to explanations or theories of musical meaning. Theories of meaning may also be divided into two broad categories. However much they may differ from one another on the surface, theories of meaning in music fall into the autonomous (also known as absolutist or formalist) and heteronomous (also expressionist) viewpoints. The first, which is defended by Eduard Hanslick in his epoch-making *The Beautiful in Music* (1854), holds that music means absolutely nothing beyond its tones, excepting perhaps the relatively insignificant extrinsic meanings derived from the imitation of natural sounds (onomatopoeia), as exemplified by passages in Beethoven's *Pastoral Symphony*. "The essence of music," says Hanslick, "is sound in motion."[6] Regarding subject matter in music, he writes (pp. 118-19) that "Music has, indeed, no contents as thus understood; no subject in the sense that the subject to be treated is something extraneous to the musical notes. . . . Music consists of successions and forms of sound, and these alone constitute the subject. Now, whatever be the effect of a piece of music on the individual mind, and howsoever it be interpreted, it has no subject beyond the combinations of notes we hear, for music speaks not only by means of sounds, it speaks nothing but sound."

The autonomous or absolutist theory has been expressed more recently by Igor Stravinsky in his *Chronicle of My Life.* The author of the *Rite of Spring* wrote: "I consider that music is, by its very nature, powerless to *express* anything at all, whether a feeling, an attitude of mind, a psychological mood, a phenomenon of nature, etc. . . . if, as is nearly always the case, music appears to express something, this is only an illusion, and not a reality."[7]

Summarizing the prevailing contemporary aesthetic attitude, Deryck Cooke states that "Music is widely regarded nowadays, not as a language at all, but as 'pure', inexpressive art, like architecture; and even those who do feel it to be some kind of language regard it as an imprecise one, incapable of conveying anything so tangible as an experience of life or an attitude towards it."[8]

The extreme form of the heteronomous or expressionist view, on the other hand, maintains that music is a kind of language, and a musical composition a sort of audial book that can not only communicate a whole range of meanings but is indeed capable of particularizing the ideas and emotions being communicated. Among the many composers who have held this or similar views, at least at some point in their careers, are those who have composed programmatic works. Richard Wagner and his disciples constitute another group who defended an extreme heteronomous viewpoint. Hanslick's arguments, as is well known, are mostly directed against Wagner and Wagnerians. For the author of *Tristan und Isolde,* as Morris Weitz explains in his introduction to Gustav Cohen's translation of *The Beautiful in Music* (p. x), "Music is a language of specific emotions, things, persons, ideas; it can be used to refer to and describe anything."

Among the subscribers to some variant of the extreme heteronomous view is Colin McAlpin. In his *Hermaia,* he attributes to music the capacity to express twenty-eight different meanings, ranging from "the expression of the self" to music as "the expression of moral development." Unlike Wagner and Wagnerians, however, McAlpin does not claim for music the ability to particularize thoughts and emotions. All his categories are as generalized or vague as the two mentioned above. McAlpin's theory of meaning is developed within the framework of the comparative expressive capabilities of the different arts, especially painting, poetry, and music. Man has a tripartite nature, McAlpin holds: physical, mental, and spiritual. Painting, poetry, and music are the respective mediums for the expression of this tripartite nature. In this theory of expressive aestheticism each art has the following role to play: "painting, poetry, and music represent, respectively, the transcription of nature, its translation and its transcendence. The first art is, then, a faithful reproduction of its model in nature; the second, though its medium differs from nature, still reproduces mentally the facts thereof; while the third and last art employs a medium and relates to a model, both of which are supranatural" *(Hermaia,* pp. 48-49). Each of these arts, McAlpin's evolutionary theory maintains, begins its own expressive career where the previous one left off. Thus, McAlpin explains (p. 28), "Painting pales into poetry; poetry melts away into music. Where the painter fails to interpret the changeful moods of nature, the poet comes to our assistance. And when words fail the poet, the musician steps in, and discarding semblance and metaphor, copes with the inarticulate and conquers the evasive emotions of man." As we can see, McAlpin's theory of musical meaning is, to a large degree, the counterpart of the divine-metaphysical theories of musical origin. It also owes much, it seems, to Walter Pater in ascribing to the sister arts an ascending measure of perfection and to music the consummate degree of expressibility. Pater writes:

> In music, then, rather than in poetry, is to be found the true type or measure of perfected art. Therefore, although each art has its incommunicable element, its untranslatable order of impressions, its unique mode of reaching the "imaginative reason," yet the arts may be represented as continually struggling after the law or principle of music, to a condition which music alone completely realises; and one of the chief functions of aesthetic criticism, dealing with the products of art, new or old, is to estimate the degree in which each of those products approaches, in this sense, to musical law.[9]

A recent and more moderate version of the heteronomous viewpoint is that of Deryck Cooke, whose book, *The Language of Music,* "is an attempt to bring music back from the intellectual-aesthetic limbo in which it is now lost, and to reclaim it for humanity at large, by beginning the task of actually deciphering its language. . . . and . . . thereby make it ultimately possible to understand and assess a composer's work as a report on human experience, just as we do that of a literary artist'' ("Preface," *Meaning of Music,* pp. xi-xii). Cooke is careful to distinguish between what music can and cannot express (p. xii):

> It is not imagined, let me hasten to add, that such assessments will take the form of philosophical discussions of conceptual arguments, since music cannot express concepts; nor that they will be "digests" of the "meanings" of various works, for the same reason; rather, since music can only express feelings, it is thought that they will probably be in the nature of interpretations of analysis perfected by Wilson Knight for the elucidation of the "images" used, and interpretation of their emotional and psychological connotations.

Deryck Cooke finishes the first chapter of his book by answering the question posed in the title, "What kind of an art is music?" "Music is," he concludes, "in fact, 'extra-verbal', since notes, like words, have emotional connotations; it is, let us repeat, the supreme expression of universal emotions, in an entirely personal way, by the great composers" (p.33).

Jorge de Sena's statement in the postface—"music does not mean anything except itself"—would seem to place him among the autonomists or absolutists. And he probably was an autonomist as far as his extrapoetical experience of music was concerned. As for his poetical experience of music, however, he was an autonomist only in principle. This contradiction between Sena's postfactory statements and the poems of *Art of Music* has been noted in the two most perceptive critical appraisals of the book: that of Óscar Lopes and that of João Palma-Ferreira. The latter expresses it thus:

> The poet's predisposition for the art of music is well revealed in his extraordinary capacity for effecting a "crystallization" from works of music into poetic forms free of the anecdotal and detachable perorations so often foreign to the nature of music. This is tantamount to saying that, although music *expresses nothing except itself,* the poet nevertheless manages to go beyond cataloguing the interminable or the inexpressible to record, through his own feelings and impressions, a moral and intellectual climate identical to the one he discovers in the musical work he "crystallizes."[10]

Óscar Lopes states that "the book does exactly that which, at every step, almost poem by poem, it proscribes doing: *it searches for meanings in music,* speaks *about* music, and speaks *instead* of music, recognizing all the while that, *music is only music"* (loc. cit.).

It is true that in the case of some works of pure music—Bach's Preludes and Fugues and *Goldberg Variations*; Scarlatti's Sonatas—the poet, search as he may for signs of "life," i.e., for verbally capturable emotions and thoughts, is compelled to admit that "a vida está ausente" ("life is absent") ("Preludes and Fugues"); and that all extramusical associations and considerations crumble and mean nothing before "abstracção como esta" ("abstraction such as this /Scarlatti's music/") ("Wanda Landowska"). Nevertheless, in the case of Bach's *Goldberg Variations* Sena does find plenty of evidence of human experience in the organization of the music. The latter may be relatively lacking in emotional—but not in intellectual content. In the case of Bach's Preludes and Fugues and Scarlatti's Sonatas, as we shall discover in due time, Sena finds many manifestations of life—both within and without the music, i.e., associated with the acoustic substance, the composer, the performer and, equally important, with himself, the listener.

When Sena experiences the music in essentially subjective and humanistic terms, as he does in these poems, and communicates that experience through the medium of language, he is perforce more on the side of heteronomists like Deryck Cooke than of autonomists like Hanslick or Stravinsky. Sena's position, as exemplified by the poems, reveals that to him all music—purely instrumental or otherwise—is in a sense programmatic. Not in the traditional technical sense that music can tell a story or paint a picture, but in the more profound sense that all music, being a human creation to be experienced by other humans, always has a story to tell. This story may be embedded in the music, i.e., inherent to it, or it may stem from the poet's discovery that this particular piece of music is totally self-sufficient, that it has no story as such. In Sena's overall poetical experience of music, not finding a story or meaning(s) in music is also an important story in itself: a story of the humanist's search for human presence and how he reacts when he finds that presence lacking. This search, as we shall see, is dramatized in poems on Bach and Scarlatti.

The role that the poet imposed on himself in these poems is to tell these musical stories as he lives and/or creates them. The story of music, let me insist at the risk of repeating myself, is not the *objective, technical* story or content of the musical compositions as might be told by a professional critic or historian of music. It is primarily the story of the musical compositions as perceived or lived by a poet who happens to be a humanist in the sense defined and explained earlier; in short, one who believes that art—all art—is an inseparable part of human experience as a whole. As I suggested when discussing a few poems of *Metamorphoses,* when Sena poetically enters a museum, it is in search of life; it is in search of life that he delves into what to him are the sometimes mysterious but for the most part relatively clear waters of music.

169

To call Sena an autonomist as far as his extrapoetical view of music is concerned and a heteronomist when it comes to the poems themselves is necessarily to simplify matters too much. His views of musical meaning as expressed in the poems are not preconceived or monolithic ones. They stem largely from and are always conditioned by the experience of a given composition. It is this specific work that informs and defines the view he expresses at this moment. Another composition will give rise to a necessarily different view of musical meaning. However, even when Sena defends, as he repeatedly does, the aesthetic integrity of music and its sometimes autonomous character, he still does not—as far as his overall experience of the music is concerned—abandon or forsake the idea that "Understanding it /music/ as a form in itself does not compel one to see it as something inhuman, devoid of contact with the reality of life and human experience, and without correlation to a cultural context" ("Postface," p. 220).

Keeping in mind its conditionality and changeability, we see that Sena's view of musical meaning follows from his view of musical creation and can be summarized thus. Music is a species of rational or intelligential discourse, a vehicle through which the composer pours his humanity and translates his experiences into living tones. In short, music is, in varying degrees, an expression of humankind's reason, emotions, aspirations, hopes and disillusionments. Sena's view of musical meaning is indeed very compatible with his views of poetic meaning. Music is also a mirror in which the listener, or better, he who experiences music, can see his or her own image reflected. The degree to which any ideas or emotions in music can be particularized is not aprioristically determinable: it depends upon the composition and predisposition of the co-participant, the one who experiences. Somewhat analogous to what happens in poetry, various types of music place emphasis on emotion, while other types stress intellectual content as reflected, for example, in formal control. Some types tend to be more expressive or referential (program music, Romantic music), others less expressive of any particularizable emotions and ideas and thus more self-contained. According to the poet, in Bach's *Goldberg Variations* floats an "ideia despojada de sentido" ("idea bereft of meaning"). However, the sonnet on Mozart's *Concerto for Piano and Orchestra,* K. 406, begins by particularizing the nature of the emotion expressed by the music—"Finíssima *amargura* ("Most piercing and subdued *bitterness")*—at the same time that it also points to the control of emotion by reason—"Finíssima amargura *recatada"*("Most piercing and *subdued* bitterness") (my italics).

Very often, then, the poems of *Art of Music* may be thought of as intermediaries between the abstract or non-representational realm of music (particularly in the case of absolute music) and the concrete plane of human experience. Although music springs from life, it tends, by its very nature, to isolate itself from life sources. Because the substance of music, tones, is the furthest (of the four sisters: painting, sculpture, poetry, music) removed from human nature and the realm of everyday existence, the humanistic experience of music and its expression through a medium like poetry builds a bridge of sorts between the abstract audial realm and the concrete stage of human reality. Music, says Colin McAlpin, "cannot directly express either physical existence or human experience, from the viewpoint of fact, since in such a case the mind must be definitely directed toward empirical circumstances and specific personality" *(Hermaia,* p. 138). But poetry can and Sena's poems often do compensate for this "insufficiency" of music: poetry can interpret, particularize, establish relationships, invest forms with ideas. It can, furthermore, create new art forms from those already existing while at the same time performing an intermediary role between the strictly musical plane of listening and the music's contextual antecedents.

A specific example of experiencing music on the strictly musical plane would be to listen to, say, Handel's *Water Music* and perceive the Allegro, the Bourré, the Hornpipe with their peculiar acoustic and formal characteristics and nothing else. Of course, the degree of musical culture on the part of the listener would determine the depth and complexity of this experience. But the latter would be confined ideally to the acoustic sphere. An example of the humanistic experience of music—and one that Sena's poem on Handel's composition actually exemplifies—is to experience the music as inseparable from its contextual elements. It is the experience of *Water Music* within the framework of its historical and human antecedents: the circumstances attendant to its performance aboard barges on the Thames, the social and cultural milieu of which the music (seen within this historical context) is a manifestation. Most of all—since the poems of *Art of Music* are not meant as high-sounding trumpets for a humanistic approach to music—it is to create a poem that constitutes a new experience for the reader; a way of discovering fresh interrelationships among different orders of experience and between two art mediums; it is, in short, to watch a work of art spring alive from the experiencing of another, utilizing techniques of another while at the same time exercising attributes that other art mediums lack or do not possess to the same degree.

It is important to point out that even Eduard Hanslick—one of the staunchest defenders of the autonomous view—concedes that

> Not long since, the fashion began to regard works of art in connection with the ideas and events of the time which gave them birth. This connection is undeniable and probably exists also in music. Being a product of the human mind, it must naturally bear some relation to the other products of mind; to contemporaneous works of poetry and the fine arts; to the state of society, literature, and the sciences of the period; and, finally, to the individual experiences and convictions of the author. To observe and demonstrate the existence of this connection in the case of certain composers and works is not only a justifiable proceeding but also a true gain to knowledge. *(The Beautiful in Music,* p. 62)

It is precisely the existence of this "connection" between some works of music and their biographical, cultural and conceptual contexts that many of Sena's poems communicate. Even though, like Hanslick, Sena upholds the aesthetic integrity and even self-sufficiency of some pieces of music, his poems show that he is always conscious and alert to the possibility that embedded in the acoustic tissue may very well be, among other things, "the individual and social dramas to which the composer reacted with feeling or that he suffered" ("Postface," p. 223).

Thus far I have dwelt on the different approaches to musico-literary criticism and to which type Sena's poems respond best (Chapter IV); and, in the present chapter, I have discussed Sena's humanistic view of music as revealed in his stance vis-à-vis theories of musical creation and meaning, and the relationship between music and its extramusical context. Very little has been said so far about the different ways in which Sena experiences distinct types of music. It is now time to clarify that, despite much overlapping in Sena's approach to all types of music, there are nevertheless significant differences that must be pointed out. The following generalizations may be made and will be borne out in the discussions of the poems. In the overwhelming majority of the poems in the first two groups—Miscellaneous, and Program Music and Opera—Sena pays as much attention to the content of the texts independently of the music as he does to the alliance of text and music. This is particularly noticeable in the poems derived from opera and compositions associated with liturgical texts, such as Mozart's *Requiem* and Beethoven's *Missa Solemnis*. In poems inspired by programmatic works, the poet again lends as much emphasis to the story itself as he does to the music or its other contextual elements. Therefore, in the majority of poems within these two broad groups Sena deals as much with a textual, i.e., literary, experience as he does with a musical one. In the case of absolute music, one of three things happens: the poet experiences the compostion essentially on Copland's expressive plane, tending toward the allegorization of its meaning (''D Minor Concerto, K. 466, by Mozart''); he experiences the composition in both acoustic and contextual terms, i.e., fuses elements derived from the audial and extramusical spheres *(''Water Music,* by Handel''); or else he experiences the composition, in part, against the backdrop of theories of musical creation and meaning (''Listening to Quartet, Op. 131, by Beethoven''). These, of course, are but sweeping introductory or preparatory generalizations which do not account for all aspects of the content, let alone the alliance of content and form, of these poems. No poem exemplifies only one approach, concentrating exclusively on the music, the dramatic or the contextual elements. Thus, contextual or extramusical elements are present in the poem on Mozart's *Concerto for Piano and Orchestra,* a sonnet that also exemplifies experiencing music on the expressive plane. And the expressive plane of listening is also reflected in the poems on Handel and Beethoven which contain, respectively, much contextual information and meditations on theories of musical creation and meaning. These last poems, as noted earlier, also exemplify the poetic adaptation of musical forms and other structural devices. There is also a reason, to be discussed later, why the poem on Mozart's Concerto is cast in the form of a sonnet.

Surveying the major types of approaches or modes used by Sena in all the poems of *Art of Music,* we come up with at least five major ones, some of which have been referred to above. The outlining of these modes will serve as a guideline for the discussion of the individual poems later on. Although some of these modes characterize poems derived from a given type of music more so than other types, some of the modes typify many or most of the poems. Also, a given poem may illustrate two, three, or more modes. No poem is limited to only one. And I believe that the most effective poems are those which necessarily blend a number of modes, which is to say different ways of experiencing or perceiving a given model composition. These modes will be called *descriptive, imitative, interpretive, textual,* and *personal.*

When exercising the descriptive mode—which he does often but always in conjunction with other modes—Sena comes very close to dwelling exclusively on the acoustic experience as such. This mode, to the extent that it can be isolated from others, is the one that probably most reflects Copland's sheer musical plane, as previously noted. The poet concentrates primarily on what the music is doing. This mode is thus exemplified by descriptive passages in the poems. Sena gives us as objective a description of the behavior of the music as is possible within the confines of (his) poetic exigencies. More description and the poem might become restricted to the audial event, subservient to it. Less objective concentration on what the music is doing, and the poetic metamorphosis might become almost independent of or disconnected from the composition on which it is avowedly based. In very general terms, Sena describes for the most part the music's melodic and harmonic configurations as he perceives them, comments on the musical texture, identifies a group of instruments or a single instrument sounding at the time, notes the 'dialectical interchanges' among them. These descriptions-as-the-music-develops, along with the titles of the poems—"Listening to Quartet . . .," "Octaves: Listening to Brahms's First Symphony"—help to create that notion of on-the-spot listening that I spoke of earlier, i.e., that listening to the music and writing the poem are simultaneous and coterminous acts. The following lines of "Preludes and Fugues by J.S. Bach" illustrate this mode (of describing a fugue):

> *a melodia oculta e repartida*
> *em tantas sequências que se opõem,*
> *e se intercalam, contraditum . . .*

> (the occult melody, divided
> into so many interweaving,
> opposing and contradicting sequences . . .)

Another example from "Erik Satie for Piano," previously quoted:

> *As notas vêm sós por harmonias*
> *como de escalas que se cruzam*
> *em sequências descontínuas de figuras*

> (The notes go solitary through harmonies
> the way scales cross
> through discontinuous sequences of figures).

In these passages Sena approaches a kind of "technical" description of the music, as revealed by his use of technical musical terms: *melody, notes, harmonies, scales.*

In many other cases, however, Sena describes the music or what the music is doing, not in "objective" or quasi-technical terms, but in a subjective way. That is to say, instead of describing the contours of a melodic, harmonic or polyphonic configuration employing musical terminology, the poet uses subjective imagery. To be sure, his description may still be, and always is, faithful to the music. But the language in which this perception is expressed is entirely subjective and serves both a descriptive and an imagistic function. This is done in at least two ways: the musical pattern is compared to some non-acoustic phenomenon, and we end up with a simile; the musical constituent is directly converted into an expressive verbal equivalent, and we have a metaphor. (In reality, these two forms of description could also be categorized and discussed under the rubric of interpretive mode, for they partake of description as well as interpretation. Sena simultaneously captures what the music is doing /descriptive mode/ and attributes extramusical or extrinsic meaning to these patterns—the image- or meaning-creating part.) An example of musical phenomena conveyed in metaphorical terms is contained in the previously referred to first quartet of "D Minor Concerto, for Piano and Orchestra, K. 466, by Mozart":

> Finíssima amargura recatada
> que exasperadamente se contém
> de gritos e lamentos mas devém
> doçura tensa tão dialogada.

> (Most piercing and subdued bitterness
> that controls itself exasperatedly
> with screams and laments but comes to be
> a tense and so dialogued sweetness).

The line "São como vagas vindo no perlado" ("Notes on a string of pearls move / like small waves"—which describes the 'movement of sounding musical notes' in "Erik Satie for Piano"—exemplifies the simile version of this type of description. (In music, *notas perladas* also means "executed with perfection.")

Mention must also be made of the use of naming and verbal suggestion (of musical patterns, instruments, etc.) as a descriptive device. As Calvin S. Brown points out, poetry cannot always effectively describe, say, the melodies or the tone color of a given composition; however, it can go a long way by recalling them to the reader's mind through naming and suggesting.[11] Naming and suggesting, alternating with other types of description such as quasi-technical and imagistic, can actually function as a compensatory device for language's poor ability to convey information about, and much less re-present, the acoustic quality of music. For example, are the sounds /kr/, /tr/, and /i/ in "Crepitam trompas e destilam flautas" ("Horns crackle and flutes distil") *("Water Music,* by Handel")* precise analogues of the timbres of the instruments mentioned, to say nothing of the melodies they are playing? If so, does the stressed /i/ of *crepitam* and *destilam* refer both to the brass and woodwind instruments, or does each /i/ coupled with its respective consonants refer only to the named instrument? Independently of the naming of the instruments the answer might be difficult. However, since the poet uses the sounds mentioned in conjunction with the naming of the instruments, the reader may still not experience the verbal equivalent of those tone colors—but he or she is at least persuaded to recall them to mind. The reader may not feel that *crepitam* and *destilam* ("crackle," "distil") are adequate verbs to describe what the music is doing, but he certainly has a suggestion upon which to engage his imagination (and acquaintance with the music). Through this device of naming and suggesting, the poet can evoke an entire music piece or a section of a composition: "brisa" ("breeze") (the Air in *Water Music); "música da morte" ("music of death") (Dies Irae* in Mozart's Requiem). Tempo and dynamic descriptions are other devices employed by Sena to recall the music: "os instruments tocam / virilmente lânguidos" ("the instruments virilely / languishing render") *("Water Music,* by Handel"; English version by Jonathan Griffin); "roncos e estridências lacrimosas" ("in shrieks and tearful dissonances"), "crescendos delirantes" ("delirious crescendos") ("The Death of Isolde").

In the imitative mode we are dealing neither with a quasi-technical or subjective description of the music, nor with evocation through naming or suggesting. In this case the poet's aim is to approximate some aspect of the music's formal design and structural techniques. Enough has been said before (Chapter IV) about the approximate rendition by Sena of these formal techniques of music. I shall discuss these imitative devices in connection with the analyses of the poems. The use of word music might also be included under this heading, although with the reservations already pointed out in Chapter IV. Suffice it to add here that, in some poems, Sena utilizes yet another type of formal imitation—this one the easiest to accomplish and detect. I am referring to the strophic or sectional arrangement of the poem so as to match the number of movements or sections of the model composition. "Brandenburg Concerto" and "Creation, by Haydn" are cases in point. It must be emphasized, however, that all the poems of *Art of Music* are complete units—even when they are based on multiple compositions or finales or single operatic scenes. That is to say, the inspirational work may be multiple or sectional, but the experience it represents for the poet is a complete one. This is another compelling suggestion that the poems' primary intention is not to imitate the model piece of music—otherwise the poems, like the music, would be somewhat fragmented—but to translate into artistic form the whole and complete experience that the music constitutes for the poet.

The interpretive mode is an approach—usually employed in conjunction with several others—in which the poet reacts to the music by striking a critical, i.e., interpretive, pose. In this case, the music does not provoke in the poet only the desire to describe or imitate one or more of its constituents: it instills in him the understandable urge to evaluate, explain, and judge. "Music induces introspection, suggestions to search within ourselves for possible meanings the sounds may have" (Portnoy, p. 133). This introspection—which in *Art of Music* tends to be more often provoked by absolute than other types of music—necessarily involves criticism or judgment of the music's artist and/or human nature and worth. When Sena evaluates or judges, his appraisal of the composition can be personal, i.e., original, or, as happens in some cases, reiterative of, or fairly identical with, traditional professional critical opinions. When employing this evaluative approach, the poet asks (implicitly) and answers (explicitly) questions such as: Does Schubert's music add to the poems of Wilhelm Müller what they lacked, or did they already embody theretofore undetectable greatness? Do Schumann's music and Heine's poetry form the perfect alliance? How good a composer and how original is Anton Bruckner?

The poems on Schubert and Schumann's lieder—they are, respectively, settings of Müller's *Die schöne Müllerin* and *Winterreise,* and Heine's *Buch der Lieder*—both have something in common and also differ from each other in the emphasis they place on the music or the poetic texts. Both constitute critical reflections on the inspiring works; although, as the titles indicate, the first focuses primarily on the music, while the second lays equal or perhaps greater emphasis on Heine's poetry than on Schumann's music. "Lieder by Schubert on Texts by Wilhelm Müller" follows very closely traditional critical opinions on this work, a fact which Sena makes quite clear from the beginning:

> Eram poemas para o sentimentalismo vácuo
> sem nenhuma categoria que os dignificasse,
> Diz a crítica . . . .
>
> (They were poems to serve vacuous sentimentalism
> without any dignifying quality,
> Say the critics . . . .)

Müller's *Die schöne Müllerin* has indeed been called "a cycle of harmless poems."[12] And, according to the same critic, although the poems comprising *Winterreise* "rank higher than the first group" (p. 95), nevertheless, Oskar Bie adds: "never did Schubert do so much with such small means" (p. 105). Regarding *Die schöne Müllering,* Bie simply states that "Everything has been turned into sound. The words are ashamed of their limited powers" (p.87). And he concludes: "my good Wilhelm Müller, you scarcely know how little you contributed to bringing about this transformation" (p. 88). Sena expresses similar ideas in a language reminiscent of Bie's:

> *Como é possível? Como foi possível? Deu a música*
> *aos poemas o que não tinham? Ou eles*
> *tinham o que às vezes poesia pode ter sem*
> *bem ser poesia: a falta dela*
> *que a música pode compor e criar?*
> *Tantas vezes grande música se fez com má poesia,*
> *e tão raras vezes foi feita com poesia grande!*
> . . .

> (How is it possible? How was it possible? Did the music give
> the poems what they didn't have? Or did they have
> what poetry can sometimes have without
> really being poetry: a lack of what
> music can compose and create?
> How many times has music been made out of bad poetry,
> and how rarely out of great!
> . . .)

One of the rare instances of the ideal marriage of great music to great poetry occurs, according to Sena (and musical critics in general), in the case of Schumann and Heine:

> *Nunca talvez tão grande poesia encontrou sua grande música.*

> (Never perhaps has such fine poetry met its fine music.)

As stated above, in this poem Sena gives (progressively) more attention (and hence importance?) to the poetry than to the music. This is done perhaps in conscious or unconscious opposition to Schumann, who "believed poetry to be an inferior art form ⟨to music⟩. The poem . . . must be crushed and have its juices expressed like an orange; it must wear the music like a wreath; or yield to it like a bride."[13] In Sena's poem the music does not surpass, but enhances, the poems—these "pequeninos dramas líricos" ("little lyrical dramas") which bring forth, not Schumann's love for Clara (with which some of the *Dichterliebe* have been associated; see Sams, pp. 22-23), but Heine's otherwise unconfessed biographical drama. The "little lyrical dramas":

> *são a poesia funda que não disse o homem*
> *que brincou perseguido, exilado e traído,*
> *com tudo o que perdia mas na voz ganhava.*

(are the deep poetry that was never spoken by
the persecuted, exiled, and betrayed man who toyed
with everything he lost and everything a voice regained.)

Let me hasten to reiterate that, despite containing statements that can be construed as judgmental, the poems of *Art of Music* are far from being musical criticism or statements of opinion on music in the guise of poems. What Sena said regarding the poems of *Metamorphoses*—that they are not "literary essays, moralistic meditations, impressionistic art criticism . . ."—also applies to *Art of Music*. All of Sena's interpretations and critical appraisals will be discussed within his overall humanistic experience of music and how they relate to it—independently of their extrapoetic accuracy or value (and I am sure they have both). The critical pose must be seen, I believe, as yet another component in Sena's multifaceted experience of music. In fact, underneath the apparent musical criticism of the poems runs a more profound current of criticism of life, in the Arnoldian sense of the phrase, even though the poet imagines the songs superseding this criticism. The last passage quoted above strongly suggests that Sena was more interested in searching out Heine's "drama" embedded in the poems and accentuated by Schumann's music than he was in celebrating the perfect aesthetic marriage of the two arts. Indeed, there is even a second important dimension to those lines: "the persecuted, exiled, and betrayed man who toyed / with everything he lost and everything a voice regained" is also Sena himself, or better, his conception of his own life, which he so often expresses in other poems. These lines fit perfectly Sena's view of himself as the "persecuted, exiled" poet who, only through his art, can gain what life "denied" him, can indeed transform misery into song. As we shall see below, this personal identification on the part of Sena with the human beings whose dramas are embedded in the music he poetizes is one of the constants of *Art of Music*.

What I have termed the interpretive mode is by no means restricted to judgmental statements, however. It deals also with coherent interpretations of the music. These interpretations are drawn from the following three areas in varying degrees or combinations: the musical substance itself (this type of interpretation is roughly reflective of Aaron Copland's expressive plane of listening); the relationship between the music and the life of the composer; and the musical work viewed against the background of history in general. In accordance with these three variants of the interpretive mode, Sena poses and answers questions such as these: How viable are certain theories of musical creation and meaning when applied to specific works like Beethoven's Quartet, Op. 131? To what extent is

Beethoven's *Missa Solemnis* a solemn religious work, and to what degree is it an expression of the composer's own metaphysical anxieties? How is Tchaikovsky's *Romeo and Juliet* relatable to some aspects of the composer's personality and to his own life? To what degree is Turandot—the character in Puccini's *Turandot*—a personification of the composer's own death? When the interpretive mode deals with the historical as opposed to the biographical antecedents of the composition, questions such as the following come into play: What do Mozart's *Concerto for Piano and Orchestra*, Berlioz's *Symphonie Fantastique*, and Schoenberg's *Piano Concerto*, Op. 42, tell us about their respective times? In what sense is Mozart's *Requiem*, not his "song of death," but his song of life? What does Haydn's *The Creation* have to say to the secular humanist of today?

The next mode I wish to discuss is the textual. When utilizing this method of expressing his experience of a musical composition, Sena is approaching the model in part by taking into account the libretto or text (in the case of opera, oratorio, or Mass) and the intended dramatic story (in the case of program music). As was noted before, in some instances—and the poems on Wagner's operas are cases in point—Sena does not dwell on the entire content of the work, but chooses specific humanly charged episodes or scenes. When it comes to the literary elements depicted in a programmatic work, Sena either follows or acknowledges the intended dramatic line or utilizes the composition's dramatic content as a point of departure for the elaboration of his own "program." This is the case, respectively, with *"Symphonie Fantastique*, by Berlioz" and "'Fêtes,' by Debussy."

The last mode I wish to discuss is the personal. By personal I mean Senian, reflective of his own human personality, involving aspects of his own life. This approach to the poetization of musical experience is in a way the most important one of all for it usually underlines all the others. It is also the most difficult to explain, except in relation to specific poems. Sometimes it is more implicit than explicit; and in some cases it can best be discerned by comparing the poem in which it appears with poems from other Senian works.

According to John Hospers, "there do seem to be mysterious affinities between life-experiences and musical ones; for music does evoke in us experiences sufficiently like some experiences in life to make us use the same characterizing adjectives in describing them, inadequate as they are, and to do so with considerable regularity and insistence."[14] These "mysterious affinities" also exist between the life experiences and personalities of different artists. These experiences and personality traits very often find their way into works of art. When we discover them, they tantalize us; they beckon to us with friendly, or less friendly, signs of our common humanity. Sena loved to answer these callings and exploit them poetically. The art of music is a most fertile ground for the cultivation of these correlations between shared or common experiences.

Music—in the sense of audible tones, and not merely in the sense of notes written on a score—results from the combined efforts, however separate in time and place, of the following entities: the composer who translated his thoughts and feelings and committed them to musical notation; the performer who re-creates his or her version of the composer's message; and the listener whose experience of the music completes the process. This experience can be passive (one merely hears the music but hardly pays it any attention; one merely allows oneself to be enveloped by the music's sensuous sounds), and it can be active, i.e., colored by the dynamics of participatory intellectual and emotional response. Since Jorge de Sena is not only a listener but a poet who communicates his experience of the music in artistic terms, he actually combines two entities: that of highly responsive listener, and that of re-creator of the musical experience in the poetic medium. When I say re-creator I do not mean this in the sense that a performer re-creates the composer's message. I mean re-creator in the sense that we could say that every intelligent and sensitive listener of music is a re-creator of the artistic event in his or her own terms. The work of music, as it relates to the composer and performer might, for the sake of argument, be considered as being separate from the listener, objective, out there. However, when the music penetrates the sphere of the active listener, it begins to surrender some of that objectiveness as far as that listener is concerned. According to Julius Portnoy, "A listener must also be able to project, transfer his feelings, and endow tones and rhythms with *his* life's experience. A listener whose life is not burdened with tragedy and given to hope will find no joy or sadness in music" (*Music in the Life of Man*, p. 104, my italics). Portnoy adds (p. 106) that "a listener's response to a musical work depends on his age and maturity, his beliefs and convictions, prejudices and sympathies, and the mood he happens to be in at the moment." These statements support the contention that when a listener is actively engaged in the experience of music, the "joy" or "sadness" (or any other emotions or ideas) he perceives therein may be partly inherent to the music, i.e., instilled into it by composer and performer, and partly a projection or reflection of the listener's world view, personality and momentary disposition. The dynamics of response operate, of course, in the experience of all works of art. However, since music (and particularly absolute music) is necessarily the least precise in the presentation of its paraphraseable content (some would even question if it has any such content), the amount of input provided by a listener probably exceeds that of readers or viewers of poetry, painting or sculpture. On the basis of response alone, a heteronomous theory of musical meaning is justifiable. Although one could always question the objective *presence* in the music of particular thoughts and feelings, who has a right to question the fact that the listener may project those feelings and thoughts? And that this projection is a legitimate component of the dynamics of art experience?

Since Jorge de Sena fuses into one the roles of active listener and artistic re-creator of the enriched listening experience, the degree and variety of his input into the overall perception of music is understandably greater that it would be for the average active listener, if it be licit to postulate such an entity. As the poet, listening or experiencing as poet, situates himself on the crossroads of multiple avenues of awareness in regard to the music; as he suffuses his experience with his particular world view; as he brings to bear upon this experience extraneous elements that a "normal" listening process might not allow for; as he fashions all these products into self-sustained poems and not merely stylized reports on other works of art—the story that a given composition ends up by telling is as much (and sometimes less) its own story as it is Sena's very own story.

If we add to all this the fact that Sena loves to establish parallels between other artists' lives and his own; that he often utilizes other poets' words (Camoens's, Pessoa's) to tell his own story or to strike uncanny analogies, then we shall understand better the autobiographical dimension of "'La Cathédrale engloutie,' by Debussy" and the implicit parallels between some of Debussy's and Sena's life experiences; we shall be in a better position to discover the autobiographical elements in "Final 'Potpourri'" as well as those implicit in "*Symphonie Fantastique*, by Berlioz," "Chopin: An Inventory," "To Piaf," "'Socrates,' by Satie." We shall not, furthermore, find it unusual that a poem inspired by a musical paean to Bohemia (Smetana's *Má Vlast*) should turn out to be in part a comment on life in Portugal. We shall find it, if not entirely acceptable, at least understandable that Sena should view in totally secular terms Mozart's *Requiem* and Mahler's *Resurrection Symphony*, thus inverting and perverting their authors' avowed religious intentions and the well-established consensus of musical critics. We shall, finally, understand why Sena sings, not what is present in Wagner's Liebestod of *Tristan und Isolde*, but what is absent from it, i.e., that Sena should sing what he himself *placed* there; and why he praises Richard Strauss for *failing* to accomplish in *Zarathustra* what he avowedly set out to realize.

In conclusion, it can be said that Sena's unique experience of music does not betray the latter's aesthetic integrity, but neither does it forget that human creation, including the most evanescent and "inhuman" of the arts, can hardly hide humans from sight; can hardly fail to project their image while remaining a mirror on which those who would look upon it see themselves reflected. Thus, the descriptive, imitative and some of the variants of the interpretive mode fundamentally dwell upon the audial substance as such. The other modes, including some aspects of the interpretive, bring to bear upon the musical event a variety of elements extraneous to music as such. Some of these elements—the textual, the programmatic—are inherent to the works of music. Others, while related to the composition in some way, are, properly speaking, outside the immediate realm of the models. Although Sena recognized and acknowledged extrapoetically the self-sufficiency and self-referring nature of music, as a poet he seldom looked upon music as mere highly structured tones floating upon the river of time. This is so even when he poetically celebrates music's "abstracção" ("abstraction"), or the fact that from some works of music "a vida está ausente e alheia" ("life is absent and alien"). He looked upon music as a product of human experience and, as such, a phenomenon highly interpenetrated by life. To search out what is living, what is thought, feeling, joy of life and drama in and around the substance of music, and in himself as he reflects upon and actively participates in the musical events; and then to express all this in viable poetic form, in poems capable of standing by themselves as entities with deep roots in the musical works but with a life entirely of their own, is the fundamental purpose of *Art of Music*. The purpose of the next three chapters of this book is to show how this is done, by discussing representative examples of the three groups of poems identified earlier: miscellaneous, program music and opera, and absolute music.

The poems that will be analyzed at length (about half of the poems of *Art of Music*) have been carefully chosen as examples of the most representative thematic, as well as formal, constants in the book. Although some of the best poems of *Art of Music* are among those I chose to analyze, many of those that have been mentioned only in passing and will again be discussed briefly in the last chapter of this study are also among the best. Therefore, the choice was not made on the basis of my perception of the poems' aesthetic quality.

VI

Miscellaneous Poems

The Miscellaneous group consists of twelve poems. Eight will be discussed in this chapter. They are: "'La Cathédrale engloutie,' by Debussy," "Listening to Songs by Dowland," "Creation, by Haydn," "'Requiem' by Mozart," "*Missa Solemnis*, Op. 123, by Beethoven," "Chopin: An Inventory," "To Piaf," and "Final 'Potpourri.'" Some comments have been made regarding some of the other four poems in this group: "Lieder by Schubert on Texts by Wilhelm Müller," "Listening to Poems by Heine as Lieder by Schumann," "Poor Bruckner," and "*Das Lied von der Erde,* by Mahler." Of these twelve poems, four are based on art songs even though *Das Lied von der Erde*, which I place in this category, may be considered, and has been considered, a "symphony"; three are inspired by works allied to sacred texts, two of them being liturgical; two are derived from general impressions of composers' lives and works; one is a meditation on the biography, personality and, to a lesser extent, the works of a popular singer; the two other poems, the first and last in the book, were implicitly termed "non-metamorphic" by Sena. The reason for this is that these two poems are not based to the same extent as the rest on works of music. They are both largely personal poems. The most ostensibly autobiographical, however, is the opening poem of *Art of Music.*

"'La Cathédrale engloutie,' by Debussy"

Although the title of this 64-line free verse poem places the musical composition in the forefront, the poem is primarily about Sena's personal story associated with this piece of music: how he was inspired seriously, albeit unsuccessfully, to write poetry for the first time upon hearing this musical work on the radio; and how this composition awakened in him the desire to follow a poetical career. Thus, of all the musical compositions that Jorge de Sena poetized, none had as great an impact upon his life as did Debussy's mystic Prelude. As indicated in the subtitle of *Art of Music*, Sena refers to this poem as "prelude." Given the poem's overall function in the book, however, the word "prelude" must not be understood in the Debussyan sense of character piece, but in the pre-Romantic denotation of opening or introductory piece. Or—and Sena's poem lends itself to this—the word "prelude" may encompass these two meanings simultaneously. It is an introduction to *Art of Music*; but it is also a "character piece." In describing poetically his first attempt at writing poetry, Sena also presents his views regarding the interrelation of personal experience and poetry in general, and that of poetry and music in particular. But "'La Cathédrale engloutie,' by Debussy" is much more than this.

Sena begins the poem by stating that he will never forgive the music for having instilled in him the desire to become a poet. He goes on to say that he played the piano, however amateurishly; he even contemplated pursuing an avocational interest in music. The young Sena—he was then 17—had read, since childhood, popular literature (Verne, Salgari), as well as erudite writers (Eça de Queiroz, Teixeira de Pascoaes). He even recalls having read a French book, published by Larousse for children much younger than he was then, about the famous Breton legend of the city of Ys. One day, in 1936 (the date is not part of the poem; it is supplied by Sena extrapoetically), Sena heard on his grandmother's radio Debussy's Prelude on the same legend. The music not only brought back memories of those early readings, but awakened in the young man, right then and there, the desire and resolve to become a poet. Although the poem does not mention this, Sena had probably written poems and most likely had tried his hand at prose fiction prior to this day. But it was upon hearing that piece of music that he was seriously, officially, as it were, born to a career that was to be his for the rest of his life. Sena attempted, upon hearing the music, to write a poem based on that experience. The poem was unsuccessful. "'La Cathédrale engloutie', by Debussy," which bears the composition date 31 December 1964, is, in a sense, the poem that Sena could not write in 1936.

What is extremely important to point out, however, is that Sena's compulsion upon hearing the music was not to snatch the subject matter for the poem out of a vacuum. In other words, he did not try to use the music as a pretext for, say, the creation of arbitrary imagistic tours de force. The music did not—as its mystical programmatic content might readily have lent itself to—induce in the young man any religious thoughts. Nor did the music move him to try to imitate verbally what the piano was playing. Rather, it inspired him to communicate, through the medium of poetry, his composite experience of the music. This composite experience includes particularities, both tonal and programmatic, derived from the inspiring work. Most important of all, the music compelled the young poet to establish some equivalence between purely tonal structures and concrete human experience. The images from the program of Debussy's Prelude merge with other images—derived from early readings, particularly Pascoaes; from Sena's physical surroundings—as the young poet tries to find his way from musical experience to experiential poetry. That is to say, Sena's first poetic encounter with music, although much more Romantic than it was to become later, already was in part what it would be: a humanistic one.

The tenth of Debussy's first set of *Douze Préludes* (1910), *La Cathédrale engloutie* is a piano piece with an a posteriorily determined impressionistic program. The sinful inhabitants of Ys, so the story which has inspired numerous artists goes, drowned when their city was entirely submerged as divine punishment. Debussy's Prelude is an attempt to suggest audially the momentary rising of the Cathedral of Ys—the priests intoning the Gregorian chant, its bells tolling—and the subsequent resumption of the cathedral's centuries-old slumber at the bottom of the sea. Musically, this work is noted for three principal ideas: "one suggestive of plain chant and the organ, as if played by phantom fingers; another representative of the quiet sea; the third like the slow swelling of the waves."[1] These elements are all evoked in Sena's poem. However, what especially grasped the young poet's attention, then as later, was the music's dissonance. The dissonant tones were interpreted thus:

> . . . *eram a imagem tremulante*
> *daquelas fendas ténues que na vida,*
> *na minha e na dos outros, ou havia ou faltavam.*

> (. . . formed the shimmering image
> of the thin fractures that in life,
> my own life or that of others, are there or are missing.)

The rest of the poem is a fusion—and, I might add, an often impressionistic fusion with somewhat blurred contours—of different elements stemming from reminiscences of early childhood readings, dramatic constituents, and autobiographical memories. Sena welds all these elements together and—reflecting upon these adolescent experiences from the adult viewpoint—tells of the impact of this music upon his life; of what it was like to want to write a first serious poem and not be able to; and then he goes on to tell what it has been like to be a poet ever since. The poem is, then, a mini-autobiography of Sena's life as a poet. Sena utilizes two extremely vivid strands of imagery to convey metaphorically the initial impact of the music upon him and his first experience at poetizing. One strand is derived primarily from the program of Debussy's Prelude; the other is a cluster of images associated with a Chinese vase broken by the maid. Both groups of images are thus drawn from experience: *Bildungserlebnis* and vital experience. Both are transformed or metamorphosed into metaphoric substance.

The poet writes of what he felt upon hearing *La Cathédrale engloutie* on the radio:

> Foi como se as águas se me abrissem para ouvir os sinos,
> os cânticos, e o eco das abóbadas, e ver as altas torres
> sobre que as ondas glaucas se espumavam tranquilas.
> Nas naves povoadas de limos e de anémonas, vi que perpassavam
> almas penadas como as do Marão e que eu temia
> em todos os estalidos e cantos escuros da casa.

> (It was as though waters parted and I heard bells,
> canticles, echoing vaults, and saw lofty towers
> beneath gray waves becoming tranquil foam.
> In naves peopled by lichens and anemones, ghosts moved
> like those of Marão that I feared
> in all the cracking and dark corners of the house.)

These parting or opening waters are simultaneously evocative of the dramatic content of the music and constitute a most viable extended metaphor for the unveiling of a new, deep and mysterious dimension of experience for the 17-year-old Sena: the encounter with the mysterious depths of Art. The evocation of the music's program fuses with the "ghosts" derived from Pascoaes's poetry, and are reinforced by the young man's own fears of the unknown. Be it mentioned in passing that, as Mrs. Mécia de Sena has told me in private conversation, Jorge de Sena remained affected by these fears of "cracking and dark corners of the house" all his life. The young man tries to set down—but how impossible!—what memory, fired by music and imagination, can so easily assemble. Sena was unable to express all this in poetry. Only the music, which he then played on the piano, taught it to him but without words. He had to wait another 28 years before he could adequately communicate poetically his complex experience of Debussy's Prelude.

Later on in the poem, the idea of the sea—still associated with the program of the Prelude, but also with autobiographical memories—recurs. Sena writes:

> *Submersa catedral inacessível! Como perdoarei*
> *aquele momento em que do rádio vieste,*
> *solene e vaga e grave, de sob as águas que*
> *marinhas me seriam meu destino perdido?*

> (Sunken, inaccessible cathedral. How can I forgive
> that moment when you emerged from the radio,
> solemn, vague, deep, from those oceanic
> waters that would be my lost destiny?)

This reference to a 'lost maritime destiny' is clearly autobiographical. Sena spent five years in the service: the first year as a cadet in the naval academy, the last four in the army. Sena's life's dream at that time was to pursue a naval career (his father had been a commander in the merchant navy). Upon his dismissal from the navy—which occurred after the eventful journey in the *Sagres*, which took him to different parts of the world and provided him with precious material that he would later transmute into short stories compiled in *The Grand-Captains*—the young man was faced with the choice of two different careers that each of his parents wanted for him. A compromise was reached and the future writer and university professor became a civil engineer. It is interesting to note that Sena and Debussy have something in common regarding their careers. Sena was most likely aware of this as he wrote the above lines. Debussy's parents wanted their son to be a sailor. They changed their minds only when young Claude's precocious musical talents became obvious.[2] It is still more interesting to point out, however, the role of the sea in Sena's life. Young Sena's vocational goals were oriented towards a naval career—towards the sea. He did not succeed in this. However, the work of art that awakened in him the serious desire to become a poet—his true career—is a work of music intimately connected with the sea. No wonder that Sena's poetry, which is not particularly superabundant in Nature imagery, nevertheless abounds in sea imagery.

Still another reference to the sea appears at the end of the poem. Again it evokes both the music's program and Sena's biography, this time in a much broader scope, for the poet's traveling perspective throughout the poem now encompasses all his life up to the moment of writing, 1964. The passage reads in part:

> Ó catedral de sons e de água! Ó música
> sombria e luminosa! Ó vácua solidão
> tranquila! Ó agonia doce e calculada!
> Ah como havia em ti, tão só prelúdio,
> tamanho alvorecer, por sob ou sobre as águas,
> de negros sóis e brancos céus nocturnos?

> (O cathedral of tones and water! O somber
> and luminous music! O hollow and undisturbed
> solitude! O sweet and calculated agony!
> How could there have been in you, only a prelude
> a bursting dawn beneath the waters and above,
> a bursting dawn of dark suns and white nocturnal skies?)

Sena simultaneously addresses Debussy's music and reflects upon his own life as a poet, a life which, as the passage clearly indicates, is inextricably connected with this work. The major thrust of these lines is their emotional and antithetical imagery: "somber and luminous," "sweet and calculated agony," "dark suns," "white nocturnal skies." The imagistic building blocks of the passages are drawn both from the program and Sena's "lost" and then regained destiny ("beneath the waters and above" alludes, respectively, to the submerged cathedral and the sea highways which Sena lost by not fulfilling his career dream). But the images now function primarily as metaphors to express Sena's perception of his life as a poet—both the negative, dark, and painful side, as well as the positive, luminous, and joyous one.

Turning to the second major cluster of images in the poem—the imagery associated with the broken vase—we again notice a transformational process throughout the poem, whereby the images encompass ever wider meanings and ever wider circles of experience. There is at the core of this image cluster the same basic idea that underscored the aquatic images derived from the legend of the city of Ys. We recall that the waters opened up ("It was as though waters parted and I heard bells . . .") before the young poet's eyes as he heard the music. He then poetically plunged into those waters to explore their secrets. As for the vase, it, too, is broken into pieces—to reveal for the poet its inner contents.

190

The first time the poet uses the imagery related to the broken vase is to describe the chaotic or fragmented results of his first attempt at writing a poem on music:

> . . . Escrevi. Como o vaso da China,
> pomposo e com dragões em relevo, que havia na sala,
> e que uma criada ao espanejar partiu,
> e dele saíram lixo e papéis velhos lá caídos,
> as fissuras da vida abriram-se-me para sempre,
> ainda que o sentido de muitas eu só entendesse mais tarde.

> (. . . I wrote. Like the pompous Chinese vase,
> covered with dragons that was in the parlor
> until the maid broke it while dusting,
> and out came trash and old papers,
> and though I only understood later,
> the fissures of life were forever opened before my eyes.)

The object that Sena seizes upon to express metaphorically his experience is a truly appropriate one. The "pompous dragons" suggest the self-assuredness, the arrogance of the 17-year-old; and the pieces of broken vase and its contents are the metaphorical equivalent of the results. One most positive thing results from this experience, however: the "fissures of life," i.e., its most impenetrable dimensions, began to open before the adolescent's eyes even though the meaning of it all he would only understand much later in life. In other words, the poet does not yet see, but he is beginning to learn where to look and how to look.

This image of the broken vase recurs later in the poem as Sena reflects on the broad scope of his poetical career. We note that at the end of this passage there is a clear intent on Sena's part to integrate once again the images of the vase with recollection of the music's program. This underlines the notion that, although the poet's mind and imagination do travel about, their wanderings are always within the gravitational sphere of the music:

> Passei a ser esta soma teimosa do que não existe:
> exigência, anseio, dúvida, e gosto
> de impor aos outros a visão profunda,
> não a visão que eles fingem,
> mas a visão que recusam:
> esse lixo do mundo e papéis velhos
> que sai de um jarrão exótico que a criada partiu,
> como a catedral se iria em acordes que ficam
> na memória das coisas como um livro infantil
> de lendas de outras terras que não são a minha.

191

(I became the stubborn aggregate of what doesn't exist:
demand, yearning, doubt, the taste
of imposing on others deep vision,
not the vision people pretend having
but the one they resist:
the world's trash and old papers
that fall from a big exotic vase the maid broke,
as the cathedral would vanish in chords staying
in our memory of things like a child's book
with its legends of lands not my own.)

We need but recall what has been said about Sena's poetry in earlier chapters to realize that many of the fundamental concepts expressed in this poem are repeatedly treated elsewhere: the poetical career, and life itself, being shaped to a large extent by destiny ("Soube-me sempre a destino a minha vida" — "My life always smacked to me of destiny"; "Wanderer," *I*, p. 63); the desire to "impose" his humanistic view of life on others (cf. "Pamphlet," *I*, p. 112); the use of imagery of debris and trash derived from real experiences and used as far-reaching metaphors ("Cubicle," *I*,p. 44; "Sewer," *I*, p. 93); the dark and lonely side of being a writer (cf. "Solitude Visits Me," *I*, p. 208); and this view counterbalanced by the sun-bright joys of being a creator ("One Who has Seen Much," *III*, p. 50). In connection with Sena's propensity to turn real impressions into poetically viable metaphors—a tendency which, as this poem indicates, begins very early indeed—one is reminded of Goethe's remarks in *Dichtung und Wahrheit*. "And thus began that habit," writes the author of *Faust*, "from which I could not break away my whole life through—the habit of turning into an image, into a poem, whatever delighted or troubled, or otherwise occupied me . . ."[3]

Sena presents in "'La Cathédrale engloutie,' by Debussy" not only a dramatization of his struggle to become a poet, but the kind of poetry he pursued from the earliest stages of his career. From his first attempt to write serious poetry to the very last poems he penned, Sena was a poet *engagé* with life. He always drew impressions from one sphere of experience and made them applicable to another. His was always a poetry of metamorphosis of reality—not a type of transformation that casts a disfiguring mask upon the face of reality, but one that heightens vital experience by magnifying the way it appears to us and the voice with which it speaks to us. This poem also establishes the autobiographical tenor of much of *Art of Music*. It foreshadows the intromission of Sena's self in many other poems of the book; it points to the appropriation by him of someone else's artistic language as instrument to express *his* own story. If there is an ever-present impulse in *Art of Music*—indeed, in all of Sena's poetry, as has been repeatedly pointed out—it is the impulse to render personal everything he poetizes.

This poem sets the philosophical and aesthetic path to be followed in the other poems of *Art of Music*. Later on in life Sena was to tell of his encounter with musical works much the same way that he attempted to tell it in 1936. He could not have done so in those early days because life had not built up and consolidated within him a plentiful reservoir of experiences; he had not developed the artistic know-how that would allow him to sort out and express what he intuitively already perceived in a piece of music. This poem, then, is a true and fitting prelude or introduction to what one finds in *Art of Music*. But it is also a complete and coherent spiritual and poetical autobiography. No wonder, therefore, that the poet used it as his opening piece even though, chronologically, there are several poems in the book that preceded it and, on the basis of the chronological order by composers, it could have been one of the last.

"Listening to Songs by Dowland"

This is the second poem of *Art of Music* and the first in the series that Sena calls "metamorphoses." Of the four poems inspired by art songs (again, for convenience's sake, I am including in this category the poem inspired by *Das Lied von der Erde*), this is the most atypical, for here, unlike in the other three, the poet pays relatively little attention to the poetic texts—or so it appears. In "Listening to Songs by Dowland" Sena seems to concentrate, almost exclusively, upon one "artistic" constituent: the structure. By "structure" Sena means, undoubtedly, the structure of the poems and the structure of the music which, in Dowland, are for the most part one and the same. Referring to two of Dowland's songs, Walter R. Davis writes: "The two examples of 'Shall I sue' and 'Flow my teares' suggest that the structure of the poems Dowland set and the structure of his music are inseparable. Just as the poems present one idea elaborated through several emotional variations to a powerful climax, so too his typical musical structure consists of a single motif that is varied or expanded until it reaches its final and most compelling form."[4]

In the note to the poem, Sena writes: "The oldest of the series, this poem came to me after listening on the radio, unexpectedly, to a recording by the tenor Peter Pears singing works by the great English composer of the end of the 16th and first quarter of the 17th century, who was named 'lutenist' of King James I, in the same year (1616) in which Shakespeare and Cervantes died" (*II*, p. 235). The British tenor

Peter Pears did record many of Dowland's songs on several occasions; yet, prior to 1960, the year in which Sena's poem was written, he had recorded only three songs by John Dowland, accompanied by Benjamin Britten on the piano and Julian Bream on the lute.[5] These songs were issued in an album (London LL 1532, 12 in., 1956) which includes works from the Elizabethan Age and the present century. Of the 19 songs in this album, Sena's poem could refer only to the three by Dowland therein contained: "I saw my lady weep," "Awake, sweet love," and "In darkness let me dwell." In subject matter and mood these songs range, respectively, from the joyous awareness of love being reciprocated, to the tender love song, to the expression of almost tragic melancholy. "O let me living, living die, till death do come" is the last line of the last song. These moods are evoked by Sena even though the poem does not refer to any of the texts specifically: "a melodia que ondulante toca / falsamente a emoção"; "sobretudo uma melancolia" ("the melody that, undulating, plays / falsely the too prompt emotion"; "especially a melancholy").

Sena's poem, besides these subtle allusions to the textual content of the songs, concentrates on what he terms the "structure" hidden under the melody. According to the poem, this structure embodies the whole meaning and essence of the songs. The poet's perception of, and attention to, the music not only bypasses the melody and harmony—"que progride arguta / suscitando pretensas marginais ideias" ("that progresses, sharp, / arousing pretended marginal ideas"—but the rhythm as well—"que é permanência / enganadora do que flui, dissolve" ("that is permanence, / the deceiver of what flows and dissolves"). Of course, the poet is knowingly engaging in a contradiction. He does not totally discard these elements. Indeed, he translates them into human terms. But it is most obvious that he does not dwell on them. False ready-made emotions, a harmony that awakens marginal ideas, a rhythm that bespeaks deceptive permanence—all these are passed by hurriedly; they are fleeting images on either margin of the river of music. For the poet is only intent on relentlessly pursuing that "nítida estrutura" ("clean structure"); he must stay with it; he cannot allow any distractions to sway his attention.

As his perceptive faculties become aware of the different elements of the music and refuse to dwell on them, the poet comes, time and again, to an element of the musical experience which in other poems he can seldom resist, but which here he feels he must: the extramusical realm. We have already seen that the harmony occasioned suggestions of ideas. Now the poet writes:

> *. . . e outras eras e lugares*
> *ocorrem pressurosos: mas não ouço*
> *nada de antigo ou novo, dissipado ou*
> *presente ainda no que resta em mim.*
> *Apenas ouço uma estrutura: . . .*

> (. . . and other eras and places
> quickly rush to me: but I hear
> nothing old or new, dissipated or
> still present in what remains in me.
> I hear only a structure . . .)

The rejection of these elements that would connect the music with the human sphere—the texts per se (which are only subtly alluded to), the historical suggestions awakened by the music and then immediately suppressed—creates the impression that Sena is experiencing Dowland's songs on the plane of a single element: the interaction of the texts with Dowland's music. It seems that the poet has not only ousted all the other components that together make up these songs, but he is especially keen on severing or not acknowledging any ties between Dowland's songs and human reality. This is far from being the case, however.

It is in the last eight lines of this 20-line free verse poem that the poet and the reader find what the former has been so obsessively pursuing: the "clean structure" actually undergoes a metamorphic process and becomes a magnificent vision; the sense of hearing progressively yields to the sense of sight; the phonic mirror reflects a visual image:

> *Apenas ouço uma estrutura: um*
> *gesto silencioso, um movimento,*
> *e sobretudo uma melancolia.*
> *Uma estrutura: como um deus que a face*
> *encosta pensativo à mão e o cotovelo*
> *ao joelho soerguido, e assim, medita. Em quê?*
> *Como é difícil ser-se humana! El' sabe.*

> (I hear only a structure: a
> silent gesture, a movement
> and especially a melancholy.
> A structure: Like a brooding god who
> leans his face on his hand and his elbow
> on a slightly raised knee, meditating. On what?
> How difficult it is to be human! He knows.)

All the "human" elements that one felt were being discarded, passed by, at the beginning of the poem are accumulated in these last lines: a gesture, a movement, melancholy, a divine figure meditating on how difficult it is to be human. Whose figure is being evoked here? Dowland's? A personification of all that is human in Dowland's songs? Is it the poet's self-awareness of his own demiurgic image meditating on Dowland's compositions? All of these at the same time? The poem's ambiguous nature on this point provides the best possible answer by providing no definitive answer at all. This ambiguity endows the songs with a double function for the poet: they are windows through which the poet looks; they constitute a phonic mirror, progressively metamorphosed into a visual one, upon which the poet sees himself reflected, as well as everything that this music means to him. Upon reading the above analysis, Mrs. Mécia de Sena asked: Could Jorge de Sena be thinking of Rodin's *The Thinker*, even if he was doing so subconsciously? The similarity between the image that Sena "visually" perceives embedded in Dowland's songs and Rodin's statue more than justifies this question.

The very structure of this poem, with its accumulation of "human" elements at the end, suggests that one has to delve into the "depths" of music to find its true meaning at the "bottom"; that in doing so one looks for one's fellow man, as well as for oneself. Finally, it suggests that, in this poem, Sena's *perception* and *pursuit* of a "clear structure" and his *creation* of one—are one and the same. Stated in other terms, what Sena pursued all along was his own poem, and he found it at the end.

The very structure of this poem is, therefore, a perfect analogue to Sena's experience of the essence of Dowland's songs, as well as of his poetic expression of that experience. The poet's humanistic experience of music follows a rather more oblique or circuitous route in this poem than it does in others; but it is nevertheless present and is presented with force. Sena captures the solidity of human presence in the fluidity of musical form. Language alchemizes this fluidity and transforms it into a visual image replete with meanings. A sculpture, as it were, emerges from tones, thus evoking the traditional association between musical form and the plastic arts. Sena seems intent on applying to music, using the medium of poetry, the classic story of the image asleep in the amorphous block of marble until the sculptor disengages it and gives it form. Here it is the poet who performs the miracle. The figure in Sena's poem not only acquires form, but is actually endowed with the highest attributes of human life: thought, feelings, and concern for other fellow humans. Perhaps no poem of *Art of Music* is more deserving of the epithet "metamorphic" than

"Listening to Songs by Dowland." Certainly not many of them convey Sena's humanistic approach to music so subtly, so effectively, and so beautifully.

"Creation, by Haydn"

Sena's brand of humanism versus the religious philosophy embodied in Haydn's *The Creation* is the fundamental thematic focus of this poem. "Creation, by Haydn" is inspired by a composition that Sena both admired for its artistic excellence and repudiated for its philosophical content. In the note to the poem he writes: "This poem was written in the auditorium of the London School of Economics, where my friends Suzette and Helder Macedo had taken me to attend a benefit (and horribly amateurish) execution (that's the word) of the magnificent oratorio which has always been, among those great baroque and rococo choral-symphonic works . . . one of those I have admired most" (*II*, p. 236). However much the poet may admire *The Creation* for other reasons, he is not moved by the content of a work that embodies a supernaturalistic view of life while implicitly relegating this earthly reality to a secondary position.

For in "Creation, by Haydn" it is the content of the libretto, more so than Haydn's music per se, that draws and retains the poet's attention. Sena only makes the vaguest of references to the music through the verbs "compor" ("compose") and "cantar" ("sing"). But in the context of the poem even these words could be considered allusions to the verbal content. The fact that the poet does not dwell ostensibly on the music (and he may fail to do so in part because of the "horribly amateurish execution" he spoke of in the note) may account for the somewhat conflicting attitudes regarding *The Creation* as expressed in the note and in the poem itself.

The Creation, where Haydn is said to have striven to effect a masterpiece worthy of Genesis, is based on the Bible and on Baron von Swieten's German translation of a Poem compiled by Lidley from Milton's *Paradise Lost*. The oratorio consists of three sections rather than the traditional two of Italian oratorios. The first and second parts celebrate the six days' work culminating in the appearance of man, the "crown of creation." The third part—which is really an appendix to the entire body of the work—sings of the bliss that Adam and Eve experienced prior to the Fall. Sena's poem, although following primarily the textual mode, also exemplifies the imitative mode to some degree. Not only is the poem divided into three strophes, but even part of the content of each of its sections parallels or matches the thematic development of the libretto. Thus, the first strophe evokes the Creation out of Chaos ("cânticos do criar do mundo"—"canticles on creating the world"); in the second strophe the human pair makes its appearance ("e o par humano pisava sem pecado / o jardim paradisíaco"—"that human pair strode without sin the paradisal garden") (trans. by George Monteiro). In the third strophe, however, the poet expresses his inability (and unwillingness) to accept the supernatural views embodied in the work ("não podemos"—"we cannot"), whereas in the third section of the oratorio the angel Uriel tells about Adam and Eve as the latter express their thanks to the Lord.

Martin Stern has called the libretto of Haydn's oratorio a portrait of an era. He writes that, "If one reads the letters of gratitude and the reports on those performances which were sent to Haydn, and circulated and/or published by listeners and critics, one begins to get the impression that in this libretto the wishes and dreams of a whole generation were realized."[6] Despite its changes in fortune throughout the years as far as critical opinion is concerned, Haydn's oratorio now rivals in popularity Handel's *Messiah*. This popularity is due as much to Haydn's artistry as it is to the religious content of the work. By the turn of our century, says Martin Stern, this eighteenth-century work could still move "thousands and thousands of listeners to tears of emotion" (op. cit., p. 344). Haydn himself was religiously moved by the text he set to music. G. A. Griesinger relates the story that when Emperor Francis II, on the occasion of the performance of *The Seasons*, asked Haydn which of the two oratorios he preferred, the composer replied: "*The Creation* . . . in *The Creation* angels speak and tell of God; but in *The Seasons* it is only Simon talking."[7]

Two entirely different world views are in conflict in this poem: the one expressed by *The Creation* and the one espoused by Sena. The latter must always be kept in mind when reading the poem. The poet's reference to "estes homens que podiam escrever da Criação" ("those men who could write about Creation") is not limited to Haydn, but encompasses the Biblical writers, von Swieten, Lidley, and possibly even Milton, as well as the entire generations of people these men represented. These men could soar above the human condition and sing of Biblical Creation and paradisal bliss. The poet can understand and perhaps even admire ("Felizes estes homens . . ." — "Happy those men . . .") the faith and aspirations embodied in their works. But he cannot—not now—identify with, nor accept, the philosophical view that gave impetus to their flight. Theirs is an art whose content turns its back on life, on their own human suffering. Sena's repudiation of their philosophical outlook extends beyond his non-belief in sin, i.e., his rejection of a religious ethics of morality. It encompasses a much wider humanistic perspective: the poet's desire—as exemplified by all his poetry—to immerse himself in the here and how of true human reality rather than take refuge in the mythical past; his commitment to dwell artistically on the human condition, no matter how painful this may be, rather than turn his back on it. The poet implicitly offers faith in man in place of faith in God.

This poem is, therefore, as much an implicit expression of Sena's own secular world view as it is an overt repudiation of the religious view crystallized in *The Creation*, a work which he otherwise deeply admired. Again, Sena poetically bypasses his extrapoetically expressed admiration for this work as artistic realization in order to concentrate on what to him is the work's more pressing dimension: its human implications. But "Creation, by Haydn" can be read as more than a poetic dramatization of the conflict between Sena's individual secular humanism and the religious perspective expressed in Haydn's oratorio. By using the third person plural in the first line of the poem ("Felizes estes homens que podiam . . ." — "Happy those men who could . . .") and the first person plural in the last ("não podemos"—"we cannot"), Sena not only views "these men" as the spokespersons for their era, but places himself—using perhaps a bit too much liberty here—as the spokesman for his. The plural "we" means the poet in collaboration with, or as a spokesman for, his fellow humanists. The first person plural becomes especially important in this poem in light of the fact that it is relatively rare in all of Sena's poetry. The difference and distance between "their" view and "our" view, their "past" and our "present," is further accentuated by the strategic use of verbal tenses. Nearly all the verbs in this 12-line free-verse poem are in the imperfect: *podiam, era belo, era bom, era perfeito, o par humano pisava* (*could, was lovely, was good, was perfect, that human pair strode*). However, the very last word of the poem is a verb in the present tense: it bespeaks a *now* as opposed to a *then*; it is, furthermore, in the negative: it negates the pastness explicit in those other verbs:

> *Nós nem mesmo em momentos únicos,*
> *raríssimos, epifânicos*
> *—e não só por não crermos no pecado—,*
> *não podemos.*

(Not even in moments that are unique, of the rarest kind,
Epiphanic—and not only because we do not believe in sin—
Can we so sing.)

(trans. George Monteiro)

In "Creation, by Haydn" Sena has both dramatized the conflict between his and *The Creation's* brand of humanism *and* encouraged the reader to view the poem as dealing with a wider conflict between two eras, two universal modes of seeing the world, two stages in the spiritual development of humankind. Is there a note of sadness in the "não podemos," i.e., in the poet's confessed inability to share in the faith of those men of the past? I believe not. This is one instance in which a confessed 'weakness' and an apparent sadness are really a sign of strength and a sigh of joy.

"'Requiem' by Mozart"

"'Requiem' by Mozart" and *"Missa Solemnis*, Op. 123, by Beethoven" are the only other poems in the Miscellaneous group that are inspired by compositions associated with religious texts. In both poems the fundamental theme is the conflict between secular and religious humanism. Sena's longest poem on Mozartian compositions is based on the *Requiem*, K. 626, the composer's final and unfinished work. Mozart is said to have completed only a little over half the Mass. His disciple Süssmayr, in addition to supplying the orchestration for the sections already written, provided the music for the last three: The Sanctus, the Benedictus, and the Agnus Dei. Sena refers to this fact in the note to the poem; but in the poem itself he looks upon the entire *Requiem* as Mozart's own work. The poem is composed of four sonnets, each with a different rhyme scheme, the last sonnet containing fifteen as opposed to the normal fourteen lines. As I stated before, the exploitation of word music in this poem is one of the richest, if not the richest, in *Art of Music*. It is also one of the most emotional poems in the book. Indeed, it may be said to be dripping with emotion. But it is not raw, unintellectualized emotion. The evocative and exclamatory lines bespeak an incendiary emotion always allied to an intellectualized perception of the music, not to unanalyzed sensuality. Perhaps the word music in the poem stems from its emotional nature. It is not an attempt to imitate what the music is doing.

The poem draws upon and fuses into an organic whole information derived from four major sources of inspiration. Three are related to the composition. They are: Mozart's music as music, i.e., the acoustic substance more or less independent of the liturgy; the text of the Eucharist itself; and biographical elements connected with Mozart's death. The fourth sphere or source of inspiration has to do with the power of music in moving the human spirit and is inspired by Fray Luis de León's ode "A Francisco Salinas" ("To Francisco

Salinas''), itself a poem inspired by music. Sena quotes as one of the epigraphs to *Art of Music* the following lines from Fray Luis de León's poem:

> *Oh desmayo dichoso!*
> *oh muerte que das vida! oh dulce olvido!*
> *durase en tu reposo*
> *sin ser restituido*
> *jamás aqueste bajo y vil sentido!*

> (O blessed ecstasy!
> O life-giving death! O sweet forgetfulness!
> could I but rest in your bosom
> without being brought
> ever again to this low and mean state!)

Although the spirit of these lines might apply to other poems of *Art of Music* as well, it fits best the work under consideration.

Sena indicates in the note to the poem that the latter is partly based ''not only upon the performance of the *Requiem* of Karl Richter, directing the Munscher-Bach Chorus and Orchestra, but also upon the bitterly painful words spoken by Mozart'' (*II*, p. 237). These words of Mozart, which Sena quotes in part in his own Portuguese translation, are contained in one of the last letters written by the composer. In it he refers to the *Requiem* and to his imminent death. This letter of September 1791, written two months before the composer's death, is thought to have been addressed to Da Ponte in response to the latter's suggestion that Mozart should leave Vienna and move to England. The part of the letter quoted in Sena's note to the poem is given here in an English translation by E. G. Dent from the original Italian. Mozart writes:

> I know from what I suffer that the hour is come; I am at the point of death; I have come to an end before having had the enjoyment of my talent. Life was indeed so beautiful, my career began under such fortunate auspices; but one cannot change one's own destiny. No one can measure his own days, one must resign oneself, it will be as providence wills and so I finish my death-song ⟨the *Requiem*⟩; I must not leave it incomplete.[8]

As for the liturgy itself, the first sonnet probably corresponds in part to the first movement of the *Requiem*, Introit and Kyrie. I say *probably* because there is only one element, as we shall see, that could be related to these liturgical items. The same doubt is not raised, however, regarding the second sonnet. It relates unquestionably to the

Dies Irae. In the third sonnet there is an unequivocal allusion to the Offertory. The fourth sonnet contains an implied reference to the Agnus Dei, the last item of the Mass. What is important to stress from the outset is that "'Requiem' by Mozart" always reflects an unecclesiastic view of the liturgy. Indeed, the latter's symbolic meaning—whenever it is evoked in the poem—is inverted or humanized. By the same token, when Sena draws inspiration from or intertextually engages the ode "To Francisco Salinas," it is once again the strictly human import implicit in the ode, not its religious implication, that wins his attention.

Turning to the discussion of the first sonnet, we note that such is the feeling aroused in the poet by Mozart's music (and here it seems to be the music as such, i.e., the tonal event quite independently of any other considerations) that the latter is perceived, right from the beginning, as rising from the human to the cosmic level but maintaining, nevertheless, indissoluble ties with the human sphere. To the poet, Mozart's music projects itself into an other-wordliness that is still of this world. Sena adapts a mystical language reminiscent of Fray Luis de León's, not to suggest the music's disengagement from the human sphere, but to stress its power in elevating the human spirit. As the music rises, it carries with it the human spirit, which is represented by the "potente amor / que em teu ouvir-te queda esvoaçante" ("potent desire / that hovers about you as you sound").

There is in this sonnet a possible allusion to the principal object of the Requiem Mass, which is, according to the Reverend Nikolaus Gihr, "to implore for the suffering souls eternal rest in the bosom of God and the light of heavenly glory."[9] This light is part of the Introit: "Requiem aeternam dona eis." The notable difference between the liturgical symbolism of "light" in the Introit and the "luz" ("light") in Sena's sonnet is that in the latter the "light" is materialized by its association with "steel":

> *Ouço-te lá pousada, equidistante*
> *desse clarão cuja doçura é de aço.*

> (I hear you there, set down
> as far from sweetly steeled clarity.)

I shall return to this image later. The rest of the paraphraseable content of this sonnet bears a greater resemblance to Fray Luis de León's ode than it does to elements of the liturgy. This similarity is particularly noticeable in the "rise" of the music as perceived and felt by the two poets:

Fray Luis:

> *Trespasa el aire todo*
> *hasta llegar a la más alta esfera.*

> (Pierces the air
> until it reaches the highest sphere.)

Sena:

> *Ouço-te, ó música, subir aguda*
> *à convergente solidão gelada.*

> (I hear you, music, sharply rising
> to convergent solitude of ice.)

In Fray Luis's ode, Salina's music, which is human music, bears the soul ("la alma") upwards, until the latter reaches the "highest sphere" and there the soul hears another kind of music—"música que es de todas la primera" ("music that is first among all"). This is cosmic music or "música de cielos" ("heavenly music"), as Fray Luis calls it in a passage of *Exposición del Libro de Job* (xxxviii, 37) (*Explanation of the Book of Job*). From the auditory human plane the music has risen to the silence of the spheres; it has become merged with the All. The soul's feeling when this happens is one of mystic swoon, which Fray Luis expresses in the lines that Sena quotes as epigraph. Yet, the soul does not forget or forego, as one might expect, the human sphere, as the next five lines of "To Francisco Salinas" clearly indicate:

> *A aqueste bien os llamo*
> *gloria del apolíneo sacro coro,*
> *amigos a quien amo*
> *sobre todo tesoro*
> *que todo lo demás es triste lloro.*

> (To this good,
> the glory of the Apollonian sacred chorus,
> I summon you,
> friends whom I love
> above all treasures
> for all else is sorrowful weeping.)

What the cosmic music brings out of the poet is the desire to share the state he is experiencing with his fellow humans. He does not experience a severing of ties with them, but rather deepens those ties through the love enkindled, originally, by Salinas's music.

Sena's sonnet expresses basically similar ideas with regard to Mozart's music, albeit without the eschatological implications of Fray Luis's ode. Mozart's music, Sena suggests, has become transfigured to his, the poet's, perception of it; it has become audible more to the inner than the outer ear. But it remains enveloped in the love that Mozart imparted to it. It is this human love that gives it soaring wings. It has become a species of cosmic music—again without religious overtones—not because of any extra-human qualities or even due to its association with an item of the Mass—but because of the human love that it harbors and in turn is capable of awakening in the poet. The latter feels compelled to share this love with others, as Fray Luis felt compelled to share his. Hence "'Requiem' by Mozart."

This first sonnet—which is the most detached from the Eucharist and the excerpt from Mozart's letter—celebrates the mystical power of Mozart's music as music. However, to understand what Sena is and is not celebrating we have to distinguish between two types of mysticism: religious and secular. The first is divinely inspired; the second is humanly inspired. One leads to God; the other points to the direction of man. As Charles T. Smith points out, "When people say a composer's music is divinely inspired they mean that it provides a profoundly moving experience wherein they are lifted out of themselves by a spiritual force emanating from above" (*Music and Reason*, p. 45). St. John Chrysostom, too, spoke of this power of music when he wrote, "Nothing raises the soul and gives it soaring wings and frees it from the earth, nothing so frees it from the bonds of the flesh and makes it philosophise, . . . as music and the rhythm of divine song."[10] Secular mysticism, on the other hand, stems from music's ability to transport us, not away from ourselves and into a world beyond, but toward a tighter union with the cosmos and the depths of our own being. Music's mysterious human powers are sung—not the power of God. The spiritual uplift produced by music is common to Sena and Fray Luis de León. But music leads the two into quite different realms. Fray Luis's path leads to God; Sena's leads to man's discovery of his own spiritual self, by broadening man's consciousness of that self. "Music demonstrates its mystical qualities when it extends the areas of our consciousness and broadens our life experiences. A spiritual quality exists in music when as a result of having listened to it we experience life more keenly than we had ever been capable of previously. The mysterious element, of course, is in us" (Julius Portnoy, op. cit., p. 248). Fray Luis's "alma" ("soul") rises toward *heaven;* Sena's spirit rises toward the *sky.* The Portuguese poet stresses this contrast between heaven and sky with the phrases "convergente solidão gelada" ("convergent solitude of ice"), "vácuo centro" ("hollow center") "doçura é de aço" ("sweetly steeled"). In other words, the poet emphasizes that his is the "heaven" of astronomy, of materiality. "Aço" ("steel") bridges the gap between this "heaven" and the earth. Indeed, the poet suggests that his "heaven" is weighed down with "steel." It sinks toward the earth because it is one with it.

As noted earlier, there is no doubt that the second sonnet of the poem corresponds to, and clearly evokes, the *Dies Irae*, the second section of the *Requiem*. The exclamatory lines—"Ó música da morte, ó vozes tantas . . . / Ó música da carne amargurada" ("O music of death, o voices so many . . . / O music of flesh made bitter")—are still stylistically reminiscent of Fray Luis de León's ode, though. As far as the subject of death itself is concerned, Sena is referring to the general idea of death embodied in the traditional *Dies Irae*, but more specifically still to Mozart's own death, in accordance with the composer's reference to the *Requiem* as his own "death-song." The lines "Ó música da mente espedaçada / de tanto ter sonhado o que entretece" ("Music of the mind so often broken / by having dreamt what it halfway weaves") most probably constitute an allusion to Mozart's reported state of exhaustion as he penned his last song. Several other allusions throughout the sonnet evoke other biographical elements. Indications that Sena steers clear of any ecclesiastic implications—indeed, that he secularizes all religious notions of the *Dies Irae*—are scattered throughout the sonnet also. First, the poet relates the *Dies Irae* to the "carne amargurada" ("flesh made bitter"), i.e., to Mozart's physical suffering and death, not to his fear of facing the wrath of God. An equally overt secularization of this item of the Mass is contained in the last two lines:

Amor que as asas sobre o corpo nu
fecha tranquilas no possuir da sorte.

(Love that folds its wings calmly
over the naked limbs embraced by destiny.)

Isn't Sena suggesting that it is the pagan god of love, Cupid, who presides at Mozart's death? that it is fate that takes his breath away? These lines probably constitute an interpretation of Mozart's words—"one cannot change one's own destiny"—in totally pagan terms, i.e., destiny as *fatum* and not God's will.

In the third sonnet, which corresponds to and evokes the Offertory (Domine Jesu and Hostias), Sena dwells both on the symbolic meaning of this section of the liturgy, as well as on the music as such.

The Offertory is the moment when the bread and wine are transubstantiated into the Body and Blood of the Lord. The first quartet of the sonnet reads:

> Além do falso ou verdadeiro, além
> do abstracto e do concreto, além da forma
> e do conceito, além do que transforma
> contrários pares noutros pares também
> . . .
> (Beyond false or true, beyond
> abstract and concrete, beyond form
> and conceit, beyond what transforms
> contrary pairs into other pairs
> . . .)

As the Reverend John Cuthbert Hedley states, the Offertory "is a conversion, or change, of one thing into another, which is outside of the order of nature, and it is the only one of its kind whether in the natural order or the supernatural."[11] Sena's third sonnet is the most iconoclastic of the poem. It suggests that Mozart's music, a human creation involving the transformation of tones into meaningful musical forms, transcends the transubstantiation itself; that *it* is the only one of its kind. This music, the poet goes on to imply, rises above all mystico-religious meaning to that plane Sena spoke of in the first sonnet: a realm reserved for music which, in and of itself, is capable of simultaneously partaking of the terrestrial and cosmic spheres, and which is perceivable by the outer as well as the inner ear—"lá onde ouvir e não-ouvir se igualam" ("where to hear or not are the same").

The Reverend Nikolaus Gihr writes that "In Requiem Masses the position of Agnus Dei /is the moment during which/ we twice implore from the Divine Sacrificial Lamb 'rest' for the suffering souls from their pains and torments, and the third time we implore for them 'eternal rest' in heaven" (op. cit., p. 718). In Sena's fourth sonnet, Mozart's death continues to be conceived in strictly naturalistic terms and in relation to his Art. His death, the poet suggests, is as much a beginning as it is an end; it is as much a birth as it is a death. That is why Sena brings together the themes of death and propagation of life, employing quite explicit sexual terminology:

> Tudo se cala em ti como na vida.
> Tudo palpita e flui como no leito
> em que se morre ou ama, já desfeito
> o abraço do momento que, sustida
> a sensação da posse conseguida,
> a carne pára a ejacular-se atenta.

(In you as in life, everything falls silent.
Everything pulses and flows as in the bed
where we die or love, already dissolved
the momentary embrace in which flesh will end
by attentively ejaculating, having sustained
the feeling of consummated possession.)

Having imparted so much of his being into his "death-song," and being the superb artist he is, Mozart *rests* assured that he will go on being reborn in his Art. His feeling of *peace* stems from the knowledge that, although he dies a corporeal death, his spirit will go on living in his music. This shall happen even if Mozart the man should one day be forgotten. But no paraphrase can begin to convey the power and beauty of this passage:

> *Tudo é prazer em ti. Quanto alimenta*
> *esta glória de existir, trazida*
> *a cada instante só do instante ser-se*
> *reflui em ti, liberto, puro, aflante,*
> *certeza e segurança de conter-se*
> *na criação virtual o renascer-se*
> *agora e sempre pelo tempo adiante,*
> *mesmo esquecido. Em ti, o conhecer-se*
> *deste possível é a paz do amante.*

(In you everything is pleasure. What feeds
this glory of existing, carried
each instant by life's being an instant only,
flows again in you, swelling, pure, free:
the certainty and sureness that being born again
is contained in virtual creation
now and in the time that will never cease
even when forgotten. In you, knowledge
of this possibility is the lover's peace.)

The last line of this sonnet—an extra line, for it is the sonnet's fifteenth—is a fitting finale for this poem. Its three most significant words are "possível," "paz" and "amante" ("possibility," "peace" and "lover"). They bespeak Mozart's *hope* for the future glory of his music; *peace* in that certainty; and *love*—the love he imparted to the music and which the poet receives. The poem ends with an appropriate allusion to the sexual act, the supreme moment of postcoital repose. Mozart's *Requiem* was not, after all, his death-song: it was his last *petite mort*-song—one from which there is awakening.

Although Sena's poem is divided into four more or less self-contained sonnets, it possesses thematic unity: it integrates its four most important sources of inspiration by wholly translating them into humanistic terms. The poet goes to the extreme of removing from the liturgy all mystical sense and replacing it with human meaning. In essence, Sena re-creates Mozart's *Requiem* in his, Sena's, own terms. In a sense, the composition becomes Sena's *Requiem*, but one possessing a totally different meaning from that traditionally associated with Requiem Masses. To Sena, in " 'Requiem' by Mozart" as elsewhere, the most sacred entity in the universe, indeed the only sacred one, is man. All religious mystical symbolism, all supernaturalistic notions, crumble before the majestic presence of human life and human creation. Although it is inspired by a composition that deals exclusively with death, an outpouring of vitality, of emotion, of hope, suffuses the entire poem. It is not a poem about death, but about survival. It is a celebration of Art's—not only Mozart's, but all true Art's—inherent power to conquer oblivion. This is an idea that has been expressed innumerable times: from Horace's "Exigi monumentum aere perennius," to Ricardo Reis's "Seguro assento na coluna firme" ("Firmly I rest upon this firm column"). Jorge de Sena expresses it again in the presence of death itself. One wonders whether Jorge de Sena was also thinking of his own death and his own art as he wrote the last sonnet of "'Requiem' by Mozart."

"*Missa Solemnis, Op. 123, by Beethoven*"

This poem exemplifies the interpretive, descriptive and personal modes. Sena begins with a critical assertion regarding the general character of the composition, proceeds with references to specific elements of the musical work that he deems confirmatory of his critical statement, and then goes on to offer his own interpretation of the meaning of the music. This essay-like development of "*Missa Solemnis*" also characterizes other poems of *Art of Music*, as we shall see. Sena's critical comment—expressed in the first two lines of this 31-line free-verse poem—parallels the opinion of many musical critics regarding this work, which Beethoven himself is said to have considered his greatest:

> *Não é solene esta música,*
> *ao contrário do nome e da intenção.*

> (This music is not solemn,
> contrary to its name and its intention.)

> (trans. F. G. Williams)

One of the most controversial of Beethoven's works, the *Missa Solemnis* (composed 1818-1823) indeed has been considered to embody a dramatic or theatrical mood instead of the expected and more proper liturgical solemnity explicit in its title and inherent in the purpose for which it was composed: the enthronement of Archduke Rudolph of Austria as Archbishop of Olmutz (Moravia), scheduled for March 8, 1820. Beethoven's Masses (the much earlier C Major Mass and the *Solemnis*) are "frankly concert pieces, and more effective outside than inside a church," opines Charles Rosen.[12] Paul Nettl is of the same opinion when he writes, referring to the *Missa Solemnis*, that "The importance of music is so overwhelming that it places the liturgy in the background."[13]

The elements and characteristics of Beethoven's composition that Sena mentions, and with which he supports his critical statement, are contained in these lines:

> *Clamores portentosos, violência obsessiva*
> *(por sob apelos doces, lacrimosos)*
> *de um ritmo orquestral continuado,*
> *tanta paixão gritada, tanto contraponto*
> *que teimosamente impede que na tessitura*
> *das vozes e dos timbres se interponha hiato*
> *não de silêncio mas de um fio só*
> *de melodia, por onde a morte*
> *penetre interrompendo a vida.*

> (Portentous clamors, obsessive violence
> (from under sweet appeals, lacrimonious)
> of an orchestral rhythm continued,
> so much passion shouted, so much counterpoint
> which stubbornly impedes that in the tessitura
> of the voices and timbres be interposed a hiatus
> not of silence but of one strain only
> of melody, through which death
> may penetrate interrupting life.)

In these lines Sena continues to echo opinions similar to those expressed by musical critics. John N. Burk refers to the *Missa's* "intense feeling, . . . not designed with any thought of average receptivity."[14] Sena's reference to the composition's textural thickness could be construed as an allusion to the Credo, where the words "Et in unam sanctum catholicam et apostolicam ecclesiam" are, in the words of Denis McCaldin, "tucked away in the middle of the verbal texture and are therefore generally inaudible."[15]

The question of whether the *Missa Solemnis* synthesizes a

response to a religious or secular stimulus is generally resolved in favor of the latter, despite concessions to the former. Critics are then wont to turn to explanations and interpretations of the work. What is the intellectual and emotional content of this music which, in the words of John Burk, "conforms phrase by phrase to the text, and yet remains musical logic, self-contained and inevitable" (op. cit., p. 326)? While agreeing on the non-liturgical nature of the work, Sena departs from critical interpretations of Beethoven's Mass. One of these interpretations is Paul Nettl's, which attempts to reconcile both the religious and secular aspects of the work. He writes:

> The text of the *Missa*, as treated by Beethoven, is not strictly liturgical. The Master was a deist, and looked upon God as an architect and creator of the world. He attributes to God heroic qualities and we may say that the *Missa Solemnis* expresses ideas similar to the Eroica Symphony exalted to metaphysical magnitude. It represents a reasoning with his God which is best understood by the grandiose columns of the Kyrie, the representation of God's deeds as illustrated by the Credo, the mysticism of transubstantiation, the exalted jubilation of the Gloria, the mournful melody of the Passion and humble prayer for peace. Beethoven inscribed the "Dona nobis pacem" with the words "Bitte um inneren und ausseren Frieden." These words alone show the subjectiveness of Beethoven's work. The entire Mass is a unique human document. (*Beethoven Handbook*, p. 145)

Sena's poem agrees that the *Missa* is a unique human document. The poet does not feel, however, that Beethoven's work is either an attempt "to reason with God" (irrespective of a specific conception of God), a "representation of God's deed," or a representation of the mysticism of transubstantiation. According to Sena, the *Missa* is not even a

> *piedosa tentativa para captar um Deus*
> . . .
> *Não é também, com tanta majestade,*
> *a exigência de que Ele exista,*
> *porque mereça quem assim O inventa.*

> (pious attempt to capture a God,
> . . .
> Neither is it, with so much majesty,
> the necessity that He exist,
> because he deserves it who thus invents Him.)

In this last section of the poem Sena not only refers to the Agnus Dei but actually paraphrases this prayer to some degree. It is clear, however, that what the poet understands Beethoven to be asking is God's (should He exist) intervention in human life as such—not after death, but in the here and now. Sena seems to have drawn some inspiration from Beethoven's own words inserted in the score: "Prayer for both inner and outer peace." Most important of all, the poet believes that the composer's hope, his "desperate hope," is that "our own greatness" as humans, and especially as artists, remain standing in the interval between a possible God and music itself. According to the poet, Beethoven's work is not one that humbles man before his Creator, but a courageous affirmation of man's humanity and of *his* capacity as creator. To a large degree, therefore, Sena's interpretation of Beethoven's *Missa Solemnis* is yet another statement of his own humanistic philosophy, his own metaphysical quests and doubts, his own belief in the artist's powers. In other words, the ideas behind Sena's interpretation of Beethoven's *Solemnis* are to be found as much in the composition and in the existing criticism as they are contained in the poet's own doubts and beliefs—doubts and beliefs which he repeatedly expresses elsewhere in his work. In short, Sena utilizes the "language" of the composer to tell his own story. Or, what amounts to the same thing, the *Missa* is a phonic mirror upon which Sena projects his own image.

"Chopin: An Inventory"

The last three poems to be discussed within the Miscellaneous group—"Chopin: An Inventory," "To Piaf," and "Final 'Potpourri'"—also exemplify, to varying degrees, the personal mode. That is to say, they harbor projections of Sena's own biography and personality disguised in the first two of these poems as meditations—which they are, first and foremost—on someone else's biography and works.

"Chopin: An Inventory" may be an inventory, but it is also a kind of verbal portrait of the man drawn against the background of contemporary and subsequent history, particularly relevant aspects of the history of Chopin's Poland and France, and the history or fate of his music. Sena begins his poem with a lengthy enumeration of Chopin's general titles ("Quase sessenta mazurcas; cerca de trinta estudos," etc.—"Almost sixty mazurkas; about thirty etudes"). By the seventh line of the poem, however, the list of titles gives way to another type of enumeration—this time of the biographical and historical constituents of the portrait:

além de umas dezassete canções para canto e piano; uma tuberculose mortal;
um talento de concertista; muitos sucessos mundanos; uma paixão infeliz;
uma ligação célebre com mulher ilustre; outras ligações sortidas;
uma pátria sem fronteiras seguras nem independência concreta;
a Europa francesa do Romantismo; . . .

(besides some seventeen songs for voice and piano; a fatal case of tuberculosis;
a talent for concertizing; many mundane successes; an unhappy passion;
a celebrated liaison with a famous woman; other assorted liaisons;
a country without sure borders or definite independence;
the French Europe of Romanticism; . . .)

Sena goes on itemizing—in a matter-of-fact way, as if there were no categorical differences among them—biographical and historical elements; commenting on the often unhappy fate of Chopin's music ("prato de não-resistência para as pessoas que julgam / que gostam de música mas não gostam"—"a pièce de non-résistance for those performers who play for those who believe they like music but really don't"); offering synthetic critical comments, e.g., "uma arte de escrever música como quem escreve um poema" ("a knack for composing music as one writes a poem"). It is perhaps no mere coincidence that André Gide also refers to Chopin's compositions as poems and says that "remarks which I might make about Chopin are equally applicable to Baudelaire, and vice versa."[16] In the note to the poem Sena states that his contradictory admiration for Chopin "only turned positive for me after the beneficial reading of André Gide's little book" (*II*, p. 238). Gide's major thesis—that Chopin's music has been "misunderstood . . . betrayed . . . intimately, totally violated" (op. cit., p. 20)—is also echoed in Sena's poem, as the lines quoted above indicate.

The poem ends with a reference to Chopin's main instrumental medium: the piano. In a sense, the structure of Sena's poem, i.e., the order of distribution of its constituent elements, places Chopin's "life" (as represented by the biographical references) between (the enumeration of) his compositions and (mention of) the piano. But this spatial distribution of elements is not entirely clear-cut. The elements of the portrait—bibliographical, biographical, historical—are at times interwoven with one another. These two ways of ordering the elements of the poem, the unscrambled and the partially scrambled, seem to suggest 1) that Chopin's extra-artistic life was somehow squeezed between those two (more important?) activities: composing and performing; and 2) that Chopin's art, both as composer and as performer, is so intertwined with his life and with his epoch that to speak of one is tantamount to speaking of the other. Thus, Sena's positioning and mixing of the "colors" of the portrait achieve thematic importance in their own right. The length of "Chopin: An Inventory" is also most important thematically and in perfect accordance with my reading of the poem as a portrait of Chopin: 39 lines, one for each year of Chopin's life (1810-1849).

Gastão Cruz may be partially justified in censuring the poem for its prosaism even though, as stated earlier, a recital of the poem will reveal more word music in it than a silent reading or a mere visual glancing over it might indicate that it possesses. But the poem's overall viability was perhaps never meant by Sena to reside in its musicality—but on what it did with its "prosaic" elements; not on effecting a poetic statement illustrative of a traditional conception of "pretty" poetry, but one which conforms to his desire to transmute human experience by altering its appearance without negating it, by heightening its voice without muffling it—in short, by rearranging it so that it fits the framework of Art without betraying life.

Sena's poem may also be viewed as a sort of biography of Chopin as man and artist. But in these notes on Chopin's life one also perceives echoes of Sena's own self. Some of the experiences and characteristics that both men share in common are included in the poem; others are not. But even the latter are guided by the poem into the mind of the reader who is familiar with Chopin's and Sena's biographies and personalities.

On the human side both were men who deeply loved their country but chose to live in exile: Chopin in Austria and France; Sena in Brazil and the United States. Both remained, all their lives, deeply patriotic (in the broad sense of this word) and consumed, each in his own way, by homesickness. Both, as fate would have it, died in foreign lands. Although Sena's poem calls Chopin "um pedante convencido da aristocracia que não tinha" ("a pedant sure of an aristocracy he couldn't claim"), the Portuguese poet, too, claimed an aristocratic background (although I am not denying the veracity of this claim). Both may be said to have made some incursions into the other's artistic province: if, as André Gide says and Sena's poem reiterates, Chopin composed "poems," Sena studied the piano and, as he writes in the postface to *Art of Music*, "In early adolescence, I imagined myself an illustrious pianist and composer, giving concerts for groups of intimate friends and close family members, in which there would be thundering chords and emotion-laden (though I wouldn't say emotion-provoking) 'smorzandos'..." (*II*, p. 216). As artists both men used their love of country and homesickness as mainsprings of inspiration. Chopin's first piece of music, composed at age 8, was a polonaise; his last a mazurka. As Adelaide Murgia says, Chopin recaptured the flavor of ancient Slavic legends in his ballades and his last polonaises.[17] Chopin's last Etude (No. 12), known as the *Revolutionary*, was inspired by the Polish revolution of 1831. In his letter rejecting the offer of court pianist, extended to him by Czar Nicholas I, Chopin wrote: "Even though I did not physically take part in the Polish revolution of 1831, my soul participated in it, and I aspire to no other title than that of *emigré*" (apud Murgia, p. 33).

Jorge de Sena, as noted in earlier chapters, always carried Portugal in his soul. Like Chopin, not only does he draw inspiration from ancient Portuguese "traditions" as exemplified by *The Wondrous Physician* and other works, but he also, in a manner basically identical to Chopin's, participated from afar in the Portuguese revolution of 1974 and wrote a long series of patriotic (again in the broad sense of the term) poems on it. Of course, these and several other similarities between the two men should not be taken too far, for the simple reason that such points of contact exist between most men. Although both men are patriotic and great lovers of their country, Sena's love of country is often mixed with hatred, whether justified or not. Hatred of his own country, in whatever form, was never an attitude publicly espoused by Chopin. Also, the differences between the two men—some explainable by the different times and places in which they lived, others attributable to their personalities—are perhaps even more noteworthy than any similarities between them. Sena was never a dandy, nor did he have love affairs with women who used male pseudonyms. He was a respectable *pater familias*, albeit without "the patriarch's vocation." But the fact that some similarities between the two men do exist and that their lives and creative works are so interwoven with one another constitutes an invitation to at least a partial autobiographical reading of "Chopin: An Inventory." If the titles of Chopin's works were substituted by Senian titles; if the biographical and historical allusions were appropriately rearranged—the structure of the poem would be a most adequate frame to accommodate a self-portrait. For Sena's life, too, was to a large degree squeezed between his creative productions and his "performance"/teaching of literature. And who would deny that to speak of Sena's life as an artist is tantamount to speaking of his life as man, and vice-versa?

"To Piaf"

Perhaps still more autobiographical than the poem inspired by Chopin is "To Piaf," a work which is ostensibly about the biography, personality, and to a lesser degree the works of the popular singer. With relatively minor change, however, most of what Sena says concerning Piaf can and does apply to himself. No less a writer than Jean Cocteau said of Edith Piaf:

> Look at this little woman, whose hands are like lizards darting amongst the ruins. Look at the Bonaparte-like forehead, her blind eyes that have recovered their sight. What will her voice be like? How will she express herself? How will she be able to bring all the sorrow of the night out of that narrow little chest? And yet she sings, or more like a nightingale in April, she brings forth her love song. Have you ever heard a nightingale? He toils, he hesitates, he rasps, he chokes, he begins and falters; then suddenly he finds the note. He sings and his voice overpowers you.[18]

It is this voice, more than anything else, that Sena's poem celebrates,

> *Esta voz que sabia fazer-se canalha e rouca,*
> *ou docemente lírica e sentimental,*
> *ou tumultuosamente gritada para as fúrias santas do "Ça ira",*
> *ou apenas recitar meditativa, entoada, dos sonhos perdidos,*
> *dos amores de uma noite que deixam uma memória gloriosa,*
> *e dos que só deixam, anos seguidos, amargura e um vazio ao lado*
> *nas noites desesperadas da carne saudosa que se não conforma*
> *de não ter tido plenamente a carne que a traiu,*
> *esta voz persiste graciosa e sinistra, depois da morte,*
> *como exactamente a vida que os outros continuam vivendo*
> *ante os olhos que se fazem garganta e palavras*
> *para dizerem não do que sempre viram mas do que adivinham*
> *nesta sombra que se estende luminosa por dentro*
> *das multidões solitárias que teimam em resistir*
> *como melodias valsando suburbanas*
> *nas vielas do amor*
> *e do mundo.*

> (This voice that could make itself canaille and coarse,
> or sweetly and lyrically sentimental,
> or tumultuously loud in holy frenzies of "*Ça ira*,"
> or simply recite broodingly intoning the lost dreams
> of one passionate night that leaves behind a glorious memory
> or those other dreams that, long after, leave behind sorrow and emptiness
> in desperate nights when yearning flesh can't believe that
> it never fully possessed the flesh it was betrayed by—
> this graceful and sinister voice persists, after death,
> just like the life that others keep living
> in front of eyes that become throat and words
> to say not what they always saw but what they divine

in the shade that spreads a half-light in the hearts
of lonely masses who stubbornly resist,
like melodies waltzing
suburban in the backstreets
of love and the world.)

What attracts Sena to Piaf is not her popular music, but her music of humanity, i.e., the life embedded in that music, the suffering and the joy. Indeed, Sena states in the postface to *Art of Music* that folk and popular music only interested him in rare moments and, when it did, it was because of the human personalities associated with it. "The fado, the samba, the flamenco, etc., are extremely repugnant to me: which doesn't mean that I do not like to hear an occasional fado to while away the time, but I would not consider it typically 'national' or even representative of anything other than the vulgar taste of a decadent aristocracy and a so-called bourgeoisie, who impose it commercially beyond the shadowy borders of a mythical Alfama" (*II*, p. 221). In the note to "To Piaf," Sena writes: "Since Edith Piaf is a personality and not a composer, the poem does not refer to specific songs. This, actually, may help to clarify what is said in the postface. Indeed, the American song, or the French song, etc., is not what interests me, but the personalities who, interpreting the song, render it humanly autonomous—but with this difference: in serious music it is the works of the great composers that represent that human autonomy" (*II*, p. 244).

Sena celebrates the French singer's voice because Piaf was "a singer of songs about real life" (Berteaut, p. 17), including her own life. Since Jorge de Sena, too, was a singer of real life, he is also celebrating his own voice. Both Piaf's and Sena's were voices often dominated by a spirit of accusation. Both intoned their "Ça ira." But if Sena was capable of singing the bitterest of diatribes ("Camoens Addresses his Contemporaries," "In the Land of Pricks"), he was also capable, like Piaf, of intoning the sweetest of love songs, like "I know the Salt" and "You Are the Earth" (*III*, p. 235). Both artists were, or considered themselves to be, victims of society and witnesses of society. Both used their respective mediums to fight back. One cannot help but be struck by some of the social vignettes that Sena transformed into poems, e.g., "Cubicle," "Sewer," and "Sunny Day," and the social world of which Piaf was a part during her childhood and adolescence, a world that she so often transposed to her songs. Piaf was literally born on the pavement, raised in a brothel and learned to sing in the streets. "My music school is the street, my intelligence is instinct," Piaf once said (apud Berteaut, p. 180). That is why her voice is one "that you feel has been washed in all the waters of the gutter," as Pierre Loiselet aptly describes it (apud Berteaut, p. 241); or, as Jorge de Sena puts it in the poem, "Quem tinha assim a morte na sua voz / e na vida" ("She had so much death in her voice / and in her life").

As Sena alludes to the thematic content of Piaf's better-known songs (in the passage quoted above, which comprises 17 of the poem's 23 lines), a content which is inextricably interwoven with the fabric of her own life, Sena is simultaneously referring in part to some of the major thematic strands in his own life and works: lost dreams, sweet and bitter memories of love, the persistence of the artist's voice after death, i.e., the faith in art and the artist's power to rescue from oblivion the life he sings. Some elements mentioned in the passage quoted above are indeed strikingly similar to experiences poetized or fictionalized by Sena. Doesn't the "amores de uma noite que deixam uma memória gloriosa" ("one passionate night that leaves behind a glorious memory") evoke the love celebrated in the avowedly autobiographical novella "The Great Canary" of *The Grand-Captains*? Doesn't the "noites desesperadas da carne saudosa que se não conforma / de não ter tido plenamente a carne que a traiu" ("desperate nights when yearning flesh can't believe that / it never fully possessed the flesh it was betrayed by") bring to mind the previously quoted "digested scraps, lives not begotten" of the poem "Sewer"; and the "smell of unfulfilled promises, a smell of flesh yearning for the love that wasn't, the love postponed, refused, not consummated" of the short story "Child's Cry"? Doesn't the "multidões solitárias que teimam em resistir" ("lonely masses who stubbornly resist") constitute yet another ray of hope in an otherwise love- and hope-barren world, a ray of hope that makes us think of the "pequenina luz bruxuleante / . . . indefectível próxima dourada" ("little flickering light / . . . indefectible close golden"; trans. Don Bartell)? Sena finishes the poem "To Piaf" with these words which apply both to himself and Piaf, the same way that the words he places in Camoen's mouth in "Camoens Addresses his Contemporaries" are at the same time Sena's speech to *his* contemporaries:

> . . . Quem como ela perdeu
> toda a alegria e toda a esperança
> é que pode cantar com esta ciência
> do desespero de ser-se um ser humano
> entre os humanos que o são tão pouco.

(. . . Only those who have lost
all joy and hope can sing,
as she has with the despairing science
of being human among people
of so little humanity.)

In Chapter IX, I shall return to this poem and discuss the thematic importance of its strategic placement in *Art of Music* right after "Concert for Piano, Op. 42, by Schoenberg."

"Final 'Potpourri'"

Sena refers to the first poem of *Art of Music* as a prelude. He uses another musical term for the title of the last poem. *The Harvard Dictionary of Music* defines "potpourri" as "A medley of popular tunes, operatic airs, patriotic songs, etc. which are played in succession, connected by a few measures of introduction or modulation."[19] The link between the different pieces may be thematic, chronological, or even alphabetical, as in Karl Komsák's *ABC-Potpourri*. Sena employs a similar pastiche technique. The poem is a patchwork formed with pieces and bits of musical, geographical, literary and historical allusions, as well as verbatim quotations (all of which Sena identifies by name of author in the note to the poem). Sena uses *thematic* links from one allusion or quotation to another. All these quotations are used with a referential meaning that conforms more to the thematic exigencies of "Final 'Potpourri'" than to the referential meanings the passages possess in the original works of which they are a part. Indeed, those original contextual meanings are, for the most part, perverted in Sena's poem. In addition to these allusions and quotations, the poet uses English and French words, sometimes effecting humorous puns; and creates, in a manner reminiscent of "Four Sonnets to Aphrodite Anadyomene," a couple of lines with words derived from ancient Greek. This seemingly unlikely hotchpotch is contained within an imagined conversation between the poet and the composer Carissimi. This "encounter" and "conversation" is what, in part, renders the poem logical, and it is to it that we must look to attempt to determine the meaning and function of what may well be the most hermetic, and certainly the strangest, poem of *Art of Music*. Indeed, one's temptation after reading the other poems of *Art of Music* and then reading this one is to ask the question that has been raised by some critics in connection with the "Four Sonnets to Aphrodite Anadyomene" vis-à-vis the poems of *Metamorphoses*: Does "Final 'Potpourri'" belong to, or was the poet well advised in including it in, *Art of Music*? I will try to justify a positive answer to this question.

Giacomo Carissimi (1605-1674) was a priest known primarily as a composer of liturgical and non-liturgical sacred music even though he also composed secular vocal chamber music. Sena's reference to Carissimi, right at the beginning of the poem—"compositor de opereta / para violoncelo de igreja" ("composer of operetta / for a churchman cellist")—is both ironic and irreverent. This biting, and satirical attitude with respect to the composer and his music sets the tone for the rest of the poem. The latter may be construed as an epilogue to *Art of Music*, a sort of farewell to music as poetic inspiration. But it is much more than this.

Turning to the "encounter" between poet and composer, we note that the latter arrives and greets the poet. The poet, in addition to identifying Carissimi with the remarks just quoted, adds by way of reply to his greeting: "*—Cameta adinomata apropictéron.*" These words—loosely derived from Greek *kameta*, 'toils,' 'labors'; *adynamos*, 'without strength'; and *apropikteron*, which includes the notion 'cast off'—could be tentatively translated thus: "I don't want any trouble and refuse your offer." What offer? First, Carissimi proposes a homosexual act, which compounds the irony with which the composer is conceived in the context of the poem: Carissimi is not only a composer of "operetta for a churchman cellist" but a homosexual, i.e., a double symbol of decadence (cf. Petronius's *Satyricon*, where homosexuality is used as a symbol of Roman decadence; cf. Sena's own short story "The Brothers," a story in part inspired by the *Satyricon*, where homosexuality is used as a symbol of decadent fascist Portugal). Other images of "decadent" European culture will occur later in the poem. Second, Carissimi attempts to initiate a conversation with the poet. The latter explains:

> *Quando tudo acabou, para ganharmos tempo*
> *era mister que falássemos. De quê?*
> *Trifles, trifles. Bagatelles. Como*
> *se conta assim a infância que não tivemos.*

> (When everything was done we had to speak
> to save time. About what?
> Trifles and trifles. Bagatelles. As if
> narrating the childhood we didn't have.)

This last statement, a reference to a non-existent or painful childhood, is clearly autobiographical. Various aspects of the poet's childhood are artistically documented in the short story "Homage to the Green Parrot" of *The Grand-Captains*. We thus have, and practically in the same breath, *true* autobiographical elements (the allusions to childhood) and *pseudo*-autobiographical elements (the encounter with Carissimi). The significance of these two elements being included in the poem side by side will be discussed below. This and other true autobiographical intrusions in a poem that is, in many ways, humorous (in accordance with the light entertainment value of a pot-pourri) means that Sena looked upon "Final 'Potpourri'" as an essentially serious poem. Indeed, realizing its potential for being taken as farcical, Sena warns in the postface that the poem is only "apparently farcical" (*II*, p. 220). Next, Carissimi offers the poet music:

> *Adinomata—e sussurrei, atento*
> *aos dedos que avançavam, música.*
>
> (Adionamata—and attentive to the fingers
> reaching toward me, I whispered music.)

Carissimi represents European culture, especially sacred musical culture. Other composers associated with religious music are also evoked: Mozart and Palestrina, particularly the latter's *Missa Papae Marcelli*. This poem is thus a repudiation of the culture that Carissimi epitomizes, to be sure. But it is also motivated by a sense of satiety on the part of the poet in regard to culture in general, and European culture in particular. This is in contrast with the other poems of *Art of Music* which are inspired by an attitude that is fundamentally reverent regarding that culture. In a sense this poem revives and carries to its ultimate consequences an attitude already present in "'La Cathédrale engloutie,' by Debussy." Then the poet expressed it thus: "Música literata e fascinante, / nojenta do que por ela em mim se fez poesia" ("Literary and fascinating music, / nauseating because of that through which in me was made poetry"). The poet attempts to cast off a burden that he both loves and loathes, accepts and rejects; a burden which in "'La Cathédrale engloutie'" he expressed in part with the astronomical images "de negros sóis e brancos céus nocturnos" ("of dark suns and white nocturnal skies"). Sena's contradictory desire or need to assail and befoul the culture that he deeply lived and loved is also typical of poems in other books, for example "In Crete, with the Minotaur," where the poet refers to Greece as "esta merda douta que nos cobre há séculos" ("that learned shit that has covered us for centuries"; trans. George Monteiro).

After mention of Mozart and Palestrina there is a transition in the poem to a non-musical "theme," a line from Leopardi: "*Sempre caro mi fu quest'ermo colle...*" This is the first line of a short poem entitled "L'Infinito" (*Canti*, 1836), where Leopardi sings of this "hidden knoll" ("quest'ermo colle") in his native Reconati and ponders the eternal and bygone or dead seasons ("l'eterno"; "le morte stagione") as the wind drowns out his thoughts. However, neither Leopardi's agnostic-atheistic philosophy, so akin to Sena's, nor the theme of this poem, which harmonizes with that philosophical stance, seem to have an important thematic function in Sena's poem. The verse was probably suggested by the name "Carissimi," which leads in the poem to several puns: *Carissimus, Carissimo* ("Dearest"), and finally *Sempre caro...* ("Always dear...") of Leopardi's verse. The next reference is geographical: "Pff... *Piazza d'Espagna*." In this case, the association probably traveled this route: Carissimi—Mozart—Leopardi—Italy—Piazza d'Espagna, with the interjection "Pff" synthesizing the poet's scornful, if playful, attitude. It is interesting to note that in the section entitled "Rome" of the poem "Roaming Around Europe, Nothing Sentimental" (*Exorcism*, written in 1971 or nine years after "Final 'Potpourri,'"), Sena's attitude toward Piazza d'Espagna remains as it was in the earlier poem.

The next thematic strand in Sena's potpourri, possibly suggested by the association Rome-Roman Empire (with the underlying notion of decadence always present), is the Latin *dicta "Ave Caesar, morituri te salutant."* These words, which according to Suetonius (*Claudius*, 21), were used by the gladiators, are also quoted, in English, by George Bernard Shaw in Act II of his *Androcles and the Lion* (1912). That is probably why Sena alludes to Shaw's play in the line immediately following the *dicta:*

> Andrócles, então, escuta, escuta,
> converteu o leão ao catolicismo.
> Romano? Pois se foi em Roma.

> (Well, listen, listen, Androcles,
> he converted the lion to Catholicism.
> Roman? Of course, it happened in Rome.)

This reference to Catholicism—which is, in and of itself, quite irreverent—leads to a still more iconoclastic tirade, the first three lines of which culminate in a verse ("*avec l'assentiment des grand héliotropes*") from Rimbaud's "Oraison du soir" (*Poésies*), itself an irreverent poem where Rimbaud, in one of his typical moods to befoul, pictures himself furiously and shamelessly urinating in a café garden. The word *héliotropes* of Rimbaud's verse is going to recur further on in Sena's poem ("se o heliotrópio é cucurbitácea?"—'is the heliotrope in the cucumber family?"). The idea of *piazza* (cf. *Piazza d'Espagna*) will also be recalled in the form of an allusion to Antonio Machado:

> *... Esqueci a botânica,*
> *pela mesma época em que—la plaza tiene una torre—*
> *descri por completo das noções de posse.*

> (... I forgot botany
> at about the same time that—*la plaza tiene una torre*—
> I put aside notions of possession.)

Although the connection between Piazza d'Espagna-*plaza* (of a Spanish poet) and Catholicism-*torre* "tower" may account for Machado's verse *La plaza tiene una torre* ("The square has a tower"), it does not explain, I believe, the reference to *posse*. The following explanation may be ventured. Obviously Sena is referring to two kinds of *possession*. In the context of "Final 'Potpourri'" he is referring to sexual, or more precisely homosexual, possession. But in a more serious and autobiographical vein Sena is probably alluding to three other lines by Antonio Machado that he deeply admired and quoted as epigraphs to the third section of *Persecution*:

> *No es el yo fundamental*
> *eso que busca el poeta,*
> *sino el tú esencial.*

> (It isn't the fundamental I
> the poet seeks
> but the essential you.)

We may choose to interpret these lines as referring precisely to the opposite of possession, i.e., the poet does not seek to gratify the self but to search for other beings. He does not possess others; he gives and shares. We could—without barring other interpretations of Machado's enigmatic verses—interpret them as synthesizing Sena's humanistic philosophy: his search for, and preoccupation with his fellow man. This interpretation is reinforced by the next quotation Sena uses: Terence's "*Nil humani* (ou vice versa) *a me alienum puto*." Here, however, we have the poet undermining the statement that best defines his philosophy. This is done in accordance with the mock-serious spirit of the poem.

A series of puns follow until Sena, still playing on Carissimi's homosexual proposal, quotes an appropriate verse (i.e., appropriate to the "encounter" between the poet and Carissimi) from

Shakespeare's *King Lear* (V, 3): "Undo this button. Thank you." What follows next is one of the most logical of all associations in the poem. The Shakespearean line being about the last words that Lear utters before dying, it naturally enough suggests to the poet the idea of death. That is why Sena quotes to this thematic effect the line from Álvares de Azevedo's poem of the same name, "Amanhã... se eu morrer amanhã" ("Tomorrow... If I should die tomorrow").

The allusion to Álvares de Azevedo—the first in the poem to a New World figure, a Brazilian to be exact—also acts as a kind of transition to the farewell between the poet, i.e., Sena, and Carissimi:

> *Addio! O "Mayflower" apita.*
> *Ouvem-se as fanfarras do Novo Mundo (a sinfonia,*
> *feita com temas do Velho). Vai, não percas*
> *a passagem, as estribeiras, a cabeça:*
> *as pradarias esperam-te.*
> *Pasta nelas.*
> *E, para mim mesmo, murmurei: Carissimi!...*

> (Good-bye! The "Mayflower" sounds its horn.
> You can hear the fanfares of the New World (the symphony,
> made with themes from the Old). Go, don't lose
> your passage, your temper, or your head;
> the prairies wait for you.
> Go and graze on them.
> And to myself I murmured: *Carissimi!...*)

The poet takes leave of Carissimi and the world of European culture, musical culture especially. But here again enters an autobiographical allusion of a special kind. Sena mentions the "Mayflower," the most famous of the ships that carried the English pilgrims to America in search of freedom. Is Sena not referring subtly to his own departure from his native land in search of liberty? In the context of the poet's farewell to European culture, the allusion to Dvořák's Ninth Symphony represents an irony that also applies to Sena. He could not fail to be aware of it. Although Dvořák's symphony bears the title of New World Symphony and indeed incorporates songs modeled after those of the American Negroes and Indians, some of this material, as is well known, is charged through and through with Bohemian, i.e., European, musical culture. And we ask: What is *Art of Music* but a work written totally in the New World but with "themes" from the Old? Indeed, what is "Final 'Potpourri'" but a medley comprised of a few "themes" from the New World but the majority from the Old?

After the poet rejects all of his offers, Carissimi tells him to go "graze" on the immense prairies of the New World. This is simultaneously an allusion to the freedom that those prairies can afford the man, and to the inexhaustible possibilities they can provide the artist with. But, as in the case of Dvorák's music, the Old World "themes" will remain forever present and latent in Sena's poetry, even when he ostensibly writes of the New World. It is in moments such as this that Sena's poem is fundamentally autobiographical and bears a close relationship to "'La Cathédrale engloutie,' by Debussy." The latter dealt with the poet's *encounter* with music. The last poem is meant, in part, as the man's *farewell* to Europe in the hope of finding freedom in the New World; and the poet's *addio* to European culture as poetic inspiration. The former, i.e., personal freedom, Sena accomplished to some degree and for some time, as autobiographical statements quoted earlier clearly show. The farewell to European culture was impossible—and too much to ask.

I believe, however, that this autobiographical dimension of the poem releases only one, and not necessarily the most important one, of its meanings. The poem's most important function and meaning in the entire context of *Art of Music* is this: "Final 'Potpourri'" is an act of demythification. Sena drew much poetic inspiration from his own life and personality: in this poem he mixes the truly and pseudo autobiographical to underline the fact that all art, even that inspired by true experience, is also invention. Throughout the book he presented himself as the humanist imbued with European culture and assumed an essentially reverential posture before it: in this poem he strikes a playful attitude before it. He drew inspiration from musical compositions and only permitted his imagination to move within the orbit of those inspirational sources: in this poem he gives free rein to his imagination. In all the previous poems everything had an aura of nobility and moved within a high-brow sphere: here we have a potpourri, a lowering of the high-brow to the low-brow. The Italian critic Giuseppe Tavani has explained Sena's tendency to demythify everything he comes in contact with in these terms:

> The dominant, tormenting, obsessive motive is that of demythification: the demythification of social and human idolatry, religion (which contradicts again his stated atheism), time, "civil progress" and ecological death (the latter being the cause of social misery and the result of arbitrariness and political coercion), maternity (endured with an impetus of love-hatred), nationalistic myths (Camoens). All this is expressed in an ironic-sarcastic tone which characterizes all his contacts with a reality that is disheartening and banal, with the absence of freedom, with capitalism, with cultural commonplaces.[20]

In no way, though, do Tavani's just remarks and "Final 'Potpourri,'" where those remarks are to a large degree exemplified, invalidate what has been maintained all along in this study regarding the tenets of Sena's humanism and his conception of poetry. The paradoxical and demythifying nature of much of Sena's poetry indeed constitutes a strengthening of those tenets and of that conception of art. For it all means that to Jorge de Sena no views were ever static; no truths ever failed to contain within themselves their antitheses; no institutions were sacred; no creeds were sacrosanct. Stasis of thought, the enthronement of present truths, and the divinization of any institutions whatsoever are the mortal enemies of true humanism. "Final 'Potpourri'" represents in *Art of Music* an exorcism, a flight from everything—except from poetic imagination and from freedom itself.

VII

Poems on Program Music and Opera

Art of Music contains six poems on ostensibly programmatic compositions and seven on operatic works. The poems on program music are "*Symphonie Fantastique*, by Berlioz," "'Má Vlast,' by Smetana," "'Romeo and Juliet,' by Tchaikovsky," "'Fêtes,' by Debussy," "'Thus Spake Zarathustra,' by Richard Strauss," and "'Verklärte Nacht', by Schoenberg." The first five will be analyzed in this chapter. The seven poems on opera are either based on complete works or draw inspiration from particular sections of the model compositions. Six will be discussed here: "The Death of Isolde," "Finale of 'The Valkyrie,'" "Siegfried's Funeral March of 'Twilight of the Gods,'" "'La Bohème,' by Puccini," "Principessa di Morte," and "Listening to 'Socrates,' by Satie." The seventh poem on opera is "'Boris Godunov.'"

"Symphonie Fantastique, by Berlioz"

This poem combines, in varying degrees, the textual, descriptive, interpretive and personal modes. The poet dwells on the programmatic and acoustic substances and vies to determine what in the composition is expressive of Berlioz's personality and what is expressive of, and a reaction to, the composer's epoch. Sena also stamps his own personality upon the poem. The latter's four major thematic constituents—the program, the tonal matter, the biographical aspect, and the music's historical dimension—are all tightly interwoven in the poem. For ease of exposition they will be dealt with separately.

Berlioz's *Symphonie Fantastique* (1830), subtitled "Episode of the life of an artist," is generally considered prototypical of musical Romanticism. Its programmatic content—inspired by the composer's unsuccessful suit for the British actress Harriet Smithson (who later became his wife)—is outlined in the titles of the composition's five movements: "Dreams and Passions," "A Ball," "Scenes in the Country," "March to the Scaffold," and "Dream of a Witches' Sabbath." Although unrequited passion is the overall theme of the program, the latter does encompass many other thematic bands common to the Romantic spectrum. Ernest Newman summarizes the plot thus: "The story was that of a young artist who, in the first movement, romanticises over his beloved, in the second meets her at a ball, in the third finds her presence a disturbance of the peace brought to his ravaged soul by the beauty and quiet of the country, in the fourth dreams that he has killed her and is being led to the execution and in the fifth sees her as not the least horrible part of the grotesque horror of a Witches' Sabbath."[1] In short, the program presents a novelistic plot with an array of contrasting themes and atmospheres—within the same movement or from movement to movement—being the rule: waking reality and the world of dreams induced by opium; waves of objectless joy and maelstroms of despair; pastoral scenes and death on the scaffold; silence and the roar of thunder; the image of the beloved converted into a witch in the midst of a crowd of ghouls and monsters.

Musically, the *Fantastique* is particularly noted for its original and brilliant use of color for expressive effects; a melody which Berlioz called *idée fixe* and which he uses in every movement to represent the beloved; shattering climaxes followed by moments of eloquent silence; a waltz to represent the ball; tonal imitation (through the use of timpani) of distant thunder; an almost brutal interruption of the *idée fixe* to portray the decapitation at the end of the fourth movement; the transformation, in the last movement, of the *idée fixe* into a caricaturesque dance to suggest the metamorphosis of the beloved into a witch; and, finally, the slow and frightening *Dies Irae* against the rapid and powerful witches' dance.

Sena's poem characterizes the entire composition—taking into account the programmatic and tonal substances—before dwelling on the relationship of the work to the composer and to his times. The first three lines of the poem synthesize the most Romantic aspects of the *Fantastique*—those which Sena treats with poignant irony: the program in general, and the guillotine passage and the witches' dance in particular:

Programas, poetas, sonhos de ópio,
pastores pipilando, e as guilhotinas,
e o sábat das bruxas ao som do Dies Irae,
. . .

(Programs, poets, opium dreams,
shepherds piping, and the guillotines,
the Witches' Sabbath to the sound of the *Dies Irae*.
. . .)

As a rule, the stories of the programmatic compositions that served as models for poems of *Art of Music* are satirized by Sena. In this and other poems it is quite apparent that Sena did not take the idea of program music very seriously. Yet, as noted earlier, Sena renders nearly every type of music he comes in poetic contact with programmatic—in the sense that he reads coherent ideas into it, in the sense that all compositions, programmatic or not, had a story to tell the poet.

The poem's next two lines—"comédia melancólica e sarcástica / de romantismo sentimental e crítico" ("sarcastic and melancholy comedy / of critical and sentimental romanticism")—are most significant. Not only do they reemphasize the poet's ironic view of the *Fantastique*—it is a comedy, not a drama—but point to what Sena considered most positive in the composition: its worth as music, independently of the program; and its documental, i.e., its extramusical import. The crossing of the adjectives—*melancólica-sarcástica / sentimental-crítico*—is probably meant to suggest the inextricable bond in the symphony between its strictly biographical and wider historical dimensions.

What is biographical in Berlioz's *Fantastique*? To answer the question (for it is implicit in the poem) Sena relies primarily on the evidence provided by the program and the tonal substance itself. Nevertheless, his answers also echo elements derived from the composer's biography and from the criticism on his music. The poem strongly suggests that Sena was very familiar with both. To the poet the *Fantastique* embodies many of the characteristics we have come to associate with Romantic personalities: egoism, madness, solitude. Are they conventional poses or real traits? In the case of Berlioz, the poet considers them genuine, although displayed in a hyperbolic fashion. Sena is echoing traditional critical opinions regarding the composer. Ernest Newman writes that "The big effects at which /Berlioz/ aimed in his music were, indeed, only one form of manifestation of a curious faculty that was always leading him to the grandiose. The ordinary orchestra, the ordinary chorus, the ordinary concert-room would never do for him; everything must be magnified, as it were, beyond life-size" (*Berlioz, Romantic and Classic*, p. 43). And Newman adds (p. 51): "We may just note that Berlioz's early life was in every way calculated to produce both the inflation of the prose style that we see in his letters and the eccentricity and exaggeration that we see in some of his early music." There is perhaps no greater example of this tendency toward the hyperbolic than the *Symphonie Fantastique*. Sena's poem communicates this sense of exaggeration through an ironic use of adverbs, as he translates into the verbal medium the expressive qualities of the music, describes in very general terms its tonal configurations, and subtly alludes to the composer's biography. Sena vies to convey a double simultaneous impression: what is genuine and what is pose in Berlioz's life and work. Berlioz's is a romanticism "*desesperadamente* triste de si mesmo" ("*desperately* sad with itself"); his music is "*violentamente* / música. *Agressivamente* / música" ("*violently* /music. *Aggressively* / music"); his solitude is "solidão romântica *imensamente* pública—mas solidão / . . . amargura romântica *tremendamente* amena—mas uma amargura" ("romantic solitude *immensely* public—but still solitude / . . . romantic grief *tremendously* mild—but still grief") (my italics). The reference to a genuine but "tremendously public" solitude probably constitutes an allusion to the composer's intention to make public his unrequited love for the Shakespearean actress by displaying it in a concert hall by means of a preposterous program.

According to Sena's poem, the *Fantastique* is also an example "Da raiva de não ser o mundo uma obra de arte" ("of rage that the world is not an artwork"). This statement, too, is biographical and required, on the part of Sena, a close acquaintance with the literature on the life of Berlioz. If ever there was a man whose affective and artistic lives merge into each other, whose desire to bring art into life and carry life into art forever preoccupied him, that man was Hector Berlioz. Ernest Newman points out (op. cit., p. 70) that the composer complains in his letters about the flatness and ugliness of the world, a world which his sensibility would love to convert into a work of art in many ways reminiscent of the world of the *Fantastique*: "colorful worlds of sultans and odalisques and houris and hashish and pirates and brigands, worlds of magnificent rapes and assassinations and tortures, of wine drunk out of enemies' skulls, and so on." And above and beyond its genuine character, what is Berlioz's pre-matrimonial relation to Miss Smithson but an attempt to live, in his personal life, a Shakespearan "tragedy," and then convert it into a true dramatic work in the *Fantastique*? Regarding this celebrated love episode in the composer's life, Berlioz's biographer Jacques Barzun writes that it was always "colored by Shakespearan associations." The composer, Barzun adds, "clung to the idea, if not of Harriet, at least of the Ophelia she had incarnated—a sad beloved, remote but poetic. The thought plunged him into Hamlet-like reveries mingled with tempestuous passion.''[2]

But as far as Sena's poem is concerned, the *Fantastique* is not only a personal document: it is a historical one, as well. Somewhat paradoxically, the poet sees it as a reflection or partial duplication of an era and, simultaneously, a reaction against, and negation of, that same world which it mirrors. Surely the composition exhibits some of the artificiality that characterized the post-Revolution Philistine world in France:

> *bastante vulgaridade, muito efeito fácil,*
> *e um colorido por vezes novo rico*
> *como os cristais e as pratas dos barões banqueiros.*

> (sufficient vulgarity, the easy effect,
> and at times a nouveau-riche coloration
> like crystals and silver of bank barons.)

But notwithstanding this, the *Fantastique*, as its very title indicates, does aim to fill a void—a deep void left precisely by a

> . . . *mundo burguês sem fantasia,*
> *sem mais maravilhoso que o da infâmia,*
> *sem mais espanto que o da hipocrisia.*

> (. . . bourgeois world with no fantasy,
> with nothing more marvelous than scandal,
> and nothing more wondrous than hypocrisy.)

These same characteristics that Sena perceives/experiences in Berlioz's work were pointed out by Jacques Barzun (op. cit., p. 8): "⟨Berlioz⟩ transcended as well as embodied his time, and his greatness for us lies precisely in this, that he gives us text and commentary in one living shape: at all key points his life and art furnish an explicit critique of his age.'' Barzun goes on to add (p. 21) that "to pomposity and pedantry Berlioz opposed wit and irreverence; on easy optimism and the trumpery faith in progress he turned a scornful glance; and against Philistine commercialism he raised a religion of art . . .''

The poet identifies with the composer at the end of the poem. He, too, reacts against the Philistines of today on behalf of Berlioz. If today some people fail to perceive the human dimensions of Berlioz's music, as well as its artistic merits, it is because they lack that humanity and a corresponding sensibility; it is because "a grosseria / cresceu à escala cósmica'' ("grossness / grew on a cosmic scale''). Sena conceives of Berlioz as being at once a herald and critic of his age. We may ask: Was not Jorge de Sena a herald and critic of his? The voice of irony and accusation that Sena detects in the *Fantastique*—"Música pungente, irónica, raivosa" ("Pungent, ironic, raging music")—is also to be heard throughout his own works. Art as a weapon was common to both Hector Berlioz and to Jorge de Sena. In this 35-line free-verse poem, Sena reveals an experience of the music for its own sake, it is true. But he also does so primarily as a window through which he can peer into the composer's soul and the reality of his times, as well as the reality of Sena's own times. For the relationship between the artist's world and the world of Philistinism has not changed very much from Berlioz's day. The music is both a human and a humanizing factor: a means through which Berlioz transmits his humanity; a means through which the poet tightens his fraternal bond with another artist. Berlioz's *Fantastique*, Sena's poem holds, arises from a context that is at once personal and historical. Correlating the music with the man and history, i.e., with human life, can only heighten, not minimize, one's enjoyment of it. Perhaps the most notable aspect of this poem is how Sena brings together into a coherent thematic whole elements derived from different spheres both musical and extramusical; from both types of reaction, critical and laudatory—with his perception of the tonal substance itself acting as a nexus among them. In a sense, the poem ends up being imitative of the composition in a very special way: the *Fantastique*, too, may be considered in part a tonal distillation of distinct vital experiences that once lay outside the province of music; and it, too, reconciles apparently mutually exclusive attitudes on the part of Berlioz.

"'Má Vlast,' by Smetana"

If the relationship between life and music was in part responsible for Sena's poetic interest in the *Fantastique*, this same relationship in the form of intense love of country—the major impetus behind Smetana's *Má Vlast*—may account for the presence of the latter work among the inspiring sources of *Art of Music*. Although the poem takes into account the general content of the program and contains references to Smetana's personal tragedy—"um músico surdo e louco e desprezado" ("an insane, deaf, and despised musician")—nevertheless what interests Jorge de Sena the most is the composer's relation to his country, Bohemia. This relation leads Sena to draw parallels between the Bohemian and Portuguese states and to reveal his own feelings toward Portugal. "'Má Vlast,' by Smetana" is a title with a double meaning: *Má Vlast* means "My Country"—but the country that the poem dwells upon is Sena's own, not Smetana's. Indeed, had Sena not been intent on calling attention to *his* country, he might have entitled the poem "'Die Moldau,' by Smetana"; for, as he tells us in the note to the poem, the latter refers primarily to the second of the six symphonic poems that comprise *Má Vlast*.

Smetana's masterpiece was inspired by, and constitutes a hymn to, the natural beauty, history, legends, as well as folk songs and dances of Bohemia. Like Rimsky-Korsakov's *Russian Easter Overture* and Sibelius's *Finlandia*, *Má Vlast* (composed 1874-79) is a musical expression of the nationalistic feelings that swept Europe following the French Revolution and Napoleonic Wars. However, Smetana's nationalism probably runs deeper than a mood or trend of the times. It found more than justifiable reason in the past and present history of Bohemia. In a letter dated 11 March 1860, Smetana writes to a former student: "I need hardly repeat that I am a Czech, body and soul, and that it is my pride to be the heir to our glory. I am therefore not ashamed to answer you in my mother tongue, albeit imperfectly, and I am glad I am able to show you that my homeland means more to me than anything else."[3] In 1861, Smetana co-founds a Prague choral society, whose motto is "Through song to the heart, through the heart to the homeland." As early as 1848 he had written "Song of Freedom"; and upon his return in 1862 from exile in Sweden, his homeland-oriented works continued in *The Brandenburgers in Bohemia* (1863) and *The Bartered Bride* (1866) before culminating in *Má Vlast*. "At one of the saddest periods of his life," writes Brian Large, "Smetana managed to overcome adversity, concentrating his creative powers to celebrate, in *Má Vlast*, the glories of Bohemia. In this cycle he transforms shadows of personal darkness and misery into a paean of praise."[4]

The program of these symphonic poems does constitute a paean to Bohemia's past. But it is also the embodiment of the musician's hope to see his land free from the oppressive Austrian yoke. Paraphrasing Smetana's own words, the first poem is an evocation of the glory of old Bohemia. The second tells of the flow of the Vltava as it sweeps through groves and meadows, as well as sites full of legend and history, past the St. John's rapids and on to Prague before merging with the mighty Elbe. *Sarka*, the third poem, evokes the legend of the Czech amazon who swears revenge on men for the infidelity of her lover. The fourth draws inspiration from Bohemia's meadows and forests. The fifth pays homage to the "pride and glory and the unbreakable nature of the Hussites." *Blaník*, the last and most prophetic of the poems, bears the name of a mountain near Prague where the old Bohemian heroes slumber, awaiting the propitious moment to rise again and bring about the resurrection of the Czech nation.[5]

A little over two thirds of Sena's poem (lines 1-13) deals with the above mentioned aspects of Smetana's biography and Bohemian history as contained in the program of *Má Vlast*. Not all the elements are mentioned by Sena, but all are more or less evoked and need to be taken into account for an adequate reading of the poem. In the last three verses—the most important in the poem—Sena refers to his own country. The poem has a curious structure that contributes much to its overall meaning. This unusual structure concerns the rhyme scheme and the poem's sequential or discursive logic.

"'Má Vlast,' by Smetana" is comprised of sixteen lines rhyming *aabbccdaaeeffdgg*. There is nothing unusual about this scheme until we realize that there exists a displacement of rhyme *d*, i.e., that line 7 rhymes with line 14, and not with line 8 as expected. More important still, we notice that this displacement also occurs in the logic of the poem. In other words, what "should" have followed line 7 are the last three lines of the poem, thus:

> . . .
> *senso de que só escravo se torna quem o era já.*
> *Mas nós não temos de estrangeiros outros mais que nós. Não dá*
> *portanto o que pensamos para tais doçuras.*
> *Pois de nós mesmos—porcos—não brotam pátrias puras.*
> (. . .
> perception that only those who were already slaves end up as slaves.
> But we have no foreigners except ourselves.
> Our thoughts don't open out into such sweetness.
> And so from our porcine hearts no pure homelands bud forth.)

After taking into account this displacement, it is easier to understand these otherwise somewhat enigmatic three lines (in a poem ostensibly inspired by *Má Vlast*) and determine their full implications in the context of the poem. The stated and implied content and "message" of "'Má Vlast,' by Smetana" is, therefore, this: Portugal, like Bohemia, has a glorious past. (But in this poem Sena is not directly concerned with that past.) Unlike Bohemia, however, Portugal is not suffering under the yoke of a foreign power. The "foreign" oppressors of the Portuguese people *are the Portuguese themselves*. Sena cannot imagine, as Smetana could for his country in his cycle of symphonic poems, especially *Blaník*, a "pure" Portugal rising from a self-generated and self-propagated "filth,"

And so from our porcine hearts no pure homelands bud forth.

Mrs. Mécia de Sena has brought to my attention the passage in Byron's *Childe Harold's Pilgrimage* (I, 216-24), where the author of *Don Juan* refers to the citizens of Lisbon in terms that might have suggested to Sena the epithet "swine":

> But whoso entereth within this town,
> That, sheening far, celestial seems to be,
> Disconsolate will wander up and down
> 'Mid many things unsightly to strange ee:
> For hut and palace show like filthily;
> The dingy denizens are rear'd in dirt;
> Ne personage of high or mean degree
> Doth care for cleanness of surtout or shirt,
> Though shent with Egypt's plague, unkempt, unwash'd, unhurt.

Of course, what Sena says about Portugal in this context gains its true significance only when read in contrast to Smetana's prophetic hope. We also must realize that the poem was written in 1964, therefore when Portugal was still very much under fascist rule. This poem is an example of Sena's feeling of hopelessness, awakened in the face of Smetana's extreme hopefulness, regarding the political future of his country—a hopelessness that contrasts markedly with poems like "A Very Little Light" and "Those Who Have It."

"'Má Vlast,' by Smetana" was published in 1968, when fascist censorship was very much operative in Portugal. Could Sena's fear of censorship also account in part for the displacement just mentioned, a displacement that constitutes a mild disguise of Sena's protest? Be that as it may, this poem is yet another example of a meditation on a work of music that transcends the latter's tonal and programmatic boundaries.

"'Romeo and Juliet,' by Tchaikovsky"

This is another poem that takes into account the program of the famous Overture-Fantasy, as well as some aspects of the composer's biography and personality. It is one of the prime examples in *Art of Music* of the interpretive mode. One of the major problems of musical criticism has always been, understandably enough, the biographical approach. How does music (and I am now referring exclusively to non-programmatic instrumental music)—that is solely abstraction, indeed an "art form that thinks without the aid of ideas,"[6] reflect, with any degree of accuracy and verifiability, its composer's life?

Contrasting the biographical approach in the study of literature and music, Edward Lockspeiser states: "The fact is that literary critics pay the greatest attention to biography. They are always /sic/ attempting to find out how it came about that that man, with all his indefinable complexities, was able to produce that particular work. This, surely, is the sole purpose of biography. Biographers of musicians cannot quite take this view, possibly because music, by its nature, is far too nebulous to be associated with biographical events'' (*Music and Painting*, pp. 83-84). Lockspeiser goes on to add, however, that "this strikes me as strange because the broad problems of the creative mind with which we have to deal are the same." What needs to be especially emphasized, I think, is the difference between applying a biographical approach to purely instrumental or absolute music, on the one hand, and to program music, on the other. Although the latter partakes, as instrumental music, of the abstraction and "nebulosity" Lockspeiser referred to, its declared programmatic content is by definition representational. Being so, program music is to a degree akin to literature and thus an appropriate province for biographical criticism, or at least less risky a venture than with absolute music. We know, for example, that the program of Berlioz's *Fantastique* was influenced by biographical events even though we may always disagree as to whether or not the music as such reflects those events and, if so, to what degree and how.

We are also aware that certain circumstances in Tchaikovsky's life played a significant, if not decisive, role in his decision to write a composition on Shakespeare's work and thus we can, to some degree, relate the music to those personal circumstances. It is this relation which allows Lawrence and Elizabeth Hanson to write of Tchaikovsky's Overture-Fantasy that "The score is dominated by a controlled rapport between composer and subject; he understood the fate which would part the lovers but he felt the love too and recreates it with a touching blend of compassion; never before had the fire and poetry of young love been communicated with such truth and charm."[7]

"'Romeo and Juliet,' by Tchaikovsky" constitutes a poetic interpretation of the composition effected through the combination of programmatic and biographical elements. The former has to do with the love of Romeo and Juliet; the latter takes into account biographical circumstances attendant to the composition of the music (e.g., "Ele era ainda muito jovem quando imaginou este poema"—"He was very young when imagining this poem"), as well as elements of Tchaikovsky's personality—the most important of which being the composer's alleged bisexuality. Sena's poem is, therefore, a poetic equivalent of the biographical approach in musical criticism—but with a difference. As criticism of Tchaikovsky's work, Sena's poem might be susceptible to charges of impressionism even though the Jungian, as well as Freudian, basis of his interpretation makes the latter plausible enough. As a poetic meditation on his experience of that work, however, it is perfectly legitimate and coherent. In art—and let us always remember that these poems, no matter what perspective they assume, are strictly *poems*—truth is not necessarily factual or empirical: it can be intuitive. Sena's poem, although it applies a method akin to biographical musical criticism—tries to make poetic, not necessarily critical, sense. Also, Sena's poem is as much motivated by a desire to provide a poetic psychological interpretation of the Overture-Fantasy as it is by his intent to make yet another ironic statement regarding program music. As noted earlier—and as revealed by Sena's poem on Berlioz and other poems on program music which we will momentarily discuss—Sena's view of program music was nearly always partially satirical. Tchaikovsky himself is Romeo and Juliet—"Por isso pôde conceber / Tão belo cântico . . ." ("That's why he could create / A canticle full of beauty . . .")

> . . . *Não canta a união de Romeu*
> *e de Julieta; canta do que seriam ambos*
> *na união, no amplexo em que foram um só corpo*
> *bem mais que uma só alma; canta do que eram ambos*
> *antes de os sexos serem dois, na infância.*
> *Canta da paz e da certeza, antes do bem e o mal.*
> *E sonha e faz sonhar, nesta grandeza tão sonora e fútil,*
> *do horror de ser-se e de não ser-se dois.*

> (. . . It doesn't sing the union of Romeo
> and Juliet; it sings what they would be
> if joined, in the embrace of being one body
> even more than one soul; it sings what they both were
> before childhood split into two sexes.
> It sings of peace and certainty, before good and evil.
> And it dreams and causes us, in this sonorous futile greatness,
> to dream of the horror of being and not being two.)

I mention in passing that Sena's fascination with the theme of androgyny is not restricted to this poem. The first poem of *Metamorphoses*, "Metamorphosis," constitutes Sena's own poetic dream of hermaphroditism. The poet wonders regarding the creature that his poetic vision perceives upon the sands of a primeval beach:

> . . . *Deus ou deusa?*
> *Há quanto tempo ali dormia? Há quanto?*
> *Ou não dormia? Ou não estaria ali?*
> *Ao pé dos cardos, junto à solidão*

que quase lhe tocava do areal imenso,
do imenso mundo, e as águas sussurrando—
—ou não estaria ali?... E um deus ou deusa?
Imagem, só lembrança, aspiração?
De perto ou longe não se distinguia.

(. . . God or goddess?
For how long had he slept there? For how long?
Or wasn't he sleeping? Or wasn't he there?
Near the thistles, close to the solitude,
which almost touched him of the immense sands
of the immense world and the waters purling—
—or wasn't he there? And a god or goddess?
Image, mere remembrance, aspiration?
From nearby or from afar one couldn't tell.)

As we can see, Sena's interpretation of Tchaikovsky's *Romeo and Juliet* is very complex indeed. It is a partially biographical, partially satirical "reading" of Tchaikovsky's work, but it may also be a projection of Sena's own poetic dream. This point deserves much more attention than the scope of this book permits.

"'Fêtes,' by Debussy"

In contrast to "'Romeo and Juliet,' by Tchaikovsky," "'Fêtes,' by Debussy"—inspired by the second of the three symphonic poems collectively entitled *Nocturnes*—does not contain a single allusion to the French impressionist composer's biography. Nor does it draw from Debussy's program but a subtle suggestion. Sena's poem may, in fact, be considered an invented program for *Fêtes*. Sena states in the note to the poem that "the suggestion of a festival or Renaissance 'triumph' is provided by the composer himself" (*II*, p. 241). However, a consultation of the score reveals that what Sena took from Debussy was the mere suggestion of an old-time festival and a procession with music. The particularities of the festival, its specific time and place, as well as the historical figures mentioned in the poem, are all Sena's own.

Edward Lockspeiser summarizes the intended program of *Fêtes* thus: it "gives us the vibrating atmosphere with sudden flashes of light. There is also the episode of the procession (a dazzling fantastic vision) which passes through the festive scene and becomes merged with it. But the background remains persistently the same: the festival, with its blending of music and luminous dust, participating in the cosmic rhythm" (*Painting and Music*, p. 189). Still according to this critic, Debussy's inspiration for the procession evoked in the music was not a Florentine Renaissance triumph, but a "recollection of old-time public rejoicings in the Bois de Boulogne attended by happy, thronging crowds; the trio with its fanfare of muted trumpets suggests the former drum and bugle band of the Garde Nationale, beating the tattoo as it approached from afar and passed out of sight" (Lockspeiser, pp. 189-90). Debussy's music draws on pictorial associations, but not realistic ones; his is an impressionistic festival of atoms and light, the vision of a fantastic procession. As Oscar Thompson says, "the pictures presented are not the literal ones that musical realists would have essayed. They are evocations rather than descriptions, reflections rather than specific images" (*Debussy: Man and Artist*, p. 318).

We may ask: How did Sena conceive the idea of describing a Florentine triumph on the basis of a mere suggestion of a phantom procession and an old-time festival in the Bois de Boulogne? The answer may be, in part, Sena's deep interest in the history of Florence. Indeed, when the poem was written (1964), Jorge de Sena had recently been steeped in the study of Machiavelli and the history of 15th-century Florence, which resulted in the publication, in 1963, of his essay "'The Prince,' by Machiavelli."[8] Unlike Debussy's impressionistic evocation of a festival of atoms and light disturbed by the passing of an equally fantasmagoric procession, Sena's poetic technique is one akin to a realistic pictorial presentation. It has been suggested that *Nocturnes* owes its title to Whistler, and that Renoir and Monet were probable sources for the pictorial content of the symphonic poems. Sena's pictorialness is closer to the Gozzoli of *The Procession of the Magi* than it is to the French impressionist painters, say, Renoir's *Moslem Feast in Algiers*.

Sena's poem is indeed a *tableau vivant* of the Florence of Machiavelli, Gozzoli, Botticelli, Lorenzo the Magnificent, and Poliziano. The last two, great friends that they were, are actually mentioned in the poem by name. In Book VIII of his *Istorie fiorentine*, where he gives a brief estimate of Lorenzo, Machiavelli refers to the festivities for which Florence was justly famous all over Europe: "in times of peace, his country enjoyed festivals; where were frequently seen plays based on events and ancient triumphs. His objective was abundance in the city, the unity of his people, the honoring of nobility. Lorenzo the Magnificent loved wonderfully all excellence in the arts, favoring the men of letters."[9] Among these men of letters, Lorenzo favored Poliziano, author of *Stanze della giostra* of another Medici, Giuliano. As for poetry, Lorenzo the Magnificent loved particularly the lewd kind, as his own *Canti carnascialeschi*, celebrating sexual love, indicate. Sena evokes all this in the poem.

The latter consists of two extended similes, one within the other: "É como se as ruas de Florença . . ."; "como congelados no tempo" ("It's as if Florentine streets . . ."; "as if frozen in time") (l.1 and 14, respectively). Sena often prefaces his poetic associations awakened by music by an "as if..." or "as though..." These careful comparisons point to his belief that no entirely satisfying verbal parallel for music can ever be found. But the very fact that he goes on to supply those words stresses his still greater belief that supplying associations is one of the few recourses the poet has if he should discourse on music, and one way to bring music in close contact with life.

As mentioned above, the poem is essentially realistic in its descriptions of the action and characters comprising the invented program. However, the poem also contains elements suggestive of impressionistic paintings:

> O cortejo porém passa e todos adormecem,
> num suspenso gesto, num detido amplexo,
> como congelados no tempo e feitos invisíveis

> (The procession vanishes; everyone dozes off
> in a suspended gesture, in a delayed embrace,
> as if frozen in time and made invisible.)

This suggestion of arrest in time, the capture of the evanescent moment about to escape, is indeed very typical of impressionist painters, many of whom are so fond of representing fleeting forms and figures seemingly on the verge of disappearing from the canvases and vanishing into thin air (Degas's *L'Etoile, Portrait of Hortense Valpiçon, Le Foyer, Laundresses*; Renoir's *Dancer, Gondola in Venice;* Monet's *Wild Poppies, Boating on the River Epte;* etc.).

By referring thus far only to the program of *Fêtes*, I have probably conveyed the notion that Sena does not heed the tonal substance at all. Not so. As the entire poem implies, it is the sound of the music that sets the whole procession in motion. Sena's narrative renders spatial, as it were, the music's temporalness. But the poem's narrative progression parallels the temporal flow of the music. Presumably the entire scene set in motion in the poem had remained frozen in the river of time, awaiting the life-giving performance/hearing of the music to bring it deliverance. But the festival can only be awakened for a brief period of time. When the music comes to an end—and it does so all too soon!—the river is once again congealed. The figures imagined by the poet are once again arrested in timeless suspension—until the music sounds anew. In no poem of *Art of Music* is the reciprocal and mutually enhancing relation of the two sister arts stressed more subtly, convincingly and beautifully. Music, the poem suggests, gains "life" by its alliance with poetry; poetic imagination comes to an end when the music stops. The progressively shorter lines of the last section of the poem convey the conclusion of the music, as well as this progressive freezing over of the river of time—and poetic imagination, which ceases when the sound merges with silence:

> Mas o tempo falta
> para acabarem gestos,
> concluir a posse
> iniciada
> outrora.

> (But there is no time
> to finish the gestures
> or conclude the lovemaking
> initiated
> yesteryear.)

Constant Lambert has written of *Fêtes* and *Sirens* that the former's "wild exhilaration . . . is the exhilarating bustle of wind and rain, with nothing in it of human gaiety. And the icy waves that lap the siren's rock are disturbed by no Ulysses and his seamen."[10] And Lillian Baldwin has said of Debussy's music that "It is too intensely personal, too withdrawn from life to have universal appeal. It gives. It gives us wind and wave, moonlight, clouds, children's toys, and legendary saints, but never man. The human element is completely lacking, even in his opera."[11] Perhaps Sena's intention on substituting a Renaissance triumph for Debussy's program was the poet's desire to instill human life into his experience of the musical composition—not with impressionistic vagueness, but with realistic detail. To Debussy's essentially atemporal and ageographical associations, Sena opposes a particular time and place. More important still, Debussy's dance of atoms and light and phantom procession yield to human activity: to a "massa de povo, nos salões, / onde todos rolam e se apertam rindo" ("mass of people who sway / in the salons and collide laughing"). In "'Fêtes,' by Debussy," the music of dust particles and dream-like processions has been metamorphosed into waking, living reality: the streets of Florence

> cheias de gente e colgaduras e festões de flores,
> para passarem nelas grandes carros alegóricos,
> ao som de charamelas e canções, enquanto

241

Il Magnifico e o Poliziano nas tribunas,
rodeados de damas e de pagens,
lêem poemas de alegria pagã,
maliciosos e obscenos.

(full of people and tapestries and wreaths of flowers,
for great allegorical chariots to pass through
to the sounds of shawms and songs, while
on the dais, surrounded by ladies and pages,
Il Magnifico and Poliziano
read malicious and obscene
poems of pagan joy.)

Before leaving "'Fêtes,' by Debussy" it is important to add that no unidimensional reading of this, or of any other poem of *Art of Music*, can do it entire justice. The unique "program" that Sena creates—following the suggestion of Debussy's intended program, but deviating markedly from it—reveals once again Sena's ironic attitude toward program music. Sena's "program" suggests that any program fits equally well a piece of programmatic music. Indeed, who would deny that Sena's program is vastly superior to Debussy's? In other words, Sena goes along with the programmatic idea and extracts a most viable and beautiful poem from that idea. But he does not fail to strongly imply that, in strictly musical terms, program music perhaps ought to be taken with a grain of salt.

"The Death of Isolde"

The three poems on Wagner's operas—"The Death of Isolde," "Finale of 'Valkyrie,'" and "Siegfried's Funeral March of 'Twilight of the Gods'"—all have something in common: they are based on some of the most dramatic and human episodes in the three music dramas. So consistent with the philosophical principles that inform *Art of Music* (and all of Sena's poetry) are these poems; and so thematically unified are they with one another, that they actually constitute a kind of trilogy of their own. The unifying thematic principles that tie the poems together are the celebration of love conceived in a humanistic frame, and the affirmation of the overall supremacy of empirical man over supernatural entities. When Wagner's conception of human love is alien to Sena's own (as in the Liebestod, the source of "The Death of Isolde"), the poet rejects it. When the human experience depicted by Wagner (as in the two model scenes of the other two music dramas) is consistent with Sena's philosophical views, the poet joins the composer in upholding and celebrating it. These three poems exemplify different modes of experiencing opera: they place

242

more or less emphasis on the tonal or dramatic components, or attempt to effect a verbal synthesis of both to the extent that this is possible.

"The Death of Isolde" fuses the descriptive, textual and personal modes, and to a lesser degree the imitative. It evokes elements from the entire opera and contains at least one allusion to an aspect of the medieval story which Richard Wagner did not incorporate in his music drama: the burial of the lovers in separate graves. As the title indicates, however, the poem concentrates primarily on the Liebestod, Isolde's song of love and death at the end of the opera. The poem is both a re-creation of the tonal and dramatic constituents of the Liebestod and an expression of Sena's reaction to the kind of love portrayed by Wagner. The human side of the episode—not the latter as a detached and self-contained aesthetic entity—is what attracts and retains the poet's attention throughout the poem.

Tristan und Isolde (produced in 1865) is the first of Wagner's new-style music dramas in which the old operatic style yields to a lush harmonic vocabulary, leading motives (which will become even more prominent in the *Ring*, although part of the latter precedes *Tristan*), and the so-called endless melody. The work is generally considered one of the greatest exponents ever of musical eroticism. "This is a long opera about love and about almost nothing else: sexual passion is expressed with the full force of Wagner's newly enlarged orchestra."[12] But what kind of love and what kind of passion does it portray? Guido Pannain summarizes it thus: "*Tristan und Isolde* is the poem of yearning (*desiderio*) which perpetuates itself through yearning and comes alive with death to continue its incompleteness. The ideas of love and death, of sorrow and joy, are dissolved in mystical elusiveness and cross over to music. The music attains exactly the essence of being, the *Urgrund des Seins*."[13] Mystical love and the love-death theme portrayed by Wagner versus Sena's concept of humanistic love or the love-life theme constitutes the essential subject matter of the poem.

Ernest Newman is also of the opinion that the principal expressive medium of the opera is the music itself. "Throughout the poem," he writes, "Wagner restricts himself to the barest minimum of words—sometimes no more than two or three to a line of verse,—having no need of speech beyond what is necessary to concretize the emotion being poured out by the prime expressive instrument of the work, the music."[14] Sena's poem also lends maximum importance to the tonal substance. Indeed, as the poet re-creates the content of the Liebestod, he first concentrates on the music. Then, almost imperceptibly at times, he allows his references to the dramatic constituents to become fused with the musical. In this way, Sena effects an inseparable alliance of music and text that accords perfectly with the design of Wagner's music drama. The poem's very important references to the dramatic content, however, make it necessary for us to recall the principal elements of the action.

Tristan und Isolde is based on Wagner's own libretto. His version of the story, drawn mostly from the text of Gottfried von Strassburg, is considerably altered and condensed to suit his dramatic purposes. When Act I opens, Isolde, her attendant Brangaene, and Tristan are on board the latter's ship bound for Cornwall, where the Irish princess is to marry the aging king Mark. Isolde hates Tristan, her escort, as the killer of her former betrothed, Morold of Ireland. But she is also secretly in love with this fair man whom she nursed back to health after the very combat that took the life of the Irish knight. Grieving, she orders her servant to prepare a poisoned drink that would put an end to hers and Tristan's life. But Brangaene intentionally substitutes a love-potion for the lethal brew. Act I comes to an end as the ship arrives in Cornwall and as Tristan and Isolde, whose concealed love for each other has now become uncontrollable, fall in each other's arms. The lovers sing passionately as shouts echo through the ship that King Mark, Tristan's uncle and friend, is coming aboard to greet his bride.

In the numerous versions of the story of Tristan and Isolde it is not always clear whether the love between them already existed before the philtre or whether it was brought about by it. In Wagner's opera, however, there is no doubt whatsoever that the two loved each other and that the potion only intensified their passion and made them impervious and oblivious to the conventions of their society. Sena's poem departs from Wagner's libretto when the Portuguese poet writes: "palpita a frustração do amor maldito / porque de um filtro só nasceu" ("the love that was cursed for being born / from only a potion is palpitating"). It is doubtful that Sena was unaware of Wagner's handling of the love-potion. Sena's reading serves the thematic intentions of his poem just as Wagner's handling of the love-potion served his. Wagner could not accept the naive explanation that the love of Tristan and Isolde sprang from a mechanical contrivance. Sena chooses to believe it in order to further accentuate the unnaturalness of that love when contrasted with human love conceived in naturalistic terms.

When Act II begins, it is night. The setting is a garden outside the king's castle. As sounds of a hunt are heard, Isolde awaits the arrival of Tristan. But the ever-watchful Brangaene suspects treachery from a courtier. Oblivious of time and everything that surrounds them, the lovers engage in a duet—"O sink upon us, night of love."

Brangaene's suspicions were justified: King Mark and the courtier Melot do surprise the lovers. The king's soliloquy expresses his grief at being betrayed by his trusted nephew and friend. Tristan asks Isolde to accompany him to the dreary land of his birth. The answer is affirmative. But in the struggle that ensues between the courtier and Tristan, the latter is wounded and sinks to the ground as Isolde, in tears, flings herself upon her beloved's breast.

The scene of Act III represents an old manor, Tristan's home in Brittany. Gravely wounded, Tristan can think only of Isolde whom he anxiously awaits. Upon being told that her ship is approaching, Tristan is seized with frenzied despair and tears the bandage from his wound. Isolde arrives in time to see him die. Meanwhile another ship arrives bringing King Mark. Tristan's men prepare to defend themselves, but needlessly. The king, who now realizes that Fate is to blame for the lovers' uncontrolled passion, comes to offer his pardon and to unite them. But Tristan is already dead, and Isolde, transfigured by love and her own imminent death, sings the passage that begins "Mild und leise / Wie er lächelt" ("Mild and softly, how he smiles") to the melody of the Liebestod theme first introduced in Act II by Tristan. At that point Tristan had suggested that they should never part from each other and had proposed that they die together. In Wagner's own words, "Isolde, as if glorified, sinks gently in Brangaene's arms down upon Tristan's body."[15] King Mark blesses the dead.

The poetry of the Liebestod is an explosion of erotic and mystical imagery. Isolde does not see Tristan as being dead. She sees him smiling, feels his heartbeat, smells his sweet breath, as if they were truly engaging in sexual union. She senses herself being enveloped by erotic billows and breezes which she sips and drinks. As she sinks into death, she rises in a whirlwind of passion to the heights of ecstasy. The lovers have thus achieved in death or consummated mystically the union they had never experienced in life.

Sena's poem contains 34 lines of free verse. The first 23 comprise five segments of lines that always start with references to the music before subtly incorporating elements of the text. The first segment (lines 1-7) translates the erotic nature of the music and text of the Liebestod, suggests the "unending" love melody that stretches from Act II to Act III, and clearly conveys the mystical nature of the love being protrayed. Sena relies on erotic imagery as heavily as does Wagner. In this passage, form is in perfect harmony with content: enjambment reinforces the hyperbolic eroticism and "unending" love melody expressed by the image "como um longo sexo" ("like a long sex"). This image of a monstrous sex wrapping itself around the world without penetrating it, is a stroke of genius. It is the exact objective correlative for the eroticism of music and text of the Liebestod, and the most expressive image that Jorge de Sena could have used to communicate the protagonists' mystical love.

The image is obviously an allusion to Ouroboros, the serpent or dragon biting its own tail. Only here there is no union: there is but strangling death, denial of the life announced in the phrase "tecido vivo" ("living weave"). This interpretation, that Sena is alluding to Ouroboros, is confirmed later on in the poem by a further reference to the "eternal serpent." As Ouroboros, the serpent has at least two main symbolic values. As a Gnostic and alchemical symbol, it represents eternity, "expresses the unity of all things, material and spiritual, which never disappear but perpetually change form in an eternal cycle of destruction and re-creation."[16] Sena's poem, as we shall see, invokes this meaning. Another symbolic value of Ouroboros, and one that suits even better Sena's use, is explained by Thomas Inman: "The serpent and the ring indicate *l'andouille* and *l'anneau*," he writes. "The tail of the animal which the mouth appears to swallow, is *la queue dans la bouche*. The symbol resembles the *crux ansata* in its signification, and imports that life upon the earth is rendered perpetual by means of the union of the sexes."[17] Sena looks upon the love of Tristan and Isolde precisely in this broad context of 'love upon the earth'; and his reaction to their *modus amandi* is that of a humanist who conceives of love in a holistic sense, one which includes love as a vehicle for the propagation of life. Tristan's and Isolde's love, lines 1-7 suggest, is life-denying, barren sensuality. It is a misguided serpent which, instead of uniting mouth and tail for the life-affirming union, wastes its energy and strangles human life. It is self-consuming love, flight from reality, copulation in the mind. (It is important to stress, at the risk of emphasizing the obvious, that Sena is not arguing with Wagner's artistic handling of his chosen subject matter. The Portuguese poet is responding to the human implications of the story.)

In the next four segments of the poem (lines 8-20), Sena continues to bring together elements derived from the music and text. As for textual references, the poet comes very close at times to paraphrasing lines from Isolde's song. The "volutas de uma chama ambígua" ("spirals of an ambiguous flame"), for example, constitute an important reinforcing metaphor for the aroused but misguided serpent; but they could also be construed as a subtle paraphrase of the mystical billows and breezes that envelope the heroine. In this passage Sena also synthesizes his subjective reaction to the love in the Liebestod with lines such as "nesta fluidez sem tempo não há gozo algum" ("in this timeless flow there is no joy whatsoever"); "é cópula mental" ("is copulation in the mind").

As for references to the music, this portion of the poem constitutes a kind of listening outline, with particular emphasis given to dynamics. Stressing this aspect of the music is important, for what Sena is trying to bring out in the poem is, on the one hand, the erotic furor of music and text, and on the other the non-consummatory nature of that love in natural terms. The "roncos e estridências lacrimosas" ("shrieks and tearful dissonances") (second segment, lines 8-10), besides being yet another ironic reference to the hyperbolic but sterile eroticism of the Liebestod, could also refer to the sorrowful voice of a clarinet that joins Isolde's voice. The "crescendos delirantes" ("delirious crescendos") of the third segment (lines 12-15) are probably a verbal translation of the dynamic swelling which begins with the words "Heller schallend, / mich umwallend" ("Growing brighter, flowing over me") and grows to a point of near paroxysm. Isolde's emotions as well as the dynamics subside as she approaches the end of her song of love and death, which terminates on a high note on the word "Lust" ("bliss"). In Sena's poem this is suggested by the phrases "que se exaspera e expira em tão agudas posses" ("exasperatedly expiring in such piercing acts of possession"). The last segment of the poem is comprised of line 19 and half of line 20: "Nesta doçura que ao silêncio imóvel acaba retornando . . ." ("In this sweetness that finally returns / to a still silence . . ."). As the last half of line 20 (to be discussed later) shows, Sena is simultaneously alluding to "postcoital" repose, i.e., to the dramatic content, and to the silencing of Isolde's voice, before the gentle music of the violins takes over to last until the curtain falls.

So far Sena has dwelt on the re-creation of the love depicted in the Liebestod and on the characterization of this love from a humanistic viewpoint. This is why he has vied simultaneously to express what the Liebestod embodies and what it lacks. Starting with the second half of line 20, Sena initiates a post-auditory reflection on Isolde's song. In this part of the poem we have a much more emphatic expression of love in a humanistic frame than in the earlier part. Sena does not define or explain his own conception of holistic love: he supplies a concrete example of it (emphasis added):

> . . . Não há uma paz dos rostos que se pousam,
> enquanto os sexos se demoram penetrados
> no puro e tão tranquilo esgotamento da chegada
> que só ternura torna simultânea.
> *Não há, mas só tristeza infinda e fina*

e tão terrível de que, estrangulado,
o amor no mundo é morte impenetrável: dois
seres que o sexo destruiu,
estéreis como o sopro da serpente eterna.

(. . . there is not the peace of resting faces
when their sexes remain penetrated
in the pure and calm exhaustion of climax
that only tenderness makes simultaneous.
There is not—only a boundless, acute sadness
so terrible that love strangled in the world
is impenetrable death: two
beings that sex destroyed,
sterile like the breath of the eternal serpent.)

Sena's entire poem develops and revolves around a series of contrasts, the most important of which are mystical and sexual love, sad and joyous love, life-denying and life-affirming love. Thus, mystical ecstasy and peace in death are implicitly contrasted with postcoital plenitude and repose. The misguided and life-strangling Ouroboros, the sterile serpent, has been compared with life-sustaining sexual love. This reference to the sterile breath of the serpent evokes a function of the serpent among the Sethians of ancient Egypt who believed that it was from the breath of the serpent that generation began. Human love, Sena suggests, is the only vehicle capable of performing this miracle. The "impenetrable death" of Tristan and Isolde is a death without awakening. From the penetrable death (*la petite mort* of sexual love) there is awakening for the individual and eternal re-creation for humanity itself. Sena has thus suggestively united the two primary symbolic functions of Ouroboros: eternity for human life, as well as joy, resides in sexual, not mystical, union. At this point, the Liebestod has become, paradoxically, a point of departure for a celebration of sexual love. It is not a celebration of strictly lustful or libertine love in a manner that is also typically Sena's. Here we have a much more comprehensive view of love: love as a fusion of the biological and emotional sides of humankind (cf. "ternura torna simultânea"—"tenderness makes simultaneous"); love as a source of joy but also the very spring of life upon the earth; a love that, because it is sexual, is pure, genuine. For, as Jorge de Sena tells us in "Art of Love" (*Exorcism*),

Que gestos há mais belos que os do sexo?
Que corpo belo é menos belo em movimento?
E que mover-se um corpo no de um outro o amplexo
não é dos corpos o mais puro intento?

(*III*, p. 126; emphasis mine)

248

(What lovelier gestures are there than of sex?
What beautiful body's less lovely in movement?
What stir of one body in another's hug
is not those bodies' *purest* aiming moment?)
                                    (trans. Jonathan Griffin)

It is, in short, the celebration of the kind of love that Sena also sings about in the poem appropriately entitled "Love" (*Peregrinatio*):

> *Amor de amor de amar de amor tranquilamente*
> *o oleoso repetir das carnes que se roçam*
> *até ao instante em que paradas tremem*
> *de ansioso terminar o amor que recomeça.*
> *Amor, amor, amor, como não amam*
> *os que de amar o amor de amar o amor não amam.*
>   *(III, p. 75)*

> (The love of the love of loving of loving tranquilly
> the oily repeat of the flesh that rubs
> until the moment when it, trembling, halts
> in the anxious finishing of the loving that starts anew.
> Love, love, love, how they don't love
> those who the loving of love of loving the loving do not love.)

"The Death of Isolde" began in a brutal and inhuman erotic note: with the world-strangling serpent that translates into symbolic terms the love portrayed in the music and text of the Liebestod. The poem went on to sound the contrasting sweet human music of postcoital fulfillment and tenderness. It ends in an outcry of human feeling. What the poet is left with is a "taste of pity" for Wagner's lovers and a desire to finish and redo their story: to bury them, not in separate graves (as happens, for example, in Joseph Bedier's *Le roman de Tristan et Iseut*), but in the same grave, as in the much more human story of Sena's own wondrous physician and Urraca (cf. *The Wondrous Physician*), "p'ra que talvez na morte—imaginada—se conheçam / melhor do que se amaram" ("so that maybe in some imagined death they might know each other / better than they loved"). Most of all, what remains in the poet, for whom love is always *mature commitment to life*, is a shared feeling of impotence—"de uma impotência que se quis só sexo / virgem demais para um amor da vida" ("of an impotence that only wanted virgin sex / too excessively for a love of life").

"Finale of 'Valkyrie'"

This poem does not contain a single allusion to the musical substance of *Die Walküre*. It is a re-creation of the dramatic episode announced in the title. The subject matter of the poem is again human love, this time paternal love. Sena seizes upon what is perhaps the most human and tenderest of moments in the second drama of Wagner's tetralogy: the moment when Wotan—torn between his godly duty to uphold the oath made to his wife Fricka and his fatherly love for his favorite daughter—reluctantly kisses away the godhood from Brunhilde and reduces her to the condition of simple woman, thus setting the stage for future human tragedy and the eventual collapse of the gods:

> *cavalo ardente de Valquírica amante*
> *que o pai sofrendo humanamente triste*
> *condena ao sono não de eternidade mas*
> *da enércia solitária de quem espera*
> *o amado herói que há-de tocar-lhe os lábios*
> *soprando-lhes ardências de fatal destino.*

> (fiery steed of a loving Valkyrie
> whom her father, suffering humanly sad,
> condemns not to an eternal sleep, rather
> to the solitary rest of one who awaits
> her beloved hero who will brush her lips
> wafting upon them burning kisses of fatal destiny.)
> (trans. Jack E. Tomlins)

Although the poem deals primarily with paternal love, it is quite obvious that sexual love is strongly implied in the images Sena uses: "fiery steed," "wafting upon them burning kisses." These sexual motives establish a close intertextual bond between this poem and "The Death of Isolde."

However, in this poem—unlike in "The Death of Isolde"—Sena does not oppose the kind of love depicted by Wagner. Instead he joins Wagner in celebrating it. For it is the human-love aspect of the episode that once again attracts Sena, as the passage just quoted indicates and as he explains in the note to the poem. Sena was drawn to Ferdinand Frantz's interpretation of *Die Walküre* (with the Vienna Philharmonic Orchestra, directed by Furtwängler) because, according to this interpretation, "Wotan is, at once, a god and a human father full of sadness when he must condemn Brunhilde" (*II*, p. 239).

The first four lines of this 15-line free-verse poem seem to have little or nothing to do with *Die Walküre* and even less with the specific episode of Act II, Scene II, to which the title refers:

Deuses podiam de um Valhala em chamas
sumir-se nos escombros quando o Reno
cantante como o fogo inundaria verde
o palco e o catafalco dos heróis.

(Gods could disappear in the ruins
of a flaming Valhalla when the singing Rhine
like the fire would engulf with green
the stage and catafalque of heroes.)

But these four lines do fulfill two extremely important functions in the poem: 1) they anticipate or foreshadow the conflagration that is going to destroy Valhalla after the death of Siegfried (the subject of Sena's next poem on *Die Götterdämmerung*), and 2) they point to the vulnerability of the gods, thus setting the psychological stage, as it were, to the subject matter of the present poem. The vulnerability of the gods manifests itself in at least two ways: in *Die Walküre* (and in Sena's poem on it) it produces the conflict between godly duty and human paternal love, on the one hand, and the thorough humanization of Brunhilde, on the other; in *Die Götterdämmerung* (and Sena's corresponding poem) it leads to the gods' destruction. Therefore, if read by itself, "Finale of "Valkyrie"" is yet another celebration of human love. When read vis-à-vis "Siegfried's Funeral March of 'Twilight of the Gods'" (as the thematic relation between the two poems indicates it should), its humanistic import becomes even wider in scope: it is the ultimate affirmation of humankind before the supernatural.

"Siegfried's Funeral March of 'Twilight of the Gods'"

This poem on Siegfried's Funeral March begins with these lines:

Na tarde que de névoas se escurece
escuto a marcha que ao herói transporta
fúnebre e doce, tão violenta e fluida,
à sua pira onde arderá cadáver
a cinzas reduzido. . . .

(In the afternoon darkening with mist
I hear the march, funereal and sweet,
fluid and violent, carrying the hero
to the pyre where his corpse will be burned
and reduced to ashes. . . .)

The first line brings to mind the opera's stage scene. In Wagner's own stage directions, "Mists rise up from the Rhein and gradually fill the whole stage up to the front."[18] The next lines just quoted, besides referring to the funeral cortege itself, also constitute a poetic re-creation of the solemn theme with which the March begins. The rest of the poem, however, does not follow very closely either the verbalizable content of the March or the dramatic substance of *Die Götterdämmerung*.

The March, as Sena himself states in the poem, is a "mostrar por música" ("this spectacle in music"). Wagner dispenses with words and endows the orchestra with the power of speech. As Albert Lavignac puts it, the Siegfried Funeral March is no march at all, but an eloquent "funeral oration."[19] In this oration the entire life of the hero is reviewed through musical motives. The listener is reminded of the heroism of the Volsungs, to which Siegfried belongs; the unhappy lives of his parents, Siegmund and Sieglinde, and the several key episodes in the hero's own life. But Sena does not concentrate on translating these motives. Rather than re-creating the specific circumstances depicted in the Funeral March, the poet meditates on the general relationship of the gods to humankind and, more particularly, on the music's underlying theme and mood: death. Whose death? The heroes', who die such a human death; the demigods', who enjoy life, suffer and finally die just as we humans do. Most important, it is a meditation on the death of the gods themselves who, being human creations, "aos heróis mortos / nunca sobrevivem" ("never outlive / dead heroes"). If Sena's poems on *Tristan und Isolde* and *Die Walküre* celebrate different aspects of human love, this one, in spite of being inspired by an operatic episode dealing with death, sings of human earthly redemption: the disintegration of godhood and the triumphant supplanting of the gods by humankind.

Poetic justice: Sena begins his poetic trilogy on Wagner by opposing the kind of love depicted by the composer; he goes on to join Wagner in celebrating paternal love in the second poem; he ends the trilogy by uniting his voice to Wagner's once again. Together they intone the ultimate and most far-reaching form of human freedom: freedom from the supernatural, a freedom loudly proclaimed in the collapsing roar and the consuming fires of Valhalla. In Sena this type of freedom is sung again and again: throughout *Art of Music*, throughout his entire poetic corpus. In the case of Wagner, this is one of the few instances—perhaps the most significant of all—when he comes down from his mystical heights and sounds the humanistic trumpet of ultimate human liberty!

From the legendary world of medieval romance ("The Death of Isolde") and the mythological heights of the *Ring*, Sena's next poem on opera brings us right down to the Real Life of Puccini's *La Bohème*. As for the nature of the worlds portrayed and the beings who inhabit them, no greater dissimilarity could be expected within the same genre than the one which exists between Wagner's operas poetized by Sena and this work of Puccini's. Yet, the impression one is left with after reading these four poems on opera is that Sena is always dealing with the same basic phenomenon: the power that musico-dramatic art has in bringing us into close contact with life. The poetic techniques that Sena uses in "'La Bohème,' by Puccini," however, are considerably different from those utilized in the case of Wagner's operas. To begin with, the poet does not, and need not, aim his poetic lens at the most dramatic or human scenes of the opera.

"'La Bohème,' by Puccini" takes into account the entire composition and starts from the understandable assumption that, as far as its dramatic elements are concerned, nothing whatsoever in this opera lies outside the sphere of common human experience—however romanticized this experience may be. The poem may be construed as an answer to an implied question: How can a work that utilizes numerous facile recourses of literary and musical art still move us so, both aesthetically and humanly?

La Bohème (1896), whose libretto by Giuseppe Giacosa and Luigi Illica derived from Henri Burger's picaresque novel *La vie de Bohème*, is one of the most successful operas ever written. Surprisingly, what in part accounts for its appeal, the libretto, ought to have rendered the work a colossal failure. From a strictly literary viewpoint, *La Bohème* is a concoction brewed with a great many of the ingredients one has come to associate with ultraromantic and melodramatic literature. The plot, for example, is transparently simplistic and shockingly bathetic. A Bohemian playwright, who shares a Parisian garret with a "philosopher" and two other equally inartistic and equally hungry Bohemians, meets a girl under the most stereotypically contrived of circumstances, and they automatically (one might even say, mechanically) fall in love with each other. They live and party together for some time and then separate on account of the Bohemian's jealousy. At the end of the opera, after she has lived with a viscount who kept her, Rodolfo and Mimi get back together and she dies of consumption in the apartment where they first met.

Yet, woven into this boy-meets-girl plot are a number of really touching human situations; a series of characters who are strangely real, convincing and charming despite their artificiality; a great deal of thematic variety, oscillating between the sorrows and joys of existence. Aesthetically noteworthy are the concentration of the action, the effective integration of imagery, for example the imagery of cold and heat (the cold in the Bohemians' apartment and lives and Mimi's "gelida manina"; the heat produced by the burning manuscript and Mimi's death in the "warmth" of the apartment, etc.); and, finally, the dazzling visual spectacle of some scenes of the opera.

And then there is Puccini's music: the lyrical style throughout, the famous melodies, the unforgettable arias ("Che gelida manina"; "Me chiamano Mimi"; Musetta's "Quando me'n vo' soletta per la via"), the lightness of texture that offsets the "heaviness" of the melodrama, the superb orchestration. Both dramatically and musically there is more than enough in the opera to allow the spectator or listener to forget that his emotions are being played with and for him or her to be convinced that the whole aesthetic and human impact of a work of art often transcends what one might expect from the sum total of its components individually and intellectually considered. Spike Hughes writes of *La Bohème* that "perhaps for the very reason that the story is simple and tells itself, Puccini was able to concentrate more fully on the purely musical enjoyment to be had out of the opera than in anything else he ever wrote. He found in it opportunities for humour and horse-play, for charm, for descriptive music, for love songs, quarrels, comedy and wit. His characters are human, his crowds are picturesque, and there is a genuineness in the pathos of the last act which survives all sneers at the composer's sentimentality."[20]

Sena's poem, which is essentially exemplificative of the critical, i.e., interpretive, mode, constitutes a double response to *La Bohème*: an intellectual, objective, disinterested or analytical response that dwells on some of the opera's dramatic and musical elements and techniques; and a considerably more subjective response that focuses on the overall aesthetic and human impact of the work. The poem's formal elements and tone are carefully orchestrated to enhance the communication of this double response. Although the poem is not strophically divided into parts, it does contain three quite distinct, albeit thematically integrated, sections: 1) lines 1-9 comprise the first section. This free-verse part is discursive. Its diction is akin to that of musical criticism; its tone is "smilingly sarcastic," to quote Sena's own characterization of the poem (see Note, *II*, p. 241); 2) lines 10-21 constitute, in much more *musical* and in some instances rhyming verses, a more positive and more emotional response to the whole opera; 3) in lines 22-31 the poet returns to strictly free verse and a discursive style to confess his surrender to Puccini's manipulation of his emotions. The poem is thus a partial analysis and criticism of the opera, as well as an analysis of the poet's own double and somewhat contradictory response.

The prosy, discursive lines of the first section of the poem follow an essay-like structure. Sena begins with a sweeping declarative statement (first line) and then proceeds to develop/substantiate his assertion by referring to both the music and the drama:

> É "romântica", sentimental, mesmo piegas,
> na opulência melódica de uma osquestração habilíssima,
> em que não há recurso desonesto da escrita musical
> que não seja usado para enternecer
> ou para fazer sorrir um satisfeito sorriso triste
> por conta da "tragédia" inevitável,
> com vidas fáceis, muita miséria alegre,
> o "quantum satis" de imoralidade, e o bacilo
> de Koch, herói do Romantismo. . . .

> (It's "romantic," sentimental, even maudlin,
> in the melodic opulence of an extremely capable orchestration,
> in which no dishonest recourse of compositional technique
> is not used to make us wistful
> or leave us smiling with a satisfied mournful smile
> since the "tragedy" is inevitable,
> with its easy lives, and quite happy wretchedness,
> with the immoral quantum satis, and Koch's bacillus
> a Romantic hero. . . .)

The tone of these lines is critical, cold, and obviously "smilingly sarcastic," particularly in the choice of adjectives and in the enumeration of the constituent elements of the opera, which are meant to suggest (cf. "the quantum satis of immorality") that Puccini did indeed follow some kind of melodramatic operatic recipe calculated to produce certain results.

But in the next section of the poem this derisive tone changes to one of greater acceptance. The poet begins to indicate this transition with the conjunction "mas" ("but"), which serves to express opposition, or at least reservations, to his own initial, more intellectual, response:

> ....Mas...
> jamais se foi tão fundo ao fundo da vulgaridade,
> jamais se fez tão terna e doce a irresponsabilidade,
> jamais se comoveu tanta gente dura com a realidade,
> transformando-as em convenções tão líricas.

E jamais tão bem se anestesiaram as pretensões do gosto
com esta coisa tão simples
que é como bondade,
como que tristeza,
como que morte,
e é uma alegre fúria de fugazmente viver,
sensível, inútil, condenada,
mas que sempre pungente viverá nesta música.

(......................................Yet...
never have we been so deep into the depths of vulgarity,
never has irresponsibility been so tender and sweet,
never have so many hardened people been moved by reality
transformed into lyrical conventions.
And never were pretentions of taste so well numbed
by such a simple thing
which is a kind of goodness,
a kind of sadness,
a kind of death,
and is a glad rage to live ephemerally,
emotional, useless, condemned,
and always pungent and alive in this music.)

Not only the tone but also the formal elements of the poem have changed. The discursive, forward-moving language of criticism has not entirely disappeared, but has also partially yielded to qualities compatible with true word music: repetition and rhythmic variation, rhyme and ample use of alliteration—all suggestive of lyricism, subjectivity, emotionality. The latter two qualities are also reinforced by the fact that the enumeration develops by accretion, not by rigorous analytical order, as exemplified by the first line of the poem: "'romantic,' sentimental, even maudlin." Now the poet evokes the real-life qualities embedded in the opera: goodness, sadness, death. Most of all, the poet finds and seizes upon an element which is an attribute of most works of music as far as he is concerned and one which is to be found in many of his own works: *La Bohème* expresses the joy of life even in the presence of death.

Of course, we must always avoid overly linear or unidimensional interpretations. It is undeniable that this section extends the irony made more obvious in the first. Indeed, the insistent (one might say, purposely exaggerated) use of rhyme might be construed as being derisively imitative of the saccharine melodramaticism of *La Bohème*. In other words, in this section the poem continues to be "smilingly sarcastic," but with a significant difference: here, unlike in the first section, the accent is on *smilingly*, not on *sarcastic*.

256

In this second part of the poem, the poet's intellectual, analytical faculties are not in abeyance, but they are balanced by emotional ones. In the last section of the poem, Sena returns once again to a more emotionally detached critical stance, only this time he does so in order to survey his own emotional response, his being won over by Puccini, despite himself:

E, quando cai o pano sobre a morte de Mimi,
mal sonha a maioria dos espectadores conspícuos
a que ponto, com a lágrima no olho,
pagaram a conta do café aos Marcelos e aos Rodolfos,
e compraram sapatos mais largos a Museta.
E isto faz que perdoemos a Puccini tudo,
e lhe concedamos o lugar que merece em nós
como o coração que perdemos, e ele,
sem vergonha e sem escrúpulos,
nos restitui.

(And when the curtain falls on Mimi's death,
the majority of conspicuous spectators hardly dream
how much they, with tears in their eyes,
have paid the café bill for the Marcelos and Rodolfos,
and have bought Musetta's wider shoes.
And so we forgive Puccini everything,
conceding to him a deserved inner place
like the heart that we lose and that he,
shamelessly and without scruples,
gives back to us.)

Sena's critical stance toward *La Bohème* coincides exactly with Puccini's own artistic aims and with the better informed critical opinions on his operas. "I love small things," Puccini often said, "and the only music I can or will make is that of small things . . . so long as they are true and full of passion and humanity, and touch the heart."[21] Sena's poem also agrees with Ernest Newman's opinion of Puccini: his "genius is a very limited one, but he has always made the very most of it. His operas are to some extent a mere bundle of tricks: but no one else has ever performed the same tricks nearly so well."[22] But Sena's poem does more than strike a critical pose: it is, more than anything else, a celebration of the humanizing power of art. Reading "'La Bohème', by Puccini" one gets the feeling of having shared with the poet the latter's live experience of the opera: how his intellectual faculties reacted, how his emotional ones intervened to play their role. Perhaps most important of all, one comes to share in the poet's realization that a work of art, if it is to work its full aesthetic and human effect upon us, must be responded to intellectually, emotionally, and with human understanding, in short, with our whole, undivided being.

"Principessa di Morte"

Puccini's operas exhibit varying degrees of conformity between their subject matter and the composer's life and personality. Yet, the single most irresistible attraction for the biographical-minded critic probably remains *La Bohème*. Most people acquainted with Puccini's biography cannot fail to be struck—and many a critic has been—by the similarities between the lives of the garret dwellers and merrymakers of the Café Momus and the composer's own "Bohemian" experiences during the years he attended the Milan Conservatoire. This all-too-obvious relationship could account for the fact that Sena steered clear of the biographical approach in "'La Bohème', by Puccini." When the poet utilizes the biographical mode, he usually does so by establishing the kind of far-reaching association that would be too risky or outright untenable for the music critic, i.e., one that produces viable poems instead of mere versified or stylized musical criticism. A case in point is the relationship Sena perceives between Tchaikovsky's bisexuality and his choice and treatment of subject matter in *Romeo and Juliet*. Another example of a poetically justifiable and satisfying but perhaps critically farfetched interpretation informs "Principessa di Morte," where Sena goes so far as to see Puccini's death as an integral part of his last opera, *Turandot*. For the reader "Principessa di Morte" is one of the easiest poems of *Art of Music* to follow. However, for it to be allowed to work its magic upon the reader, the latter must be familiar with the subject matter of the opera in general, and the characterization of the protagonists, Turandot and Calaf, in particular.

Turandot (first performed in 1926), divided into three acts and five scenes, is the only one of Puccini's twelve operas that deals with a fairy tale. The libretto is by Giuseppe Adami and Renato Simoni, although Puccini, as his letters to Adami clearly demonstrate,[23] so closely supervised every single line of the text that the latter bears the stamp of his personality to a remarkable degree. The story is derived from Carlo Gozzi's *Turandotte* (1762), a tragicomedy in five acts, which in turn was based on a French version of a Chinese fable from *A Thousand and One Nights*. (Mrs. Mécia de Sena informs me that Jorge de Sena translated, in 1960, the story "As 99 cabeças" ⌐"The 99 Heads"⌐, which is the story of Turandot, for the Editorial Estúdios Cor's edition of *A Thousand and One Nights*.) As is the case with several of Puccini's operas, when the composer decided on this story, it was already well known and had inspired several literary and musical works, the best known being Schiller's play, presented in 1804, and Ferruccio Busoni's opera also entitled *Turandot* (1917). Puccini's version differs from the others in very important details, however. Some of the most noteworthy are that the impassive princess is mellowed and won over by love, and the riddles that are presented to the suitors differ markedly and significantly from those utilized by Schiller and Busoni. Most important perhaps, the character Liù, one of the greatest of Puccini's creations, is totally unique to his version. *Turandot* exhibits the transparent simplicity of plot common to Puccini's greatest operas. The story is set in an exotic, fairyland Peking. Turandot is really a victim of psychopathic chastity even though she ostensibly assumes the role of avenger of the dishonor of an ancestor who perished at the hands of cruel invaders. The cold and despotic Turandot delights in condemning to death all suitors who are unable to solve her mysterious riddles. When the Unknown Prince's turn comes and he successfully does so, his life still remains in danger. For he, although justly victorious, magnanimously grants the impassive Turandot that, should she learn his name by morning, he shall relinquish the right to her hand and willingly submit to the fate that befell all the others. The little slave girl Liù is the only person, besides the Prince's own father, in possession of the secret and therefore becomes the victim of Turandot's cruelty. But because she loves Calaf—"Because once, in the Palace, you smiled at me"—Liù takes her own life for fear of divulging the secret under torture.

Puccini composed the music up to this dramatic moment of Liù's death. Fate would have it that his own death prevented him from completing the Act III love duet and the finale, for which he had merely outlined the music. It was on the basis of this sketch that Franco Alfano composed the opera's last fourteen minutes of music. We know that Puccini agonized over the music he did not live to write; that he envisioned it as a kind of mini swan song; that he even hoped to make it "like Tristan," as a note scribbled on one of the sketches of the duet indicates. However, the libretto, as it stood then and as it stands today, gives a good idea of the dramatic climax the composer had in mind. Calaf and Turandot stand alone on the stage. Her face is covered by a veil meant to protect her from the horror of Liù's suicide. After accusing Turandot—"Principessa di morte! Principessa di gelo!"—of causing Liù's death, Calaf rips aside the veil concealing her face and kisses her passionately. At this point the cold Turandot voluntarily, although only momentarily, also drops the veil of her contrived impassivity and confesses to always having loved him. Confident of the power of love, Calaf defiantly reveals his name, knowing full well that this action can still mean his death. In the last scene of the opera the court assembles to witness the divulging of the anxiously awaited secret. Turandot, to everyone's but Calaf's (and the opera's audience's!) surprise, joyously announces that his name is "Love."

Mosco Carner's Freudian interpretation of the relationship between Puccini and his characters casts some important light upon the possible reasons behind Sena's poetic interpretation of *Turandot*.[24] Carner's theory, in very simplified terms, is this: Puccini, he argues, chose the subject matter of his operas for three reasons: the musical suitability of the stories, the dramatic suitability of the stories, and certain affinities he perceived between the subjects and his inner self or unconscious fantasies. The foremost among the latter was a fixation on his mother, which manifests itself, as far as the composer's personal life is concerned, in his avoidance of superior women (symbols of the powerful Mother) and his pursuit of socially inferior women (who allowed him to feel dominant and secure, as well as free from the terrible shackles of Mother). In Puccini's works, this leads to the creation of a gallery of "poor little girls," placed far below the pedestal occupied by Mother. Puccini falls in love with these characters and, as a compensation for giving them a low social and moral status and inflicting pain and death upon them, he also attributes to them extremely positive human qualities. His is a classical example, says Mosco Carner, of the psychological ambivalence described by Freud in the statements "I should like to enjoy your love" and "I should like to murder you." Turandot, who in more ways than one is the great exception among Puccini's female characters, is the very symbol of the exalted, cruel and feared Mother. This theory is made particularly attractive when, as Mosco Carner notes, we realize that Puccini's male characters are also symbolic projections of the composer: "in the tenors he is the romantic lover, in the baritones he is the killer of his heroines."

In Sena's poem, Turandot and Calaf also acquire a symbolic significance that transcends the opera itself: Calaf is Puccini's alter ego, and Turandot his own death. By bringing the composer into his own opera, Sena has broken down the barriers between dramatic, i.e., literary, and empirical reality. The poem recalls the moment of Liù's death, goes on to describe some aspects of the music and of the general character of the opera—"Estrondos exóticos de orquestra e pompa, / as árias transformadas em conjuntos / que oscilam sempre entre o humor e o drama" ("Exotic crashes of orchestra and splendor, / arias transformed into ensembles / always wavering between humor and drama"); Sena even strikes a note of source criticism: "tudo cheirando a *Boris Godunov*" ("smacking entirely of *Boris Godunov*"), which is probably an allusion to Puccini's use of the chorus in *Turandot*. But, as far as the overall essential message of "Principessa di Morte" is concerned, all this remains ancillary to the last of the third strophic sections of the poem:

> *Mas Turandot, apesar de posta nesta música,*
> *não era apenas a heroína de uma história fantástica,*
> *uma peça de Gozzi, que podia dar pretexto*
> *à ressurreição da grande ópera em termos de ironia.*
> *E, quando Puccini ergueu a mão de um* alter-ego
> *para rasgar-lhe o véu que lhe escondia o rosto,*
> *não foi já música nem canto ou formosura*
> *o que ele viu, mas a caveira lendária*
> *da* principessa di morte, principessa di gelo,
> *que o aguardava para devorá-lo.*

> (But Turandot, though placed in this music,
> was no simple heroine of a fantastic story,
> a play by Gozzi, providing the pretext
> for the resurrection of grand opera in ironic terms.
> And when Puccini raised the hand of an alter-ego
> to unveil her face,
> it was no longer music or song or beauty
> he saw, but the legendary skull
> of the *principessa di morte, principessa di gelo,*
> waiting to devour him.)

What motivates Sena to equate Turandot with Puccini's own death and Puccini with the protagonist Calaf? Could it have been ideas similar to those expressed by Mosco Carner? Could it be that Sena, notwithstanding the cruelty of the idea, saw Puccini's death as a kind of poetic justice? Aren't Puccini's operas strewn with the corpses of his female victims—Ana, Fidelia, Manon, Mimi, Tosca, Butterfly, Angelica, Liù? Is it not befitting and just that one of his own creations, Turandot, "avenge" the death of the others? Isn't Turandot conceived as the avenger of the cruelty inflicted upon other women and the very symbol of death? Doesn't Calaf's (Act I) twice-repeated cry "Turandot" provoke the same choral response "La Morte"? Aren't the very riddles—"Hope, Blood, Turandot/Death"—also an invitation to Sena's interpretation? Finally, doesn't Puccini's simultaneous struggle with his own death and the rush to finish *Turandot* suggest, indeed make *inevitable*, the associations that Sena establishes in his poem? The latter is so much enriched by the fact that Sena makes the associations while omitting all explanations as to what led him to do so. This way the reader can—and, if he is to savor the poem, he must—search for his own answers in Puccini's opera and life. Sena's poem is an invitation to itself, as well as an invitation to revisit Puccini's opera.

But the poem is also a tribute to Puccini's memory. As is well known, at the first performance of *Turandot*, Arturo Toscanini refused to conduct beyond the point immediately following Liù's death. He laid down his baton and said to the audience: "Here ends the opera left unfinished by the Master, for at this point the Master died." Isn't Sena also suggesting that Puccini's death was his last creative act, one which his last work not only anticipated but incorporated to the point where one act becomes the completion of the other? In other words, isn't Sena also suggesting that Alfano's music need not be played because Puccini's opera is "complete" without it? Whatever explanations one chooses to come up with for Sena's interpretation, one thing is most certain: "Principessa di Morte" compels us to look at the intimate, if not necessarily direct or readily apparent, relationship between Art and Life.

"Listening to 'Socrates,' by Satie"

The last poem of *Art of Music* inspired by an operatic work is "Listening to 'Socrates,' by Satie." In the note to the poem, which was previously quoted, Sena writes: "Inspired by the opera, particularly its text, which is based on Plato's 'dialogues,' the poem centers especially on Socrates (and on what Satie's music says about him, as synthesized in the last two lines)." Sena's poem captures both the content and manner of Satie's *drame symphonique*: it scarcely goes beyond the dramatic content of *Socrate* and even reproduces verbatim (in Portuguese translation) lines from the drama; it expresses these dramatic elements with the essentially unadorned "linearity" and the "sort of Greek perfection" that, according to critics, characterizes the music of *Socrate*. But "Listening to 'Socrates,' by Satie" is not a mere imitation of some dramatic and musical constituents of Satie's work. The poem is, above all else, a re-creation and restructuring of those elements, particularly the dramatic ones. In addition, the last two lines of the poem—the ones that Sena particularly singles out in the note to the poem—suggest that the latter may be read in part not only as a portrait of Socrates but a portrait of Satie—and a portrait of Sena himself.

Satie's symphonic drama is divided in three parts, each respectively based on Victor Cousin's translation of the *Symposium, Phaedrus,* and *Phaedo.* Satie shortened the dialogues considerably by omitting all the technical philosophical passages. He also removed from Cousin's version what seemed to him a poetization of Plato's prose. Part I is entitled "Portrait de Socrate." As we recall, each of the guests at the Banquet is asked to speak in praise of love. When Socrates's turn comes, he claims to have been taught by the priestess Diotima that love can assume an intellectual guise, manifesting itself, for example, in the creation of poetry. But Plato's philosophy of love, which is almost wholly contained in the *Symposium* and *Phaedrus*, does not appear in *Socrate* at all. Satie concentrates instead on Alcibiades's speech in praise of Socrates. The drama opens with Alcibiades's famous similes: Socrates is like a Silenus, the little figure that was depicted as holding a flute or Panpipe and that could be opened down the middle to reveal the images of the gods inside; Socrates is like Marsyas the Satyr, the only difference between them being that Socrates makes music with words and not with musical instruments. He, Alcibiades, cannot help but be overcome and shed tears whenever he hears Socrates speak. To which the philosopher replies, as if he were not the subject of Alcibiades's praise, that it is now his own turn to praise the man sitting to his right. Part II of *Socrate*, entitled "Bords de L'Ilissus," omits the discussion on the two types of rhetoric and focuses on Socrates's invitation to Phaedrus to walk with him along the riverside until they find a pleasant and quiet place to talk. They come to rest by a "charmant lieu de repos! Comme ce platane est large et élevé."[25] Socrates tells Phaedrus the legend of Boreas. Part III, "Mort de Socrate," is by far the largest of the drama. Satie includes Phaedo's account of everything Socrates did and said during his final hours, but once agains omits the philosophical discussions on the immortality of the soul, the doctrine of ideas and the theory of reminiscences.

It is obvious that Satie's primary intention, as far as the text is concerned, was to present a composite but concise portrait of Socrates, the man and the philosopher, from as human a perspective as Plato's dialogues allowed. Why dwell to any greater length on his philosophy per se if all of Socrates's words and deeds, no matter how trivial they may seem, are the embodiment of his philosophical ideals of virtue and human excellence? Socrates, as Jean Brun says and as Satie's text (and Sena's poem on it) suggests, "lived only through conversation, through contact with disciples from whom he received as much as they received from him."[26] Satie gives us the living Socrates rather than the incorporeal ideas. Socrates presents himself or is presented by his friends. Satie seizes upon the most revealing elements possible: Alcibiades's similes, which give us simultaneously the outer and inner Socrates; the conversation with Phaedrus, one of the rare instances in which Socrates, the dweller and lover of the city, shows himself enamored of the countryside as well; the plain but earthshaking last words, which both Satie's drama and Sena's poem could not resist including: "Criton, we owe Asklepios a cock. Don't forget to pay this debt." The music of *Socrate* and the knowledge and imagination of the reader complete the portrait of Socrates.

In a letter to Valentine Hugo, dated 6 January 1917, Satie wrote: "I am very busy with *La vie de Socrate*. I'm frightened to death of bungling this work. I want it to be as white and pure as antiquity."[27] This purity informs the text of *Socrate*, which is smooth fluidity and utter simplicity—so much so that even the simple and direct dialogues of Plato are further simplified. But what about the music itself? James Harding sees a perfect harmony between text and music: "Like Racine, who drew his magical effects from the use of a severely limited number of simple words, Satie restricts himself to a tiny vocabulary. The slim filament of sound which opens the 'drame symphonique' may widen a little as time goes on, it may shift rhythm almost unnoticeably and change colour with a slight variation of nuance, but the tone remains the same throughout: cool, lucid, fluent." Harding adds that the "reticent, austere, dignified" *Socrate* achieves a "sort of 'Greek' perfection" (*Erik Satie*, pp. 179-80). And Rollo H. Myers sees in "the simple and limpid style of this reflective work which flows quietly and inevitably in an uneventful stream," the apotheosis of the "linear conception of music" to which most of Satie's previous works had aspired.[28]

The textual "purity" and tonal "limpidity" of *Socrate* are mirrored in Sena's poem: the purity of the poem's essentially unadorned descriptions of Socrates and in the naturalness of the diction; the limpidity in the conversational tone; the frequently alliterative and flowing enjambed verses; and, particularly, in the forward-moving linearity of the syntax. The latter contains relatively few of the figures of speech and rhetorical devices that often lend a labyrinthine quality to Sena's poetry, even to some poems of *Art of Music*. But this does not mean that the poem is not, in some instances, ambiguous, as we shall see.

A further discussion of the poem will be easier to follow if the latter is quoted in full:

> *Tão sábio, sereno e calmo,*
> *irónico e risonho, deram-lhe*
> *cicuta. Alcibíades descreve-o*
> *como um Sileno cheio*
> *de suaves imagens divinas.*

Fazer que os homens se nascessem
de si mesmos no contido
ardor de um diálogo incorpóreo
era o seu mister. Não ensinava
nada senão o mais além
de em nós—o juvenil
interrogar do corpo até à morte
sem responder-lhe nunca.
"Críton, devemos a Asclépios
um galo. Não te esqueças
de pagar esta dívida". E calou-se.
Havia amado a terra e os homens
como se os deuses não
fizessem mais que existir:
"Que encantador lugar para o repouso!
como este plátano é tão alto e forte!"
Um sátiro: "Que fascínio exerce
em mim a flauta dele", disse Alcibíades.
A música soprada e linear
do espírito que fala e não se entrega.

(So wise and serene, calm,
so ironical that he smiled when given
hemlock. Alcibiades describes him
as a Silenus full
of suave and godly images.
It was his duty
to make men give birth to themselves
in the contained passion
of an incorporeal dialogue. He taught
nothing except what is beyond
in us—the youthful
questioning from body to death
without ever providing any answers.
"Criton, we owe Asklepios
a cock. Don't forget
to pay this debt." And then silence.
He'd loved the world and men
as if the gods
did nothing but exist:
"What an enchanting place to rest!
how tall and strong this plane tree is!"
A satyr: "What fascination his flute
works upon me," said Alcibiades.
The musical breath and line
of the spirit that speaks and never yields.)

Sena paraphrases or quotes specific passages from each of the three parts of *Socrate*. He also elaborates on them. His is the kind of response that *Socrate* necessarily provokes. The dramatic elements given by Satie are so few but yet so far-reaching that one feels irresistibly compelled to elaborate on what they suggest. They are mere fragments of Socrates's person. We want to complete the portrait by going beyond them. This is what Sena's poem does to some degree. Lines 6-11, for example, constitute a description of Socrates's practice of philosophy, something that is not stated in the drama but is implied in the fragments of conversation given. The same can be said regarding lines 17-19. All the passages that Sena derives or quotes from *Socrate* contain verbs conjugated in the present tense. The elaborate passages are given in the past tense. This oscillation between the present and the past is in keeping with the experience of the drama. The latter gives us Socrates now. Memory, as it reaches for more, must draw from the well of the past. Socrates is as he was; he was as he is.

As noted earlier, Sena not only paraphrases and quotes passages from *Socrate*—he also reorganizes them in the poem. In other words, there is in Sena's poem a shuffling of the sequential order of the dramatic elements as presented by Satie. This shuffling is thematically significant. To begin with, Sena starts the poem where Satie ends the drama: with the death of Socrates. In the second half of line 3, the poet recalls Alcibiades's speech, which occurs in the beginning of Part I of *Socrate*. The first direct quotation from the drama, which is taken from Part III, comes next. The verses "'What an enchanting place to rest! / how tall and strong this plane tree is!'" are drawn from Part II. But "A satyr: 'What fascination his flute / works upon me,'" is again from Part I of *Socrate*. What is the thematic significance of the shuffling of these elements? By starting with the death of Socrates, Sena is probably emphasizing that it is the ultimate lesson to be derived from his philosophy, whose primary aim was to teach men how to die. The reorganization of the other elements suggests that, no matter how one organizes Socrates's words and deeds, the result is basically identical—for Socrates lives in every sentence he ever uttered and in every action he ever performed, including the taking of the hemlock. Sena also creates new, unexpected meanings for the quotations drawn from *Socrate* by forcing them into new contexts that are aesthetically most satisfying. For example, "'What an enchanting place to rest! / how tall and strong this plane tree is!'" comes to refer, in the context in which it appears in the poem, to Socrates's eternal resting place or grave (a befitting grave for him), and not to the spot by the Ilissus as it did in Satie's drama and, of course, in Plato's dialogue. In short, Sena's poem is not only an imitation of Satie's portrait of Socrates; it is a re-creation of that portrait, indeed a new kind of portrait.

In the last two lines of the poem, the text of *Socrate* recedes into the background. The spirit of Socrates is now wholly expressed by the music (as Sena tells us in the note to the poem). The poet suggests that the text of *Socrate* can give us the physical particulars of the man. But the medium that is best suited to express his spiritual essence is the music:

> *A música soprada e linear*
> *do espírito que fala e não se entrega.*

> (The musical breath and line
> of the spirit that speaks and never yields.)

In the whole context of the poem, the word "music" is ambiguous, however: it refers to Satie's music but simultaneously evokes the music of Socrates's words as described by Alcibiades. Could these two lines be ambiguous in yet another sense? Couldn't the spirit "that speaks and never yields" be at once construable as the spirit of Socrates, of Satie, and of Jorge de Sena himself?

Both Rollo H. Myers and James Harding have perceived striking similarities between Socrates and Erik Satie. Harding is of the opinion that Satie's special sympathy for Socrates's character is probably due to an affinity between the two men as fas as their personalities and experiences are concerned. Socrates was condemned for bringing in alien gods; Satie was criticized and "condemned" for introducing strange music. "Socrates lived a plain and simple life. He refused luxury and riches. They left him indifferent. He was the sort of man whom admirers describe as uncompromising in his ideals and whom enemies attack as quixotically stubborn. With all this he had a sharp sense of humour. These traits were to be found in Satie" (Harding, p. 175). The similarities that Rollo H. Myers perceives between Socrates and Satie are even more relevant to Sena's poem. "Both were ironists," he writes, "both had questing, inquisitive, 'gad-fly' dispositions, both concealed under a mocking exterior a profound disillusionment; both, in their different ways, were thinkers pursuing a lonely path, obstinate in their convictions and undeterred by the incomprehension and even hostility of their fellow-man" (Myers, pp. 56-57). In short, both had the kind of spirit that "never yields," no matter what the consequences. The last two lines of Sena's poem could, therefore, also apply to Satie.

But wasn't Jorge de Sena himself this kind of obstinate gadfly who, as a writer (and to some extent as a man), made enemies more readily than he made friends, although he had many friends? Wasn't he sarcastic, biting, accusing? Didn't he introduce a "new" kind of poetry, one that disconcerts some critics, so much so that they insist on calling it prose and worse? Wasn't he, for the most part, uncompromising? Didn't he suffer the consequences of his stubbornness and obstinacy? Isn't it befitting and just to apply to Jorge de Sena himself, this pagan humanist, what he applies to Socrates?

> *Havia amado a terra e os homens*
> *como se os deuses não*
> *fizessem mais que existir.*

> (He'd loved the world and men
> as if the gods
> did nothing but exist.)

It was stated earlier—and I am not the first to say so—that the accusing voice of Camoens, in "Camoens Addresses his Contemporaries," is simultaneously the voice of Sena. And that the "Ça ira" he perceives in Piaf's life and songs is also typical of his life and work. In the poem "L'été au Portugal," Sena's accusing voice manifests itself in terms almost identical to those of Socrates's and Satie's in the last two lines of "Listening to 'Socrates,' by Satie." After the furious diatribe against the socio-political conditions in his country and the self-denying apathy he sees in the Portuguese people; after rhetorical questions such as "Que Portugal se espera em Portugal?" ("What Portugal can one expect in Portugal?") Sena concludes, perverting Camoens's lines "Que morrer de puro triste, / Que maior contentamento?" ("What greater happiness, / Than to die of pure grief?"):

> *É tarde, e estão contentes de tristeza,*
> *sentados em seu mijo, alimentados*
> *dos ossos e do sangue de quem não se vende.*
> *(III,* p. 180)

> (It's late, and they are happy in their sadness,
> sitting in their own piss, feeding
> on the bones and blood of those who won't sell themselves.)

Isn't "The musical breath and line / of the spirit that speaks and never yields" yet another symbolic projection of the same accusing voice that will not quit, that will never compromise, no matter what the consequences may be?

VIII

Poems on Absolute Music

Of the 44 poems that comprise *Art of Music*, 20 are based on works of so-called absolute or pure music. (One of the works of music, Mahler's Second Symphony, actually has a brief program and choral passages that lend it a programmatic meaning. However, Sena's poem on that composition will be discussed in this chapter.) For the poet, these poems on absolute works present somewhat different problems of poetic transposition from the poems discussed in the two previous chapters. These problems have to do with the "content" of pure music. Sena usually handles or "resolves" these problems by dramatizing them in the poems themselves.

So much stays in our minds after a truly significant immersion in music. Yet, so little of the tonal event per se seems recordable except in the film of memory. How does one impart to others the content and meaning of music? (For the time being, I will distinguish between apprehending and communicating the content and meaning of music as such, and having and expressing a *musical experience*. The former is ideally confined to the tonal substance; the latter, as has been repeatedly noted, in addition to involving our own subjective response, may include elements extraneous to the music.) Does music have content or subject matter the same way that a novel or a poem do? Are "content" and "meaning" the same thing? One can, with relative ease, share some aspects of the content of a novel, a poem, an opera, or even a programmatic musical composition by dwelling on their paraphaseable, verbalizable, components—action, characters, imagery, a melodic or rhythmic figure that suggests and is said to represent, say, the trickling of water in a stream, as in the beginning of Smetana's *Die Moldau.* Much literary criticism is dedicated to apprehending and verbalizing the meaning of a novel, a play, a poem. However, in the case of pure music, where there is precious little or nothing paraphraseable for the mind to seize upon; where content, meaning and form are one and the same thing to a degree unparalleled in any other artistic medium, how does one go about defining and conveying that meaning? Beethoven, when asked what was the meaning of the Eroica Symphony, so the story goes, is said to have gone to the piano and played the first bars of the work, thus emphasizing that music is its own meaning. Except for the work of the musical critic—who, in many cases, concentrates on describing, explaining and interpreting musically, i.e., technically—is silence the only thing left for us where pure, absolute, instrumental music is concerned? The poet Jorge de Sena says yes—and no.

All the poems of *Art of Music* seem to be predicated on two principles: a significant musical experience must be recorded and preserved lest it be lost to silence and oblivion; there are elements, particularly *human* elements, embedded in certain works of music that the poet feels compelled to celebrate and to share with other people. If the sounds of music—Sena asks in the poem "Bach: Goldberg Variations"—are not gratuitous but guided by intelligence into well-structured and meaningful patterns; if this happens as though it were accomplished effortlessly; if the music comes to resemble less a well-integrated temporal structure than sculpted stones, a curved wall; if music, furthermore, translates the joy of living into cascades of sound; if music can accomplish all this and much, much more, HOW (and the poet capitalizes this interrogative) can the poet keep silent about the music? In this poem, Sena also focuses upon some of the ideas he deals with in the postface and which were discussed in earlier chapters. There are two ways of speaking about music: technically and poetically. To speak of music technically, as a professional critic does, is inadequate as far as allowing the reader to "experience" the composition in all its rich complexities. It is tantamount, the poet says in "Bach: Goldberg Variations," to describing a painting by referring to colors, forms and volumes without showing the painting itself—or without having even seen it. The only adequate way of talking about music, i.e., of "presenting" its richness verbally, is by utilizing the medium of poetry. Although, as Sena would be the first to admit, poetry is incapable of expressing or re-presenting music as such, it can re-create a composite experience that has as stimulus and nexus a particular musical work. The poem can, furthermore, create an objective correlative for the content and meaning—as perceived by an informed and poetic sensibility—which the reader "experiences" to a degree he cannot by reading the critic's comments *about* the music.

These are indeed tall claims for the power of poetry and for the nature of music. The analogy with painting and the images the poet perceives as he experiences Bach's *Goldberg Variations* imply that there is—when pure music is poetically experienced, at any rate—a content and a series of meaningful images susceptible of being apprehended and presented by poetic language. In other words, poetry can render the audial, visual; and the temporal, spatial. But, can poetry draw sense directly by transposing purely tonal structures, or does it have to go beyond the realm of sound hoping to find some indirect way of conveying that sense? Is this sense induced from the music, i.e., read out of it, or is it read into it? These and similar questions and the aesthetic problems they raise were, given the objectives of this book, sufficiently dealt with in Chapters IV and V. The reason for reiterating them here is that the poems I will be discussing in the present chapter implicitly raise these questions and aesthetic problems all over again—not in merely theoretical, but practical or applied, terms. Therefore, besides whatever else they are, most of the poems on absolute music also constitute dramatizations of the very aesthetic and philosophical problems involved in the poetization of purely instrumental music. In problematic conflict are: the strengths and limitations of the poetic medium in capturing and particularizing the general thoughts and feelings lodged in music; and the viability or lack of viability of certain theories of musical creation and meaning vis-à-vis the poetic experience, here and now, of a given work. Also problematic are several questions. How close to the musical fabric of a composition can poetry stay and still have something to verbalize about? How far can the poet wander away from the tonal realm as such and still effect a convincing verbal transposition of the model piece of music? How can poetry appropriate to itself some of music's formal techniques without aspiring to be music-like and, most of all, without compromising its essential attribute: intellegential discourse? And, lastly, how can poetry discourse about all this and still remain, not musical or aesthetico-philosophical criticism in stylized form, but viable poetry in and of itself?

The representative selection of poems on pure music will be presented and discussed in an order different from the chronological order in which the poems appear in the book and which was followed, within the two general types (Miscellaneous, and Program Music and

271

Opera), in the two previous chapters. The reasons for this will become apparent. I shall discuss, first, a poem inspired by Scarlatti: "Wanda Landowska Playing Sonatas by Domenico Scarlatti." In this poem Sena dramatizes the power of attraction and retention that pure music has over him versus his tendency, operative in many other poems on absolute music, to depart from the music into realms extraneous to the audial phenomenon per se. This poem is thus a good introduction to the discussion of the groups of poems dealing with absolute music even though it is preceded in *Art of Music* by several other poems on absolute works. In two poems to be discussed, "Preludes and Fugues by J. S. Bach" and "Listening to Quartet, Op. 131, by Beethoven," Sena comes probably closest in all the poems of *Art of Music* to concentrating on the strictly tonal dimension vying to capture the content and meaning embedded therein. In "*Water Music*, by Handel," the poet reconciles aspects of the tonal and extramusical properties to effect a poetic metamorphosis which is, in my view, the crowning glory of *Art of Music* and one of the most beautiful poems Jorge de Sena ever wrote. Finally, in "Mahler: Resurrection Symphony" (based on the last movement, which is partially choral) we shall see how Sena, in sharp contrast with the music's intended meaning, conveys what is perhaps the strongest humanistic statement made in *Art of Music*: the ultimate meaning and function that great music, according to Jorge de Sena, has and represents for humankind.

"Wanda Landowska Playing Sonatas by Domenico Scarlatti"

As noted above, the strictly acoustic properties of absolute works can exert such gravitational pull, as it were, over the poet that he feels unable (or unwilling) to extricate himself from the realm of sounds. The tones become the only object of his attention. Therein he searches for, and finds, meanings, either by inducing them from the music, or by projecting them onto it. Those meanings, insofar as they are verbalizations, do necessarily implicate extramusical factors. The important point, however, is that the meanings are solely conditioned by the acoustic event and not derived from any ostensibly extraneous elements. In other words, the poet experiences the music on Copland's expressive plane of listening (see Chapter IV). But there are works of music—and for Sena Scarlatti's Sonatas constitute good examples—which bear little or no reading out of or into, i.e., that impose themselves as meaningful but "unmeaning" abstractions. Are these "unmeaning" works severed from life experiences, cut off from life? What can poetry say about such works? The poem on Scarlatti implicitly poses these very questions.

A work of absolute music can, on the other hand, act as a sort of catalyst that stimulates the poet's associative faculties, thus impelling him beyond the music without releasing him altogether. When this happens, the poem oscillates between one and the other pole, i.e., between transposing from or reading into the music as such and gathering what the music stirs up: historical associations, philosophical reflections of a general nature, elements related to the lives of the composer and performer, etc. In this case, the poem comes close to being a poetic analogue of the kind of composite or impure music experience that most people probably have, the irritations and preachings of tonal purists nowithstanding. This centripetal versus centrifugal force that music can have over the poet—and, as I said earlier, most of the poems on pure music follow one or the other of these two tendencies—is dramatized in "Wanda Landowska Playing Sonatas by Domenico Scarlatti." In this poem, Sena reconciles two seemingly mutually exclusive factors: he unequivocally proclaims the tonal integrity and self-sufficing abstractness of music, at the same time that he builds a bridge leading from life to the music and from the music back to life. Implicitly dramatized in this poem is also the difficulty of conveying through the medium of language this "unmeaning" abstraction that is the music. The poem affords, therefore, a good opportunity for the reader to look at the poet's workshop, to share in some of the difficulties and solutions involved in the process of extracting poems from musical experience.

Further discussion of the poem requires that the latter be quoted in full:

> Ouço-a tocar estas sonatas
> anos depois que já está morta,
> e mais de duzentos anos
> depois que Domenico morreu.
> É isto agora a nossa humanidade,
> com que a vida se prolonga
> e os sons que alguém vibrou
> como estes que ressuscitavam
> um instrumento abandonado.
> Seria tão fácil o imaginar
> daquele Madrid de cabeleira
> com a princesa portuguesa que
> o levara consigo e às
> harmónicas cantigas
> que se hispanizaram
> nesta elegância doce.
> Mas não. Nem o perfil

pontiagudo da cravista que
tão severamente
moveu tão delicada
os dedos duros
nessas teclas de preterido som.
Tudo isso nada é perante
abstração como esta
de morta música
num morto cravo
tocado pela morta
nesta apoteose
de ressurreição
que eu posso, com um toque,
demiurgo e mago,
conclamar a que
me submerja em vida
percutindo
a solidão
triunfal.

(I hear her play these sonatas
years after she died,
and more than two hundred years
after Domenico died.
This is now our humanity,
with which we prolong life
and the sounds someone struck
like these that revived
an abandoned instrument.
It would be so easy to imagine
that bewigged Madrid
with the Portuguese princess who
carried him off and the
harmonious songs
that were Hispanicized
in this sweet elegance.
But no. And not the sharp-pointed
profile of the clavierist who
so severely
moved her so delicately
firm fingers
over these keys
of suspended sound.
All this is nothing before
abstraction such as this
of dead music
in a dead clavier

                    played by a dead woman
                    in this apotheosis
                    of resurrection
                    that I can accompany,
                    demiurge and mage,
                    shouting for it
                    to submerge me in life
                    striking
                    the solitude
                    of triumph.)

The poem's subject matter develops in the order in which it was announced in the title: "Wanda Landowska Playing . . ." The poet
enters into the music from the side of life, i.e., by acknowledging the
'living presence' in the music of the performer and composer who are
now dead. As noted earlier, all musical experience—and Sena's poem
reveals that he knows this very well—is the result of the collaboration
among three entities: the composer, the performer, and the listener.
The first two entities, performer and composer, are mentioned at the
beginning of the poem. There is perhaps some logic in mentioning the
performer first, for she is the one that the listener is most directly
aware of as he enters into the musical experience. The third entity, the
listener, is of course implicitly present throughout the poem, but is actually mentioned—"that I can . . ."—at the end of the poem. (In a
second poem on Scarlatti, also inspired by these same compositions—but which, for the sake of economy, will not be
discussed—Sena again treats of this interrelationship among performer, composer and listener, concentrating this time on the relationship between the last two.)
    But let us follow "Wanda Landowska Playing Sonatas by
Domenico Scarlatti" chronologically. An important theme, related to
performer and composer, is announced at the outset and reiterated:
death. Following this, the poet pauses to meditate on human life and
death and on art's ability to transcend death or somehow extend life.
The second important theme of the poem, resurrection, is introduced
in connection with the music and the musical instrument itself, the
harpsichord. Death and resurrection are thus the poem's thematic
poles, thesis and antithesis—which will resolve in a synthesis. So far
the music itself, the Sonatas, have only been alluded to in the vaguest
of terms. What the music has done so far is bring to the poet's consciousness the human fate of performer and composer, which in turn
has occasioned reflections leading to the classical theme of the survivability of humankind through its own artistic creations. Poetry, so
the poem strongly suggests up to this point, is much more at ease

discoursing about ideas and tangible things connected with the music than about the music as such. How easy it would be, the poet tells us, to continue in this vein: to talk about Scarlatti in Madrid; the eighteenth century and its customs ("that bewigged Madrid"); the Hispanicization of Scarlatti's music, a debt mentioned by all critics of his music; the relationship between Scarlatti and his famous pupil and protectoress, Princess Barbara, daughter of John V of Portugal and future Queen of Spain. How easy and comfortable for poetry, in other words, to continue talking around the music. But is the poet being fair to the music? Does Scarlatti's music warrant this kind of centrifugal approach? The poet, who approaches the music from the outside, as it were, finally reaches the sea of pure sounds.

Finding himself immersed in the tonal fluidity, the poet feels as if guilty (this feeling of guilt is even much clearer in the second poem on Scarlatti)—guilty about having concentrated on all those extraneous elements and forsaken the music, the "suspended sound." None of those extramusical factors he mentioned—the poet now realizes—matter very much before "abstraction such as this." The music, he now implies, is everything; it is capable of standing by itself. Its significance for us rests on its "touching our entirely empty ego, the self without further content," to quote one of Hegel's opinions regarding the function of music.[1] But, if this is so, how can poetry speak about an entity that, by definition, has no verbalizable content? In other words, if, as Sena implies in the lines "All this is nothing before / abstraction such as this," the significance of music lies in its abstract organization—what can poetry do except proclaim this truth and afterwards confine itself to silence? This is, indeed, what happens in the poem. After proclaiming the abstract and self-contained significance of music, poetry does remain silent. It does not say anything else about the music per se. What poetry can still do is talk about the overall experience of listening—of listening to something that has high significance but no verbalizable meaning. The poet goes on talking about the overall experience of listening by returning to the tangible elements with which he started—those that 'did not matter before abstraction such as this': *dead clavier, played by a dead woman*, etc. It is this music created and performed by entities now dead, in a "dead" instrument, the very same music that is capable of submerging the poet in *life*. Whose life and what life? The life that the music in and of itself possesses, that abstractness the poet spoke of, or the life that was imparted onto it by Scarlatti and Landowska and that the poet receives and feels embraced by as a listener? The poem seems to suggest—despite some hints to the contrary—that it is the latter. The poem also implies, however, that this life is, in part, the life that the poet himself, demiurge-like, has just imparted to the music. This "abstraction" is meaningful and self-contained, not because it has managed to isolate itself from life, but precisely because it comes enveloped in life and is capable of stirring and, like a magnet, attracting more life into its center.

This poem is, therefore, as much about Scarlatti's Sonatas per se as it is a poetic meditation, inspired and conditioned by these compositions, on the legitimacy of cluttering the musical experience with extramusical associations. In a sense, what Sena does is play devil's advocate with himself by questioning the very approach to absolute music which the overwhelming majority of his other poems exemplify. We might say, in fact, that in this poem Sena comes close to undermining the humanistic foundation on which all of *Art of Music* rests. But, as might be expected, the poem comes to paradoxical conclusions. We might say that the poet explicitly defends one thing and the poem as a whole indicates quite another. The poet proclaims the self-sufficient abstraction of the Sonatas. Yet, what he does is begin by reconstructing the bridge that led from life to the music and, after pausing to proclaim the music's self-containedness, he goes on to admit feeling submerged by the life contained therein. Whence did that life come if not from the composer and performer—and, of course, from the poet himself? In this poem Sena has dramatized, I think, the two basic dimensions of music and has vied to uphold both: its strictly tonal integrity and its roots in life, a life which was instilled into it by composer and performer now dead; a life which the poet-listener, through the miracle of phonorecording and through the still greater miracle of poetic imagination, "can accompany, / demiurge and mage."

It was stated above that the poem implicitly recognizes the role of the three most important entities in the total musical event: the composer, the performer, and the listener. But a fourth can be added: the critic. The latter is the listener who possesses an uncommon understanding of the music and who, in addition, is capable and willing to verbalize his thoughts. However, if what one wants to draw from musical experience is not merely technical understanding but a parallel work of art, the role of listener merges with that of artist. Sena, as poet of music, combines into one three distinct roles: those of listener, critic (understood here as one who has understanding of music primarily as a cultural phenomenon, as distinct from a highly technical knowledge), and artist. The last is the most important, for the poet can theoretically fail to be a good listener and a good musical critic and still write a viable poem based on his experience of the music. By the same token, it is theoretically possible for him to understand a work of music and be able to articulate valid critical opinions on it and still produce an indifferent poem. In "Wanda Landowska Playing Sonatas by Domenico Scarlatti," we have a good example of how Sena can draw a most viable poem from his experience of music without striking a particularly notable critical pose. In this poem, the only thing that comes close to a critical comment is the recognition that these particular sonatas do not lend themselves, as other compositions might, to elaborate analysis on an expressive plane of listening; and that Scarlatti's music was influenced by Spanish music. What the poet does instead is fuse the role of listener with a historical ear with that of artist to dramatize the difficulties and possibilities involved in that composite role a far as creating a parallel work of art is concerned. What might be considered by some to be a listening weakness—the extramusical associations—is converted into poetic strength. This poem is viable not so much because Sena understood or failed to understand the music, or said or did not say anything critically valid about Scarlatti's sonatas, but because he re-created his complex experience of the music as poetry.

The poem is viable, furthermore, because it makes a humanistic statement that transcends any and all particularities of Scarlatti's sonatas, save their status as great art. This statement, which constitutes the poet's all-encompassing human response to the music, is this: contact with any great work of art is one of man's ways of experiencing spiritual transcendence, paradise—a paradise that is not only accessible to him in this earthly reality, but one which is actually of his own making. We note that Sena expresses this idea with words that have religious overtones: *resurrection, demiurge*, and *triumph*. However, these religious overtones are strictly applied to the human sphere. Art, a human creation, is capable of submerging us in life because it is a species of life—it is the extension of its creator's living breath in another form. He who experiences art is witnessing the resurrection of his fellow man and, as man, is sharing in the artist's immortality. The poet, who artistically fixes this portentous experience for the future, enters into this stream of latent eternal life that will be resurrected when someone reads him. As the poet was able, "demiurge and mage," to stir the life pulsating in Scarlatti's music, so will a future reader resurrect the lives embedded in the poem. If the reader should artistically re-create his or her experience for posterity, this cycle of art-inspired and art-propagated life will go on indefinitely. This theme of man's immortality through his creations — one of the most frequently recurring themes in all of Sena's poetry — is even more explicitly stated in the next poem I shall discuss.

"Preludes and Fugues by J. S. Bach, for Organ"

Before turning to the discussion of the poem, however, we may ask: What determines whether Sena incorporates in these poems on pure music elements extraneous to the tonal substance, for example the composer's biography, or concentrates solely on the composition's structural techniques and sonorous configurations? We may establish as a general principle that the extent to which Sena goes in relating the musical composition to any extramusical ideas is determined, it seems, not by any intrinsic demands of the poem, as it were, but by the nature of the inspiring work. The famous contextual circumstances associated with Handel's *Water Music* make it almost inevitable that Sena should incorporate them in his poem on that work, as we shall see later. On the other hand, Bach's pure music is as self-contained and self-sufficient as any music could possibly be. Albert Schweitzer tells us that Bach is one of those objective artists whose works stem "solely from the stimulus of their outer experience, we need not seek the roots of their work in fortunes of its creator. In them the artistic personality exists independently of the human, the latter remaining in the background as if it were something almost accidental. Bach's works would have been the same even if his existence had run quite another course."[2] By omitting any references to the composer's biography, or any other elements of an ostensibly contextual nature, Sena's poem implies as much.

As its title indicates, "Preludes and Fugues by J. S. Bach, for Organ" lacks the inspirational specificity that characterizes, for example, the poem on the Brandenburg Concerto, No. 1 or the poem on Beethoven's Quartet, Op. 131. "This poem," Jorge de Sena writes in the note, "refers to the series of complete works for organ by J. S. Bach, recorded by Carl Weinrich for Westminster, particularly to the preludes and fugues S 531, S 539, S 541, S 543. That Bach represents for me music par excellence will be made evident by this poem and others that deal with works by him" (*II*, p. 235). The poem is divided in three sections of 22, 19, and 18 lines, each section being separated by Roman numerals. Despite this division, however, and despite the fact that it was inspired not by a single but multiple compositions, the poem possesses thematic unity. Its content is tantamount to the thoughts, questions and answers that come to the poet's mind as he strives to discern the meanings embedded in the mass of subjects, answers and countersubjects that comprise these organ pieces.

This is the only poem of *Art of Music* inspired by fugal works. To what extent does Sena's poem reflect the fugue's structural techniques? Nothing in the poem reveals that Sena was as intent on suggesting a fugal scheme here as he was in the poem "Fugue on a Strophe by Gastão Cruz" discussed in Chapter IV. The only suggestion that Sena's poetic meditation on Bach's compositions was influenced by the contrapuntal nature of the fugue is the fact that the poem, instead of a forward-moving linear discourse, represents instead a halting discourse, i.e., it keeps pausing or turning back upon the ideas presented earlier, thus conveying a mild suggestion of contrapuntal texture. In other words, instead of a series of imitative techniques ostensibly advertised as in the poem on Cruz's strophe, here the fugal suggestion is incorporated into the thought processes themselves. As the latter are presented, recaptured, left behind and picked up again; as the poet now affirms one thing and later comes to question or modify his affirmation, he conveys the comings and goings of the fugal subjects which, as he meditates with the music, carry and shape his thought processes. Thus, if Sena was indeed influenced by the fugal forms at all, this influence is revealed in a subtle and not readily detectable way. Another suggestion that the poet is dealing with that musical genre is conveyed by the poem's diction.

The poem opens by establishing two important analogies. Sena's verbal equivalent for the musical sound is the most basic and unique of human attributes: speech. His poetic analogue of the fugue's structural techniques is the most human of human experiences: conversation. "Conversation" is, of course, an apt way to categorize a musical genre that uses *voices*, states *subjects*, provides *answers* and proposes *countersubjects*. But—and Sena is already dealing, not with the technical musical terminology, but with the human import of "voice" and "conversation"—speech presupposes a speaker; and conversation implies an exchange of ideas, the imparting of recordable information. The entire poem may be construed as an attempt on the poet's part to identify the proprietor of this "voice" that engages in such wordless conversation and to decode the kinds of utterances it makes. Will poetry be successful? This poem is, once again, as much a meditation on given works of music as it is a dramatization of the relative strengths and weaknesses of music as a means of communication; and of poetry as a mediational vehicle trying to do what it does best: particularize thoughts and feelings which, in the realm of music, exist basically without names or labels.

In the first part of the poem, Sena tells us that the "voice" that pleases him is that of man as musical artist. The "harmonious conversation" he is being witness to is made up of phrases that God does not speak, either because He cannot, knows how but chooses not to, or because He does not exist. It does not matter which. This music —of this we are absolutely certain—is man's. The sounds are a species of the humanly divine. Nothing matches this sonorous breathing (notice the life-imagery) that proudly, although without pretense or show, affirms itself; that creates in the listener—as the fugal melody splits up, turns on itself, or intertwines with other melodies—what amounts to an experience unsurpassed by that of any paradise his yearning spirit might envision. But the music, a product of reason, was not created merely to please—but rather to cause the poet to reflect. As he does so, he realizes that the music imposes itself as an example of *ex nihilo* creation. Of course, in his poems *de laudabis musicae* the poet may be excused a bit of exaggeration. No one, including the composer, creates *ex nihilo*. But if any artist in any medium can convey the notion of creating out of nothing, that artist is definitely the composer and that medium is unquestionably music. This part of the poem is, therefore, a celebration of the music—one which spills over, as it were, into becoming one of Sena's most daring celebrations of humankind. This blazing optimism is going to be considerably modified, however, in the next section of the poem, much as a fugal subject takes on new dimensions as it is picked up by different voices.

This second part begins with the verse "Dulcíssima—e agreste, não perdura" ("Most sweet—and rough, it doesn't last"). The antecedent of these adjectives could be the "melody" mentioned twelve lines earlier or it could be the "music" in general, or the "conversa harmónica" ("harmonious conversation") of the opening of the poem. The theme introduced by this line, however, is quite clear: it is the idea of transitoriness—of the fugal themes, to be sure, but also and particularly of human life, as the rest of this section clearly suggests. The poet's vision of man awakened by the music has traveled quite a distance away from the optimism of the first section of the poem. In accordance with the rationality perceived in the music, the poet, always guided and impelled by the attributes of his medium, pries into the patterns of sounds he hears. Conversation, thoughts, feelings—yes. But what is being said? Thoughts of what? What feelings and for whom? Are the thoughts in the music, or are they in the listener? These are the implied questions. And the poet concedes that, although it "talks," reasons, and feels, music does so nonreferentially. But he does seize upon a musical phenomenon that he senses is transposable verbally: sonorous tangibility or the presence of sound versus its absence. He translates 'presence' and 'absence' of sound into "being and nothingness," "beginning and end." Ah, but these—and here enters language's connotative versus denotative meaning, the language of common discourse and of poetic discourse—are symbolic analogues of the fate of man, no longer as demiurge capable of divine speech and of creating his own paradise out of nothing, but man as an ephemeral and mortal being. This thought is uncomfortable, however. And so the poet wanders off, away from it.

Music implicates one sense: hearing. But hearing is weak. Sight, which is much stronger, imposes itself. Visual analogues of the sounds and tonal structures are attempted:

> *E no entanto, há como que um dançar de luzes,*
> *ou pássaros despertos pela aragem fria.*

> (And yet, there is a kind of dancing of lights,
> or birds stirred up by the cold breezes.)

These lines, in the context of this section, represent two things. On the one hand, they reflect a logical and very common human tendency by coming to terms with the meaning of music through recourse to visual associations. But there is a more profound reason for them here: they represent a minor interlude, a momentary refuge, to the thought of death awakened a little earlier by the music. We pause to note that Sena is conveying an authentic, live experience of music, and not an aposteriorily conceived meditation. He expresses thoughts as they might occur to any sensitive listener at the moment of listening, one thought leading to another or contradicting it as the music flows on. As noted above, the fugal form, whose basic structural principles are presenting thoughts, splitting them up and re-organizing them, probably acts as a very strong analogue or model for the poet's thought processes. The images of dancing lights and awakened birds quickly vanish, though, for the music moves on and the strictly audial phenomenon exerts an overpowering attraction over the poet. The latter backs off from his imagistic greener pastures almost apologetically:

> *Apenas como que. Pois nada é como nada,*
> *e é isso mesmo o que este canto ensina,*
> *ao, sendo ouvido, nunca ser cantado,*
> *em sopros sucessivos que se extinguem.*

> (Something like that. For nothing is like anything else,
> and it's this the song teaches,
> in the hearing, not the singing, of it
> in successive gusts that die away.)

In the third section of the poem, the poet goes on experiencing the frustration of listening to a "conversation" without words. His medium is language. Language is a mediational vehicle. It must talk about something. As the poet tries to convey the essence of music—these well-structured thoughts of thoughts, these well-organized feelings without causes and without names—he is always faced with the same recurring question:

> *São contra a morte, ou contra a vida, as vozes*
> *que tão fugatamente desconversam?*
>
> (Are they against death or life, these voices
> that dissimulate so fugue-like?)

To this and similar questions, the only answer the poet can provide is "Não sei" ("I don't know"). But, as the tonal panorama is always changing, new questions arise to which previous answers no longer apply:

> *Numa estridência uma alegria vibra?*
> *Ou treme uma amargura asfixiante?*
> *E nestes graves que ressoa: a dor*
> *ou uma serena e firme complacência ignota?*
>
> (Is joy vibrating in sharpness?
> or is an asphyxiating bitterness trembling?
> And what resounds in these low notes: pain
> or hard serene, unknown complacency?)

To these last questions the poet feels there is an answer:

> *Oh não. Que a vida está ausente e alheia,*
> *lá onde, como aqui, os sons são ela mesma*
> *tornada um tempo que nos flui mental,*
> *concreto, ciente, e reduzido a nada.*
>
> (No. For life is absent and alien
> where, as here, sounds are life itself
> turned into time that flows in our minds,
> concrete, conscious, and reduced to nothing.)

Do these last four lines carry a positive or negative implication regarding what music can and cannot communicate and, more particularly, regarding the content of Bach's music? Is the poet celebrating the fact that life is reduced to sounds flowing in the river of time and memory, or is he lamenting the idea that, search as we may, in this music "life is absent and alien"? Do these lines contradict or reaffirm the thought-content of the initial section of the poem?

They probably have a double implication, but lean heavily toward the positive and optimistic. There seems to be some regret on Sena's part that music, in order to live and triumph as the meaningful but non-referential sonorous entity called music, must necessarily shun the kind of particularized thoughts and feelings that language is used to discourse about. To be sure, Bach's music is a species of thought, of rational discourse. It also contains feelings. But when we try to particularize these thoughts and feelings, they are found to be disembodied, slipping away, as the tones themselves slip away into silence. A few tangibles remain—such as the phenomenon of sound-silence itself—and to these poetry clings and around them weaves its living web, supplying what the music may lack. Another thing is most certain about the music—and this one is most worthy of celebration: music, as represented by Bach, is an act of creation that rivals divine creation itself, nay, one that stands for what divine creation is said to represent. For, as divine creation is said to have done, music starts from nothing and, out of this void, brings to life a universe. Much more than this: it brings to life the kind of universe that constitutes a heaven, a paradise, for the spirit of humankind. In this paradise the "voice" heard is not the accusing voice of a God, but the self-affirming voice of humankind itself. Could there be any greater message for music than this? Could any art form communicate as much even if it had an ability, greater than music's, to particularize and cognize?

"Listening to Quartet, Op. 131, by Beethoven"

In this poem there are two inextricably interrelated aspects to consider: the subject matter and the subject manner. The poet experiences the composition within the mental framework of well-known theories of musical meaning and musical origin. (This type of approach also characterizes the poem "Bach: Goldberg Variations.") Sena starts the poem by evoking an aesthetic theory of music, repudiates it, and then goes on to discuss that theory's implications and lack of viability vis-à-vis the musical work to which he is listening. He concludes the poem by offering his own opinion of the "meaning" of Beethoven's Quartet. But the poet does not only meditate *on* the music; he also meditates *with* it, i.e., he allows his poem to be shaped by the music's formal design. "Listening to Quartet, Op. 131, by Beethoven" constitutes a close, albeit much simplified, poetic analogue of the ABA or sonata form in which Beethoven's Quartet is primarily cast (Op. 131 is in sonata form, except for the last of its seven movements). Sena's poem is thus a meditation on the meaning of this composition and an adaptation of its overall design to poetic structure.

Described as simply as possible, the sonata form has three sections: the Exposition, in which the composer "exposes" or presents two contrasting themes or ideas; the Development, where the composer extracts the maximum effect from the two initial thematical groups; and the Recapitulation, where the initial ideas are recalled for final brief treatment and resolution. The first section of the sonata form is in the tonic key. This gives way or modulates to the dominant key in the Development section. In the last or Recapitulation section the dominant yields to the tonic or "home" key. Sena found adequate structural and syntactical analogues to suggest these musical constituents of the sonata form, the simplest outline of which could be schematized as follows:

A
Exposition
theme 1   theme 2
Tonic key (often Dominant key)

B
Development
Both themes developed
Dominant key

A
Recapitulation
theme 1   theme 2
recapitulated
Tonic key

There would normally be a double bar separating the Exposition from the Development sections, indicating that the former is repeated. This repetition lends the sonata form an AABA design. Sena's poem follows a simpler ABA structure. Also, the key relationships in the above scheme have been grossly oversimplified. Once again, I mean to indicate that Sena's poem conveys a strong suggestion of sonata form in its simplest terms. In no way is this meant to imply that he literally duplicates in the poem the sonata form in its general outlook, and much less that he attempts to imitate that form as it is specifically exemplified in Beethoven's Quartet.

The poem is divided into four sections of, respectively, 20, 15, 21, and 10 lines. The first section contains two main ideas expressed in declarative/affirmative statements, which I have interpreted as a poetic suggestion for the tonic. This is the Exposition. The next two sections of the poem, which together comprise the Development, elaborate on the two main idea groups introduced in the first section of the poem. The two middle sections amount to 36 verses, all organized into 15 questions. These questions represent a striking departure from the *affirmative* "tonal center" of the initial section and, I believe, a convincing analogue for modulation in music. In the very last section of the poem, Sena returns to the "key" of *affirmative*, i.e., non-question statements, and brings the initial "themes" of the poem, as well as the latter's entire argumentation, to a final resolution. Thus, the poem contains four strophes, possibly suggestive of *quartet*, which resolve into three:

Introduction	20 lines; 2 main ideas or "themes" (declarative/affirmative)
Development:	36 lines; elaboration of A (questions of a rhetorical nature)
Recapitulation:	10 lines; resolution (declarative/affirmative)

The relative length of the poem's Introduction, Development and Recapitulation sections is also in accordance with the sonata form, particularly as practiced by Beethoven, with whom the Development section grew to a length unknown in earlier composers. The ABA form lends Sena's poem—as it also does to a piece of music in which it is applied—an essay-like quality. The poet cites an idea and refutes it. He proceeds to develop the full implications of that idea and strives to substantiate his assertion by gathering supporting evidence from the music. He concludes by reiterating his original belief—this time, however, no longer in the more or less generalized fashion that characterized his introductory statement, but with the strong conviction accorded by the "evidence" already surveyed.

Turning now to a section by section analysis of the poem, we note the striking contrast between its two initial ideas or "themes." This contrast is also very typical of the sonata form. The first main "theme" of Sena's poem, an idea against which the entire rest of the poem is pitted, is the following:

A música é, diz-se, o indizível
por ser de inexprimível sentimento
da consciência, ou um estado de alma,
ou uma amargura tão extrema e lúcida
que passa das palavras para ser
apenas o ritmo e os sons e os timbres
só pelos músicos cientes de harmonia
e de composição imaginados. . . .

(Music is, we say, the unsayable
for being the ineffable twinge
of conscience, or of the soul's condition,
or of a sorrow so extreme and lucid
that it surpasses words to be
simply rhythm and tones and timbres
imagined only by musicians
learned in harmony and composition. . . .)

In these lines Sena synthesizes one of the better known and perhaps least controversial theories (we might even say, clichés) held by music aestheticians, composers, and even poets who have meditated on the meaning of music: the conviction that music, as a form of expression, begins its career where the power of words is incapable of penetrating. This implies—as Sena also indicates in the passage quoted—that music is a special kind of "language"—spoken only by the highly initiated—"musicians / learned in harmony and composition." To the rest of us mortals, who are used to employ more intelligential vehicles of communication, music remains incomprehensible. This view, or versions thereof, which is defended by, among many others, Richard Wagner, Matthew Arnold and Colin McAlpin (for the latter's view, see Chapter V), claims for music a degree of extremeness in expressibility that clearly places music beyond the reach of intelligential verbal discourse. According to this theory, music is the embodiment of unintelligibility in terms other than itself or the most generalized of thoughts and emotions, paradoxically not because of any lack of expressibility, but due precisely to an excess of it, as it were. The same way that an extremely high-pitched sound escapes detection by the human ear, so does music's expressive infiniteness evade the grasp of common language and common perceptibility. Richard Wagner, who emphasizes a predominantly emotional role for music, while maintaining that music can express specific emotions and ideas, also holds, somewhat paradoxically, that music "is the inarticulate speech of the heart, which cannot be compressed into words because it is infinite" (apud McAlpin, p. 148). In his poem "Epilogue to Lessing's

Laocoön,'' Matthew Arnold lends poetic support to music's ability to extend the power of words to an ''infinite'' degree. Inspired in part by a conversation he had with a friend about ''Lessing's famed Laocoön,'' as they walked through Hyde Park, Arnold's long poem is a defense of music, and reads in part:

> ''*Miserere, Domine*!
> The words are utter'd, and they flee.
> Deep is their penitential moan,
> Mighty their pathos, but 'tis gone.
> They have declared the spirit's sore
> Sore load, and words can do no more.
> Beethoven takes them then—those two
> Poor, bounded words—and makes them new;
> Infinite makes them, makes them young;
> Transplants them to another tongue,
> Where they can now, without constraint,
> Pour all the soul of their complaint,
> And roll adown a channel large
> The wealth divine they have in charge.
> Page after page of music turn,
> And still they live and still they burn,
> Eternal, passion-fraught, and free—
> *Miserere, Domine*!''[3]

The second or contrasting idea of this expositional part of the poem constitutes a blunt refutation and repudiation of the view that the expressive power of music lies beyond the scope of intelligential discourse. If music were a form of abstruse or obscurantist expression—a deduction to which that theory readily lends itself—then, the poet reasons, music would or could clearly appertain to the irrational, absurd and possibly to what is evil in human nature. Sena writes, in the continuation of the passage from ''Beethoven's Quartet'' (my italics):

> ....*Mas,*
> *se assim fosse, eles só dos homens*
> *saberiam mover-se nos espaços*
> *que a humanidade abandonada encontra*
> *nos desertos de si. Começariam*
> *onde a expressão verbal não se articula*
> *por impossível. Viveriam sempre*
> *na fímbria estreita à beira da maldade*
> *e do absurdo, como que suspensos*
> *na solidão da morte sem palavras.*
> Não é, portanto, a música o limite
> ilimitado dos limites da linguagem,
> para dizer-se o que não é dizível.

(............................But
if this were so, they alone would know how
to move in spaces
that a forsaken humanity finds
in the deserts of itself. They would start
where verbal expression articulates itself
as impossible. They would always live
in the narrow margin on the edge between evil
and absurdity, as though suspended
in the solitude of wordless death.
So music is not the limitless
limit of the limits of language
to say what is not sayable.)

In the second and third strophes of the poem—the equivalent of Development in the sonata form—Sena elaborates on the introductory statements. He develops the second idea or "theme" of the poem in the second strophe; and the first idea or "theme" in the third strophe. As would be the case with the essayist, it is now up to the poet to clarify his initial statement. Some of Sena's questions in the second strophe (for, as we recall, in the second and third strophes, all arguments are presented in the form of essentially rhetorical questions) are a development of the initial "theme" but also and simultaneously, descriptive of the music. That is to say, the poet seeks evidence for his thesis—that the music is *not* infinite, unintelligible expression—in the concrete example before him. Sena concentrates primarily, and logically, on the "discursive" aspects of the music: its emotional, conscious, rational, purposive nature. This second strophe ends with the following questions, which synthesizes the poet's argument:

> *Como pode uma coisa que sentimos tão medonha,*
> *tão visionariamente séria e pensativa,*
> *ser irresponsável?*

> (How can something we find so frightful,
> so serious and thoughtful in its vision,
> be irresponsible?)

I note in passing that the kind of philosophical tone that characterizes this poem is also typical of many other poems on pure music. And this is understandable; absolute music induces introversion, i.e., an inward, introspective search for what it all means, while in the case of music allied to texts or programs there is a greater incentive for extroversion or greater interest in phenomena out there.

The third strophe, although it is a logical continuation of the second, also hearkens back to, and develops, the initial idea or "theme," i.e., the theory against which the poet is vying. If, as that view contends, music is a vehicle for the expression of the unutterable and unintelligible,

> Será que nos diz do aquém, do abaixo,
> do infra, do primário, do barbárico,
> do animal sem alma e sem razão?

> (Does it speak to us of what is down below,
> of the infra, the primary, the barbaric,
> the animal without soul or reason?)

In other words, Sena continues to insist on the idea that that theory may mean both that music is undescribable sublimity, or—and this is the reverse of the same theoretical coin, as far as the poet is concerned (of course Sena is being ironic here)—animalistic infra-consciousness. Here Sena seems to be evoking Darwin's biological theory of musical creation, which states, in part, that "musical notes and rhythms were first acquired by the male or female progenitors of mankind for the sake of charming the opposite sex,"[4] i.e., that music is a developed form of the sexual call of animals. The poet rhetorically (and more seriously) asks:

> Não há então tristeza alguma nesta
> vida transformada em puro som,
> em homogénea outra realidade?
> Não é de angústia este rasgar melódico
> da consciência antes de criar-se humana?
> De que, portanto, vem este triunfo
> que se precepita, contraditório, nas arcadas
> dos instrumentos conversando essências?
> É simples convenção? É artifício?
> Silêncio irresponsável?

> (Is there no sadness in this
> life transmuted into pure sounds,
> into a homogeneous other reality?
> Doesn't this melodic tearing apart of conscience
> before it humanly creates itself come from sorrow?
> And from what comes this contradictory
> triumph hurling essential dialogue
> into instrumental arcs?
> Is it simply convention? Artifice?
> Irresponsible silence?)

The purpose of the last section of the poem is to supply Sena's unequivocal opinion of what Beethoven's Quartet means or represents to him. This part of the poem is also analogous to the general purpose or function of the Recapitulation in sonata form: to recapitulate the themes of the exposition and to emphasize the return home after the tour into other areas. Sena's poem does indeed come home in the "key" of affirmative statements, which return once again. Music, the poet concludes, is not an expression of the unutterable. It is not unintelligible mystery:

> Se há mistério na grandeza ignota,
> e se há grandeza em se criar mistério,
> esta música existe para perguntá-lo.
> E porque se interroga e não a nós,
> ela se justifica e justifica
> o próprio interrogar com que se afirma
> não quintessência ela, mas raiz profunda
> daquilo que será provável ou possível
> como consciência, quando houver palavras,
> ou quando puramente inúteis forem.

> (If there is mystery in hidden greatness
> or any greatness in creating mystery,
> this music exists for the asking.
> And because it asks itself and not us,
> it justifies itself and justifies
> the questioning with which it affirms
> it is not quintessence, but the deep root
> of what will be probable or possible
> as conscience, when there are words
> or when there will be no use for words.)

Sena's Recapitulation requires some explanation, for it is obvious that, in this last part of the poem, he does not merely reintroduce the initial "themes" in the "key" of affirmation. It is undeniable, however, that he succeeded in recalling those "themes": "mistério" ("mystery") (first "theme"), and "não quintessência" ("not quintessence") (second "theme"). Understandably, the poet could not allow himself, using the medium of language, the same kind of repetition that music tolerates and even demands.

Sena's opinion of what Beethoven's Quartet "means" is also not a list of clear-cut propositions comparable to those we might formulate in response to a question such as, What does that poem mean? The last section of the poem does, however, make a series of statements that convey the overall significance of Beethoven's

Quartet, in clear opposition to the theory stated in the first lines. And it is this: Beethoven's Quartet not only lies within the scope of conscious reason, but is indeed a species of rational and meaningful discourse in tonal language—one capable of being apprehended and conveyed by human speech. It is neither, as music is so often held to be, an outpouring of transcendental or supersensuous consciousness, nor a vehicle for subliminal or infra-conscious discharge. If it were any of these—these last verses imply, in accordance with what was clearly stated earlier on in the poem—then music would fail to move us in the way that it does. Music is indeed "life transmuted into pure sounds." Though the language of music is not ostensibly empiric, yet it is not impermeable to poetry. Indeed, it is the latter that has been discoursing on, revealing, translating into words the significance of music and, most of all, upholding its humanistic integrity. If it finds its verbal match, then music's secrets can indeed be apprehended. If adequate language does not exist, then music's meaning is music itself. This is what Sena means by "when there are words" (i.e., when music is apprehended by poetry), "or when there will be no use for words" (i.e., when music is left to "explain" itself).

Implicit in this poem, as in many other poems of *Art of Music*, is the complementary nature of the two sister arts even though Sena never fails, here as elsewhere, to uphold the aesthetic individuality of either music or poetry. Despite the fact that the structure and rhetorical devices of Sena's poem do convey a suggestion of musical form, the poet is far from aiming at a duplication or translation of tonal into verbal language. What the poet does is, by exercising the most unique attribute of poetry—its ability to discourse rationally and empirically about anything whatsoever—to reveal the humanistic essence diluted, as it were, in music's non-verbal but rational and meaningful language. It aims, furthermore, to rescue music—this particular composition at any rate—from theories that would almost dehumanize it by placing it outside the realm of this-wordly experience and human logic.

"Water Music, by Handel"

In this poem the centripetal and centrifugal attractions exerted over the poet by the audial and extramusical phenomena associated with Handel's composition are finely reconciled. In the note to "*Water Music*, by Handel," Sena states that "This poem cannot be related to a specific interpretation of a work that was always dear to me (as most of Handel's music is), since the composer became known to me, still in my childhood, through the famous *Largo*, transcribed for piano, from his opera *Xerxes*" (*II*, p. 236).

292

It is not clear from the note or the poem itself whether the latter is inspired by the two loose suites known as *Water Music*, which amount to over twenty pieces or whether it is based on the currently most often heard suite arranged by Sir Hamilton Harty, consisting of six little pieces: Allegro, Air, Bourré, Hornpipe, Andante, and Allegro deciso—the last being another Hornpipe. Mrs. Mécia de Sena informs me that Jorge de Sena had several editions of *Water Music* in his library. He could have drawn inspiration from any of them. By not mentioning any version in particular, the poet suggests that this was a work he listened to very often and in different interpretations. For purposes of this analysis, it is not important to identify the exact version of *Water Music* that served as inspiration for the poem.

"*Water Music*, by Handel" is a poetic metamorphosis resulting from the fusion of two related but distinct experiences, which the poet succeeds in conveying simultaneously: the experience of listening to the music and the verbal re-creation of the circumstances associated with the music's performance. Sena also communicates the philosophical and aesthetic, as well as social, ethos that marked the Augustan Age (ca. 1700-1745) in England.

One of the most celebrated of Handel's instrumental works, *Water Music* is almost equally famous for the circumstances associated with its performance aboard barges on the River Thames for the entertainment of George I of England and his retinue. While he was Elector of Hanover, so the often disputed but delightfully romantic story goes, the future king gave permission to Handel, his Kapellmeister, to visit England, where Handel had been before, with the condition that he return within an agreed period of time. But the composer chose not to honor this commitment. When, after the death of Queen Anne, the Elector became George I, Handel sought appeasement and reconciliation with the monarch by composing and offering him *Water Music*, which Handel himself directed on a barge that accompanied the king's. When told that the music was Handel's, George I is said to have called the composer to his presence and given him his pardon. This is supposed to have happened in 1715. "What is more probable," writes Lillian Baldwin, "is that the Water Music, as we know it, a suite taken from twenty-five pieces of Water Music, represents Handel's contributions on various occasions. And what is more important is that it was, unquestionably, performed at those brilliant water parties for which the Thames was famous."[5] A second water party, this one well documented, took place on 17 July 1717. The pomp and circumstance attendant to this festival at which *Water Music* was played is conveyed in the two following accounts. The first is a report published in the London *Daily Courant* of 19 July 1717:

> On Wednesday Evening, at about 8, the King took Water at Whitehall
> in an open Barge, wherein were also the Duchess of Boltan, the
> Duchess of Newcastle, the Countess of Godolphin, Madam
> Kilmanseck, and the Earl of Orkney. And went up the River to
> Chelsea. Many other Barges with Persons of Quality attended, and so
> great a number of Boats, that the whole River in a manner was
> covered; a City Company's Barge was employ'd for the Musick,
> wherein were 50 Instruments of all sorts, who play'd all the Way from
> Lambeth (while the Barges drove with the Tide without
> Rowing, as far as Chelsea) the finest Symphonies, compos'd express
> by Mr. Hendel; which his Majesty liked so well, that he caus'd it to be
> plaid over three times in going and returning.[6]

A second account of the festival, a report written to Berlin by the
Prussian resident Bonet, mentions the instruments used: "Next to the
King's barge was that of the musicians, about 50 in number, who
played on all kinds of instruments, to wit trumpets, horns, hautboys,
bassoons, German flutes, French flutes, violins and basses" (apud
Deutsch, p. 77).

As stated above, what Sena does in the poem is convey the composite experience of listening to the music while simultaneously utilizing the time-machine power of poetry to transport himself (and the
reader) to the past and feast his other senses on the circumstances of
the aquatic festival. This at the same time that he also re-creates the
philosophical, aesthetic and social ethos of the Hanoverian Era. But
before analyzing the techniques by which Sena communicates this
three-layered experience, i.e., music, festival, times, let us quote the
poem in full and then try to follow, as far as possible, the development
of *Water Music* in the text:

> *Sobre o rio descem*
> *cordas e madeiras*
> *a remos de metais.*
>
> *É como sol nas águas, no arvoredo verde*
> *que as águas reverdece de verdura e sombra.*
>
> *Crepitam trompas e destilam flautas*
> *na crespa ondulação que as proas tangem*
> *e morre em margens de oboé e bombo,*
> *cadenciando o choque das remadas de ouro.*
>
> *A brisa flui*
> *serena e fina*
> *em cabeleiras*

e em rendas que
ondulam
risonhas e solenes
sobre os bordados esparzidos, prata
que dança e salta enquanto
as barcas se meneiam
na transparência opaca de águas como céu
azul que a tarde por silêncios tece
em majestade eterna e momentânea
dos astros em seu curso.

Habitados só
por deuses e pastores
gerados na saudade
da simples harmonia
contrapuntada na invenção da vida,
os planetas pisam
abstractas órbitas
à luz de um sol de que recebem foco.

E as barcas descem temporais o rio
de cujas águas são flutuante forma
da eternidade do destino ignoto.
Com pompas e sorrisos
os instrumentos tocam
virilmente lânguidos
a circunstância de uma festa aquática:
secreta e oculta uma melancolia
dessas grandezas que ordenadas fluem
a remos de metais no efémero perene
de que o eterno faz a sucessão de instantes.

Os últimos acordes como vénias passam.
O sol dardeja sobre as frondes. Tronos
dourados se dissolvem no reflexo de águas
que a música prolonga em gloriosas tardes.

E a glória se dilui de etéreas trompas
que as cordas acompanham sobre os rios
de música tão régia que a existência vive
o acto de pensar na ordem recriada.

(Downriver glide
strings and woodwind
to oars of brass.

It's like sun on the waters, on the green grove
that greens again the waters with verdure and shadow.

Horns crackle and flutes distil
on the crisp ripples the prows play
and there dies on banks of oboe and bass drum
rhythmically the shock of the strokes of gold.

The breeze flows
serene and fine
over hair
and over lace that
undulate
above the splashed embroideries, silver
that dances and leaps whenever
the boats sway
on the opaque transparency of water like a blue
sky which the afternoon weaves through silences
in the eternal and momentary majesty
of stars on their course.

Inhabited only
by gods and shepherds
engendered in the longing
for simple harmony
counterpointed to the invention of life,
the planets tread
abstract orbits
by the light of a sun that gives them center.

And the boats glide temporal down the river
whose waters are a fluctuant form of
the eternity of unknown destiny.

With pomps and smiles
the instruments virilely
languishing render
the circumstance of an aquatic festival:
secret and mystical a melancholy
of those grandeurs that, orderly, are flowing
to oars of brass in the ephemeral perennial
from which the eternal makes the succession of instants.

The final chords go past like bows.
The sun is shooting over leaves. Gilded
thrones are dissolving in reflection of waters
which music prolongs to glorious closes.

And the glory dilutes through ethereal horns
that the strings accompany over rivers
of music so royal that existence is living
the act of thinking in order recreated.)

(trans. Jonathan Griffin)

To begin with, each segment of the poem—most with their own strophic, metrical and phonic, i.e., word-music, particularities—suggests a different movement or piece; and the poem as a whole might be construed as a kind of suite. Indeed, as is also the case with the different pieces of *Water Music*, these sections of the poem could almost stand individually by themselves and be read as minute pieces inspired by music on the theme of Nature with added philosophical reflections. Some of these poetic pieces, in subject matter, are actually reminiscent of haikus. They are clear pictures which arouse distinct emotional and philosophical insights—in this case on the passage of time and on the transitoriness of life:

> *Sobre o rio descem*
> *cordas e madeiras*
> *a remos de metais.*

> (Downriver glide
> strings and woodwind
> to oars of brass.)

But, again in a manner reminiscent of *Water Music*, the poetic pieces function primarily as parts of an organic and harmonic whole, their thematic unity stemming from their 'outdoor' quality, their subdued festive mood, punctuated here and there by a touch of melancholy, and their majestic air.

Perhaps it is not too farfetched to suggest a parallel between the vibrant festive Allegro in F (I am referring to the suite arranged by Harty) and the section comprised of lines 6-9. The climax of the musical piece is particularly emphasized in the last two lines:

> *e morre em margens de oboé e bombo,*
> *cadenciando o choque das remadas de ouro.*

> (and there dies on banks of oboe and bass drum
> rhythmically the shock of the strokes of gold.)

The noun *bombo* ("drum"), where the resonance of the long nasal /om/ is imitative of the named percussion instrument, strategically placed at the end of an end-stopped line, is brilliantly suggestive of a musical climax, particularly considering that this climax had already been semantically anticipated by the *morrer* ("to die") at the beginning of the line. But this climax suggested by Sena is not abrupt, for the following line—"cadenciando o choque das remadas de ouro" ("rhythmically the shock of the strokes of gold")—suavely prolongs it, as well as calling attention to the river, i.e., the visual scene.

This is, of course, little more than a guess, because the emphasis on *bombo* actually might be more appropriate to suggest the climax of the Allegro deciso, the last piece in Harty's suite, where that percussion instrument is used more liberally than in the Allegro. The segment comprising verses 10-22 seems evocative of the Air, which is possibly one of the most famous and most often heard of Handel's melodies. The sweet, dainty, almost evanescent Air for violin, followed by the melody for oboe and other woodwinds, is suggested by the word "brisa" ("breeze") (which, as we shall see, also refers to the breeze blowing through the hairpieces of the "Persons of Quality"). Lillian Baldwin states that in this Air "Handel shows the delicacy always rather surprising to those who think of him as the composer of majestic oratorios." And she adds: "The Handel Air is a fragrant, lace-frilled nosegay for a pretty lady" (op. cit., Vol. I, p. 53). Sena seems to suggest as much by his references to "bordados esparzidos" and "prata que dança e salta" ("splashed embroideries" . . . "silver that dances and leaps"). These images, once again, refer to the attire of the royal and noble personages, but they are also adequate poetic images for this piece of music. From here to the end of the poem it becomes more difficult to identify, however tentatively, the poetic references to the different pieces of *Water Music*. It may be pointed out, however, that the Bourré, a 17th-century woodcutter's dance and one of the most famous pieces in the Harty-arranged suite, is probably being evoked in the section comprised of lines 23-30, especially the pastoral lines "habitados só / por deuses e pastores" ("Inhabited only / by gods and shepherds"). The lines also refer to the 18th-century feeling for Nature, which I shall discuss later. In addition, could the section comprised of lines 34-36 be suggesting, particularly in the lines "os instrumentos tocam / virilmente lânguidos" ("the instruments virilely / languishing render"), the slow tempo of the majestic D Minor Andante? Whether or not we choose to engage in illusory correlations and risky parallels, the presence of the music is constant throughout the poem. The music is constantly being evoked by musical vocabulary, naming of instruments, indications of tempo and dynamics, and suggestions of climaxes. These references to the music, however, are not in and of themselves the most important aspect of the poem. The poetic function of these musical references and images is only truly revealed when they are seen in conjunction with extramusical allusions and imagery.

How, then, does Sena communicate the notion of simultaneity in the poem, the feeling that he is both listening to the music and "watching" the festival on the Thames? (The third "layer" of the poem's thematic content—the *Geistesgeschichte*—is also conveyed simultaneously with the other two "layers." For ease of exposition, however, I will discuss it separately.) The poet utilizes two techniques to render this composite experience. These two techniques produce two corresponding effects on the reader. The first technique is the use of words that simultaneously denote, or refer to, the music and the river scene, i.e., to two different orders of experience perceived with different senses. This technique produces an effect somewhat analogous to counterpoint in music, as will be shown below. (We note in passing that its polyphonic texture is one of the outstanding features of *Water Music*. Sena actually indicates this when he writes "da simples harmonia / contrapuntada . . ."—"for simple harmony/counterpointed . . ."). The second is the technique of alternating between passages in the poem where prominence is given to the aural side of the experience, i.e., to the music, with passages that refer primarily or even exclusively to the visual or river scene. This technique creates the impression on the reader that the music is now more prominent, now fades temporarily into the background without ceasing altogether, relinquishing primary importance to the scene. However, the music always returns in the following verses. The first technique, i.e., simultaneous presentation is, in my view, a much greater poetic accomplishment from the viewpoint of its effect on the reader and I now turn to a discussion of it.

Referring to harmony and counterpoint in music and how these relate to literature and literary imitation of musical structural techniques, Calvin S. Brown states that these two elements

> need not be distinguished, since both are the results of simultaneously produced tones. They have fascinated poets, and numerous devices have been tried in attempts to find some literary equivalent, but invariably the problem of simultaneity has proved an insuperable barrier. We shall not find it necessary to consider harmony and counterpoint separately unless we find that literature has some way of producing two things at the same time, for it is clearly unnecessary to look for the species in literature if the genus itself does not exist. (*Music and Literature*, p. 39).

What would constitute in literature an equivalent of counterpoint, in which two or more melodies sound together with each maintaining its own character? An example would be simultaneously written, and of course simultaneously read, speech, i.e., two (or more) different strands of utterances going on at the same time and conveyed by the writer and perceived by the reader as sounding in simultaneity. Ideally, Brown is careful to point out (op. cit., p. 40), these two parts "must be at the same time separate—almost independent—and yet related." (We have to emphasize *written* conversation, because *spoken* conversation, as in the theater, can imitate counterpoint even though, says Brown, the idea of counterpoint applied to the theater has not been exploited to its full potential.) Among the techniques that writers have employed to imitate counterpoint, Calvin S. Brown mentions the following two. One technique used by the poet Sacheverell Sitwell (in his poem "On Hearing Four Bands Play at Once in a Public Square") is to print the poem in four different columns on the page, each column referring to what one band was doing, presumably to be read at the same time—thus producing the effect of counterpoint (op. cit., p. 40). Another literary device apparently aimed at a rough equivalent of "counterpoint" was employed by ancient Icelandic bards and consisted "in the habit of alternating the phrases of two different sentences, so that both ran simultaneously" (Brown, p. 41). In a four-line stanza that Brown quotes, "the part in parentheses is one sentence, and the rest is another" (idem). Again, if read simultaneously, and only then, this would convey a rough analogue of musical counterpoint.

Other literary adaptations of counterpoint employ totally different techniques. For example, in his novel *Point Counter Point* (1928), Aldous Huxley sets the events happening around Philip Quarles in contrapuntal relation to those he plans to utilize in his own novel. A similar technique can be found in Eça de Queiroz's novel *A Ilustre Casa de Ramires (The Illustrious House of Ramires)*, where the novel-within-a-novel device is employed and where certain events happening within the protagonist's own novel spill onto, or are in contrapuntal relation to, the life of the protagonist in Eça's novel. But, are any of these literary techniques—both those avowedly intended as imitations of musical counterpoint, as well as those that seem aimed at some approximation of it—really anything close to that musical phenomenon? Only one thing is clear: all these devices are different ways of doing the impossible. As Steven Paul Scher states, "the idea of sequentiality and simultaneity is achievable in music but only conceivable in literature" ("Literature and Music," p. 234).

In accordance with his ever-present tendency toward literary experimentation and his interest in the interrelation of the arts, Jorge de Sena too seems to have preoccupied himself with the phenomenon of counterpoint—even beyond *Art of Music*. In his novella *The Wondrous Physician* (1966), written at the same time as many of his poems on music, Sena utilizes techniques and devices akin to Sitwell's and the Icelandic poets'. One of them is rendering, in parallel columns, what one character says (left column) and what the other character understands that the speaker is saying (right column), thus conveying contrapuntally the conflict between spoken words and unspoken thoughts. Here is an example:

Eu era muito moça e muito inocente quanto meu pai me casou com Gundisalvo.	*Eu era muito moça, mas dia e noite sonhava com os homens, desde que uma vez vira meu pai nu.*
(I was very young and very innocent when my father married me off to Gundisalvo.)	(I was very young but, ever since the time I saw my father naked, I dreamt about men night and day.)[7]

The other technique used by Sena in the same novella is what may be termed simultaneous narration running together. This consists in alternating sentences within the same paragraph, each sentence alluding to what is happening to different characters at the same time but in different places. Thus, in the example (*The Wondrous Physician*, p. 139)

Depois que se banharam no rio, deitaram-se à sombra.
Logo que o outro desapareceu, ficaram aterrados,
incapazes de se mexerem.

(After bathing in the river they lay in the shade.
After the other fellow disappeared, they became
petrified with fear, incapable of moving.)—

the first sentence refers to one group of characters and one place, while the second sentence alludes to another group of characters at the same time but in a totally different place.

However, in neither of these two instances, which are apparently aimed at approximating counterpoint or something similar to it, did Sena achieve a perfect analogue of that musical phenomenon. For the effect of counterpoint to be entirely successful, the reader would have to read the two parallel columns and the alternating sentences *at the same exact time*—something which is, needless to say, clearly impossible. In "*Water Music*, by Handel," on the other hand, Sena comes as close to creating a verbal equivalent of counterpoint as I believe is possible in literature. When the poet writes

> *Sobre o rio descem*
> *cordas e madeiras*
> *a remos de metais,*

> (Downriver glide
> strings and woodwind
> to oars of brass),

we the readers are simultaneously aware, as the poet was, of both music and scene. For the nouns *cordas* ("ropes"), *madeiras* ("wood"), and *metais* ("metals") refer both to the musical instruments, respectively the strings, woodwinds, and brasses (thus alluding to the acoustic event), and also to the barges and boats, because the nouns *cordas, madeiras,* and *metais* (particularly considering that the last item is preceded by *remos de* ("oars of") are logical metonymies for the river craft associated with the aquatic festival. This simultaneous referral is made especially convincing when we take into account the first line—"Sobre o rio descem" ("Downriver glide"). This image, "Gliding downriver," applies simultaneously to the movement of barges and boats gliding down the Thames, as it does to the movement of the music in time, since *river* is a universal symbol of time and music a temporal art par excellence. Sena seized upon two extremely felicitous coincidences which, of course, he can be said to have created by recognizing their poetic viability and employing it: the intimate relationship between the *Water Music* and its contextual circumstances; and a semantic coincidence that allows the terms used to convey at once two strands of meaning which are simultaneously different and self-sufficient but, within the overall musical and extramusical context of *Water Music*, also inextricably and logically interrelated. A pause is necessary here to reflect further on what Sena does vis-à-vis counterpoint in music. Counterpoint is the simultaneous sounding of two or more different and yet harmonizing melodic lines. Sena's verbal analogue does not employ different orders of experience, no matter how related to each other. This is what he does in the two types of techniques I discussed in connection with *The Wondrous Physician*. What the poet does in "*Water Music*, by Handel" is different from what polyphonic music does—only the effect is basically identical, and the only hope that poetry has of ever truly approximating counterpoint without becoming servile to music: Sena uses the same set of words to *denote*—and this last verb is the key: to *denote* and not merely connote—two different and yet related and "harmonizing" sets of referents, an audial and a visual.

The simultaneous conveying of the festival and music is not restricted to the first three lines of the poem. The process is used throughout the text. In lines 6-9, for example, the technique is again employed:

> *Crepitam trompas e destilam flautas*
> *na crespa ondulação que as proas tangem*
> *e morre em margens de oboé e bombo,*
> *cadenciando o choque das remadas de ouro.*

> (Horns crackle and flutes distil
> on the crisp ripples the prows play
> and there dies on banks of oboe and bass drum
> rhythmically the shock of the strokes of gold.)

In this case, the contrapuntal effect is created by the deft pairing of nouns and verbs, as well as by simultaneous double referral. In the phrase "proas tangem" ("prows play"), *proas* ("prows") refers to the barges or boats and *tangem* ("to play a musical instrument") refers to the music. In "margens de oboé e bombo" ("banks of oboe and bass drum"), *margens* ("river banks") once again recalls the river scene and the rest of the line refers to the music. The references to the two types of experience are in the order festival-music. This order is reversed in line 9. "cadenciando o choque das remadas de ouro" ("rhythmically the shock of the strokes of gold"). Here, *cadenciando* (from "cadence") refers to the music, but also strongly implies the movement of the barges solemnly and rhythmically gliding downriver with their "Persons of Quality" on board—an idea which *remadas de ouro* ("strokes of gold") emphasizes. In line 10—"A brisa flui" ("The breeze flows")—we have very possibly a reference to the Air, as noted earlier, as well as a clear allusion to the breeze blowing through the wigs of the noble personages. The "simples harmonia / contrapuntada" (lines 26-27) ("simple harmony / counterpointed") not only constitutes a reference to the music ("harmony," "counterpoint"), but also to the idea of harmonious co-existence or order of the universe and human society—an echo of the philosophico-aesthetic ethos or *Geistesgeschichte* of the Augustan Age, as we shall see later. The beautiful simile embedded in line 42—"acordes como vénias" ("chords . . . like bows")—is an extremely effective way of simultaneously connecting the music ("chords") with the social graces of the nobility: *vénias* ("bows," i.e., to bend the head or body as a sign of respect).

Sena employs different variants of this same technique of simultaneous double referral throughout the poem, but what has been said about the process suffices. I now turn to the second device of alternating the two experiences. This technique is not always entirely separable from the one just discussed. It is distinct enough, however, to warrant separate treatment. Whereas lines 1-3, for example, were said to refer both to the music and to the scene at the same time, that music seems to have somewhat faded by the time we reach lines 4-5. In these two lines, no explicit reference to the music exists. (We can right-ly claim that these two lines are magnificent examples of word music; however, this "music" is that of poetry and not a reference to *Water Music* per se.) When the poet writes

> *É como sol nas águas, no arvoredo verde*
> *que as águas reverdece de verdura e sombra,*
>
> (It's like sun on the waters, on the green grove
> that greens again the waters with verdure and shadow),

the impression the reader gets is not that the music has entirely vanish-ed from the poet's consciousness, but that it has merely faded, thus allowing the visual dimension of the composite experience to predominate. The simile itself—"É como sol nas águas . . ." ("It's like sun on the waters . . .")—acts as a bridge or imagistic ligature be-tween the acoustic-visual plane (lines 1-3) and a predominantly visual one. In the next four lines (6-9) the music becomes prominent once again—only to fade once more in lines 10-22, where the only more or less clear reference to the music is contained in the noun *brisa* ("breeze," i.e., Air). In this long section the imagery is mostly visual and pertains to the river scene. It is also the first time in the poem that the poet acknowledges human presence. (The reference to astronomy—"dos astros em seu curso" /"of stars on their course"/—will be discussed later.) In lines 23-30, only *harmonia* ("harmony") and *contrapuntada* ("counterpointed") recall the music, whereas in lines 31-33 the music fades again, thus yielding prominence to the scene and allowing the poet to reflect philosophically on what he "sees." (These philosophical reflections, too, are part of the third "layer" of the poem.) From line 34 to the end of the poem, a mixture of the two techniques discussed here is used, both so interwoven with each other that it is sometimes difficult to determine where one stops and the other begins.

But, as noted earlier, Sena's poem is not confined to fusing the music, i.e., the audial component of his composite experience, with visual elements that evoke the circumstances associated with the performance of *Water Music*. The music and the aquatic festival are themselves reflections of something that transcends both. The philosophical and aesthetic, as well as social, *Zeitgeist* of the dawn of the Hanoverian Age in England. As Charles T. Smith says, "Listening to music which necessitates a projection of the mind into a past period—listening with the historical ear—is possible to the extent that one is prepared to make a deep study of the contemporary social culture" (*Music and Reason*, p. 34). "*Water Music*, by Handel" reflects such cultural awareness on the part of Sena. Indeed, the poet may be said to experience *Water Music* with an audial, visual and historical ear. His poem captures—and sometimes simultaneously with the audial and visual dimensions of the experience—the spirit of the times.

What spirit? We must, of course, distinguish between at least two quite distinct human "worlds" in the England of the beginning of the eighteenth century. London itself, prototypical, was a microcosm of these two worlds. On the one hand, there was the world of the dispossessed masses, whose despair is captured in part in Hogarth's prints of London life. This is the London whose squalor and filth are also described in John Gay's *Trivia, or the Art of Walking the Streets of London* (1716) and in Samuel Johnson's *London* (1738). This London, however, does not appear in Sena's poem, for it is not the London of the aquatic festivals on the Thames for the delight of royalty. The latter London, which is represented by the *Water Music* and partially captured visually by Canaletto's *The Thames and the City of London* (1747), is the world of the Augustan Age, the Age of Reason and of faith in man. The scientific and mathematical achievements of the previous century, particularly Newton's achievements, were bearing fruit. The old idea of a biblical universe had given way, at least in many circles, to the conception of a mechanistic universe set in motion by a deistic God, who then retired and allowed it to run according to universal laws that could be and were being explained. It was the age of optimism because science and reason could penetrate—so many people thought—not only the secrets of nature but the nature of human society and of man himself. And penetrate them they did—to discover order everywhere: from the cosmic order of the heavens, to the order of human society. Where diversity was perceived, unity was sought and found in the establishment of hierarchies. This organic order was transferred to the arts: the classical principles of discipline, clearness, formal beauty and self-control reigned supreme. Most thinking people agreed with the deistic ideas expressed in Alexander Pope's famous "An Essay on Man" (1733-34) and responded positively to the relative simplicity and clearness of its heroic couplets:

All Nature is but Art, unknown to thee;
All Chance, Direction, which thou canst not see;
All Discord, Harmony not understood;
All partial Evil, universal Good:
And, spite of Pride, in erring Reason's spite
One truth is clear, WHATEVER IS, IS RIGHT.[8]

This was a period also, and understandably, marked by the pursuit of happiness—a happiness that could be found in this world, for example in the enjoyment of art: literature, theater, plastic arts, and music; and in the enjoyment of Nature—but not the wild Nature that some Romantics would later celebrate;

Not Chaos-like together crush'd or bruised,
But, as the world, harmoniously confus'd:
Where order and variety we see,
And where, tho' all things differ, all agree,

as Pope tells us in "Windsor Forest" (1713).[9]

This world of universal harmony, of orderly Nature inhabited by gods and shepherds, of refined pleasure-seekers (even though George I was much more interested in the sensual type of pleasure than in the more "refined" ones) is also captured in Sena's poem. As the royal flotilla of golden barges glides majestically downriver to the sound of *Water Music*—possibly indifferent to or in "harmonious co-existence with" the boats of simple folk which also plied the waters of the Thames—in the heavens above

os planetas pisam
abstractas órbitas
à luz de um sol de que recebem foco.

(the planets tread
abstract orbits
by the light of a sun that gives them center.)

This "Newtonian" sun (with small letters) is a far cry from Milton's "Luminary," the visible symbol of God:

. . . the great Luminary
Aloof the vulgar Constellations thick,
That from his Lordly eye keep distance due,
Dispenses Light from afar...

(*Paradise Lost*, III, 576-79)

Handel's *Water Music*, Sena's poem suggests, speaks one of the important variants of the language of its time and place: the language of order and harmony, the language of the classics, the language of overall optimism. However, amidst all this, there is a note of sadness: the sadness that arises from the consciousness, paradoxically awakened by the music and the aquatic festival, of the transitoriness of all things, including human life. The line "secreta e oculta uma melancolia" ("secret and mystical a melancholy") probably refers to this consciousness, which was beautifully and more literally conveyed a few lines earlier:

> *E as barcas descem temporais o rio*
> *de cujas águas são flutuante forma*
> *da eternidade e do destino ignoto.*

> (And the boats glide temporal down the river
> whose waters are a fluctuant form of
> of the eternity of unknown destiny.)

Here the noun *rio* ("river") is not merely an allusion to the Thames or the temporal nature of the music. It is a symbol of life's flow. The *barcas* ("boats") are no longer just barges, they are suggestive of the ships of death. In the last two sections of the poem, this passage of time—and in this case it coincides with the end of the music itself—is reemphasized. But the poem ends on a positive note, because one thing remains: "o acto de pensar na ordem recriada" ("the act of thinking in order recreated"). What order? The order of all things human and extra-human: from the order of the cosmos, to human society, to the world of art as represented by *Water Music*. Sena may also be referring—and this is nothing more than a guess—to the order and harmony reestablished between Handel and his king. The poet is, undoubtedly, also referring to the order he perceives, i.e., the order of a bygone era which the music reawakened within him before returning to silence. But something remains: the poem itself, where that sense of order and balance are forever preserved, forever locked in a circular structure, the ultimate symbol of order. For the words with which the poem begins—*rio, cordas, trompas* ("river," "ropes," "horns")—are once again repeated in the last section. The circle is closed. "The act of thinking in order recreated" is also the poet's own thought about his re-creation, in poetry: a new order of order.

"*Water Music*, by Handel" is a semantic tour de force. In its communication of different and yet intimately related and inextricably unified orders of experience it comes as close to creating an analogue of polyphonic syntax as is possible in literary art. By incorporating three orders of experience—the audial, the visual, and the historico-cultural—Sena has verbally re-created a truly composite experience of *Water Music.* Once again, the poet has demonstrated that his poetic experience of music shows the latter, not as a phenomenon dissociated from life, but as an integral part of it.

I think this poem is particularly successful because of the predominance in it of word music, and because it fuses into a cohesive and aesthetically most satisfying whole so many different and yet logically related orders of experience. Its effectiveness stems in part from the multiplicity of referents for the language used. Although it is one of the most fluid, i.e., syntactically unencumbered, if rhythmically varied poems of *Art of Music,* it is also one of its densest or most polyvalent (much more could, of course, be said about this polyvalence if space allowed). It is also especially satisfying aesthetically (at least to this reader) because of the profusion of images employed throughout.

"Mahler: Resurrection Symphony"

The last poem I shall discuss in this chapter is "Mahler: Resurrection Symphony," which, according to Sena's note, and as the content of the poem itself indicates, is based on the finale of this Mahlerian work. This poem reiterates one of the most important ideas expressed, more or less implicitly, in "Wanda Landowska . . ." and, more explicitly, in "Preludes and Fugues by J. S. Bach, for Organ." This idea maintains that art, particularly musical art in this case, holds for man the promise of an earthly paradise. Although this humanistic constant is quite prevalent in literature—and, as far as Sena's poetry is concerned, it is not even restricted to *Art of Music*—the theme does attain unusual vehemence in this poem. For here it is expressed in sharp blasting contrast with the music's programmatic meaning.

Mahler's Second ("Resurrection") Symphony is the first in a series of three symphonies belonging to the *Wunderhorn* period, so called because of their links with the composer's setting of poems from *Des Knaben Wunderhorn (Youth's Magic Horn),* an anthology of German folk-poetry published between 1805 and 1808 and from which Mahler derived much inspiration.[10] The *Resurrection* is a symphony in five movements, the first three being wholly instrumental, and the last two for soloists, chorus and orchestra. The idea for the finale is said to have occurred to Mahler while he attended the funeral of Hans von Bülow at which he heard Klopstock's hymn "Auferstehung" ("Resurrection"). This hymn, to which Mahler added verses of his own, not only lends the symphony its title, but is also the climax of the composition's programmatic meaning. For Mahler's Second Symphony, including the non-choral movements, embodies a program—a fact which the composer later attempted to deny for fear of being classified as a program symphonist.

Mahler's music is widely considered largely autobiographical and reflective of the two sides of his personality: the gloomy and the affirmatory. The former, associated with the last years of his life, found musical expression in, for example, *Das Lied von der Erde*. The period of Mahler's life represented by this work is one in which faith in God no longer held sway. Although the *Song of the Earth* (a song cycle inspired by ancient Chinese poems and cast in the form of a symphony) sings the beauty of Nature and the joy of living, many of its thematic strands—both poetical and musical—are all too obvious reminders of man's mortality and his impending doom. The more affirmatory side of Mahler's personality, and one which is well illustrated by the Second Symphony, is connected with the composer's religious feelings where metaphysical anguish is assuaged by a belief in God or the strong desire to believe—as the following verses which he added to Klopstock's hymn clearly indicate:

> *O glaube, mein Herz, O glaube:*
> *Es geht dir nichts verloren!*
> *Dein ist, was du gesehnt!*
> *Dein, was du geliebt,*
> *Was du gestritten!*

> (Believe, my heart, O believe:
> Nothing at all shall be lost!
> Yours shall be what you desired!
> Yours what you lived for
> Yours what you strove for!)[11]

Following Mahler's own indications, Michael Kennedy summarizes the entire program of the Resurrection:

> The first movement is the funeral rite of the 'Titan' of the First Symphony ⁄the Titan is a young, romantic character, Mahler's alter ego⁊; it asks ⁄in Mahler's own words⁊: 'Why did you live, why suffer? Is it all nothing but a huge terrible joke?' The second and third movements are nostalgia, happy and bitter; for the fourth movement a voice leads the soul to God and in the colossal finale there are the Day of Judgment, resurrection and love. Death and transfiguration, in other words. (*Mahler*, p. 97)

Sena's very brief poem on this finale captures at once the thundering outpour of Mahler's religious emotion and transforms it into his own (i.e., Sena's) purely humanistic message. The poem reads:

> Ante este ímpeto de sons e de silêncio,
> ante tais gritos de furiosa paz,
> ante um furor tamanho de existir-se eterno,
> há Portas no infinito que resistam?
> Há Infinito que resista a não ter portas
> para serem forçadas? Há um Paraíso
> que não deseje ser verdade? E que Paraíso
> pode sonhar-se a si mesmo mais real do que este?

> (Before this impetus of sounds and silence,
> before such shouts of furious peace,
> before this furor grand enough to co-exist eternal
> could there be Gates in boundless space that might withstand?
> Could there be boundless space which might resist not having gates
> that could be forced? And could there be a Paradise
> that would not wish to be true? And what Paradise
> could dream itself more real than this?)

"Mahler: Resurrection Symphony" is a poem of exultation just as the tremendous finale of Mahler's Symphony is music and words of exultation. But each artist rejoices for quite different, and even contrasting, reasons. Sena's Biblical language, particularly the image "Gates of the infinite/Infinite" (I am translating more literally than did Frederick G. Williams), captures the religious essence of the Klopstock/Mahler hymn; the violent image of "forcing the gates" suggests the apocalyptic "roar" of the musical climax and of the very notion of Day of Judgment implicit in the programmatic idea. One hears in Sena's poem echoes of Jesus's own words: "I am the door: by me if any man enter in, he shall be saved, and shall go in and out, and find pasture" (John, 10:9). But these words are not simply evoked by Sena. They are perverted, undermined by Sena's own view of what constitutes paradise. The latter, according to the poet, is not to be found in the Lord's House after death. It exists here and now; it is a creation of man's intellectual and emotional faculties: it is the living music that Mahler created. What Paradise, the poet repeatedly asks, could possibly wish not to be true if only to justify such powerful and sublime expression of hope and faith as contained in this music? And what Paradise, the poet concludes, could possibly be more real—and more accessible—than that very hope and faith turned music, right here, before my very ears?

Frederick G. Williams is correct when he writes that art stimulated Jorge de Sena, as seen in "Mahler: Resurrection Symphony," "where his contemplative spirit is set on fire by the beauty of the music, which in turn excites his mind with an appreciation of the grandeur and majesty of eternity. Still, he does not give himself over fully to faith in the resurrection, but is nonetheless compelled to declare belief in some sort of paradise."[12] What needs to be emphasized is that "the grandeur and majesty of eternity" is not only a result of the beauty of the music, but also, and primarily, an idea suggested and conditioned by the programmatic meaning of the Symphony. More important still, what needs to be especially stressed is the fact that Sena's idea of paradise has none of the eschatological implications that can mistakenly be inferred from the religious imagery and tone of the poem. The religious dimension of Mahler's Symphony is actually perverted or underminded. Sena's idea of paradise—here and elsewhere in *Art of Music*—rests on his faith in humankind, not God. It is a product of humankind's creativity, not God's. It concerns this-earthly reality, not any world beyond. I dare say that if the humanist Jorge de Sena is ever charged with the deification of humankind—a "crime" often imputed to humanists by non-humanists—"Mahler: Resurrection Symphony" is the single most incriminating piece of evidence.

IX

Art of Music: A Point of Arrival

The present chapter will address itself to the following questions. First, what major themes run the entire length of *Art of Music*, if we consider all of the book's 44 poems and not merely some representative examples? And how do these general themes relate to Sena's whole poetic corpus? In other words, what is the thematic profile of *Art of Music* and to what degree does it extend or deviate from the thematic concerns of Sena's entire poetic production? (I am using the word "theme" in the broad sense, as synonymous with "topic" or "orders of subject matter," such as love, death, etc. More restricted uses of the term will be made clear in the discussions.) Second, as far as Sena's overall view and attitude regarding human life are concerned, what does *Art of Music* represent? Is it a point of arrival, an optimistic moment in the poet's journey, or yet another passage in an itinerary marked by the alternating darkness and brightness that life necessarily presents and Sena's poetry reflects? If Sena's poetry—as I have maintained throughout this book—is a poetic mirror of select aspects of his life and times, what is the ultimate message of *Art of Music*?

The answers to the first question, in addition to casting further light upon Sena's brand of humanism, will reveal that even though the subject matter of *Art of Music* is derived from, and conditioned by, the inspiring compositions, the book's major themes do represent, for the most part, not a marked deviation from, but a reiteration, with varying degrees of emphasis, of the most prevalent thematic strands that inform the content of Sena's entire poetic works. In connection with the second question posed above, I will try to defend the thesis that, if Sena's entire poetic corpus mirrors both negative and positive aspects of human experience in general, *Art of Music* is a point of arrival, for it represents the affirmatory side of Sena's humanism and personality; a moment in his poetic itinerary of 40 years when pessimism, anger, sarcasm, and condemnation yield—not totally, but considerably—to an optimistic reconciliation with, and a joyous celebration of, life. Of the over one dozen books of poetry Sena wrote, the two most optimistic ones overall, as far as Sena's view of humankind is concerned, are those inspired by art: *Metamorphoses* and *Art of Music*. Of these two, I believe the more optimistic, or least "contaminated" by negativism, to be *Art of Music*. That this affirmatory side of Sena's humanism and personality—which intermittently surfaces in all his poetry, as we saw earlier, but which reaches its high point in this work—should be allied to the experience of music is both understandable and explainable.

The following are the major thematic categories and general themes of *Art of Music*. We note that all of them have to do with the relationship between music and human experience. They are: 1) Nature, 2) history and society, 3) the self (the poet's), 4) religion, 5) emotions, and 6) death. These general topics and the more specific thematic strands into which they subdivide recur in all of Sena's poetry. Let us take them one by one, including Nature, whose relatively minor role in *Art of Music* is, in and of itself, significant, for it represents a continuation of Sena's overall attitude towards Nature as subject matter for poetic treatment.

In Chapters I and II, I discussed briefly Sena's poems on Nature in connection with the poet's statement to Frederick G. Williams to the effect that Nature as subject for poetry interested him only if human beings or human marks were upon Nature; otherwise, Sena was not interested in Nature at all. I also mentioned the element of *boutade* in this statement. It is true, however, that although Sena's corpus does include many poems on Nature and numerous other poems that utilize Nature images, in most of them that statement is clearly exemplified. Nature, when it does figure in Sena's poetry, is usually present, not for its own sake, i.e., not as an object of description or as pretext for meditation on the beauty of the natural world, but as an analogue or metaphor for human experiences and as a background or stage for human actions.

Among all the compositions that inspired *Art of Music*, works dealing exclusively or primarily with the depiction of Nature—let us say, works like Mendelssohn's *Fingal's Cave Overture*, Ravel's *Histoires naturelles*, Debussy's *Nuages*—are conspicuous by their absence. In works that Sena does poetize and in which tone painting or the celebration of Nature are important components—Debussy's *La Cathédrale engloutie*, Haydn's *The Creation*, Smetana's *Má Vlast*, etc.—the poet minimizes or ignores the presence of Nature and concentrates instead on the human dimension of the musical works. In "'La Cathédrale engloutie,' by Debussy," although Sena does mention the "naves povoadas de limos e de anémonas" ("naves peopled by lichens and anemones"), what fundamentally moved the 17-year-old future poet was that the musical dissonances were the "imagem tremulante / daquelas fendas ténues que na vida, / na minha e nas dos outros, ou havia ou faltavam" ("shimmering image / of the thin fractures that in life, / my own life or that of others, are there or are missing"). Later in life, what this same composition, and particularly its association with the sea, is going to provoke in the adult Sena is a series of reflections about his destiny as man and as poet.

However, "Creation, by Haydn" is probably an even better example of the poet's relative lack of interest in Nature per se. Arthur Komar, in his *Music and Human Experience* (p. 37), calls attention to the variety of Nature scenes in this oratorio, particularly in Parts I and II. He recalls that "after the recitative announcing that God created the earth and the sea /Part I/, the bass soloist continues by singing a formal aria describing the billowing waves, the mountains and rocks, the plains, the rivers, the little brooks. We then hear another recitative concerning the bringing forth of grass, herbs, and fruits, followed directly by the lovely soprano aria, 'With Verdure Clad.'" Sena alludes very briefly and in the most general of terms to this recently created Nature—"Era belo, era bom, era perfeito o Mundo" ("Lovely, good, and perfect was the world"; trans. George Monteiro)—and then, immediately, proceeds to focus on "o par humano /que/ pisava sem pecado / o jardim paradisíaco" ("that human pair /who/ strode without sin the paradisal garden").

"'Má Vlast,' by Smetana" and "*Symphonie Fantastique*, by Berlioz" are other examples of poems inspired by compositions that contain passages of Nature description—passages that Sena does not even mention, let alone dwell on. This omission is particularly noteworthy in view of the fact that, as Sena points out in the note, the poem on *Má Vlast* is based primarily on *Die Moldau*, the tone poem of the series in which tone painting is an extremely important element. The most glaring example in *Art of Music* of the absence of Nature and its replacement by human presence, however, is "'Fêtes,' by Debussy." In this poem, which is inspired by a work lacking almost any sense of human presence, Sena goes so far as to *people* the scene which, in the composer's program, dealt with the movements of dust particles interrupted by the passage of a phantom procession.

The fact that Sena minimizes or ignores the presence of Nature in the poems just mentioned, does not mean, of course, that he does so in all the poems of *Art of Music*. Numerous Nature images are scattered throughout the book, with sea and other water images predominating.[1] I discussed "danças de luzes / ou pássaros despertos pela aragem fria" ("dancing of lights / or birds stirred up by the cold breezes") in connection with the poem in which these lines appear, "Preludes and Fugues by J. S. Bach, for Organ." And the poet starts "Siegfried's Funeral March of 'Twilight of the Gods'" with a re-creation of the stage scene—"Na tarde de névoas que se escurece" ("In the afternoon darkening with mist"). As we saw, *"Water Music, by Handel"* is a tour de force of Nature imagery. The references in *Art of Music* constitute either an evocation of the programmatic or contextual elements associated with the model composition, or else they represent Sena's often employed technique of rendering in spatial and visual terms the temporal and audial phenomenon that music is. The important point, however, is that in all these poems—as in the overwhelming majority of cases in Sena's poetry—Sena does not engage in Nature description for its own sake: Nature is a stage upon which human life is played. And that life is the phenomenon that attracts and retains his attention.

How music relates to human experience as a whole, but particularly to human experience circumscribed to the specific time, place, and society from which it sprang and which it reflects, is one of the fundamental thematic concerns of *Art of Music*. As we recall, in his postfactory statements Sena emphasizes that two principles guide his poetic transfiguration of musical experience: the music must be understood by itself as "forma em si" ("a form in itself"); but this understanding of music as form in itself in no way compels him to experience music as "something inhuman, without contact with the reality and human experience, and without correlation to a cultural context." What Sena says regarding the Marxian view of a work of history, economics, or a work of art applies to *his* overall poetic (and critical, I might add) perception of works of art, including music. Sena writes in his essay "Marx and *Capital*": "The viewpoint that a work /of art/ must be understood in relation to its time, of which it is the result and an expression, is a Marxist viewpoint; since Marxism, while defining philosophico-cultural manifestations as 'ideology,' and while showing how these manifestations reflect the social situation out of which and in which they are created, showed that, outside *historical comprehension*, any expression of thought lacks substantive meaning."[2]

We saw, for instance, that "*Water Music*, by Handel" is an excellent example of the experience of music against the backdrop of history, both the immediate circumstances associated with its composition and performance, as well as the wider cultural context from which it derives its being and which it mirrors, as far as the poet is concerned. In "*Symphonie Fantastique*, by Berlioz," Sena once again emphasizes the relationship between the music and its epoch at the same time that he experiences it as a self-contained work of art. Sena's "portrait" of Chopin is yet another partial portrait of an era, an era which, according to the poet, is reflected both in Chopin's life and works. In "Wanda Landowska Playing Sonatas by Domenico Scarlatti," the human and cultural elements—the "presence" of the performer herself; Scarlatti and Princess Barbara in eighteenth-century Madrid; the Hispanicization of Scarlatti's music—force themselves, as it were, upon the poet's consciousness, vying for his attention with the music.

This relationship between music and its historico-cultural context has been a recurring topic throughout the chapters dealing specifically with *Art of Music*; and all of the poems I discussed in the last three chapters deal, implicitly or explicitly, with that relationship. However, the importance that Sena confers on the interrelation of an inspiring phenomenon—be the latter a work of music or an incident on the street—and its historico-cultural context cannot be overemphasized. The approach which I followed of dividing the poems into three categories based on the kinds of inspiring compositions—an approach which, as I held and hold, is defensible on many counts—actually obliterates to a large degree the very close attention that Sena paid to the alliance of history (in the broad context) and music. For the importance that Sena attributes to this alliance or interrelation manifests itself even as an organizing principle for the book. I mentioned earlier that all the poems of *Art of Music*, except for the first and last, follow a chronological order based on the lives of the composers. Sena's book can actually be construed as a kind of poetico-historical survey—with emphasis always placed upon the relation between music and human experience—of the major periods of Western music, with the exception of the Medieval. The periods represented are the Renaissance (Dowland), the Baroque, the Classical, the Romantic, and the Twentieth Century with some of its· -isms (Debussy, Schoenberg, Bartók). There is, nearly always, an attempt on Sena's part to communicate something of the period's *Zeitgeist*—even when the poem, in principle, is opposed to viewing the model composition historically or contextually. In "Listening to Songs by Dowland," we have a strong suggestion of Renaissance Humanism in the figure "embedded" in the structure of the songs, a figure who, like a god—and the implication probably is: in substitution of God—meditates on how difficult it is to be human. The mixture of "rationalism, sensuality, materialism, and spirituality,"[3] as well as the preponderance of polyphonic texture and unity of mood within each composition—all characteristics of the Baroque—inform, in one way or another, the poems on Bach, Handel, and Haydn (*The Creation*).

Another example—this one being truly magnificent—of the alliance between music and the historico-cultural context is the poem "D Minor Concerto, for Piano and Orchestra, K. 466, by Mozart." This poem represents one of the finest examples in *Art of Music* of the integration of the descriptive, interpretive, biographical, and historical modes. Unlike in other poems that employ several modes in a single composition, however, in this poem there is practically no boundary or seam between one mode and another. Sena condenses the description of the piece, and what it means to him, and the music's biographical dimension, and what the music represents within the historico-cultural period to which it belongs into a single stream of thought simultaneously allusive to these four dimensions. The single but thick filament of thought which is the poem at once describes/interprets the meaning of the piece, relates it to Mozart's life, and performs an act of music history. When the poem—which is one of only five sonnets in *Art of Music*—starts, the music already has been converted in the poet's mind into a metaphor (the interpretive mode). As the poem develops with the music, what the reader follows is this:

Finíssima amargura recatada
que exasperadamente se contém
de gritos e lamentos mas devém
doçura tensa tão dialogada

que nas mesuras fica disfarçada
a dor de ser-se, que sabemos bem
não ser este sorriso mas além
a dura soledade condenada

à morte e à desgraça. Nada mais
que o esgar tranquilo, insólito e discreto
a despontar entre insistências tais

que é como triunfo de um rigor disperso
em salpicado som órfão de afecto,
morto do amor em que flutua imerso.

(Most piercing and subdued bitterness
that controls itself exasperatedly
with screams and laments but comes to be
a tense and so dialogued sweetness

that there remains concealed beneath
deep bows the pain of being, that we realize
is not this smile but is
harsh solitude condemned to death

and to disgrace. Nothing more than
the peaceful unusual and discreet grimace
sprouting among such insistence

that it's like the triumph of a rigor dispersed
in a sprinkled affectionless tone
dying from love in which it floats immersed.)

Sena's extrapoetic opinion of this Mozartian masterpiece parallels that of music critics and helps us to understand the sonnet. He writes in the note to the poem that "The use of the piano, instead of the harpsichord for which Mozart's concertos were written (this one is No. 20), makes it obvious to what extent in this concerto Mozart abandons the conventional concerto form to give himself fully to profundity" (*II*, p. 237). Of what does this "profundity" consist? According to the poem, it consists, in part, of a latent subjectivity within the framework of classicism, a classicism where objectivity, emotional restraint, and a degree of formalism still hold sway, but no longer to the extent of masking or rendering opaque the germ of passion pulsating underneath. Classicism is here a translucid veil through which the poet peers into the life half buried in the musical tissue. Whose life? Mozart's? The "biographical" elements evoked here bear enough resemblance to those dealt with in "'Requiem' by Mozart" to suggest that it is Mozart's life that is in part being alluded to. But this biographical reading accounts for only part of the sonnet's content. To the poet, the music is also more generalized bitterness, a bitterness effectively controlled but still obvious. The music is a sorrowful outcry subdued into a tense and so dialogued sweetness, reasoned out, but nevertheless recognizable; it is a peaceful grimace so insistent that, although rendered abstract and thus somewhat camouflaged in musical tones, it still continues to be perceptible enough to the sensitive ear that hears, thinks, and feels at the same time.

Alfred Einstein has written concerning the D Minor Concerto that it is "one of the best known, in the nineteenth century, which did not understand the sublime humour of the F Major Concerto, but well understood what distinguished the D minor among all the piano concertos of Mozart: passion, pathos, drama. This Concerto made it possible to stamp Mozart as a forerunner of Beethoven . . ."4 What Sena perceives to be the latent Romanticism of the musical piece, its vulcanic power still in its pre-eruption stage, as it were, is poetically rendered with deftly paired nouns and adjectives: *amargura recatada* ("subdued bitterness"), *doçura tensa* ("tense sweetness"), *esgar tranquilo* ("peaceful grimace"), *rigor disperso* ("rigor dispersed"). In these pairs, the basic tensions and contradictions perceived in the music are transposed into verbal language. While maintaining himself within the boundaries of a poetic description of the music, Sena has also given us the music's "meaning" and has related it to Mozart's own life. Most of all, he has captured the epochal drama depicted in the Concerto: the struggle between an era, Classicism, that vies to hold its own against another era, Romanticism, that threatens to break through the classical crust of self-restraint and roar into eruption. In a sense only the sonnet is the adequate vehicle to express Sena's perception of Mozart's Concerto. The latter is emotion struggling to burst free from the constraints of classical form. The sonnet, a classical genre par excellence, is precisely the medium that Sena employed—in imitation of Mozart's use of the concerto to express his already "Romantic" emotionality?—to translate that bottled up subjectivity.

Romanticism is the period that, quantitatively, is best represented in *Art of Music*. From "Lieder by Schubert" to "Principessa di Morte" (and beyond, if we include the very late "Romantics" Mahler, Richard Strauss, and Sibelius), Sena presents a whole array of philosophical, social, and aesthetic concerns that inform Romantic music: individualism, heightened emotion, imagination, exoticism, nationalism, the alliance of music and literature, emphasis on tone color, chromatic harmony, the two extremes of form—the miniature lieder and Chopin piece; the colossal program symphony (Berlioz) and Gargantuan opera (Wagner), which Sena of course cuts down to size. As we advance chronologically through *Art of Music*, i.e., through musical history, we become aware of the progressive emergence of the composer, i.e., the ever tighter bond between the person of the artist and his work. In other words, this bond is true in the music and is also true of Sena's poems on that music. Thus, the impersonality of Bach's music yields to the latent subjectivism of some of Mozart's works ("D Minor Concerto" and "'Requiem' by Mozart"); the personal dramas of Heine; the "romantic solitude immensely public"/"romantic grief tremendously mild" of Berlioz; and the fusion (in Sena's interpretation) of art and composer's biography in Tchaikovsky and Puccini (*Turandot*). From the (relative) emotionalism of Dowland's songs, we come to the overflowing nationalism of Mussorgsky's *Boris Godunov* and Smetana's *Má Vlast*. We progress from the almost atemporal nature of Scarlatti's Sonatas to reach the "portrait" of Chopin—a portrait whose elements are a balanced blend of the composer's life, works, and times. Therefore, whatever else they are, all these poems on the Romantics also constitute successful attempts on the part of Sena to experience music in history, to capture the culturo-historical context that informs these compositions. A preoccupation with historical accuracy is always part of Sena's view of life—whether he is poetizing lived experiences or artistic ones.

Impressionism, post-Romanticism and early Twentieth Century are represented by poems on Debussy, Mahler, Richard Strauss, Sibelius, Satie, Bartók, and Schoenberg. Not all of these poems constitute ostensible efforts on the part of Sena to capture the cultural and historical reality behind the music. Some exemplify thematic concerns other than the specific relation of music to the times. "Concerto for Piano, Op. 42, by Schoenberg," however, is a poetic portrait of a moment of twentieth-century history, a verbal transposition of a portrait which Sena perceives Schoenberg as having painted in tones. In *Art of Music* the transition from the post-Romantic era to what the 1910 Manifesto of the Futurist Painters called the "vortex of modern life" is made quite abruptly and, interestingly, in two consecutive poems inspired by Schoenberg. The first of these poems is "Verklärte Nacht, by Schoenberg," which is based on the symphonic poem (1899) of the same name. "A work stemming directly from the chromaticism of Wagner and filled with the spirit of Romanticism,"[5] *Verklärte Nacht* is based on a poem by Richard Dehmel. A couple walks in the woods under the moonlight. She bears the child of the husband she does not love. However, as her sensuality and guilt become transfigured by the light of the moon, she comes to accept the child as a product of humankind's fulfilled sensuality. In his poem, Sena only makes the subtlest of allusions to this story. As he describes the music—and the poem is essentially illustrative of the descriptive mode—Sena weaves into the poem several phrases allusive to the program of *Verklärte Nacht*: "a dor dos gestos" ("the pain of gestures"), "um mar de luz sombria" ("a sea of somber light"), "formas puras / que se entregeram" ("pure forms / that ceaselessly interbreed"), "sussurros e murmúrios, gritos" ("whispers and murmurs and cries"). The poem ends with a rhetorical question:

—que humanidade resta após o dissipar-se
deste sonho de som perpetuado em cordas
vibrando assim frementemente humanas?

(—what humanity remains after this dream
sound is perpetuated by trembling human strings
throbbing and vanishing into air?)

Whereas humanity still pulsates in this post-Romantic Schoenbergian composition, it has, according to Sena's next poem, completely vanished from the *Piano Concerto*, Op. 42 (1942), a work composed in the twelve-tone system. After the experiences in atonality—where the absence of a tonal center was the musical equivalent of removing the sun from the center of the solar system—Schoenberg goes on to the twelve-tone system. The latter may be characterized as a systematization of atonality, the creation of a new law of gravity in the disarrayed solar system of music, a new order of (dis)order. If the tonal system can be allowed to serve as a metaphor for the optimism and self-confidence of the nineteenth century—"Democracy in government, brotherhood in society, equality in rights and privileges and universal education—all foreshadow the next higher plane of society to which experience, intelligence and knowledge are steadily leading," as the anthropologist Lewis Henry Morgan characterized that century,[6]—then atonality comes mighty close to being its negation. And if atonality should be taken as a metaphor of, instead of the attainment of those goals, the "vortex of modern life—a life of steel, pride, fever and speed,"[7] then, the twelve-tone system, as the consolidation of that vortex, is fragmentation legitimized, chaos codified, accepted. It is tradition and continuity pulverized, super-Nothingness enthroned. Art, and the Life it mirrors, have reached the ultimate Blind Alley. Sena's poem on Schoenberg's *Piano Concerto* perceives the music as a mirror of the times; it interprets the music along similar metaphorical lines. The poem ends this way:

Música do vácuo, do vazio, do inútil, do insensível, do sem vida,
mas, mais terrível que isso, não do nada,
já que o nada, a negação, seria
ainda um pouco de consolo dúbio,
um pouco de ternura e de ilusão.

(Music of what is vacuous, vain, useless, insensible,
but, more terrible still, music not even of nothingness,
for nothingness, negation, would offer
some trace of ambiguous consoling,
some tenderness and illusion.)

No wonder that immediately following this experience, Sena writes a poem inspired, not by any work of classical music, but by the life, personality and works of a singer of popular music, Edith Piaf. From a work in which music is "reduzida à sua mesma inumanidade" ("reduced to its own inhumanity"), "beco sem saída" ("blind alley"), Sena's poem on Piaf praises a voice possessed of "esta ciência / do desespero de ser-se humano / entre os humanos que o são tão pouco" ("the despairing science / of being human among people / of so little humanity"). The placement of the poem on Piaf right after the last poem on Schoenberg represents two things: a kind of reply to Schoenberg's "vácuo" ("vacuous") and "vazio" ("vain"); a reaffirmation of Sena's commitment to life.

Similar thematic statements achieved by the strategic placement of a poem in relation to other poems is rather common in Sena's poetry. In Chapter III, I referred to the thematic statement achieved by the placement of "*The Swing, by Fragonard*" right after a poem on death, "*The Dead Woman, by Rembrandt.*" A similar life-death contrast is also achieved in another two poems of *Metamorphoses*: "The Mask of the Poet," based on the Bronze Mask of John Keats in the National Portrait Gallery, London, and "Male Dancer from Brunei." Indeed, the presence of this poem which was inspired by a picture of a dancer published in the *National Geographic*, represents something very similar to the thematic effect achieved by the presence of a poem on Piaf. In *Metamorphoses*, we move abruptly from poems inspired by works of art and museum pieces to a work drawn from real life, more specifically from works dealing with death to works (Fragonard) or merely pictures (the dancer) that in some way affirm life; likewise in *Art of Music*, where we move from works of art—specifically Schoenberg's *Piano Concerto* which, according to Sena, denies life—to the stage of real life represented by Piaf. A final example may be mentioned of thematic statement attained by strategic placement: the poem "Glory" of *Crown of the Earth*, which I discussed in an earlier chapter. This poem immediately follows "Christmas," a poem in which Sena presents the ugly reality of war vis-à-vis the ideals of peace and rebirth associated with Christmas. In the title of the poem, "Glory," as well as in the body of the text, Sena opposes to the eschatological meaning of bliss or heaven his own unshakable faith in the destiny of humankind in this-earthly life. "Glory" may thus be construed, in part, as a follow-up poem on "Christmas," just as "To Piaf" may be read, in part, as a response to "Concerto for Piano, Op. 42, by Schoenberg."

It is interesting to note, furthermore, that of the three poems that Sena once considered including in *Art of Music*, and which are now part of *Perpetual Vision* and *Sequences*, two of them, "Ray Charles" and "In the Corridor of the 'Metro' in Paris," also would have immediately followed "To Piaf," had Sena chosen to place them following the chronological order observed in the case of the other poems. Ray Charles, whom Sena admired very much, is seen as being simultaneously the victim and propagator of those American "values" the poet deplores and satirizes. The poem about Sena's experience in the Paris Metro, which would have followed "Ray Charles," is yet another comment on life as reflected by the "vozes uivadas" ("howling voices") of the Metro singers and the song they sang. They sang the Beatles' song "Let it be," in which "Mother Mary comes to me / Speaking words of wisdom / let it be." Sena's mention of this song and the non-commitment to life it implies, is of course satirical. However, the poet also perceives something worth celebrating in this "bathroom-like sewer" of Paris. The singers may be socially irresponsible; but in their borrowed song, which they sang badly, human voices are heard, even when they themselves are not seen—"preenchendo o vácuo / por ondas de vazio musical" ("filling the void / with waves of empty music"). Once again, in their humble artistry and in their socially questionable way, these men fill a void with the sound of their human voices—a void that Schoenberg's sophisticated music could not fill and, in fact, according to Sena's poem, helped to propagate.

Still in relation to "To Piaf," we recall how the poet seems to identify with that voice "que sabia fazer-se canalha e rouca, / ou docemente lírica e sentimental" ("that could make itself canaille and coarse, / or sweetly and lyrically sentimental"); a voice that, like Sena's own poetic voice, was capable of singing the tenderest love strains and of intoning the bitterest and most diatribial "*Ça ira.*" Indeed, as I have already pointed out, "To Piaf" is but one of the numerous examples of poems in *Art of Music* upon which Sena's own self, or a self susceptible of being closely associated with Sena's own personality, is stamped. This inclination to project his own self upon the experience being poetized; to subjectivize everything his muse comes into contact with; to seize upon and explore, with relish, analogies between the personalities and experiences of the figures being discussed and his own experiences and personality; to place himself, like Velázquez in *Las Meninas*, within the portrait he is painting, is a constant of all of Sena's poetry. I believe there are at least three related yet separable reasons for this tendency: a personal, a historical, and a third which is of a psychological nature.

This tendency is, first and foremost, a direct result of the biographical character of Sena's poetry, his inclination, as noted earlier, to render autobiographical nearly everything he poetizes. In fact, all of his creative works bear the undeniable imprint of Sena's social personality. As I said earlier, the artistic and social selves—which in some writers are separable to a large degree—in Sena are, for the most part, indistinguishable. For example, from the viewpoint of his philosophy of life and his assertive, often none-too-modest and abrasive human personality, and from the perspective of his love-hatred for Portugal and his love of life and art, to mention but a few constants, to come to know the self or selves in Sena's poetry and to have known the man called Jorge de Sena is to have experienced a remarkable similarity; it is to have noted an almost seamless integration of Life and Art.

Sena was justified in, and seems to have enjoyed immensely, establishing parallels between his own life and personality and the lives and personalities of other artists. The paths of these artists' lives are very often uncannily similar to Sena's own. I have already mentioned, in connection with the poem "In Crete, with the Minotaur," that Sena identified with the *estrangeirados* ("those who imitate foreigners," "those who cater to foreign countries") Eça de Queiroz and Fernando Pessoa in considering the Portuguese language his homeland, and with the life of Camoens by claiming, as he paraphrases the author of *The Lusiads*, to "having left / his life parcelled out throughout the world in bits and pieces." Sena evokes and quotes Camoens again in "To Portugal," this time to distinguish his from the epic poet's brand of nationalism. But in "Camoens Addresses his Contemporaries," Sena once again identifies with Camoens to the point where, as has been stated, the bitterness and sarcasm with which he endows that voice could be construed as Sena's own bitterness and sarcasm, as *his* own speech to *his* contemporaries. History, which often repeats itself, provided the poet with numerous opportunities to establish contrasts and parallels between his and other artists' lives and personalities. This Sena does with gusto throughout his poetry, including *Art of Music*.

The presence in his own poetry of Sena's own self, as distinct from a poetic persona, may also be construed as the result of the poet's conscious or unconscious desire to include *his own person* within the intemporal moment that is the poem. The latter constitutes a chunk of time abstracted from temporal flow; a moment lifted, as it were, from linear temporality, i.e., from psychological time or *le temps humain*. The poet stamps his own feet upon the sands of time in the form of autobiographical projections. And then, through the intemporalizing power of poetry, he subtracts that moment from temporal flow. Thus, the poet immortalizes himself twice: once in the creative act itself (cf. Horace's "Exigi monumentum aere perennius"; Reis-Pessoa "Seguro assento na coluna firme"); a second time, because his own image, like Valázquez's in his famous painting, remains visibly imprinted in the arrested moment. In other words, every artist borrows or wins a chunk of immortality by creating a work of art. However, the artist who includes his own human image upon the moment—canvas, piece of music, poem—he subtracts from time, remains more clearly visible to posterity than the artist whose role is that of disinterested creator. As an example of this double fixation of the self as artist and man, I should like to quote and briefly discuss the poem "Sunday" (*Philosopher's Stone*):

Na orla do mar azul
de um céu quase sem nuvens,
as águas, crespas, murmuram.
Jogam ao sol as crianças
na aragem primaveril.
Já outras param pensando
as formas do corpo alheio.
Os barcos, suaves, singram
nos olhos de solitários
cujos passos hesitantes
pela praia se misturam
aos de corridas e jogos
da juventude esgotando-se.
As vozes chegam longínquas...
Meus passos deixam sinais
que a tarde, ténue, adejando,
aos outros misturará
na orla do mar azul.

(I, p. 139)

(On the edge of the blue sea
of the almost cloudless sky,
the rough waters murmur.
Children play in the sun
in the spring breeze.
Others already quietly contemplate
the shapes of another's body.
Boats sail softly
in the eyes of the lonely
whose wavering footsteps
in the sand blend with those
who race and play the games
of youth exhausting themselves.
Voices come from afar...

326

My footsteps leave prints
which the afternoon, hovering, tenuous,
shall blend with the others
on the edge of the blue sea.)

(trans. Helen Barreto)

Although the central theme of this poem is the transitoriness of life—experienced as *le temps humain* or psychological time, and not as the conventional literary modality that characterizes Pessoa's Horatian poet Ricardo Reis—"Sunday" also exemplifies several other constants of Sena's poetry. Some were discussed earlier in this chapter. To begin with, we notice a progressive humanization of Nature in the first three lines. The poet begins by creating a stage for human action and experience. The suggestion that he was not much interested in Nature per se is substantiated by the fact that "as águas, crespas, murmuram" ("the rough waters murmur"), i.e., are personified, humanized. The "edge of the blue sea," "the almost cloudless sky," the "rough waters" are all indicative of movement, of transitoriness—a transitoriness projected against the intemporality of the sea and sky, which are symbols of Time. Transitoriness and permanence, human time versus Time or intemporality, are the two polar themes of the poem. The title itself, "Sunday," underscores the idea of time, our preoccupation with measuring it.

By the fourth line, Nature has given way totally to human presence. Children play in the spring breezes; other children, already thinking of bodies other than their own, are awakening to a later stage of life. Relative to these two groups of children, the "solitary" people on the beach represent yet another stage of life—the very late stage, the autumn or winter of life which contrasts with the spring of the beginning of the poem, but also confirms the temporal linearity therein announced. The boats—of life, gliding over the river of time—softly sail. Steps of bathers are imprinted upon the sands of time. For the beach, with the sky above and the sea beyond, has been converted into a stage, a microcosmic stage, upon which the fundamental experiences of life are played: joy of youth, love, play itself, but also the inevitable solitude, the foreshadow of death. All these human creatures, children, adolescents, as well as the old, are engaged in the feverish, if unconscious, battle to defeat time. They shout their youth, show their desire to procreate, fill time with activity, and stamp their feet upon the sand. This last image, of course, underlines the futility of the human struggle against temporality. The poet, too, is engaged in the same pursuit. He has the same desire to defeat time.

For he mixes his steps with those of the actors upon this

327

microcosmic stage of life. From mere spectator throughout the poem, he has, by line 15, become an actor as well—"Meus passos deixam sinais" ("My footsteps leave prints"). The poet conceives of this act as one of fraternity. He will not remain the indifferent observer of this slice of life played against sea and sky; he is now part of it. In a fraternal bond his steps will forever be mixed with those of his fellow creatures. I say forever because his act is also a blow in the face of time, a gesture of rebellion against temporal linearity, against the consciousness of transitoriness—and against the certainty of death. By mixing his steps with those of his fellow man and, simultaneously, by exercising the power of his artistic medium to congeal this moment, the poet saves himself. Time will pass; the last cloud will vanish from the sky; the boat will disappear in the distance; the children will procreate, if they do, and die; the solitary men will find the solitude of being no more; the sea will, all too soon, erase all footsteps from the surface of the beach. But his moment will forever be preserved in the poem—and the poet's own footsteps, signifying that the poet is a physical presence who *was there*, will be preserved with it. The poem is a closed circle; its structure has a thematic voice: "On the edge of the blue sea . . . on the edge of the blue sea." Between these two fixed poles, life is transitoriness, a foreshadow of death. But before death had a chance to strike, the poet struck; he froze a portion of life that can always be reawakened; one that can, in a way, never die. So too his own footprints are immortalized.

Many poems of *Art of Music* harbor clear, or less clear but still visible, projections of Sena's social or historical self. As we recall, the very structure of the book was conceived in autobiographical terms. *Art of Music* may be compared to a huge polyptych, with the lateral panels being comprised of two highly personal poems; and the central panels constitute metamorphoses of musical experiences upon which Sena's own self is, in one way or another, always projected. I pointed out, in connection with "Listening to Songs by Dowland," that the humanistic figure meditating on how difficult it is to be human could be as much the figure of the composer as Sena's own. In "Again the Sonatas of Domenico Scarlatti," the poet actually wonders if he is being exposed to the composer's thoughts, or whether he is projecting his own thoughts upon the music:

> Nesta percussão tecladamente dedilhada como violas pensativas
> ou como pandeiretas de bailado que em requebros sapateia
> a dança desenvolta, há uma ocasional melancolia que não sei
> se é do compositor, se de quem toca, se de mim...

(In this percussion of keys fingered like pensive viols
or like tambourines that longingly beat time
for the unencumbered dance, there is occasional melancholy;
perhaps the composer's, perhaps the performer's, possibly mine...)

In "*Symphonie Fantastique*, by Berlioz," Sena identifies so much
with the composer that he seems to assume the latter's fight against
Philistinism. We also saw that in his "portraits" of Chopin and
Socrates/Satie, Sena also comes very close to portraying himself.
Smetana's nationalism provokes such a reaction in him that his own
brand of "nationalism" actually takes over: the poem, as I said, is
more about Portugal and Sena's attitude regarding his own country
than it is about Smetana's love for Bohemia. Isn't Sena making a
general claim about all artists, including himself, when he looks upon
Mozart's *Requiem* as the composer's life-song, as distinct from the
"death song" which Mozart avowedly intended to write? Mozart of-
fered his life to Life. He can never truly die. In "Meditation Before a
Gigantic Corpus" (*40 Years*), his own work, Jorge de Sena writes:

> Deste cançaso imenso... Não, não é verdade
> que seja a vida o meu maior desejo:
> se não a tivera, bem a desejara,
> mas tenho-a, e tanta, que me cansa, e vejo
> perder-se em versos, em angústia e mágoa,
> a vida inteira que eu ofereço à Vida.

(40 Years, p. 55)

(Speaking of my immense weariness... No, it isn't true
that life is my greatest desire:
if I didn't have it, I'd wish for it,
but I do, so much of it, that it tires me, and I see it
waste itself on poetry, in anguish and grief,
my entire life which I offer to Life.)

When Sena discusses the religious, philosophical, and emotional content of these musical compositions, he is discussing as much what he
perceives as being contained in them as he is meditating on his own
feelings awakened by the music. Art is a mirror that reflects as much
its own light as the outside light cast upon it, as much the soul of he
who creates it as that of he who experiences it.

To a very large degree, Sena poetizes musical compositions of a
religious character—Haydn's *The Creation*, Mozart's *Requiem*,
Beethoven's *Missa Solemnis*, Mahler's *Resurrection Symphony*—not
so much to expound on the composer's religious views, or religion in
general, but, it seems, in order to come to terms with his own religious

feelings. For religion—and, underlying the general topic of religion, the existence versus non-existence of God—is one of the most problematic topics in all of Sena's poetry, judging from the poet's obsession with this theme, and, particularly, in light of the conflicting attitudes he expresses in connection with it. I stated in Chapter I, in connection with the preliminary discussion of Sena's humanism, that the problem of God tends to manifest itself via the classical dichotomy or conflict between the emotional, tradition-bound self who wishes and, it seems, needs to believe; and, on the other, the rational, earth-bound and man-centered self who rejects any commerce with the supernatural. One or the other of these selves may dominate at any given moment, although the rational self, which also has the support of Sena's extrapoetic statements, usually has the last word. I added, however, that, on balance, it is not possible to draw any definite conclusions regarding the poet's religious beliefs, particularly if we restrict ourselves to Sena's early works of poetry, *Persecution* and *Crown of the Earth*. (As I read *Post-Scriptum II* /2 vols./ which has just been published /Lisbon: Imprensa Nacional/Casa da Moeda, 1985./, I discover that these poems written between 1936-1938 /first volume/ and 1938-41 /second volume/ reveal on Sena's part the same preoccupation with the topic of religion that one also encounters in *Persecution* and *Crown of the Earth*. This is not surprising, however, considering that many of the poems of *Persecution* and *Crown of the Earth* were written at the same time as the poems of *Post-Scriptum II* . None of the poems of *Post-Scriptum II* will be discussed in this book.)

When we consider *Art of Music* by itself, however, the problem of religion in Sena's poetry does come to a definitive solution. In this book the poet's confrontation with religion and the supernatural, specifically the supernatural associated with Christianity, seems to be aimed at resolving, once and for all, the conflicts between faith and reason ("Creation, by Haydn"), man's versus God's creation ("*Missa Solemnis*," "'Requiem'"), the human versus religious implications of Mozart's sacred music, of the Eucharist itself ("'Requiem'"), and paradise on earth versus the Christian concept of Paradise ("'Preludes and Fugues by J. S. Bach," "Mahler: Resurrection Symphony"). It is fair to conclude, therefore, that in *Art of Music* the only concession that Sena makes to religion and the supernatural is that he still talks about them. The ideas he expresses, however, represent a solidification of his secular humanistic principles and views and a repudiation of all supernaturalistic notions, this time without ambiguities.

As is the case with religion, the emotional profile of *Art of Music* is Sena's own—not the emotional profile of the composers and works he poetizes. In other words, when dealing with the range of emotions in the book, we must distinguish between, on the one hand, the kinds of emotions and feelings associated with particular compositions, e.g., love and hate in Tchaikovsky's *Romeo and Juliet* and happiness and joy in Haydn's *The Creation*, and, on the other hand, the emotions and feelings that characterize the poet's reactions to the works he is poetizing. The former are important and to some extent enter into the poetic metamorphoses. But more important still are the emotions, feelings and moods awakened in the poet by the music. Very often these emotions and feelings are in direct conflict or opposition to those feelings and emotions which inspired the music. At times, when the poet does rejoice with the composer, it is not necessarily for the same reasons, as exemplified by the poem "Mahler: Resurrection Symphony," as well as many others. Sena subjectivizes the experience of music to such a degree that, in "Siegfried's Funeral March," he looks upon the events depicted in the opera as happening to him: "o herói que assassinado me transportam" ("this hero I lost — assassinated and carried off").

Sena's corpus (and let us, for a moment, exclude *Art of Music*) embodies an immense range of emotions, feelings and personal attitudes: emotions of anger, hate, love; feelings of despair, grief, melancholy, resignation; attitudes of irony, sarcasm, contempt, and approval. The darker emotions, feelings and attitudes are provoked by Sena's poetic (and human) confrontation with the negative side of life's experiences and human nature, war, crime, neglect, human exploitation of all types, and mediocrity. However, despite a preponderance in Sena's life of reasons for lamentation (as I have said, there are more negativistic than affirmatory poems in Sena's corpus), life also rewarded him with many reasons for celebration. He rejoices—and many of his poems are proof positive of this—in the very fact of being alive; in traveling; in the happiness derived from experiencing works of art; in the supreme joy of transmuting his experiences, the good and the bad, and observations into works of art. Notwithstanding many moments of despair—he never, never abandoned his Marxian belief in the perfectibility of humankind.

The range of emotions, feelings and attitudes that characterizes Sena's corpus in general is also represented in *Art of Music*. But with a difference. Here, for once, the more negative poems are not as prevalent as in other books. There are, to be sure, feelings of melancholy in some of these poems, for example, "'La Cathédrale engloutie,' by Debussy"; anger in poems like "To Piaf"; and biting irony and sarcasm in "Final 'Potpourri.'" Sena's satirical attitude informs several of his poems based on programmatic works. Although on the humanistic plane Sena relishes the human dimension that the programmatic experiences make available to his perception, what he sang about the program, i.e., his interpretation of them, as well as the very fact that, in one case, he provides his own program, constitutes or reveals a posture that carries a parodistic and ironic sting.

Irony in Sena's poetry can tend toward biting, sardonic sarcasm, or it can appear as smiling, which very often borders on light humor. The former tendency is not as common in *Art of Music* as in many of Sena's other poetic works. The latter is more prevalent here, as for example in "'Thus Spake Zarathustra,' by Richard Strauss," which I would like briefly to discuss. Based on the famous tone poem *Also Sprach Zarathustra*, Sena's poem praises the music while denying that Strauss achieved what he set out to accomplish programmatically. The composer wrote regarding this tone poem: "I did not intend to write philosophical music or portray Nietzsche's great work musically. I meant rather to convey in music an idea of the evolution of the human race from its origin, through the various phases of development, religious as well as scientific, up to Nietzsche's idea of the *Übermensch*."[8] Sena seems to have had Strauss's grandiose evolutionary idea in mind when he wrote with smiling irony:

Nem o Zaratustra de Zaratustra, nem
o de Nietzsche, mas uma gigantesca valsa
para elefantes, em que o Cavaleiro da Rosa, o D. Quixote
            o Don Juan,
a vida e a morte dos heróis (um só ou vários), com ou sem
transfiguração, as Electras e as Salomés, e a Mulher sem Sombra
—mesmo se concebidos alguns depois desta música—, todos
fazem figura de cisnes lohengrínicos catando
às margens do Wagner o seu (deles e dele) piolhinho
de renano ouro . . .

(Neither Zarathustra's Zarathustra, nor
Nietzsche's, but a gigantic elephants'
waltz, in which the Rosenkavalier, Don Quixote, Don Juan,
the life and death of heroes (one alone or many), with or without
transfiguration, Elektras and Salomes, and the Woman without a Shadow
—even if conceived sometimes after this music—all
play the role of Lohengrinnic swans searching
on the banks of Wagner for the louse of Rhine gold
their own and his . . .)

Besides alluding derisively to Strauss's often mentioned indebtedness to Wagner, Sena also expresses one of the most common adverse criticisms of the composer's tone poem when he condemns his use of the waltz. According to Norman del Mar, the use of the waltz "revealed the less discriminating side of his genius as he had not done since his ill-fated 'Funiculi, Funiculà' in *Aus Italien*: the great Nietzschean *Tantzlied* proves to be a Viennese waltz" (op. cit., p. 142).

But it is precisely in these weaknesses that the poet seems to perceive Strauss's positive contribution, for

> . . . *Nesta intrujice*
> *o nosso retrato está de humanos:*
> *elefantes dançando a valsa ratamente,*
> *ou ratos dançando elefantinamente a valsa de outro mundo.*

> (. . . In this fraud
> stands our human portrait:
> elephants dancing their waltz like rats,
> or rats dancing like elephants the waltz of another world.)

Hence we have Sena's most appropriate allusion later on in the poem to Raul Brandão's *O doido e a morte (The Lunatic and Death)*. Contrasting Strauss's intentions with the results, the poet feels as deceived as did the Civil Governor in Brandão's farce upon opening the box supposedly containing death-dealing explosives, which turns out to be harmless cotton. The analogue to the explosives is Strauss's title and the grandiose programmatic ideas; that of the cotton is the "graça elefantina / os pescoçinhos de violoncelo se debruçam sobre as altas pautas / pifarando volúpias coloridas" ("elephantine grace / do the little cello necks crouch over the high staves / fifing colors of voluptuousness")—in short, the "ruidosa alegria de compor-se e ouvir-se música" ("the roaring joy of composing and hearing music").

In *Zarathustra*, Strauss achieves success—so the poet suggests, always emphasizing the human dimension of art—not by realizing his ambitious plans but, paradoxically, by falling short of them. We may not see man climbing up the ladder of evolution to the plateau of Superman. The greater-than-life Nietzschean Zarathustra definitely fails to show up for the *Tantzlied*. But this would only have robbed him of his humanity, anyway. Instead, what we have in *Also Sprach Zarathustra*, for the human glory of Strauss and enlightenment and joy of all of us, is an expression of our human, or as Nietzsche himself would say, *menschliche, allzumenschliche* condition. Hurray for those who sometimes succeed by failing! Besides, there is always time for art to look upon the darker side of life: "Há sempre tempo / de um Wozzeck se afogar pelintra e corno e assassino" ("There is always time / for Wozzeck—to drown himself, the wretch, the cuckold, the murderer").

The overriding emotion of *Art of Music*, however, is love, running the gamut from love of life, to love of humanity, to the kind of love that Sena opposed to the Liebestod: holistic love, which is made representative of all that binds man to his fellow humans and to the earth. And the feeling that pervades the majority of these poems is the feeling of joy that results from experiencing what Sena considered in many ways the ultimate form of art, music. It is a proud joy that stems from the fact that these are human creations. If man the destroyer, the exploiter, and the creature bent on inflicting pain, suffering and often death on his fellow creatures is the figure that, with many exceptions, draws the largest amount of the poet's attention elsewhere (particularly in early books), *Art of Music* is a book for the most part dedicated to singing of man the creator and the divine creature (without any eschatological implications) who, as Sena rightly puts it in "Bach: Golberg Variations," "é, por vezes,/ maior do que si mesmo" ("is, sometimes, / greater than himself").

And this fact is precisely what leads us to the question—does *Art of Music* represent a point of arrival?—and to the answer: in a sense it does. There is a constant tension running the entire length of Sena's poetry toward resolution in a positive, affirmatory note—where the poet could cease concentrating so much on the dark aspects of life and, without ever subtracting himself from his firm commitment to life, dedicate his energies, for once, to celebrating what in humankind is positive and worthy of praise. Most of the poems of *Art of Music* are indeed dedicated to this celebration, including "Preludes and Fugues by J. S. Bach," "Bach: Goldberg Variations," "*Water Music*, by Handel*," the poems on Dowland and Scarlatti, "'Requiem' by Mozart," "Fantasies by Mozart" (which ends with the question, "foi possível que este homem alguma vez morresse?"—"How could it be / that this man died?"); "*Missa Solemnis*, by Beethoven," "Lieder by Schubert," and "Octaves: Listening to Brahms's First Symphony." Of Brahms's work Sena sings the following praise:

> . . . *Ó triunfal*
> *dormência da verdade! Ó suspensão*
> *de todas as certezas! Ó fervor*
> *tranquilo, infrene, ardentemente frio!*
> *Ó trégua, ó paz, vitória sem vencidos!*
> *Eu te saúdo como noite eterna*
> *onde por sons se escreve que existimos.*

> (. . . O dormant
> triumph of truth! O suspension
> of all certainties! O tranquil fervor,

unrestrained and ardently cold!
O truce, o peace, victory and no one conquered!
I salute you as eternal night
where it is written in sounds that we exist.)

Sena even celebrates, in "'La Bohème,' by Puccini," the music which utilizes "dishonest" devices in order to communicate the "alegre fúria de fugazmente viver" ("glad rage to live ephemerally"), as well as the composition ("'Thus Spake Zarathustra'") which, according to Sena, is all the more human and deserving of praise because it fell short of its grandiose aims. Many other poems, could be quoted as examples of the poet's celebration of creative man. In some cases, Sena even refrains from reading any meanings into the music or from scrutinizing it in any way. Instead he pauses in an attitude of almost religious reverence and awe before such human creations:

> *"Das Lied von der Erde"—será da terra que isto canta, ou canta*
> *do que não somos terra? Eu creio que*
> *. . . para que crer ouvindo este sonhar da vida?*

> *(*"Das Lied von der Erde"—does it sing of earth, or sing
> of how we are not earth? I believe that
> . . . but why believe when I can hear this dreaming of life?)

It is understandable that this celebration of man the creator, which attains its highest expression in *Art of Music*, should be expressed in connection with the experience of music. It is logical that Sena's most optimistic book of poetry should be inspired by the most abstract and impalpable of the arts. The celebration of human creativity is a constant that runs the entire length of Sena's poetry, starting with the celebration of his own creations. There exists in these celebrating poems an implied contrast between human and divine creation, a tendency that culminates in *Art of Music* in poems like "Preludes and Fugues by J. S. Bach." We recall that in "Eternity," the last poem of *Persecution*, Sena celebrates the birth of the poem with religious imagery. The poem "Demeter" (*Metamorphoses*), inspired by the much-damaged statue in the British Museum, is another example of this type of celebration. This poem, too, is fraught with religious imagery. The poet evokes, step by step, the history of the statue, starting with its pre-artistic stage, when the stone "brotou, / vulcânica nas chamas dos primórdios dias" ("emerged, / vulcanic in the fire of primordial times"). As the sculptor works the stone, i.e., as the poet imagines the sculptor doing so, "a vida vai rompendo a casca da montanha / e do ovo sai proporcionada e pura" ("life slowly breaks through the shell of the mountain / and out of the egg it emerges pure and well-proportioned"). Man, Sena suggests, is capable of imparting "life" to an amorphous and lifeless rock. Sena celebrates both the sculptor's and the poet's creative powers. For, if the former was the first to breathe "life" into lifeless matter, the poet, by exercising the reconstructive power of his medium, is the one who reconstitutes the now headless statue to a stage of wholeness—"alada em passos de que o corpo se ergue, / e de cabelos suspendendo a altura" ("in winged-steps the body rises, / and height itself suspends from her hair").

However, neither sculpture nor poetry are yet the ultimate form of artistic creation. Poetry is made of words which, with extremely rare exceptions (e.g., "Four Sonnets to Aphrodite Anadyomene"), pre-exist the poem. What the poet does is assemble the words in new combinations; he imparts new life or a higher life, if we will, to already living entities. We have a similar situation in the case of sculpture. The stone already exists in nature. The sculptor may instill form and breathe a species of life into a formless and lifeless mass—but he does not create out of nothing. The highest act of creation, or creation *ex nihilo*, can be said (with some exaggeration!) to belong only to the composer. For tones—as opposed to sounds—do not exist in nature. The composer, like God, creates the very elements with which he fashions his musical universe. It is this species of divine human creation that Sena celebrates, as we recall, in "Preludes and Fugues by J. S. Bach."

Why should this book inspired by music be, as a whole, the most optimistic of Sena's poetic works? Are these poems not, as I have emphatically maintained, poems about life, a life which Sena relentlessly pursues in the often vague seas of music, the same life which, elsewhere in his poetry, presents both a painful and a cheerful demeanor, a dark and a bright side? Is *Art of Music* a momentary respite from the more negative side of life—given the fact that Sena once again is going to tour impossible and infectious sites of life (*Peregrinatio ad Loca Infecta*) and find enough justification to effect poetic exorcisms (*Exorcism*)? The answers to these questions require that we dwell briefly on the relation between poetry and life, the visual arts and life, and, finally, music and life.

As a poet of live experiences Sena is in immediate and direct contact with life, as it is lived, as it is felt, and as it causes pain or brings joy. The poetry which mirrors this direct contact with life—and Sena's own life, to begin with, was often very painful indeed—stands a greater chance of being gloomy than the poetry which focuses upon life as presented, for example, in the visual arts. The latter deal with life and very often heighten the live experiences therein depicted to a degree of poignancy almost approaching the authentic experiences of life. Still, the visual arts are not life. There is a *distance* between the events of the third of May and Goya's painting of that title. The experience of death that inspired Rembrandt's *The Dead Woman* has been lifted, it is true, from the realm of the particular to that of the universal. However, it also has been raised from the plane of experience to that of contemplation. Moreover, as for the depiction of life's dark or ugly side in a work of art, the viewer can choose to ignore the painful elements and concentrate only on what brings aesthetic pleasure. In modern real life only the most callous and cruel of persons could tolerate or be indifferent to slavery, for example. In his poems based on real life, Jorge de Sena wages constant battle against all types of slavery—economic, social, political, and moral. Yet, in his poem "Turner" (*Metamorphoses*), inspired in part by Turner's *Slave Ship*, the poet opts not to even mention the theme of slavery. He concentrates instead on effecting a kind of Turner pastiche by gathering images from several of the artist's paintings and verbally translating them. Some of life's most horrible experiences are captured in *Slave Ship*—but the poet ignores them. And he does so because art creates that distance between the real spectacle it depicts and its depiction. The viewer has the option of concentrating on one or the other. This option does not exist—at least for a humanist poet like Sena—in the case of real life events. (I might add that Sena's omission of any references to the content of *Slave Ship* is a rare instance indeed; his approach to art is usually more committed.)

Despite their distance from reality, however, the visual arts are still closer to real life than is music. Painting and sculture come closest, among all the sister arts, to presenting a life-like image of reality. Next to painting and sculpture—although in some particulars even more than they—literature possesses this attribute in the highest degree. As Lessing long ago demonstrated (*Laocoön*), literature cannot compete with painting and sculpture in rendering the visual dimension of reality. But neither can they match the literary arts—the thinking arts par excellence—in presenting not only the thoughts and emotions that presided at a given experience, but also how the latter came to be, step by step, what the painting or sculpture shows. Poetry could not reproduce the visual horror of Goya's *Third of May* with the same impact as the painting. But the human drama that led to what the painting shows could best be told by poetry.

However, the greatest distance by far between a given life experience and its artistic expression belongs to music, particularly absolute music. It may be true that, of all the sister arts, music is the one which appeals most directly to the heart. But it is also the one that is best suited for camouflaging the true face of pain, and best endowed with the attributes necessary to metamorphose a feeling of despair into a sigh of joy. For example, to experience death in *Pietà d'Avignon* (cf. the poem of the same name in *Metamorphoses*) is not as painful as to witness death in real life. But to experience the depiction of death in music, for example in Mozart's *Requiem*, is, according to Sena's interpretation of that work, to experience not gloom but a sense of exultation, not the ceasing of life, but its beginning or rebirth. Perhaps the very fact that music is a temporal art, and not a static spatial one, also has something to do with the life-like character of music. Painting, for example *Pietà d'Avignon*, preserves the moment of death. More than this: the medium itself, because it is static spatiality, contributes to the communication of stillness and, hence, lifelessness. Not so with music. In this medium an experience of death can only be communicated by the *coming alive* of the tones. As the tones rush through time, as they move in logical, purposive patterns, as they come and go, as they pulsate to definitive rhythms—all of these being true analogues of the attributes of life itself—the very death they may be expressing is denied. In other words, to communicate death through a medium that bespeaks life itself is, in a way, a contradiction. This fact, coupled with the truth that tones, unlike words, stones, or pigments, are the most removed from nature and common human experience, explains, at least in part, why music based on life's sorrows, even death itself, can be a source of joy, a celebration of life. Isn't this the very idea behind the following lines from "Wanda Landowska Playing Sonatas by Domenico Scarlatti"?

> *Tudo isso nada é perante*
> *abstracção como esta*
> *de morta música*
> *num morto cravo*
> *tocada pela morta*
> *nesta apoteose*
> *de ressurreição*
> *que eu posso, com um toque,*
> *demiurgo e mago,*
> *conclamar a que*
> *me submerja em vida*
> . . .
> (All this is nothing before
> abstraction such as this
> of dead music
> in a dead clavier
> played by a dead woman

in this apotheosis
of resurrection
that I can accompany,
demiurge and mage,
shouting for it
to submerge me in life
. . .)

   Death, as we saw in earlier chapters, is one of the fundamental
themes of Sena's poetry. His attitude towards death is what one would
expect from a life-loving secular humanist. The theme of death,
although it is fraught with other thematic implications, basically encompasses two modalities: natural death and unnatural death. Poems
dealing with the first modality can be further subdivided into 1) those
which express ideas and feelings regarding the poet's own death, and
2) those treating death in general. By unnatural death I mean death
brought about by crimes, war, and what could be called the death of
the spirit, against which Sena rebels, as he does in the poem "Pamphlet." Death, when it is a result of man's cruelty to man, is for Sena
the ultimate crime—one which no ideologic principle, no matter what
institution sanctions it, can justify. It is against this type of death that
"Letter to My Children on the Shootings of Goya" is pitted in part.
Regarding natural death in general, Sena's posture is often one of
rebellion. So much so that, in "Death, Space, and Eternity," he concludes that death is "not natural" for humankind; otherwise, nature
would not have instilled in us such fear of death and would not have
compelled us to desperately seek, in ever new ways, to conquer it. This
attitude, however, is not typical of those other poems in which Sena
reflects on his own death. And there are so many poems, even in his
early works, where young Sena meditates on his own death. In one of
them—the supremely beautiful "Humanity," significantly the last
poem of *Crown of the Earth*—Sena actually creates an analogue of
the moment of death. What is it like to die? How would death feel in
comparison with a life such as the one the poem talks about? In this
poem, death or oblivion comes so naturally, so surely, so inevitably; it
arrives as slowly as the smoke rises from a chimney on a calm day, and
as imperceptibly as the day turns into night. And, it seems, for once
death is as welcome as the night itself. This poem recaptures some of
the essential thematic preoccupations of Sena's poetry—his commitment to life, his unshakable hope in the future of humankind even in
the face of suffering and death. But it also reflects the poets's sense of
tiredness stemming from his daily commerce with life's cruelties. His
desire to escape it all is translated, not into flight to greener pastures
or a poetic ivory tower, but into an anticipation of the moment of

death. The analogue for approaching death is the passage of day into night, and the progressive abeyance of the poet's sense of perceptions:

Na tarde calma e fria que circula
por entre os eucaliptos e a distância,
olhando as nuvens quase nada rubras
e a névoa consentida pelos montes,
névoa não subindo por não ser
fumo da vida que trabalha e teima,
e olhando uma verdura fugitiva
que a noite no céu queima tão depressa
esqueço-me que há gente em cada parte,
gente que, de sempre, sofre e morre,
e agora morre mais ou sofre mais,
esqueço-me que a esperança abandonada,
a não ser de ninguém, é sempre minha,
esqueço-me que os homens a renovam,
que o fumo de seus lares sobe nos ares...
Esqueço-me de ouvir cheirar a Terra,
esqueço-me que vivo... E anoitece.

(*I*, pp. 125-26)

(In the calm cool afternoon that circles
among the eucalyptus and the distance,
looking at the clouds not quite blood-red
and the mist consented to by the mountains,
mist not rising for not being
smoke of the life that toils and persists,
and looking at a fugitive verdure
which night in the sky burns so quickly,
I forget there are people everywhere,
people who, as always, suffer and die,
and now more die, or more suffer,
I forget the abandoned hope,
which unless if no one's, is always mine,
I forget that men renew it,
that smoke from their hearths rises in the air...
I forget to listen to the Earth's scent,
I forget that I'm alive... And night falls.)

(trans. Don Bartell)

Art of Music contains about a dozen poems on compositions or sections of works dealing in part or totally with death: "'Requiem' by Mozart," "The Death of Isolde," "Siegfried's Funeral March," "Principessa di Morte," "Listening to 'Socrates,' by Satie," "Concerto for Orchestra, by Bela Bartók." Other poems strongly imply the

340

theme of death even though the compositions on which they are based do not focus ostensibly on death: "Wanda Landowska" and "Fantasias by Mozart." In all these poems Sena reflects on death in general. Few of them dwell on the fear of death. On the contrary, what characterizes these poems is a defiance of death, the belief, converted into poetic certainty, that man goes on living or being reborn in the works he leaves behind and into which he breathes his own life. Thus, Mozart's death-song announces a beginning, not an end, for, according to Sena, the composer dies with the "certeza e segurança de conter-se / na criação virtual o renascer-se / agora e pelo tempo adiante" ("certainty and sureness that being born again / is contained in virtual creation /now and in the time that will never cease"). Regarding the two poems on Wagner dealing with death—"Isolde" and "Siegfried's Funeral March"—Sena practically bypasses death in the first and concentrates on the theme of procreative love. Here, as in many other Senian poems, Eros defeats Thanatos. In the second poem on Wagner, Sena does dwell on death, but he affirms man's parity, nay, superiority, to the gods—"que aos heróis mortos / nunca sobrevivem" ("who never outlive / the dead heroes"). In "Principessa di Morte," Puccini's death becomes identified with, or personified in, his own artistic creation: he dies at the hands of Turandot, one of his greatest creations. This is tantamount to saying that he will live so long as his *Turandot* shall be performed. "Listening to 'Socrates,' by Satie," based on the symphonic drama that ends with Socrates's death, does not end on a note of death, but on an note of life: "A música soprada e linear / do espírito que fala e não se entrega" ("The musical breath and line / of the spirit that speaks and never yields"). It is this undying spirit that the poem understands the music to be celebrating. Although these poems on the theme of death are inspired by and constitute reflections on other artists' works and lives, they also express, perhaps primarily, Sena's own ideas regarding death and how it can be defeated by man through the death-denying power of his creations.

However, the poem in which the idea that music based on an experience of impending death is in a way the negation of that death, and indeed a veritable expression and source of joy, is "Concerto for Orchestra, by Béla Bartók." The poem is based on one of Bartók's last works and one which he composed (in 1943) with his own death staring him in the face. (Bartók was a victim of leukemia, which showed its first symptoms in April of 1942. The Concerto was started at Saravana Lake, New York, where the composer was convalescing from a recent bout with another illness.) For the premiere of the Concerto, which took place in Boston on December, 1944, Bartók provided a program which read in part: "The general mood of the work represents, apart from the jesting second movement, a gradual transition from the sternness of the first movement and the lugubrious death-song of the third to the life-assertion of the last one.''[9] Sena's poem disregards this ''sternness'' of the first movement, as well as the light-spiritedness of the second movement, and there are no allusions to the fourth, in which critics have noted a parody of Shostakovich's Second Symphony. Sena concentrates instead on the elegiac third movement and seems to borrow, at least in part, some of the triumphant spirit of the last movement. I call attention to two basic ideas in the poem: 1) the fact that the composer ''plays'' with his own death, a death which he seems to feel (and which Bartók indeed felt) was near; and 2) how his experience of impending death, when translated into tones, becomes ''música dos outros'' (''music for others'').

In the postface, Jorge de Sena claims that many musical works which he deeply admired—indeed, which he admired more than some of those he actually poetizes—never occurred to him as poems. Why? It is impossible to give incontrovertible answers to this question. The very fact that Sena claims repeatedly that poems ''occur'' to him precludes any kind of conclusive answer, for the verb implies dynamics of inspiration which Sena himself probably could not fully explain. Yet, I believe, based in part on the analysis of the general themes of *Art of Music*, that the reasons have to do with a kind of affinity between the content (understood in musical and extra-musical terms) of the inspiring works, on the one hand, and Sena's philosophical, aesthetic and personal views, on the other. There is, as we noted, a very clear thematic continuity between *Art of Music* and Sena's entire corpus. Here I could dwell only on some similarities. An in-depth study of all of Sena's poetry—indeed, of all his creative works—would reveal an even greater thematic affinity than is possible to show here. The inspirational pool from which Jorge de Sena drew was basically the same and the philosophical view that informed his perception of life was perfectly coherent—whether the model experience became a poem, a short story, a dramatic piece, or a novel. This suggests that the model musical works that did ''occur'' to Sena as poems were precisely those which, whether he was consciously aware of it or not, lent themselves to the poetic elaboration of ideas, emotions, and feelings seminal to his world view—either by conforming to them, or by provoking the kinds of reactions in him that brought forth those concerns.

Among the reasons why Sena turns to music in the first place—and he drew more poems from music than from any other sister art—we have to count the fact that in the most abstract and impalpable of the arts even the expression of the darkest of life's experiences may reach the properly predisposed listener as expressions of joy. The very experience of death can be a life-song. In one of his most negativistic poems, "At Fifty" (*40 Years*), written in 1970, therefore roughly at the same time as many poems of *Art of Music*, Jorge de Sena expresses an almost total disillusionment with life. The poem reads in part:

> . . . *Não sei*
> *se amo a vida ou a detesto. Se desejo*
> *ou não desejo continuar vivendo.*
> *Se amo ou não amo aqueles que amo,*
> *se odeio ou não odeio os que detesto.*
>
> (. . . I do not know
> Whether I love life or I hate it. If I wish
> Or do not wish to continue living.
> If I love or do not love those that I love,
> If I hate or do not hate those that I detest.)

(trans. George Monteiro)

Even spiritual beauty, the poet tells us in this same poem, no longer interests him. The only thing left for him is art, specifically poetry, but not all poetry:

> *Resta a poesia que me enjoa nos outros*
> *a não ser antigos, limpos agora do esterco*
> *de terem vivido.* . . .
>
> (There's still poetry, which nauseates me in
> Others, save only the ancients, stripped
> Clean now of the stench of having lived. . . .)

On the evidence of this poem, Sena had, by this time, reached a stage in his life when he legitimately felt the need to rest from daily contact with the realities of life, the "trash" of human existence. This understandable desire from a man who poetically toured *ad loca infecta* — *infecta* in the Latin sense of unattained, impossible, but also in the sense of infectious — is expressed in other poems throughout his corpus. But Sena was too much of a humanist, much too committed to life, to allow that feeling to dominate him for long. He always returns to life, for, as he says in several previously quoted poems, "Não posso desesperar da humanidade" ("I cannot lose hope in humanity").

What better way to take a momentary respite from the ugly realities of life—oppression, war, intolerance, mediocrity, personal injury, infectious sites—than by turning to music? In this book, as in all of his creative works, Sena's first and foremost commitment is to life. Indeed, he is determined, as we have seen repeatedly, to breathe life into works of music where he finds it lacking. What *Art of Music* represents for Jorge de Sena is the best of two worlds: a continued commitment to life and to mankind, but this time the emphasis is on the best that life and humankind have to offer. Sena, like all men and women, was always searching for paradise. Like all secular humanists, he looked for his paradise in the reality of this earth. He seems to have come the closest to it when he experienced the world of human creation and, within that world, music seems to have played a truly extraordinary role. In the postface, Sena tells us that music was for him the most fertile of all inspirational sources among the arts because, "if all the arts are as necessary for my life as the air I breath, music has always occupied, among them, a special place" (II, p. 215). In Sena's poetic world, too, music occupies a special place indeed. It provides the poet with the opportunity to celebrate humankind's creative powers at the same time that it allows him to perform one of his supreme acts of creation. It allows him to immerse himself in life, while avoiding its most negative aspects, to celebrate man at his best, and to sing of human creations while creating. This is, I think, what *Art of Music* is fundamentally about. This is Jorge de Sena's poetic way with music.

NOTES

Chapter I

[1] *The Philosophy of Humanism*, 5th ed., revised and enlarged (New York: Frederick Ungar, 1965), p. 12. Future references, to be incorporated in the text, are to this edition. References to all works cited in this book, once footnoted, will be incorporated in the text.

[2] *Ideas and Illusions* (London, 1941). Apud A. K. Stout, "Morality Without Religion," *A Humanist View*, ed. Ian Edwards (Sydney: Angus and Robertson, 1969), p. 39.

[3] *Páginas íntimas e de auto-interpretação*, textos estabelecidos e prefaciados por Georg Rudolph Lind e Jacinto do Prado Coelho (Lisboa: Edições Ática, 1966), p. 13.

[4] "Falando com Jorge de Sena," *O Tempo e o Modo*, 59 (April 1968), pp. 377 ff.

[5] (Springfield, Illinois: Charles C. Thomas, 1971).

[6] (Lisboa: Moraes Editores, 1977), pp. 19-20. All references to Sena's poetry, to be included in the text, are to the following editions by Moraes Editores: *Poesia-I*, 2ª ed. (includes *Perseguição*, 1942; *Coroa da terra*, 1946; *Pedra filosofal*, 1950; *As Evidências*, 1955; *Post-Scriptum*, 1960); *Poesia-II*, 1978 (includes *Fidelidade*, 1958; *Metamorfoses, seguidas de Quatro sonetos a Afrodite Anadiómena*, 1963; *Arte de música*, 1968); *Poesia-III*, 1978 (includes *Peregrinatio ad loca infecta*, 1969; *Exorcismos*, 1972; *Camões dirige-se aos seus contemporâneos*, 1973; *Conheço o sal... e outros poemas*, 1974; *Sobre esta praia — oito meditações à beira do Pacífico*, 1977); *40 anos de servidão*, 2ª ed., 1979; *Sequências*, 1980; *Visão perpétua* (Lisboa: co-edição de Moraes Editores and Imprensa Nacional — Casa da Moeda, 1982.) Unless it is necessary to include the specific work to which the poem belongs, references to the poems will be by brief title of volume, e.g., *III*, p. 62.

[7] *O código científico, cosmogónico, metafísico de Perseguição de Jorge de Sena* (Lisboa: Moraes Editores, 1979), p. 24.

[8] George Novack, *Humanism and Socialism* (New York: Pathfinder Press, 1973), p. 126.

[9] Fernando Pessoa, *Poemas de Alberto Caeiro*, 4ª ed. (Lisboa: Edições Ática, 1970), pp. 36-37. Future references will be to this edition.

[10] Jorge de Sena, "Amor," *Grande dicionário da literatura portuguesa e de teoria literária*, Vol. I, dirigido por João José Cochofel (Lisboa: Iniciativas Editoriais, 1977), p. 245.

[11] "Falando com Jorge de Sena," *O Tempo e o Modo*, 59, p. 418.

[12] In the poem "O beco sem saída, ou em resumo...," Vietnam is mentioned in passing, and again in "Ray Charles," "Cadastrado," "Os prazeres da juventude," and "A vida e a morte como investimento segundo as áreas geográficas," all poems belonging to the "cycle" "América, América, I love you" of the volume *Sequências*.

[13] "Posfácio — 1963," to *Metamorfoses*; II, p. 167.

[14] *O reino da estupidez-I*, 2ª ed. aumentada (Lisboa: Moraes Editores, 1979), pp. 115-126.

[15] In *On Poetry and Poets* (New York: Farrar, Strauss and Cudahy, 1957), pp. 3-16.

16 "Porque, acima de tudo... (duas entrevistas à guisa de Epílogo," *Reino da estupidez-I*, p. 213.

17 "Porque, acima de tudo...," p. 212.

18 In *The Humanist Frame*, ed. Julian Huxley (New York: Harper and Brothers, 1961), p. 34.

19 Fernando Pessoa, *Poesias de Fernando Pessoa*, 7ª ed. (Lisboa: Ática, 1967), pp. 53 and 55.

20 Stated in the already mentioned videotape interview with Frederick G. Williams; also quoted by Williams in "Introduction—Jorge de Sena: The Man and His Work," *The Poetry of Jorge de Sena*, ed. with an Intro. and Notes by Frederick G. Williams and a Foreword by Mécia de Sena (Santa Barbara: Mudborn Press, 1980), p. 15.

Chapter II

1 *English Diaries and Journals* (London: William Collins, 1943), p. 7.

2 *Le journal intime* (Paris: Presses Univ. de France, 1963), p. 598.

3 *Diário*, I, 6ª ed. (Coimbra: Edição do Autor, 1978), p. 159.

4 *Private Chronicles* (London: Oxford Univ. Press, 1974), p. 37.

5 "Introduction," *The Illustrated Pepys: Extracts from the Diary*, sel. and ed. by Robert Latham (Berkeley: Univ. of California Press, 1978), p. 7.

6 "'La religieuse' de Diderot: mémoirs ou journal intime?" in *Le journal intime et ses formes littéraires* (Genève: Librairie Droz, 1978), p. 33.

7 *Amiel's Journal, Being the Journal intime of Henri Frédéric Amiel*, 2nd ed., trans. with an Intro. and Notes by Mrs. Humphrey Ward (New York: Brentano's, 1928), p. 136.

8 See *A sátira social de Fernão Mendes Pinto: análise crítica da Peregrinação*, trad. de Manolo B. R. Santos, Prefácio de Luís de Sousa Rebelo (Lisboa: Prelo Editora, 1978).

9 *The Diary of Anaïs Nin*, Vol. VI, ed. and with a Preface by Gunther Stuhlmann (New York: Harcourt Brace Jovanovich, 1977). p. 27.

10 *Diário*, VIII, 3ª ed. (Coimbra: Edição do Autor, 1976), pp. 93-94.

11 *'O poeta é um fingidor'* (Lisboa: Ática, 1961), p. 16.

12 *The Notebook of Malte Laurids Brigge*, trans. by John Linton (London: The Hogarth Press, 1930), p. 18.

13 At the moment D. Mécia de Sena is preparing a third edition of *Poesia-I*, in which the poems will appear with dates.

14 *Antigas e novas andanças do demónio* (Lisboa: Edições 70, 1978), pp. 252-53.

15 "Notas a alguns poemas," *40 anos de servidão*, p. 233.

16 Apud "Marginália," *Poesia-I*, p. 221.

17 "La poesía social," in *La poesía de Rubén Darío: ensayo sobre el tema y los temas del poeta* (Barcelona: Seix Barral, 1975; orig. pub. 1948), p. 217.

18 "Introduction—Jorge de Sena: The Man and His Work," *The Poetry of Jorge de Sena*, p. 23.

19 *The Confessions of St. Augustine*, trans. with an Intro. and Notes by John R. Ryan (Garden City: Image Books, 1960), p. 232.

[20] "Marginália," *Poesia-I*, p. 221.

[21] See Francisco Cota Fagundes, "The Search for the Self: Álvaro de Campos's 'Ode Maritíma,'" *The Man Who Never Was: Essays on Fernando Pessoa*, ed. with an Intro. by George Monteiro (Providence: Gávea-Brown, 1982), pp. 109-129.

[22] "Jorge de Sena ou os limites da alteridade em poesia," *Linguagem e ideologia* (Porto: Editorial Inova, 1972), p. 155.

Chapter III

[1] *Pure Poetry: Studies in French Poetic Theory and Practice 1746 to 1945* (Oxford: Clarendon Press, 1971), p. 32.

[2] Jorge de Sena, "Os 'Cadernos de Poesia,'" *Estudos de literatura portuguesa*, I (Lisboa: Edições 70, 1981), p. 232.

[3] "Breve enquadramento da poesia de Jorge de Sena," *Colóquio/Letras*, 37 (Maio 1977), p. 7.

[4] "How to Read," *Literary Essays*, ed. T. S. Eliot (New York: New Directions, 1968; orig. pub. 1918), p. 23.

[5] *Structuralist Poetics: Structuralism, Linguistics, and the Study of Literature* (Ithaca: Cornell Univ. Press, 1975), p. 161.

[6] *Conversations with Eckermann and Soret*, trans. by John Oxenford (London: George Bell and Sons, 1874). p. 18.

[7] (México: Ediciones Era, 1965), p. 106.

[8] *Os Grão-Capitães: uma sequência de contos*, 3ª ed. (Lisboa: Edições 70, 1982), pp. 85-86.

[9] *As cem melhores poesias da língua portuguesa*, escolhidas por Carolina Michaelis de Vasconcelos (Philadelphia: George W. Jacobs & Co., 1938), p. 219.

[10] *Baudelaire* (Norfolk, Conn.: New Directions, 1958), p. 372.

[11] The sonnet is printed in its entirety in *Histoire illustré des lettres françaises de Belgique* (Bruxelles: La Renaissance du Livre, 1958), p. 160.

[12] *Educação e sociedade no Portugal de Salazar* (Lisboa: Editorial Presença, 1978), p. 91.

[13] Two studies dealing with the phenomenon of intertextuality in Sena's works are: Fernando J. B. Martinho, "Leituras na poesia de Jorge de Sena," *Colóquio/Letras*, 67 (Maio 1982), pp. 14-25; and Francisco Cota Fagundes, "The Transmutation of Autobiographical Experiences in Jorge de Sena's *Os Grão-Capitães*," *Kentucky Romance Quarterly*, 30 (1983), pp. 203-16.

[14] *Bulletin of Hispanic Studies*, 59 (April 1982), pp. 129-42.

[15] Gotthold Ephraim Lessing, *Laocoön*, trans. Edward Allen McCormick (New York: Bobbs-Merrill, 1962), p. 78.

[16] Apud Mario Praz, *Mnemosyne: The Parallel between Literature and the Visual Arts* (Princeton: Princeton Univ. Press, 1970), p. 59.

[17] *The Arts and the Art of Criticism*, 2nd ed. (Princeton: Princeton Univ. Press, 1947), p. 312.

[18] See "Metamorfoses," *Estado de São Paulo* (27 June 1964).

Chapter IV

[1] Colin McAlpin, *Hermaia: A Study in Comparative Esthetics* (London: J M Dent and Sons, 1915), p. 192.

[2] Cited in *In Praise of Music* ed. by Richard Lewis (New York: The Orion Press, 1963), p. 57.

[3] *Verbal Music in German Literature* (New Haven: Yale Univ. Press, 1968), p. 4.

[4] Roger Kamien, *Music: An Appreciation*, 2nd ed. (New York: McGraw-Hill, 1980), p. 37.

[5] *Tones into Words: Musical Compositions as Subjects of Poetry* (Athens: The Univ. of Georgia Press, 1953), p. 24.

[6] *Monatschefte*, 55 (1963), pp. 97-101.

[7] *The Science of English Verse* (New York: C. Scribner's Sons, 1880), p. 31.

[8] "La musicalidad del 'Polifemo,'" *Revista de Filologia Espanõla*, 44 (1961), p. 141.

[9] "Music and Poetry," *British Journal of Aesthetics*, 1 (1961), p. 137.

[10] *Poesias de Fernando Pessoa,* 7ª ed., pp. 72 and 74.

[11] *Clepsidra e outros poemas*, 5ª ed. (Lisboa: Ática, 1973), pp. 172-73.

[12] *Music and Literature: A Comparison of the Arts* (Athens: The Univ. of Georgia Press, 1963; rpt. of 1948 ed.).

[13] *Music and Reason: The Art of Listening, Appreciating and Composing* (New York: Social Sciences Publishers, 1948), p. 39.

[14] *The Unanswered Question: Six Talks at Harvard* (Cambridge: Harvard Univ. Press, 1981; rpt. 1976 ed.), p. 131.

[15] For a study of "melody" in poetry, see Bayard Quincy Morgan, "Melodic Lines in Goethe's Verse," *German Quarterly*, 26 (1953), pp. 10-16.

[16] "Literature and Music," *Interrelations of Literature,* ed. by Jean-Pierre Barricelli and Joseph Gibaldi (New York: MLA, 1982), p. 229.

[17] René Wellek, and Austin Warren, *Theory of Literature*, 3rd ed. (New York: Harcourt, Brace and World, 1956), pp. 126-27.

[18] *A poesia portuguesa hoje* (Lisboa: Plátano Editora, 1973), pp. 72 and 73.

[19] "Algumas interrogações sobre o prosaísmo na obra poética de Jorge de Sena," *Studies on Jorge de Sena*, ed. by Harvey L. Sharrer and Frederick G. Williams (Santa Barbara: Bandanna Books, 1981), p. 27.

[20] "A crítica do livro ⌈Arte de música⌉," *Comércio do Porto*, 12 Aug. 1969.

[21] "Word-Music in English Poetry," *Journal of Aesthetics and Art Criticism*, 11 (1952), pp. 151-59.

[22] "The Poetic Use of Musical Forms," *Musical Quarterly*, 30 (1944), p. 90.

[23] "Notes Toward a Theory of Verbal Music," *Comparative Literature*, 22 (1970), p. 149.

[24] *What to Listen for in Music*, rev. ed. (New York: McGraw-Hill, 1967; orig. pub. 1939).

Chapter V

[1] *Music in the Life of Man* (New York: Holt, Rinehart and Winston, 1956), pp. 1-55.

[2] Apud Charles T. Smith, *Music and Reason* pp. v-vi.

[3] Cited in *In Praise of Music*, p. 96.

[4] For a more detailed account of philosophers' ideas on music, see Julius Portnoy, *The Philosopher and Music* (New York: The Humanities Press, 1954).

[5] *The Complete Works of Shakespeare*. Illustrated by Rockwell Kent, with a Preface by Christopher Morley (Garden City: Doubleday and Company, 1936), p. 1404.

[6] Eduard Hanslick, *The Beautiful in Music*, trans. by Gustav Cohen, ed. with an Intro. by Morris Weitz (New York: Liberal Arts Press, 1957), p. 48.

[7] Apud Deryck Cooke, *The Language of Music* (London: Oxford Univ. Press, 1959), p. 11.

[8] "Preface," *The Language of Music*, p. ix.

[9] *The Renaissance*, Intro. by Lawrence Evans (Chicago: Academy Press, 1978), p. 139.

[10] "Arte de música, por Jorge de Sena," *Diário Popular* (Lisboa), 28 Nov. 1968.

[11] See Chapter II, "Imitation of Music in Poetry," *Tones into Words*.

[12] Oskar Bie, *Schubert, the Man* (New York: Dodd, Mead, 1928), p. 82.

[13] Eric Sams, *The Songs of Robert Schumann*, Foreword by Gerald Moore (London: Methuen, 1969), pp. 3-4.

[14] *Meaning and Truth in the Arts* (Chapel Hill: The Univ. of North Carolina Press, 1946), pp. 96-97.

Chapter VI

[1] Oscar Thompson, *Debussy: Man and Artist* (New York: Dover Publications, 1967; orig. pub. 1937), p. 267.

[2] See León Vallas, *Claude Debussy: His Life and Works*, trans. by Marie and Grace O'Brien (London: Oxford Univ. Press, 1933), p. 4.

[3] *Poetry and Truth*, I, trans. by Minna Steele Smith (London: G. Bell and Sons, 1930), p. 252.

[4] "Melodic and Poetic Structure: The Examples of Campion and Dowland," *Criticism*, 4 (1962), p. 103.

[5] See Don McLachlan, "Peter Pears Discography," *Records and Recordings*, 16 (1973), pp. 21-22.

[6] Apud H. C. Robbins, *Haydn: Chronicle and Works*, Vol. IV (Bloomington: Indiana Univ. Press, 1977), p. 344.

[7] *Joseph Haydn: Eighteenth-Century Gentleman and Genius*, trans. with intro. and notes by Vernon Gotwals (Madison: Univ. of Wisconsin Press, 1963), p. 188.

[8] Cited by Dyneley Hussey, *Wolfgang Amade Mozart* (New York: Harper and Brothers, 1928), p. 270.

9 *The Holy Sacrifice of the Mass: Dogmatically, Liturgically and Ascetically Explained*, 3rd ed. (St. Louis, Mo.: B. Herder, 1908), p. 389.

10 Apud James Hutton, "English Poems in Praise of Music," *English Miscellany: A Symposium of History, Literature and the Arts*, ed. Mario Praz (Roma: Edizioni di Storia e Letteratura, 1951), p. 16.

11 *The Holy Eucharist* (London: Longmans, Green, 1907), p. 48.

12 Charles Rosen, *The Classical Style: Haydn, Mozart, Beethoven* (New York: Viking Press, 1971), p. 373.

13 *Beethoven Handbook* (New York: Frederick Ungar, 1967; orig. pub. 1956), p. 145.

14 *The Life and Works of Beethoven* (New York: Random House, 1943), p. 325.

15 "The Choral Music," *The Beethoven Companion*, ed. by Denis Arnold and Nigel Fortune (London: Faber and Faber, 1971), p. 403.

16 *Notes on Chopin*, trans. by Bernard Frechtman (New York: Philosophical Library, 1949), p. 27.

17 *The Life and Times of Chopin*, trans. by C. J. Richard (London: Hamlyn, 1967), p. 4.

18 Apud Simone Berteaut, *Piaf*, trans. by Ghislane Boulanger (London: W. H. Allen, 1971), p. 155.

19 Willi Apel, *Harvard Dictionary of Music*, 2nd ed., revised and enlarged (Cambridge: Harvard Univ. Press, 1969), p. 691.

20 "Jorge de Sena," *Da Pessoa a Oliveira: La moderna poesia portoghese, modernismo-surrealismo-neorealismo*, a cura di Giuseppe Tavani (Milano: Edizioni Accademia, 1973), p. 340.

Chapter VII

1 *Berlioz, Romantic and Classic: Writings by Ernest Newman*, sel. and ed. by Peter Heyworth (London: Victor Gollancz, 1972), p. 161.

2 *Berlioz and the Romantic Century*, Vol. I, 3rd ed. (New York: Columbia Univ. Press, 1969), p. 149.

3 Frantisek Bartos, *Bedrich Smetana: Letters and Reminiscences*, trans. by Daphne Rusbridge (Prague: Artia, 1955), pp. 59-60.

4 *Smetana* (London: Duckworth, 1970), p. 261.

5 "Smetana's short outline of the symphonic poems 'My Country,'" *Bedrich Smetana: Letters and Reminiscences*, pp. 263-66.

6 Sir Kenneth Clark, apud Edward Lockspeiser, *Music and Painting: A Study in Comparative Ideas from Turner to Schoenberg* (London: Cassell, 1973), p. 52.

7 *Tchaikovsky: The Man Behind the Music* (New York: Dodd, Mead, 1966), p. 18.

8 This essay, which appeared for the first time in *Livros que abalaram o mundo* (São Paulo, 1963), is now included in *Maquiavel e outros estudos* (Porto: Livraria Paisagem, 1974), under the title "Maquiavel e o 'Príncipe.'"

9 *Istorie fiorentine*, Bk. VIII, *Opere di Niccolò Machiavelli*, a cura di Ezio Raimondi (Milano: Ugo Mursia, 1966), p. 777.

10 Apud Arthur Komar, *Music and Human Experience* (New York: Schirmer Books, 1980), p. 50.

[11] *A Listener's Anthology of Music*, Vol. II (Cleveland: The Kulas Foundation, 1948), p. 372.

[12] Arthur Jacobs and Stanley Saide, *Great Operas in Synopsis* (New York: Thomas Y. Crowell, 1966), p. 165.

[13] "Richard Wagner," *La Musica: Enciclopedia Storica*, Vol. IV (Torino: Union tipografico-editrice torinese, 1966), p. 818.

[14] *The Wagner Operas* (New York: Alfred A. Knopf, 1968; orig. pub. 1949), p. 204.

[15] *Tristan and Isolda*, vocal score Richard Kleinmichel, English version by Henry Crafton Chapman (New York: G. Schirmer, 1906), p. 301.

[16] "Ouroboros," *The New Encyclopedia Britannica, Ready Reference and Index*, 15th ed. (London, 1983), p. 634.

[17] *Ancient Pagan and Modern Christian Symbolism*, rev. and enlarged (Kennebunkport, Me.: Milford House, Inc., 1970), p. 90.

[18] *The Authentic Librettos of Wagner Operas*, Complete with English and German Parallel Texts and Music of the Principal Airs (New York: Crown Publishers, 1938), p. 300.

[19] *The Music Dramas of Richard Wagner*, trans. from the French by Esther Singleton (New York: AMS Press, 1970; rpt. from the 1904 ed.), p. 431.

[20] *Famous Puccini Operas*, 2nd rev. ed. (New York: Dover Publications, 1972), p. 51.

[21] Apud Richard Specht, "Introductory Note," *Giacomo Puccini: The Man, His Life, His Work* (Westport, Ct.: Greenwood Press, 1970; orig. pub. 1933), p. ix.

[22] Apud Howard Greenfeld, *Puccini: A Biography* (New York: G. P. Putnam's Sons, 1980), p. 277.

[23] See *Letters of Giacomo Puccini*, ed. by Giuseppe Adami, trans. and ed. for the English ed. by Ena Makin (New York: AMS Press, 1971), pp. 254-320.

[24] See *Puccini: A Critical Biography* (New York: Alfred A. Knopf, 1959), pp. 256-61.

[25] Erik Satie, *Socrate: drame symphonique* (Paris: Éditions Max Eschig, 1919), p. 29.

[26] *Socrates*, trans. by Douglas Scott (New York: Walker, 1963), p. 30.

[27] Apud James Harding, *Erick Satie* (New York: Praeger Publishers, 1975), p. 176.

[28] *Erik Satie* (New York: Dover Publications, 1968; orig. pub. 1948), p. 55.

Chapter VIII

[1] Apud Jack Kaminsky, *Hegel on Art: An Interpretation of Hegel's Aesthetics* (New York: The State Univ. of New York, 1962), p. 121.

[2] *J. S. Bach*, Vol. I, trans. by Ernest Newman, Preface by C. M. Widor (London: Adam and Charles Black, 1923), p. 1.

[3] *The Works of Matthew Arnold in Fifteen Volumes*, Vol. II (London: MacMillan; Smith, Elder, 1903), p. 15.

4 *The Descent of Man* (New York: Dodd Mead and Company, 1899), p. 585 (Note).

5 *A Listener's Anthology of Music*, Vol. I, p. 52.

6 Quoted in Otto Erich Deutsch, *Handel: A Documentary Biography* (London: Adam and Charles Black, 1955), p. 76.

7 *O físico prodigioso*, 2ª ed. (Lisboa: Edições 70, 1979), p. 68.

8 *Alexander Pope: Selected Works*, ed. with an Intro. by Louis Kronenberger, Foreword by Joseph Wood Krutch (New York: The Modern Library, 1951), p. 106.

9 Ibid., p. 17.

10 The general information concerning Mahler is based on the following three works: Marc Vignal, *Mahler* (Paris: Seuil, 1966); Michael Kennedy, *Mahler* (London: J M Dent and Sons Ltd., 1974); and Deryck Cooke, *Gustav Mahler: An Introduction to His Music* (London: Faber Music, 1980).

11 German version quoted by Deryck Cooke, *Gustav Mahler*, p. 59. The English translation is my own.

12 "Prodigious Exorcist: An Introduction to the Poetry of Jorge de Sena," *World Literature Today*, 53 (Winter 1979), p. 12.

Chapter IX

1 For an excellent and beautiful study of the importance of the sea in Jorge de Sena's works, see Maria de Lourdes Belchior, "O mar na poesia de Jorge de Sena," *Studies on Jorge de Sena*, pp. 15-23.

2 *Maquiavel e outros estudos*, p. 156.

3 Roger Kamien, *Music: An Appreciation*, p. 118.

4 *Mozart, His Character, His Work*, trans. by Arthur Mendel and Nathan Broder (London: Oxford Univ. Press, 1945). p. 306.

5 Howard D. McKinney and W. R. Anderson, *Music in History*, 3rd ed. (New York: American Book Company, 1966), p. 685.

6 Apud McKinney and Anderson, op. cit., p. 665.

7 Apud McKinney and Anderson, p. 665.

8 Apud Norman Del Mar, *Richard Strauss*, Vol. I (Chatham: W. & J. Mackay, 1962), p. 134.

9 Halsey Stevens, *The Life and Music of Béla Bartók*, rev. ed. (New York: Oxford Univ. Press, 1964), p. 280.

BIBLIOGRAPHY

I. Works by Jorge de Sena

A. Complete Poetry

Poesia-I (Perseguição, Coroa da terra, Pedra filosofal, As Evidências, and *Post-Scriptum).* 2ª edição. Lisboa: Moraes Editores, 1977.

Poesia-II (Fidelidade, Metamorfoses seguidas de Quatro Sonetos a Afrodite Anadiómena, and *Arte de música).* Lisboa: Moraes Editores, 1978.

Poesia-III (Peregrinatio ad Loca Infecta, Exorcismos, Camões dirige-se aos seus contemporâneos, Conheço o sal. . . e outros poemas, and *Sobre esta praia — oito meditações à beira do Pacífico).* Lisboa: Moraes Editores, 1978.

40 anos de servidão. 2ª edição. Lisboa: Moraes Editores, 1979.

Sequências. Lisboa: Moraes Editores, 1980.

Visão perpétua. Lisboa: Moraes Editores/Imprensa Nacional-Casa da Moeda, 1982.

Post-Scriptum II. 2 vols. Lisboa: Moraes Editores/Imprensa Nacional-Casa da Moeda, 1985. Although I include this work, it was published after this book was completed. I deal with these poems in my forthcoming book *In The Beginning There Was GENESIS: The Birth of a Writer.*

B. Complete Fiction

Antigas e novas andanças do demónio. 2ª edição. Lisboa: Edições 70, 1971.

O físico prodigioso. 2ª edição. Lisboa: Edições 70, 1977.

Os Grão-Capitães: uma sequência de contos. 3ª edição. Lisboa: Edições 70, 1982.

Sinais de fogo (romance). 3ª edição. Lisboa: Edições 70, 1984.

Génesis (contos). Lisboa: Edições 70, 1983.

"Escada" (short story). In *Sílabas: contos de escritores portugueses nos Estados Unidos.* Nota inicial de Luís de Miranda Correia, Prefácio de Eduardo Mayone Dias. Providence: Portuguese Cultural Foundation, 1983.

"Secção." (short story). In *Peregrinação,* 7 (Jan. 1985).

"Sonata," "Descobertas," "As Duas Coroas de Pétala de Neve" (unfinished). Unpublished short stories, written between June 20 and September 9, 1938.

A personagem total. Unpublished unfinished novel (1938).

C. Essays

Dialéticas teóricas da literatura. 2ª edição revista e aumentada. Lisboa: Edições 70, 1977.

Dialécticas aplicadas da literatura. Lisboa: Edições 70, 1978.

Maquiavel e outros estudos. Porto: Paisagem, 1974.

"O Poeta é um fingidor." Lisboa: Ática, 1961.

O reino da estupidez I. 2ª edição aumentada. Lisboa: Moraes Editores 1979.

O reino da estupidez II. Lisboa: Moraes Editores, 1978.

Sobre o romance: ingleses, norte-americanos e outros. Lisboa: Edições 70, 1985.

II. Criticism on Jorge Sena

A. Anthologies of Sena's works containing studies

Cattaneo, Carlo Vittorio. *Exorcismi.* Bilingual anthology of Sena's poetry. Sel., trans., intro., chronology and notes by Carlo Vittorio Cattaneo. Milano: Edizioni Accademia, 1974.

Jacobbi, Ruggero and Carlo Vittorio Cattaneo. *Su Questa Spiaggia.* Anthology of Sena's poetry. Org. by Carlo Vittorio Cattaneo, intro. by Luciana Stegagno Picchio, preface "ai lettori italiani" by Jorge de Sena, trans. by Ruggero Jacobbi and Carlo Vittorio Cattaneo. Roma: Associazioni Culturale "Portucale," 1984.

Lisboa, Eugénio. *Versos e alguma prosa de Jorge de Sena.* Sel. and preface by Eugénio Lisboa. Lisboa: Arcádia/Moraes, 1979.

——————————. *Jorge de Sena.* Anthology of Sena's poetry. Org. and intro. by Eugénio Lisboa. Lisboa: Presença, 1984.

Morna, Fátima Freitas. *Poesia de Jorge de Sena.* Anthology of Sena's poetry. Intro., sel., notes and outline for analysis by Fátima Freitas Morna. Lisboa: Comunicação, 1985.

Williams, Frederick G. *The Poetry of Jorge de Sena.* Bilingual anthology of Sena's poetry. Org., intro. and notes by Frederick G. Williams, preface by Mécia de Sena, trans. by Helen Barreto, Don Bartell, Rip Cohen, Jonathan Griffin, James Houlihan, Jean R. Longland, Suzette Macedo, Alan Sillitoe, Jack E. Tomlins, and Frederick G. Williams. Santa Barbara: Mudborn Press, 1980.

B. Anthologies of critical works on Jorge de Sena; special issues of literary reviews dedicated to Sena

O Tempo e o Modo, 59 (April 1968)

Colóquio/Letras, 67 (May 1982).

Quaderni Portoghesi, 13-14 (Spring-Fall 1983). This special issue dedicated to Jorge de Sena contains a body of studies on Sena that is probably the best assembled thus far. No study herein contained was used in my book, though. This issue of *Quaderni* appeared after my book was completed.

Studies on Jorge de Sena — A Colloquium. Proceedings of a colloquium on Jorge de Sena held at the University of California, Santa Barbara, April 6-7, 1979. Intro. and preface by Harvey L. Sharrer and Frederick G. Williams. Santa Barbara: Bandanna Books, 1981.

Estudos sobre Jorge de Sena. Comp., org. and with an intro. by Eugénio Lisboa. Lisboa: Imprensa Nacional-Casa da Moeda, 1984.

C. Interview with Jorge de Sena

Williams, Frederick G. "Jorge de Sena Reads His Own Poetry." a video-tape interview in color conducted 4 May 1978. Santa Barbara: University of California.

D. Other studies on Jorge de Sena

Adriano Carlos, Luís F. "Jorge de Sena e a escrita dos limites: análise das estruturas paradigmáticas nos *Quatro Sonetos a Afrodite Anadiómena*." Tese de Mestrado. Porto, 1986.

Augusto França, José. "Na morte de Jorge de Sena." *Colóquio/Letras*, 44 (Julho 1978), 60-66.

Bento, José. "Dois poemas de Jorge de Sena e Antonio Machado." *Brotéria*, 111 (Novembro 1980), 438-442.

Cattaneo, Carlo Vittorio. "'Genesis': Contos Juvenis de Jorge de Sena." *Colóquio/Letras*, 87 (September 1985), 71-73.

Crespo, Angel. "Fidelidade e independencia de Jorge de Sena." *Nueva Estafeta*, 6 (Junio 1969), 4-6.

Cruz, Gastão. "Jorge de Sena—*Perigrinatio ad Loca Infecta*." In *A poesia portuguesa hoje*. Lisboa: Plátano Editora, 1973, 71-87.

Fagundes, Francisco Cota. "History and Poetry as *Metamorfoses*." *Bulletin of Hispanic Studies*, 59 (April 1982), 129-42.

_____. "The Transmutation of Autobiographical Experiences in Jorge de Sena's *Os Grão-Capitães.*" *Kentucky Romance Quarterly*, 30 (1983), 202-16. A Portuguese version of this article appeared in *Estudos sobre Jorge de Sena*.

_____. Jorge de Sena, *Art of Music*. Trans. by Francisco Cota Fagundes and James Houlihan, and with an Intro. Study by Francisco Cota Fagundes. Huntington: University Editions, 1988.

Freire, Natércia. "Uma breve nota ⁄sobre *Arte de música*⁊." *Diário de Notícias*, 3 October 1968.

Lopes, Óscar. "A crítica do livro ⁄*Arte de música*⁊." *Comércio do Porto*, 12 August 1969.

Martinho, Fernando J. B. "Breve Enquadramento da Poesia de Jorge de Sena." *Colóquio/Letras*, 37 (May 1977), 5-12.

Monteiro, Adolfo Casais. "Jorge de Sena." *A poesia portuguesa contemporânea*. Lisboa: Sá da Costa, 1977, 267-280.

Morna, Fátima Freitas. "Sobre um dos Sentidos da Peregrinação na Poesia de Jorge de Sena." *Afecto às letras: homenagem da literatura portuguesa contemporânea a Jacinto do Prado Coelho*. Lisboa: Imprensa Nacional-Casa da Moeda, 1984, 179-83.

Mourão-Ferreira, David. "Na publicação de 'As Evidências.'" *Vinte poetas contemporâneos*. Lisboa: Ática, 1980, 167-171.

Palma-Ferreira, João. "*Arte de música*, por Jorge de Sena." *Diário Popular*, 28 Nov. 1968.

Prado Coelho, Eduardo. "Ler Jorge de Sena ⁄*Arte de música*⁊." *Diário de Lisboa*, 26 Sept. 1968.

_____. "Ainda Jorge de Sena ⁄*Arte de música*⁊." *Diário de Lisboa*, 10 Oct. 1968.

Rosa, António Ramos. "Metamorfoses ou a Poesia da Fidelidade Total." In *A poesia moderna e a interrogação do real*. Vol. I. Lisboa: Arcádia, 1974, 121-24.

Saraiva, Arnaldo. "Fernando Pessoa e Jorge de Sena." *Persona*, 5 (Abril 1981), 23-37.

Torres, Alexandre Pinheiro. *O código científico-cosmogónico-metafísico de 'Perseguição' de Jorge de Sena*. Lisboa: Moraes Editores, 1980.

III. Miscellany

Amiel, H. F. *Amiel's Journal, Being the Journal intime of Henri Frédéric Amiel.* 2nd ed. Trans. with an Intro. and Notes by Mrs. Humphrey Ward. New York: Brentano's, 1928.

Arnold, Matthew. *The Works of Matthew Arnold in Fifteen Volumes.* Vol. II. London: MacMillan; Smith, Elder, 1903.

Augustine, St. *The Confessions of St. Augustine.* Trans. with an Intro. and Notes by John R. Ryan. Garden City: Image Books, 1960

Brun, Jean. *Socrates.* Trans. by Douglas Scott. New York: Walker, 1963.

Centre d'études stendhaliennes. *Le journal intime et ses formes littéraires.* Testes réunis par V. Dell Litto. Genève and Paris: Droz, 1978.

Culler, Jonathan. *Structuralist Poetics: Structuralism, Linguistics, and the Study of Literature.* Ithaca: Cornell Univ. Press, 1975.

Darwin, Charles. *The Descent of Man.* 2nd ed., revised and augmented. New York: Appleton, 1909.

Dewey, John. *Art as Experience.* New York: Minton, Balch, 1934.

Fothergill, Robert A. *Private Chronicles: A Study of English Diaries.* London: Oxford Univ. Press, 1974.

Gihr, Nikolaus. *The Holy Sacrifice of the Mass: Dogmatically, Liturgically and Ascetically Explained.* 3rd ed. St. Louis: Herder, 1908.

Girard, Alain. *Le journal intime.* Paris: Presses Univ. de France, 1963.

Goethe, J. W. von. *Conversations with Eckermann and Soret.* Trans. by John Oxenford. London: George Bell and Sons, 1874.

_____. *Poetry and Truth.* 2 vols. Trans. by M. Steele Smith. London: G. Bell and Sons, 1930.

Greene, Theodor Meyer. *The Arts and the Art of Criticism.* 2nd ed. Princeton: Princeton Univ. Press, 1947.

Hedley, John Cuthbert. *The Holy Eucharist.* London: Longmans, Green, 1907.

Inman, Thomas. *Ancient Pagan and Modern Christian Symbolism.* 4th ed., rev. and enlarged. Kennebunkport, Maine: Milford House, 1970.

LeRoy, Gaylord, and Beitz, Ursula (eds.). *Preserve and Create: Essays in Marxist Criticism*. New York: Humanities Press, 1973.

Lessing, G. E. *Laocoön*. Trans. Edward Allen McCormick. New York: Bobbs-Merrill, 1962.

Machiavelli, Nicollò. *Istorie fiorentine*. In *Opere de Niccolò Machiavelli*. A cura di Ezio Raimondi. Milano: Ugo Mursia, 1966.

Mónica, Maria Filomena. *Educação e sociedade no Portugal de Salazar: a escola primária salazarista, 1926-1939*. Lisboa: Editorial Presença, 1978.

Montaigne, Michel de. *The Diary of Montaigne's Journey to Italy in 1580 and 1581*. Trans. with intro. and notes by E. J. Trechmann. London: L. and Virginia Woolf, 1929.

Mossop, D. J. *Pure Poetry: Studies in French Poetic Theory and Practice 1746 to 1945*. Oxford: New Directions, 1958.

Nin, Anaïs. *The Diary of Anaïs Nin*. 6 vols. Ed. Gunther Stuhlmann. New York: Harcourt Brace Jovanovich, 1966-77.

O'Brien, Kate. *English Diaries and Journals*. London: William Collins, 1943.

Pater, Walter. *The Renaissance*. Intro. by Lawrence Evans. Chicago: Academy Press, 1978.

Pepys, Samuel. *The Illustrated Pepys: Extracts from the Diary*. Sel. and ed. by Robert Latham. Berkeley: Univ. of California Press, 1978.

Pope, Alexander. *Selected Works*. Ed. with an Intro. by Louis Kronenberger, Foreword by Joseph Wood Krutch. New York: The Modern Library, 1951.

Pound, Ezra. *Literary Essays*. Ed. T. S. Eliot. Norfolk, Conn.: New Directions, 1968.

Reis, Carlos. *Técnicas de análise textual*. 3ª ed. revista. Coimbra: Almedina, 1981.

Rilke, Rainer Maria. *The Notebook of Malte Laurids Brigge*. Trans. John Linton. London: The Hogarth Press, 1930.

Salinas, Pedro. *La poesía de Rubén Darío: ensayo sobre el tema y los temas del poeta*. Barcelona: Seix Barral, 1975; orig. pub. 1948.

_____. *La realidad y el poeta*. Spanish version Soledad Salinas de Marichal. Barcelona: Editorial Ariel, 1976.

Sánchez Vázquez, Adolfo. *Ideas estéticas de Marx*. México: Ediciones Era, 1965.

Silva, Vítor Manuel Aguiar e. *Teoria da Literatura.* 3ª ed. Coimbra: Livraria Almedina, 1973.

Starkie, Enid. *Baudelaire.* Norfolk, Conn.: New Directions, 1958.

Torga, Miguel. *Diário.* 12 vols. Coimbra: Edição do Autor, 1941-1977.

Wellek, René, and Warren, Austin. *Theory of Literature.* 3rd ed. New York: Harcourt, Brace and World, 1956.

IV. Humanism

Ayer, Alfred Jules (ed.). *The Humanist Outlook.* London: Pemberton; Barrie and Rockliff, 1968.

Babbitt, Irving. *On Being Creative, and Other Essays.* New York: Biblo and Tannen, 1968; rpt. 1960 ed.

Blackham, H. J. *Humanism.* 2nd rev. ed. New York: International Publications Service, 1976.

Edwards, Ian (ed.). *A Humanist View.* Sydney: Angus & Robertson, 1969.

Faulkner, Peter. *Humanism in the English Novel.* New York: Barnes & Noble, 1976.

Fromm, Erich. *To have or to be?* New York: Harper and Row, 1976.

——————. (ed.). *Socialist Humanism: An International Symposium.* Garden City: Doubleday, 1965.

Huxley, Julian (ed.). *The Humanist Frame.* New York: Harper and Brothers, 1961.

Kaplan, Harold J. *Democratic Humanism and American Literature.* Chicago: The Univ. of Chicago Press, 1972.

Keyser, Cassius Jackson. *Humanism and Science.* New York: Columbia Univ. Press, 1931.

Kurtz, Paul (ed.). *The Humanist Alternative: Some Definitions of Humanism.* London: Pemberton, 1973.

Lamont, Corliss. *The Philosophy of Humanism.* 5th ed. rev. and enlarged. New York: Frederick Ungar, 1965.

——————. *The Illusion of Immortality.* 2nd ed. New York: Philosophical Library, 1950.

_____. *The Independent Mind: Essays of a Humanist Philosopher*. New York: Horizon Press, 1951.

_____. *Yes to Life: Memoirs of Corliss Lamont*. New York: Horizon Press, 1981.

_____. (ed.). *Man Answers Death: An Anthology of Poetry*. New York: Philosophical Library, 1952.

Mackail, John William. *Studies in Humanism*. New Haven: Yale Univ. Press, 1950.

Maritain, Jacques. *True Humanism*. Trans. by M. R. Adamson. Freeport, N. Y.: Books for Libraries Press, 1970; rpt. of 1938 ed.

_____. *Integral Humanism: Temporal and Spiritual Problems of a New Christendom*. Trans. Joseph W. Evans. New York: Scribner, 1968.

Mondolfo, Rodolfo. *Umanismo di Marx: studi filosofici 1908-1966*. Intro. di Norberto Bobbio. Torino: G. Einaudi, 1968.

More, Paul Elmer. *On Being Human*. Princeton: Princeton Univ. Press, 1936.

Novack, George. *Humanism and Socialism*. New York: Pathfinder Press, 1973.

Ouden, Bernard D. den. *The Fusion of Naturalism and Humanism*. Washington, D.C.: Univ. Press of America, 1979.

Parsons, Howard L. *Humanism and Marx's Thought*. Springfield, Ill.: Charles C. Thomas, 1971.

Petrosian, Mariia Isaakovna. *Humanism: Its Philosophical, Ethical and Sociological Aspects*. Trans. Bryan Bean and Robert Daglish. Moscow: Progress Publishers, 1972.

Ponce, Aníbal. *De Erasmo a Romain Rolland: humanismo burgués y humanismo proletario*. Buenos Aires: Editorial Futuro, 1962.

Rader, Melvin, et al. *Art and Human Values*. Englewood Cliffs, N.J.: Prentice Hall, 1976.

Ribeiro, Lauro. *Nova perspectiva do homem: para um mundo nôvo e uma sociedade melhor e mais justa*. Rio de Janeiro: Freitas Bastos, 1968.

Richards, Philip S. *Belief in Man*. New York: Farrar and Rinehart, 1932.

Rotenstreich, Nathan. *Humanism in the Contemporary Era*. The Hague: Mouton, 1963.

Shinn, Roger Lincoln. *Man: The New Humanism*. Philadelphia: Westminster Press, 1968.

Stalnaker, Luther Winfield. *Humanism and Human Dignity*. New Haven: Yale Univ. Press, 1945.

Tavener, Wallace B. *The Path of Humanism*. London: Lindsey, 1968.

Tierno Galván, Enrique. *Humanismo y sociedad*. Barcelona: Seix Barral, 1964.

Ulanov, Barry. *Sources and Resources: The Literary Traditions of Christian Humanism*. Westminster, Md.: Newman Press, 1960.

Wells, H. G., et al. *The Science of Life*. New York: Literary Guild, 1934.

West, Charles C. *The Power to be Human: Toward a Secular Theology*. New York: MacMillan, 1971.

V. Music in General

Baldwin, Lillian. *A Listener's Anthology of Music*. 2 vols. Cleveland: The Kulas Foundation, 1948.

Bernstein, Leonard. *The Unanswered Question: Six Talks at Harvard*. Cambridge: Harvard Univ. Press, 1981; rpt. of 1976 ed.

Buker, Alden. *A Humanistic Approach to Music Appreciation: Music and Living from Practical to Aesthetic*. Palo Alto: National Press, 1964.

Cooke, Deryck. *The Language of Music*. London: Oxford Univ. Press, 1964; rpt. of 1959 ed.

Copland, Aaron. *What to Listen for in Music*. Rev. ed. New York: McGraw-Hill, 1967; orig. pub. 1939.

Hanslick, Eduard. *The Beautiful in Music*. Trans. Gustav Cohen, ed. with an Intro. by Morris Weitz. New York: Liberal Arts Press, 1957.

Helm, Everett Burton. *Composer, Performer, Public: A Study in Communication*. Florence: L. S. Olschki, 1970.

Hospers, John. *Meaning and Truth in the Arts*. Chapel Hill: The Univ. of North Carolina Press, 1946.

Howes, Frank Stewart. *Man, Mind and Music*. London: Secker and Warburg, 1948.

Kamien, Roger. *Music: An Appreciation*. 2nd ed. New York: McGraw-Hill, 1980.

Kaminsky, Jack. *Hegel on Art: An Interpretation of Hegel's Aesthetics*. New York: The State Univ. of New York, 1962.

Komar, Arthur J. *Music and Human Experience*. New York: Schirmer Books, 1980.

Langer, Susanne. *Feeling and Form: A Theory of Art*. New York: Charles Scribner's Sons, 1953.

Lewis, Richard (ed.). In *Praise of Music: An Anthology*. New York: Orion Press, 1977.

Lippman, Edward A. *A Humanistic Philosophy of Music*. New York: New York Univ. Press, 1977.

McKinney, Howard D., et al. *Music in History: The Evolution of an Art*. 3rd. ed. New York: American Book Company, 1966.

Portnoy, Julius. *The Philosopher and Music*. New York: The Humanities Press, 1954.

_____. *Music in the Life of Man*. New York: Holt, Rinehart and Winston, 1956.

Randolph, David. *This is Music: A Guide to the Pleasures of Listening*. New York: McGraw-Hill, 1964.

Reimer, Bennett. *A Philosophy of Music Education*. Englewood, N.J.: Prentice Hall, 1970.

Sessions, Roger. *The Musical Experience of Composer, Performer, Listener*. Princeton: Princeton Univ. Press, 1971.

Smith, Charles T. *Music and Reason: The Art of Listening, Appreciating and Composing*. New York: Social Sciences Publishers, 1948.

VI. Music and the Other Arts

Aronson, Alex. *Music and the Novel: A Study in Twentieth-Century Fiction*. Totowa, N.J.: Rowman and Littlefield, 1980.

Austin, L. J. "Mallarmé on Music and Letters." *Bulletin of the John Rylands University Library of Manchester*, 42 (1959), 19-39.

Barricelli, Jean-Pierre. "Music and the Structure of Diderot's 'Le Neveu de Rameau.'" *Criticism*, 5 (1963), 95-111.

Branco, João Freitas. *A música na obra de Camões*. Lisboa: Instituto de Cultura Portuguesa, 1979.

Bronson, Bertrand H. "Literature and Music." *Essays on Interdisciplinary Contributions*. Ed. James Thorpe. New York: MLA, 1967, 127-50.

Brown, Calvin S. "The Musical Structure of De Quincey's Dream-Fugue." *Musical Quarterly*, 24 (1938), 341-50.

——————. "The Poetic Use of Musical Forms." *Musical Quarterly*, 30 (1944), 87-101.

——————. *Music and Literature: A Comparison of the Arts.* Athens: Univ. of Georgia Press, 1963; rpt. of 1948 ed.

——————. *Tones into Words: Musical Compositions as Subjects of Poetry.* Athens: Univ. of Georgia Press, 1953.

——————. *A Bibliography on the Relations of Literature and the Other Arts, 1952-1967.* New York: AMS, 1968.

——————. "The Relations between Music and Literature as a Field of Study." *Comparative Literature*, 22 (1970), 97-107.

——————. "Theme and Variations as a Literary Form." *Yearbook of Comparative and General Literature*, 27 (1978), 35-43.

——————. (ed.). *Comparative Literature*, 22 (1970). Special number on literature and music.

Caro, Ethel E. *Music and Thomas Mann.* Stanford: Stanford Honors Essays in Humanities, 1959.

Cluck, Nancy Anne (ed.). *Literature and Music: Essays on Form.* Provo: Brigham Young Univ. Press, 1982.

Conrad, Peter. *Romantic Opera and Literary Form.* Berkeley: Univ. of California Press, 1977.

Cooper, Martin. *Ideas and Music.* London: Barrie and Rockliff, 1965.

Davis, Walter R. "Melodic and Poetic Structure: The Examples of Campion and Dowland." *Criticism*, 4 (1962), 89-107.

Detweiler, Alan. "Music and Poetry." *British Journal of Aesthetics,* 1 (1961), 134-43.

Dumesnil, René. "Berlioz humaniste." *La Revue Musicale*, 233 (1957), 59-64.

Eliot, T. S. "Music of Poetry." *On Poetry and Poets.* New York: Farrar, Strauss and Cudahy, 1957.

Erhardt-Siebold, Erika von. "Harmony of the Senses in English, German, and French Romanticism." *PMLA*, 47 (1932), 577-92.

Freedman, William. *Laurence Sterne and the Origins of the Musical Novel.* Athens: Univ. of Georgia Press, 1978.

Frye, Northrop. "Music in Poetry." *University of Toronto Quarterly*, 11 (1941), 167-79.

_____. (ed.). *Sound and Poetry.* New York: Columbia Univ. Press, 1957.

Heller, Janet Ruth. "'Un tumulto de acordes': Musical Technique in *Cántico.*" *Revista de Estudios Hispánicos*, 15 (January 1981), 59-74.

Hollander, John. *The Untuning of the Sky: Ideas of Music in English Poetry, 1500-1700.* Princeton: Princeton Univ. Press, 1961.

_____. *Images of Voice: Music and Sound in Romantic Poetry.* Cambridge: Heffer, 1970.

Hutton, James. "Some English Poems in Praise of Music." *English Miscellany: A Symposium of History, Literature and the Arts.* Ed. Mario Praz. Roma: Edizioni di Storia e Letteratura, 1951.

Huxley, Aldous. "Music and Poetry." *Texts and Pretexts: An Anthology with Commentaries.* London: Chatlo & Windus, 1949; orig. pub. 1932.

Johnson, Paula. *Form and Transformation in Music and Poetry of the English Renaissance.* New Haven: Yale Univ. Press, 1972.

King, Carlyle. "Aldous Huxley and Music." *Queen's Quarterly*, 70 (1963), 336-51.

Kramer, Lawrence. *Music and Poetry: The Nineteenth Century and After.* Berkeley: Univ. of California Press, 1984.

Lanier, Sidney. *The Science of English Verse.* New York: Charles Scribner's Sons, c1880.

_____. *Music and Poetry: Essays upon Some Aspects and Interrelationships of the Two Arts.* New York: AMS Press, 1969.

Lawer, James R. "Music and Poetry in Apollinaire." *French Studies: A Quarterly Review*, 10 (1956), 339-46.

Lenhart, Charmenz S. *Musical Influence on American Poetry.* Athens: Univ. of Georgia Press, 1956.

Lockspeiser, Edward. *Music and Painting: A Study in Comparative Ideas from Turner to Schoenberg.* London: Cassell, 1973.

McAlpin, Colin. *Hermaia: A Study in Comparative Esthetics.* London: J. M. Dent and Sons, 1915.

Mellers, Wilfrid Howard. *Harmonious Meeting: A Study of the Relationship between English Music, Poetry and Theater, 1600-1900.* London: D. Dobson, 1965.

Mendl, R. W. S. "Robert Browning, the Poet-Musician." *Music and Letters*, 42 (1961), 142-50.

Michell, Joyce. "Music and its Relation to other Arts." *Criticism,* 1 (1959), 91-99.

Morgan, Bayard Quincey. "Melodic Lines in Goethe's Verse." *German Quarterly*, 26 (1953), 10-16.

──────────────. "Goethe's Dramatic Use of Music." *PMLA*, 62 (1957), 104-112.

──────────────. "Musical Pitch in Goethe's Poetry." *Monatschefte*, 55 (1963), 97-101

Moreno, Salvador. "La música en San Juan de la Cruz." *Cuadernos Hispanoamericanos: Revista Mensual de Cultura Hispánica*, 157 (Jan. 1963), 54-66.

Neumann, Alfred R. "Rilke and His Relation to Music." *South-Central Bulletin*, 20 (1960), 25-28.

O'Malley, Glenn. "Literary Synaesthesia." *Journal of Aesthetics and Art Criticism*, 15 (1957), 391-411.

Palacio, Jean L. de. "Music and Musical Themes in Shelley's Poetry." *Modern Language Review*, 59 (1964), 345-59.

Pollock, Georgiana. "The Relationship of Music to *Leaves of Grass*." *College English*, 15 (1954), 384-94.

Querol, Miguel Gavaldá. *La música en el teatro de Calderón.* Barcelona: Diputació de Barcelona, Institut del Teatre, 1981.

Ridenour, George M. "Browning's Music Poems: Fancy and Fact." *PMLA*, 78 (1963), 369-77.

Rowley, Brion A. "The Light of Music and the Music of Light: Synaesthetic Imagery in the Works of Ludwig Tieck." *Publications of the English Goethe Society*, 26 (1957), 52-80.

Sanders, Charles Richard. "Carlyle, Poetry, and the Music of Humanity." *Western Humanities Review*, 16 (1962), 53-66.

Schafer, M. "Ezra Pound and Music." *Canadian Music Journal*, 15 (1961), 15-43.

Scher, Steven Paul. *Verbal Music in German Literature*. New Haven: Yale Univ. Press, 1968.

_____. "Notes Toward a Theory of Verbal Music." *Comparative Literature*, 22 (1970), 147-56.

_____. "Literature and Music." *Interrelations of Literature*. Ed. Jean-Pierre Barricelli and Joseph Gibaldi. New York: MLA, 1982, 225-50. Includes extensive bibliography.

_____. "Literatur und Musik. Eine Bibliographie." *Literatur und Musik: Ein Handbuch zur Theorie und Praxis eines komparatitischen Grenzgebietes*. Ed. Steven Paul Scher. Berlin: Schmidt. Soon to be published (as of 1984).

Smith, C. C. "La musicalidad del 'Polifemo.'" *Revista de Filología Española*, 44 (1961), 139-66.

Smith, Don N. "Musical Form and Principles in the Scheme of *Ulysses*." *Twentieth-Century Literature*, 18 (1972), 79-92.

Springer, George P. "Language and Music: Parallels and Divergencies." *For Roman Jakobson*. Ed. Morris Halle, et al. The Hague: Mouton, 1956, 504-13.

Stanley, Patricia H. "Verbal Music in Theory and Practice." *Germanic Review*, 52 (1977), 217-25.

Suhami, Evelyne. *Paul Valéry et la musique*. Dakar: l'Université, 1966.

Taylor, Ronald. "Formal Parallels in Literature and Music." *German Life and Letters*, 19 (1965), 10-18.

Wellek, Albert. "The Relationship between Music and Poetry." *Journal of Aesthetics and Art Criticism*, 21 (1962), 149-56.

Will, Frederick. "Remarks on Counterpoint Characterization in Euripides." *Classical Journal*, 55 (1960), 338-44.

Winn, James Anderson. *Unsuspected Eloquence: A History of the Relations between Poetry and Music*. New Haven: Yale Univ. Press, 1981.

Wisnik, José Miguel. *O coro dos contrários: a música em torno da Semana de 22*. São Paulo: Livraria Duas Cidades, 1977.

Witold, Jean. "L'Humanisme de Mozart." *La Revue Musicale*, 231 (1956), 59-68.

Wright, A. J. "Verlaine's 'Art Poétique' Re-examined." *PMLA*, 74 (1959), 268-75.

Yoshida, Minoru. "Word-Music in English Poetry." *Journal of Aesthetics and Art Criticism*, 11 (1952), 151-59.

Zuckerman, Jerome. "Contrapuntal Structures in Conrad's *Chance*." *Modern Fiction Studies*, 10 (1964), 44-54.

VII. Works on Composers; Librettos, Scores, etc.

Arnold, Denis, and Fortune, Nigel (eds.). *The Beethoven Companion*. London: Faber and Faber, 1971.

Bartos, Frantisek. *Bedrich Smetana: Letters and Reminiscences*. Trans. Daphne Rusbridge. Prague: Artia, 1955.

Barzun, Jacques. *Berlioz and the Romantic Century*. Vol. I. 3rd ed. New York: Columbia Univ. Press, 1969.

Berteaut, Simone. *Piaf*. Trans. by Ghislane Boulanger. London: W. W. Allen, 1971.

Bie, Oskar. *Schubert, the Man*. New York: Dodd, Mead, 1928.

Burk, John N. *The Life and Works of Beethoven*. New York: Modern Library, 1943.

Carner, Mosco. *Puccini: A Critical Biography*. New York: Alfred A. Knopf, 1959.

Cooke, Deryck. *Gustav Mahler: An Introduction to His Music*. London: Faber Music, 1980.

Del Mar, Norman. *Richard Strauss: A Critical Commentary on His Works*. Vol. I. London: Barrie and Rockliff, 1962.

Deutsch, Otto Erich. *Handel: A Documentary Biography*. London: Adams and Charles Black, 1955.

Einstein, Alfred. *Mozart, His Character, His Work*. Trans. by Arthur Mendel and Nathan Broder. New York: Oxford Univ. Press, 1945.

Flower, Newman. *George Frideric Handel: His Personality and His Times*. London: Cassell, 1923.

Gide, André. *Notes on Chopin*. Trans. by Bernard Frechtman. New York: Philosophical Library, 1949.

Greenfeld, Howard. *Puccini: A Biography*. New York: G. P. Putnam's Sons, 1980.

Griesinger, Georg August. *Joseph Haydn: Eighteenth-Century Gentleman and Genius*. Trans. with an intro. and notes by Vernon Gotwals. Madison: Univ. of Wisconsin Press, 1963.

Hanson, Lawrence, and Hanson, Elizabeth. *Tchaikovsky: The Man Behind the Music.* New York: Dodd, Mead, 1966.

Harding, James. *Erik Satie.* New York: Praeger Publishers, 1975.

Hughes, Spike. *Famous Puccini Operas.* 2nd rev. ed. New York: Dover Publications, 1972.

Hussey, Dyneley. *Wolfgang Amade Mozart.* New York: Harper and Brothers, 1928.

Jacobs, Arthur, et al. *Great Operas in Synopsis.* New York: Thomas Y. Crowell, 1966.

Kennedy, Michael. *Mahler.* London: J M Dent and Sons, 1974.

Lang, Paul Henry. *George Frideric Handel.* New York: Norton, 1966.

Large, Brian. *Smetana.* London: Duckworth, 1970.

Lavignac, Albert. *The Music Dramas of Richard Wagner and His Festival Theater in Bayreuth.* Trans. Esther Singleton. New York: AMS Press, 1970.

Leibowitz, René. *Schoenberg.* Paris: Seuil, 1969.

Lesznai, Lajos. *Bartók.* Trans. by Percy M. Young. London: J M Dent and Sons, 1973.

Lockspeiser, Edward. *Debussy.* Rev. ed. London: J M Dent and Sons, 1963.

MacDonald, Malcolm. *Schoenberg.* London: J M Dent and Sons, 1976.

Murgia, Adelaide. *The Life and Times of Chopin.* Trans. by C. J. Richards. London: Hamlyn, 1967.

Myers, Rollo H. *Erik Satie.* New York: Dover Publications, 1968.

Nettl, Paul. *Beethoven Handbook.* New York: Frederick Ungar, 1967.

Newman, Ernest. *The Wagner Operas.* New York: Alfred A. Knopf, 1968.

_____. *Berlioz, Romantic and Classic: Writings by Ernest Newman.* Sel. and ed. by Peter Heyworth. London: Victor Gollancz, 1972.

Puccini, Giacomo. *Letters of Giacomo Puccini.* Ed. Giuseppe Adami. Trans. and ed. for English ed. by Ena Makin. New York: AMS Press, 1971.

Robbins, H. C. *Haydn: Chronicle and Works.* Vol. VI. Bloomington: Indiana Univ. Press, 1977.

Rosen, Charles. *The Classical Style: Haydn, Mozart, Beethoven*. New York: Viking Press, 1971.

Sams, Eric. *The Songs of Robert Schumann*. Foreword by Gerald Moore. London: Methuen, 1969.

Satie, Erik. *Socrate: drame symphonique*. Paris: Editions Max Eschig, 1919.

Schweitzer, Albert. *J. S. Bach*. Vol. I. With a preface by C. M. Widor, trans. by Ernest Newman. London: Adam and Charles Black, 1923.

Specht, Richard. *Giacomo Puccini: The Man, His Life, His Work*. Westport, Conn.: Greenwood Press, 1970.

Stevens, Halsey. *The Life and Music of Béla Bartók*. Rev. ed. New York: Oxford Univ. Press, 1964.

Streatfeild, R. A. *Handel*. New York: Da Capo Press, 1964.

Stuckenschmidt, H. H. *Schoenberg: His Life, World, and Work*. Trans. by Humphrey Searle. London: John Calder, 1977.

Thompson, Oscar. *Debussy: Man and Artist*. New York: Dover Publications, 1967; orig. pub. 1937.

Vallas, León. *Claude Debussy: His Life and Works*. Trans. Maire and Grace O'Brien. London: Oxford Univ. Press, 1933.

Vignal, Marc. *Mahler*. Paris: Seuil, 1966.

Wagner, Richard. *Tristan and Isolda: Drama in Three Acts*. Vocal score by Richard Kleinmichel, English trans. by Henry Grafton Chapman, with an essay on the story of the opera by H. E. Krehbiel. New York: G. Schirmer, 1906.

——————. *The Authentic Librettos of the Wagner Operas*. Complete with English and German Parallel Texts and Music of the Principal Airs. New York: Crown Publishers, 1938.

Wenk, Arthur B. *Claude Debussy and the Poets*. Berkeley: Univ. of California Press, 1976.

INDEX OF PERSONS